lonely planet

Barcelona

Damien Simonis

LONELY PLANET PUBLICATIONS
Melbourne • Oakland • London • Paris

MEDITERRANEAN SEA

FIGUERES
Journey into the surreal at the extraordinary Teatre-Museu Dalí

GIRONA
Site of an impressive medieval village

WINE COUNTRY
Visit the producers of Spain's premier wines, including cava, the local champagne

SITGES
Where the beach is long and sandy, the nightlife thumps and the shops are always fashionable

TARRAGONA
Birthplace of Pontius Pilate and keeper of a rich Roman heritage

FRANCE

ANDORRA

ARAGÓN

VALÈNCIA

To Béziers
To Toulouse
To Zaragoza
To Valencia
To Huesca
To Genoa (Italy)
To Palma de Mallorca, Ibiza & Maó
To Palma de Mallorca

PERPIGNAN
Cerbère
Portbou
Roses
L'Escala
Palafrugell
Palamós
Sant Feliu de Guixols
Tossa de Mar
Lloret de Mar
Blanes
La Jonquera
Figueres
Girona
Banyoles
Besalú
Olot
Camprodon
Setcases
Ribes de Freser
Vallter 2000
Santuari de Núria
Font-Romeu
Ax-les-Thermes
Llívia
Puigcerdà
La Molina
Combrèn
Ripoll
Bagà
Berga
Sant Llorenç de Morunys
Solsona
Cardona
Manresa
Montserrat
Monestir de Montserrat
Igualada
Vic
Granollers
Sant Hilari Sacalm
Mataró
Badalona
BARCELONA
Sabadell
Terrassa
Martorell
Castelldefels
Sitges
Vilanova i la Geltrú
Sant Sadurní d'Anoia
Vilafranca del Penedès
El Vendrell
Coma-ruga
Tarragona
Port Aventura
Reus
Valls
Montblanc
L'Espluga de Francolí
Monestir de Poblet
Cervera
Tàrrega
Agramunt
Ponts
Bassella
Organyà
Adrall
La Seu d'Urgell
Andorra La Vella
Pica d'Estats (3143m)
Sort
Llavorsí
Esterri d'Àneu
Baqueira-Beret
Vielha
Benasque
Benabarre
Monzón
Barbastro
Huesca
El Pont de Suert
La Pobla de Segur
Tremp
Artesa de Segre
Balaguer
Almenar
Lleida
Flix
Móra d'Ebre
Gandesa
Tortosa
Amposta
L'Ampolla
Deltebre
Sant Carles de la Ràpita
Ebro Delta

Costa Brava
Costa Daurada
Parc Natural de la Zona Volcànica de la Garrotxa
Parc Nacional d'Aigüestortes i Estany de Sant Maurici

Riu Ter
Riu Segre
Riu Noguera
Riu Ebro

A-9
N-114
N-9
N-116
D-115
N-II
N-260
N-152
N-141
C-25
C-1411
C-1410
C-1412
C-1313
A-18
A-2
N-340
A-7
C-241
C-242
C-233
C-251
A-7
N-230
N-II
N-240
A-138
N-125
N-20
N-230
C-230
N-420
N-232

50 km
25
0

BARCELONA METRO

MEDITERRANEAN SEA

Legend

- Metro Linia 1
- Metro Linia 2
- Metro Linia 3
- Metro Linia 4
- Metro Linia 5
- Funicular
- Teleféric de Montjuïc
- Tramvia Blau

- Station
- Terminal Station
- Interchange Station
- RENFE Station
- Ferrocarril de la Generalitat de Catalunya
- Line with disabled access
- Station with disabled access

Information supplied by ⊕ TMB

Barcelona
Ist edition – April 1999

Published by
Lonely Planet Publications Pty Ltd A.C.N. 005 607 983
192 Burwood Rd, Hawthorn, Victoria 3122, Australia

Lonely Planet Offices
Australia PO Box 617, Hawthorn, Victoria 3122
USA 150 Linden St, Oakland, CA 94607
UK 10a Spring Place, London NW5 3BH
France 1 rue du Dahomey, 75011 Paris

Photographs
All of the images in this guide are available for licensing from
Lonely Planet Images.
email: lpi@lonelyplanet.com.au

Front cover photograph
La Sagrada Família, Barcelona (Simon Bracken, Lonely Planet Images)

ISBN 0 86442 607 0

text & maps © Lonely Planet 1999
photos © photographers as indicated 1999

Printed by Colorcraft Ltd, Hong Kong

Contents – Text

Contents – Maps

The Author

Damien Simonis

With a degree in languages and several years reporting and sub-editing on Australian newspapers (including *The Australian* and *The Age*), Sydney-born Damien left Australia in 1989. He has since lived, worked and travelled extensively throughout Europe, the Middle East and North Africa. Since 1992, Lonely Planet has kept him busy writing for *Jordan & Syria*, *Egypt & the Sudan*, *Morocco*, *North Africa*, *Spain* and *The Canary Islands*. In 1999 Damien returns to Italy to update, research and write *Tuscany*, *Florence* and *Venice*. He has also written and snapped photos for other publications in Australia, the UK and North America. When not on the road, Damien resides in splendid Stoke Newington, deep in the heart of north London.

From Damien

People all over the place have helped me out on this job in many different ways. First and foremost, however, I owe a debt of gratitude to John Noble, whose work in Barcelona on the 1st edition of Lonely Planet's Spain provided me with a hefty springboard.

On the home front, Cathy Lanigan in particular and all the gang in general at LP London have helped me keep things ticking over. Thanks to Leonie Mugavin for help on travel info from Australasia and to Sacha Pearson in the USA for similar aid.

In Barcelona, I owe a lot to Rafa Perera (who became my temporary landlord on the fourth floor at Gran Via), Álvaro Picardo (in London, thanks for the contacts), Max Jacobson (also in London, with more contacts), Mar Batlló and Anabel. Susan Kempster and the gang from Carrer de Sant Pere més alt (Michael van Laake, Paloma, Natalia) welcomed me into their labyrinthine home on more than one occasion, and Michael kept a watchful eye on Gnomo during his well earned rest periods when I was in London. Susana Pellicer's friend Antonio saved my bacon during the Great Computer Meltdown – a mere 'thank you' seems inadequate.

Finally, a huge *abrazo* goes to Susana herself, *y ya sabes porqué*.

This Book

From the Publisher

This first edition of Barcelona was researched and written by Damien Simonis using Barcelona text from *Spain* written by John Noble. Wendy Owen was the coordinating editor and Jenny Joy Jones was coordinating designer. Jocelyn Harewood, Janet Austin and Ada Cheung assisted with editing and proofing, Jane Hart and baby Lauren checked the artwork, Katie Cody checked everything else, Tim Uden provided Quark support and Quentin Frayne prepared the language section. Simon Bracken designed the front cover and Mick Weldon drew some wonderful illustrations. Warm thanks to Damien for keeping his cool and coming up trumps despite his endless electronic ailments.

Foreword

ABOUT LONELY PLANET GUIDEBOOKS

The story begins with a classic travel adventure: Tony and Maureen Wheeler's 1972 journey across Europe and Asia to Australia. Useful information about the overland trail did not exist at that time, so Tony and Maureen published the first Lonely Planet guidebook to meet a growing need.

From a kitchen table, then from a tiny office in Melbourne (Australia), Lonely Planet has become the largest independent travel publisher in the world, an international company with offices in Melbourne, Oakland (USA), London (UK) and Paris (France).

Today Lonely Planet guidebooks cover the globe. There is an ever-growing list of books and there's information in a variety of forms and media. Some things haven't changed. The main aim is still to help make it possible for adventurous travellers to get out there – to explore and better understand the world.

At Lonely Planet we believe travellers can make a positive contribution to the countries they visit – if they respect their host communities and spend their money wisely. Since 1986 a percentage of the income from each book has been donated to aid projects and human rights campaigns.

Updates Lonely Planet thoroughly updates each guidebook as often as possible. This usually means there are around two years between editions, although for more unusual or more stable destinations the gap can be longer. Check the imprint page (following the colour map at the beginning of the book) for publication dates.

Between editions up-to-date information is available in two free newsletters – the paper *Planet Talk* and email *Comet* (to subscribe, contact any Lonely Planet office) – and on our Web site at www.lonelyplanet.com. The *Upgrades* section of the Web site covers a number of important and volatile destinations and is regularly updated by Lonely Planet authors. *Scoop* covers news and current affairs relevant to travellers. And, lastly, the *Thorn Tree* bulletin board and *Postcards* section of the site carry unverified, but fascinating, reports from travellers.

Correspondence The process of creating new editions begins with the letters, postcards and emails received from travellers. This correspondence often includes suggestions, criticisms and comments about the current editions. Interesting excerpts are immediately passed on via newsletters and the Web site, and everything goes to our authors to be verified when they're researching on the road. We're keen to get more feedback from organisations or individuals who represent communities visited by travellers.

Lonely Planet gathers information for everyone who's curious about the planet – and especially for those who explore it first-hand. Through guidebooks, phrasebooks, activity guides, maps, literature, newsletters, image library, TV series and Web site we act as an information exchange for a worldwide community of travellers.

Research Authors aim to gather sufficient practical information to enable travellers to make informed choices and to make the mechanics of a journey run smoothly. They also research historical and cultural background to help enrich the travel experience and allow travellers to understand and respond appropriately to cultural and environmental issues.

Authors don't stay in every hotel because that would mean spending a couple of months in each medium-sized city and, no, they don't eat at every restaurant because that would mean stretching belts beyond capacity. They do visit hotels and restaurants to check standards and prices, but feedback based on readers' direct experiences can be very helpful.

Many of our authors work undercover, others aren't so secretive. None of them accept freebies in exchange for positive write-ups. And none of our guidebooks contain any advertising.

Production Authors submit their raw manuscripts and maps to offices in Australia, USA, UK or France. Editors and cartographers – all experienced travellers themselves – then begin the process of assembling the pieces. When the book finally hits the shops, some things are already out of date, we start getting feedback from readers and the process begins again ...

WARNING & REQUEST

Things change – prices go up, schedules change, good places go bad and bad places go bankrupt – nothing stays the same. So, if you find things better or worse, recently opened or long since closed, please tell us and help make the next edition even more accurate and useful. We genuinely value all the feedback we receive. Julie Young coordinates a well travelled team that reads and acknowledges every letter, postcard and email and ensures that every morsel of information finds its way to the appropriate authors, editors and cartographers for verification.

Everyone who writes to us will find their name in the next edition of the appropriate guidebook. They will also receive the latest issue of *Planet Talk*, our quarterly printed newsletter, or *Comet*, our monthly email newsletter. Subscriptions to both newsletters are free. The very best contributions will be rewarded with a free guidebook.

Excerpts from your correspondence may appear in new editions of Lonely Planet guidebooks, the Lonely Planet Web site, *Planet Talk* or *Comet*, so please let us know if you *don't* want your letter published or your name acknowledged.

Send all correspondence to the Lonely Planet office closest to you:

Australia: PO Box 617, Hawthorn, Victoria 3122
USA: 150 Linden St, Oakland, CA 94607
UK: 10A Spring Place, London NW5 3BH
France: 1 rue du Dahomey, 75011 Paris

Or email us at: talk2us@lonelyplanet.com.au

For news, views and updates see our Web site: www.lonelyplanet.com

HOW TO USE A LONELY PLANET GUIDEBOOK

The best way to use a Lonely Planet guidebook is any way you choose. At Lonely Planet we believe the most memorable travel experiences are often those that are unexpected, and the finest discoveries are those you make yourself. Guidebooks are not intended to be used as if they provide a detailed set of infallible instructions!

Contents All Lonely Planet guidebooks follow the same format. The Facts about the Country chapters or sections give background information ranging from history to weather. Facts for the Visitor gives practical information on issues like visas and health. Getting There & Away gives a brief starting point for researching travel to and from the destination. Getting Around gives an overview of the transport options when you arrive.

The peculiar demands of each destination determine how subsequent chapters are broken up, but some things remain constant. We always start with background, then proceed to sights, places to stay, places to eat, entertainment, getting there and away, and getting around information – in that order.

Heading Hierarchy Lonely Planet headings are used in a strict hierarchical structure that can be visualised as a set of Russian dolls. Each heading (and its following text) is encompassed by any preceding heading that is higher on the hierarchical ladder.

Entry Points We do not assume guidebooks will be read from beginning to end, but that people will dip into them. The traditional entry points are the list of contents and the index. In addition, however, there is a complete list of maps and an index map illustrating map coverage.

There's also a colour map that shows highlights. These highlights are dealt with in greater detail in the Facts for the Visitor chapter, along with planning questions and suggested itineraries. Each chapter covering a geographical region begins with a locator map and another list of highlights. Once you find something of interest in a list of highlights, turn to the index.

Maps Maps play a crucial role in Lonely Planet guidebooks and include a huge amount of information. A legend is printed on the back page. We seek to have complete consistency between maps and text, and to have every important place in the text captured on a map. Map key numbers usually start in the top left corner.

Although inclusion in a guidebook usually implies a recommendation we cannot list every good place. Exclusion does not necessarily imply criticism. In fact there are a number of reasons why we might exclude a place – sometimes it is simply inappropriate to encourage an influx of travellers.

Introduction

Location, location. If Barcelona were up for sale, it would pull in a fortune for position alone. You are never more than a few hours' drive from: southern France; the Pyrenees (skiing in winter, hiking in summer); the seaside lunacy of Sitges (the gay capital of the costas, but with plenty of room for straights); Romanesque and Gothic monasteries and churches; the Penedès wine country; and the splendours of the northern Costa Brava – the Rugged Coast. Old rivals such as medieval Girona (north) and Roman Tarragona (south) are easily accessible for day trips.

Barcelona is one of the most dynamic and exciting cities on the western Mediterranean seaboard – perhaps only Marseille and Naples can compete in any way for attention – sedulously promoting itself as a European metropolis, a link between the sub-Pyrenean peninsula and the heartland of Western Europe. At its worst over the centuries, Barcelona has been an inward-looking, parochial and smugly self-satisfied

Copy of original engraving from 1851 edition of *The Iconographic Encyclopaedia of Science, Literature and Art*

bourgeois town. At its best, it displays a zest for life, artistic genius and sense of style that few cities can boast.

A city that attracts abbreviations and nicknames usually has something going for it. BCN is one of those places. The only city in the world with an underground train that goes to the local beach, this Mediterranean metropolis of 1½ million pumps life and dynamism. If some hicks from the surrounding countryside refer to the Big B as *Can Fanga* (House of Mud), it is comforting to think that behind the disparaging words lies a hint of admiration.

The Romans didn't much like the place, but they should have stuck around. Medieval grandeur left the city with one of the most impressive and varied Gothic building legacies in all Europe. True, the city's fortunes began to slide as its Mediterranean empire crumbled and Madrid enforced tighter central rule. Artistically at least, things remained rather dull for a few centuries. But then along came the Modernistas. Led by Antoni Gaudí, they cast across Barcelona an Art Nouveau splash unparalleled anywhere else in the world. Some of the greatest artists of this century put in time here – Picasso and Miró make an impressive duo, and Dalí was born and lived much of his life just up the coast.

Barcelona is not just about monuments and paintings. The city that shot into the limelight with the successful 1992 Olympic Games provides all sorts of entertainments, starting with the palate. Catalan cuisine is among Spain's best, so you're in for a treat. The wine you drink with the fine seafood probably comes from the Penedès area, barely a half-hour's drive south-west of Barcelona and home to *cava*, the prized local version of champagne.

If you thought it was time to head for bed after a meal that might not have even started until 11 pm, think again. You've barely begun. The city centre and several *barris* further out heave to the joyous rhythms of the bar-hoppers. Barcelona doesn't quite match Madrid, but it leaves anywhere else in Europe for dead with its sheer concentration of bars and cafés. And then there are the late-night bars and discos for those who seek no sleep.

In summer especially, various parts of the city seem to lose their sanity, giving themselves over to week-long *festes*. These outdoor parties feature bands, competitions, and traditional parades of giants, dwarfs and demons (*gegants*, *capgrossos* and *dimonis*). Not to mention the madness of fire-running (*correfoc*) through the narrow lanes of the old city with fire-breathing dragons during the late September *Festes de la Mercè*. It's all washed down with plenty of local wine, although this is not in any way an ugly bar-brawling style of drinking.

Barcelona is and isn't Spain. The second city after Madrid, it is also capital of the autonomous region of Catalunya, only fully incorporated into the centralised state after defeat in battle in 1714. The Catalans speak their own language, and not just literally. Viewed with suspicion and envy by some from more southern parts, the Catalans are, in a sense, to Spain what the Scots are to Britain. They're canny with money too, so they say. On the subject of money, economically Barcelona has had more comebacks than Lazarus. It is now one of the country's industrial and commercial powerhouses and conscious of its role as a European business centre.

Qué tal Barna? a friend from Madrid asked a while back. How is Barcelona? Very well, thank you. Come and see for yourself.

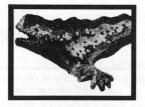

Facts about Barcelona

HISTORY

The history of the second city of Spain, though far longer than that of its brasher Castilian rival Madrid, could be dismissed as that of an also-ran, a wannabe which, at various moments, was clearly on the brink of greatness, but though its whose hopes and pretentions were all too often dashed by events beyond its control.

For centuries Barcelona shrank in the shadow of greater cities and powers. When finally it emerged from the Dark Ages as the successful headquarters of a burgeoning mercantile empire across the Mediterranean, Barcelona still failed – just – to attain the grandeur of some of its major competitors.

Absorption into unified Spain at the close of the Middle Ages meant Barcelona was relegated not only to second place behind Madrid, the newly established centre of the Spanish empire, but frequently languished well behind other urbs of greater imperial weight , such as Sevilla in the south.

Civil conflicts, revolts against Madrid and the the disaster of 1714 contributed little to the city's happiness, but a tenacious optimism helped to fuel repeated sparks of growth and activity. By the end of the 19th century, Barcelona was probably *the* leading economic light in an otherwise vexed and gloomy country, shackled by poverty, inept government and incessant infighting.

Republican defeat in the Spanish Civil War again meant relegation. Generalísimo Franco's rigid distaste for the devolutionist desires of the Catalans was most eloquently expressed by the official suppression of their language. Unsurprisingly, little love was lost between the diminutive dictator and the bulk of Barcelonins (as residents of Barcelona are called) – his demise in 1975 was greeted with palpable relief. Since the devolution process began in 1978, Barcelona has sparkled back to life.

Early Barcelona

The area around present-day Barcelona was certainly inhabited prior to the arrival of the Romans in Spain in 218 BC. By whom, is another question, and whether or not there was an urban nucleus is open to debate.

Pre-Roman coins found in the area suggest the Celt-Iberian Laietani tribe may have settled here, but without any recognisable urban centre. As far back as 35,000 BC the tribe's Stone Age predecessors had roamed the Pyrenees and begun to descend into the lowlands to the south.

Other evidence hints at a settlement established around 230 BC by the Carthaginian conqueror (and father of Hannibal), Hamilcar Barca. It is tempting to see in his name the roots of the city's own name. Archaeologists believe that any pre-Roman town must have been built on the hill of Montjuïc.

Right in the centre of old Barcelona is Carrer d'Hèrcules (Street of Hercules). Among the many feats attributed to this figure of Greek mythology is the founding of Barcelona – but it's a claim not taken terribly seriously by anyone.

The Romans

The heart of the Roman settlement of Barcelona lay within what would later become the medieval city – now known as the Barri Gòtic. Its core was a lowrise known as Mons Taber, where the temple was raised. Remains of city walls, temple pillars and graves all attest to what would eventually become a busy and lively town. Barcino (as the Romans knew it) was not a major centre, however. Tarraco (Tarragona) to the south and the one-time Greek trading centre of Empúries to the north were both considerably more important. Tarraco, in fact, became capital of the Roman province of Hispania Citerior.

It took the Romans some two centuries to fully subjugate the peninsula. Greek and

Carthaginian settlements tended not to resist, but, at times, the wilder Celt-Iberian tribes put up some stiff opposition. However, the area around Barcelona enjoyed a mostly peaceful occupation, and in 15 BC Caesar Augustus was magnanimous enough to grant the town the title of Colonia Julia Augusta Faventia Pia. Evidence from sources such as the Latin poet Ausonius suggests a picture of contented prosperity – Roman Barcelona lived well off the agricultural produce in its hinterland and from fishing. Oysters, in particular, seem to have appeared regularly on the menu in ancient times.

Barbarian Invasions

All good things come to an end and, as the grand structure that was the Roman empire began to wobble, it was only a matter of time before Hispania would feel the effects. It is no coincidence that the bulk of the Roman walls, vestiges of which remain today, went up in the 4th century AD. Marauding Franks had visited a little death and destruction on the city in a prelude to what was to come – several waves of invaders flooded across the country like great Atlantic rollers. By 415, the comparatively Romanised Visigoths had arrived and under their leader Athaulf made a temporary capital in Barcelona. This state of affairs did not last long, but it appears the town remained a privileged centre in the centuries that followed. Nevertheless, Toletum (Toledo) became the real power centre. In all Hispania (as the Iberian Peninsula was known to the Roman world) there were probably never more than a few hundred thousand Visigoths. But they would remain the ruling class – much aided by Hispano-Roman nobility and the emerging Christian clergy.

Other Visigothic rulers spent time in Barcelona and there is evidence that the population grew slowly but steadily until a new invasion, this time from North Africa.

Islamic Blitzkrieg

In 711, the Muslim general Tariq landed an expeditionary force at present-day Gibraltar (Arabic for Tariq's Mountain). After the death of the prophet Mohammed in 632 in distant Arabia, Muslims swept across Asia Minor and all of North Africa, conquering and converting as they went in an unprecedented spate of divinely inspired ad hoc empire building.

In Spain Tariq found that the Visigothic 'state' had become so rotten through internecine bickering that, in the words of a 20th century dictator with a small moustache when talking of the Soviet Union, all they had to do was 'kick the door in' and watch the whole thing come tumbling done. Hitler got it wrong, but the idea worked for Tariq & Co. They cake-walked it all the way into France, where they were only brought to a halt in 732 by the Franks at Poitiers.

Barcelona fell under Muslim sway, of course, but this situation was short-lived. Not a lot is known about this period. The town is mentioned in various Arabic chronicles but it seems the Muslims resigned themselves early on to setting up a defensive line roughly along the Ebro river to the south. Whatever the thinking at the time, Barcelona was taken by the Frankish ruler Louis the Pious in 801.

The counts (*comtes*) who were installed here as Louis' lieutenants hailed from local tribes roaming on the periphery of the Frankish empire. Barcelona was a frontier town in what was known as the Frankish or Spanish March – a rough-and-ready buffer zone south of the Pyrenees designed to keep the Muslims and other undesirables at arms' length, and to be used as a springboard for later offensives.

A Hairy Beginning

The history of Barcelona, in a sense, only truly began at this point. The plains and mountains to the north-west and north of Barcelona were populated by the people who by then could be identified as 'Catalans' (although surviving documentary references to the term only date to the 10th century). Catalan, the language (and its many dialects) of these people, was closely related to the *langue d'oc*, the post-Latin lingua franca of southern France (of which Provençal is about the only barely surviving reminder). It is not, therefore, a dialect of Castilian Spanish, as many would have us believe.

The March was under nominal Frankish control but the real power lay with local potentates who ranged across the territory. One of these rulers went by the curious name of Guifré el Pelós, or Wilfred the Hairy. This was not a reference to uneven shaving habits. According to the legend, old Will had hair in parts most people do not (exactly which parts was never specified – the mind boggles!). Son of Sunifred d'Urgell, he and his brothers went about conquering all the neighbouring Catalan bastions, including Barcelona, which by this time was something of a glorified country town, albeit a prominent one. This task was completed by 878 and Guifré entered the folk mythology of Catalunya. A great funder of religious foundations in Barcelona (none of which survive) and

Born in Blood

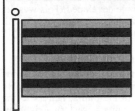

Guifré el Pelós founded the Casa de Barcelona more or less with the consent of his Frankish overlords. But what's a new political entity without a flag of some sort? As we have seen, writers of history and other tall tales hit upon a particularly gratifying account for the existence of Catalunya's national colours (apparently the following story and several different versions began to circulate some time around the 16th century).

Called upon to join the holy fight against the wicked Muslims with an army of Frankish good guys, the gutsy Guifré fell wounded in hair-raising style on the field of battle. The Frankish emperor, Charles the Bald (this is not a joke), was so touched by his vassal's loyalty that he wanted to reward him in some way. No, not with an all-expenses paid holiday to Rome or a gold-plated letter-opener. Upon seeing Guifré's bright golden shield embarrassingly bereft of a coat of arms, old Charles dipped his fingers in a pool of Guifré's fresh warm blood and drew four finger stripes, *les quatre barres*, down the shield.

So much for the story-telling. From this tale came the Catalan coat of arms, concrete evidence of which first appears in 1150 in a seal of Count Ramon Berenguer IV. The same heraldic sign (said to be the fourth oldest in all Europe) can also be made out on the coffin of Ramon Berenguer II (in the cathedral in Girona), who died in 1082. The coat of arms went on later to became that of the so-called Corona de Aragón, formed in 1137 of a coalition comprising the principality of Catalunya, Aragón, Valencia, the Islas Baleares and Roussillon (in present-day France).

The Catalan flag (in which the stripes become horizontal) is first documented in the 13th century and became the official symbol of the modern, autonomous region of Catalunya in 1979. A similar symbol to the coat of arms, but oval in shape, was concocted in 1932 and now represents the Generalitat, or regional government. The same colour combination also appears in the heraldry of the former members of the Corona de Aragón.

across Catalunya (some of which do), he astutely won for himself the benevolence of the only people who could write in those days – the clergy. They began a tradition of eulogy that has never really died since. If Catalunya can be called a nation, then its 'father' was the hirsute Willy.

The mythology is a little too complicated to go into here, but an element of it was Guifré's supposed anti-Frankish ways, seen as proof of the rise of a new and independent nation. That's putting a little too much spin on the story. Guifré's position as Comte de Barcelona (even today many refer to Barcelona as the *ciutat comtal* (or city of counts) was assured, but he hastened to seek approval and confirmation from the Franks. His successors assiduously couched their claims to legitimacy in terms of backing from the Franks, for whom they remained, technically at least, vassals.

The Comtes de Barcelona

By the late 10th century the Casa de Barcelona ruled an independent principality covering most of modern Catalunya except the south, plus Roussillon which today lies across the border in France. This was the only Christian 'state' on the Iberian Peninsula not to fall under the sway of Sancho III of Navarra in the early 11th century. One last Muslim assault came when Al-Mansur raided Barcelona in 985. His stay was short-lived and, by the time he died in 1002, the Cordoban Caliphate that had been the unifying backbone of Muslim Spain was descending into chaos. The events of these years held a special significance for the Comtes de Barcelona. Calls for Frankish aid to repulse Al-Mansur had gone unheeded, so from this time on the Comtes implicitly refused to acknowledge Frankish suzerainty. The Franks never contested the new status quo and so a new entity, 'Catalonia', began to acquire tacit recognition across Europe.

Throughout Spain, a confusion of counties, principalities and kingdoms vied, jockeyed and fought for local or peninsular domination. It was as common for Muslim

warlords to team up with Christian rulers in local spats as for Christians and Muslims to challenge one another. These were, to say the least, interesting times. Particularly so for the Comtes de Barcelona, who managed to pick up a lot of booty by judicious meddling in Muslim squabbles to the south. This booty was put to good use.

Comte Ramon Berenguer I was able to buy the counties of Carcassonne and Béziers, north of Roussillon, with Muslim bullion. Barcelona would maintain ambitions in France for two more centuries – at one point it held territory as far east as Provence. Under Ramon Berenguer III (1082-1131) Catalunya launched its own fleet and sea trade developed. This was the era of great Catalan Romanesque art, with its masterly church frescoes.

Marriage of Convenience?

In 1137 Ramon Berenguer IV clinched what must have seemed an unbeatable deal. He was betrothed to Petronilla, heiress to the throne of Catalunya's western neighbour Aragón, thus creating a joint state which set the scene for Catalunya's golden age. This state, to be known as the Corona de Aragón (the Crown of Aragon), was ruled by *comtes-reis* (in Catalan parlance) or count-kings. The title enshrined the continued separateness of the two states, and both retained many (but not all) of their own laws. The arrangement was to have unexpected consequences as it tied Catalunya to the destiny of the rest of the peninsula in a way that ultimately would not appeal to many Catalans.

In the meantime, however, Don Ramon wasn't content to lie about with Petronilla. In the course of the 1140s he wrested control of southern Catalunya from the Muslims. This southward expansion heralded a major shift in policy, which had been concerned with the north until then.

Don Ramon's son Alfons I styled himself King of Aragón, as would his successors, but already trouble had begun to brew as Catalan rulers tended to clash with Aragonese nobles. The latter looked favourably on neighbouring Castilla's endeavours to pursue the Christian Reconquista (Reconquest) of Muslim-occupied Spain, and official endorsement came in a treaty signed by Alfons II in 1179.

In the meantime, however, more pressing problems were at hand. Pere I died in the Battle of Muret in 1213 and France pounced on virtually all Catalan possessions north of the Pyrenees.

Mediterranean Empire

The French blow induced some serious thinking in Barcelona on which way to proceed next. Not content to leave all the glory of the Reconquista to the Castilians, Jaume I (1213-76) embarked on some spectacular missions of his own.

Although Barcelona's shallow, silty harbour was hardly ideal, the city's importance by now should have made it a logical launchpad for Mediterranean sea trade, at this time largely the preserve of Italian city states like Genoa, Pisa and Venice and their North African counterparts.

When winds prevailed, sailing vessels zipped across to the Islas Baleares but there was one problem. The islands were occupied by Muslim North Africans who were making a very nice living by using them as a customs staging post and as a base for piracy.

Jaume I took a while to convince the Aragonese nobility of the attractions of seizing the islands and thus opening the doors to expanded commerce, but eventually the nobles came around. In 1229 Jaume, with a kind of divine fervour, set off on an expedition that involved fleets from Tarragona, Barcelona, Marseille and other ports. His object was Mallorca, which he won. Six years later he had Ibiza and Formentera in hand. Things were going so well that, prodded by the Aragonese, for good measure he took control of Valencia (on the mainland) too. This was no easy task and was completed only in 1248 after 16 years of grinding conquest. All this activity helped fuel a boom in Barcelona and Jaume raised new walls that increased by tenfold the size of the enclosed city.

Mallorca, in particular, became a commercial centre of great importance and was quickly Catalanised. This didn't stop it from wangling a large degree of independence from Barcelona in 1276, a situation only reversed in 1343.

The party wasn't yet over and the empire-building program shifted into top gear in the 1280s. Jaume I's son Pere II (1240-85) took Sicily in 1282. Pere was married to the daughter of the last of the island's Hohenstaufen rulers, who opposed the claims of Charles d'Anjou (which had papal backing) to mastery of the island. Charles was dislodged in the night of the Sicilian Vespers and Pere moved in with his troops in a largely bloodless conquest.

The easternmost part of the Baleares, Menorca, was not so lucky, falling to Alfons II in 1287 in a bloodbath. Most of its people were killed or enslaved and the island remained largely deserted throughout its occupation. Malta, Gozo and Athens were also taken, but not held for long. A half-hearted attempt was made on Corsica but the most determined and ultimately fruitless assault began on Sardinia in 1324. The island became the Corona de Aragón's Vietnam. As late as 1423 Naples also came under the influence of the Catalo-Aragonese.

In spite of the carnage and the expense of war, this was Barcelona's golden age. The grandest city in the Catalan-Aragonese coalition, Barcelona was the base for what was now a thriving mercantile empire. The western Mediterranean had been turned into a Catalan lake and trade proceeded apace, not only among the occupied territories but also with North Africa (through which Barcelona dominated the African gold trade) and to a lesser extent in the Levant.

The Rise of Parliament

The rulers of the Casa de Barcelona and then the count-kings of the Corona de Aragón had a habit of not residing in Barcelona. Initially, local city administration was in the hands of a viscount but in the course of the 12th century local power began to shift.

Fanfare for the Common Man

Although the modern Catalan nationalist insistence on Catalunya's separateness from the rest of Spain may at times seem a trifle tiresome (it is in any case a sentiment by no means shared by all Catalans, and especially not in Barcelona), there is something to it. Perhaps that is what gets to some Castilians, whose prejudices against the Catalans (to whom they often refer as *polacos*, Pollacks) can be equally irritating.

Under the Casa de Barcelona a system of feudal government and law evolved that had little to do with the more centralised and absolutist models that would emerge in subsequent centuries in the Castilla reconquered from the Muslims. In language and politics, the Catalans tended to look northwards to France and shared the destiny of the remainder of post-Carolingian Europe.

A hodge-podge of Roman-Visigothic laws combined with emerging feudal practice found its way into the written bill of rights called the *Usatges de Barcelona* from around 1060. Dating this law code is impossible as it grew and changed until well into the 13th century. But it appears that the initial core went into effect in the reign of Ramon Berenguer I (who ruled from 1035 to 1076).

Feudalism was by and large no picnic for the lower classes. Knights more preoccupied with their own chivalry (and frequently less noble pursuits) and the ruling class of counts, dukes and lords above them spent a good deal of time extracting high taxes from overworked peasants with few rights. The Usatges, at least, encouraged what one writer has dubbed 'responsible feudalism'.

The Usatges were put together by legal experts immersed in the study of Roman law as well as the customs of the land. Although they no doubt introduced greater security for the lower classes (vassals), the aim behind these laws was a little less noble. The Comte de Barcelona was in some respects no more than one among many counts across Catalan territory. Establishing a universal law code of which the Comte should be the supreme arbiter was one means of placing the nobles in check.

In his role as supreme judge, the Comte de Barcelona was bound to protect not only his own dependents but all vassals 'unjustly oppressed by their lords'. In the code, Ramon Berenguer I decreed also 'that all princes who will succeed us in this princely office [ie Comte de Barcelona] shall have a sincere and perfect faith and truthful speech for all men, noble and ignoble, kings and princes, magnates and knights, peasants and rustics, traders and merchants, pilgrims and wayfarers, friends and enemies, Christians and Saracens, Jews and heretics...'

The roads and waterways, high points and other strategic bits of land were held to be under the Comte's jurisdiction in order to maintain peace and protect travellers. This was an extension of the older clerical *pax et treuga* (peace and truce). Before anyone spoke seriously of laws to curb lords and knights, the pax et treuga declared zones around monasteries, churches and the like to be 'circles of peace', where anyone could find refuge in time of need. The deterrent was purely moral, and fear of divine retribution frequently was not enough to hold up what was little more than banditry. The aim of reinforcing the Casa de Barcelona's clout dovetailed nicely with a general desire to curb lawlessness.

Some articles of the code could not spell out more clearly the intention of the Comtes de Barcelona to enforce their rule over all Catalan nobility: '... let none of the magnates hereafter presume in any way to either punish criminals ... or to build a new castle against the prince ... '(article 73). The same article reserves the right to judge criminal cases 'only to the rulers'.

Of course justice in those days may seem a little rough for modern tastes: '... let them (the rulers) render justice as it seems fit to them: by cutting off hands and feet, putting out eyes, keeping men in prison for a long time and, ultimately, in hanging their bodies if necessary.' Was

Fanfare for the Common Man

there an element of misogyny in the Usatges? 'In regard to women, let the rulers render justice by cutting off their noses, lips, ears and breasts, and by burning them at the stake if necessary ...'

In many cases, absence of proof meant that those sitting in judgement had to rely on oaths and violence. A series of articles weighs the value of individuals' oaths in monetary terms and according to status. For instance, 'the oaths of peasants who possess a homestead and work it with a yoke of oxen shall be believed, up to the amount of seven silver sous'. A knight's oath was valued in gold coins – owing to the dubious assumption that his rank accorded him greater nobility and probity.

Where all this was considered insufficient, the only options left in many cases were 'judicial battle' or trial by ordeal. The former involved duelling (oneself or by proxy, depending on the circumstances), while the latter involved what was tantamount to torture with boiling and freezing water.

Accusations of adultery (which only men could make) were generally resolved by judicial battle (by proxy) or ordeal of boiling water (in the case of peasants). 'If the wife is victorious, let her husband honourably keep her and make compensation to her ...'! One can only wonder what would compensate for a prolonged bath in boiling water.

The Usatges did improve the legal lot of the lower classes (it's not hard to improve on abject misery), but they hardly made it perfect: 'When a peasant suffers injury to the body or damage to his property or fief, let him in no way dare take vengeance ... but as soon as he suffers the wrong, then let him make an end to this matter in accordance with his lord's command' (article 95). Serfs, of course, barely got a look in.

The Usatges de Barcelona gained widespread acceptance in territories subsequently occupied by the Catalans, for instance in northern Valencia and the Islas Baleares. Under the Corona de Aragón the Usatges remained a pillar of law-making and by the 16th century formed the historical basis of what came to be known as the Constitucions de Catalunya. As Catalunya was absorbed into Castilian Spain, the Catalans jealously guarded the use of their own legal system.

Defeat of the Catalans by Bourbon King Felipe in the War of the Spanish Succession in 1714 spelled the end of the road for the local legal system. Felipe not only banned the use of the Catalan language, he abolished all local privileges and submerged Catalunya in the Spanish state. The Catalans can be an obstinate lot, however, and when in 1932 a Catalan statute was proclaimed, the newly refounded Generalitat resurrected the whole corpus of Catalan law. Franco's victory in 1939 reversed that decision, but by 1960 the centralist grip had been relaxed and the old laws again became the historical basis for a modern Catalan legal system.

Consellers receiving a copy of the Ustages de Catalunya (detail, after a miniature by Bernat Martorell).

Citizens of senior rank already had some say in the running of city affairs and in 1249 Jaume I authorised the election of a committee of top citizens to advise his officials. The idea developed and by 1274 the Consell dels Cents Jurats (Council of the Hundred Sworn-In) formed a kind of electoral college from which an executive body of five *consellers* was nominated to run city affairs.

In 1283, the Corts Catalanes met for the first time. It was a kind of legislative council for all of the territory of the Corona de Aragón and was made up of representatives of the nobility, clergy and high-class merchants to form a counter-weight to regal power. The Corts Catalanes met at first annually, then every three years, but had a permanent secretariat known as the Diputació del General or Generalitat. Its home was, and remains, the Palau de la Generalitat in Plaça de Sant Jaume.

Both the Corts and Consell de Cent increased their leverage as trade grew and their respective roles in raising taxes and distributing wealth became more important. As the count-kings required money to organise wars and other enterprises they came increasingly to rely on Barcelonese and Catalan impresarios who were best represented through these two oligarchic bodies.

Those citizens not considered of high enough quality to break into these clubs, but who increasingly contributed a good amount of wealth to the city and state, became restless. Occasional uprisings and riots were fomented in the streets of Barcelona and the city was roughly divided into two factions: the dominant Biga and the opposition Busca (who at times appeared to get a nudge and a wink from regal sources, just to keep a little pressure on the institutions). Barcelona was as violent as any other average medieval city, nevertheless, the lid was kept firmly on the trouble, if only because ultimate power still remained with the count-kings. They had an interest in stirring things up every now and then but not in precipitating uncontrolled power struggles that might have slipped out of control.

The Generalitat and Consell de Cent lasted until all local rights were abrogated by the Bourbon King Felipe V in 1714.

Meanwhile, Barcelona's trading wealth paid for the great Gothic buildings that still bejewel the city. The cathedral, the Capella Reial de Santa Àgata and the churches of Santa Maria del Pi and Santa Maria del Mar were all built in the late 13th or early 14th century. King Pere III (1336-87) created the breathtaking Reials Drassanes (Royal Shipyards) and extended the city walls again, this time to include the El Raval area west of La Rambla.

Decline & Castilian Domination

Like many empires, Catalunya's came to exhaust its homeland. Sea wars with Genoa, resistance in Sardinia, the rise of the Ottoman empire and the loss of the gold trade all drained the coffers. Commerce collapsed. The Black Death and famines killed about half Catalunya's population in the 14th century. Barcelona's Jewish population suffered a pogrom in 1391.

After Martí I, the last of Guifré el Pilós' dynasty, died heirless in 1410, a special council elected Fernando (Ferran to the Catalans) de Antequera, a Castilian prince of the Trastámara house, to the Aragonese throne. This, the so-called Compromiso de Caspe (1412) (Caspe Agreement) was engineered by the nobility in Aragón, who saw a chance to reduce Catalan influence over their affairs. Fernando and his successors were soon at daggers drawn with their Catalan subjects, who felt they were being exploited for Castilian interests. A rebellion that began in 1462 against King Joan II ended in a siege in 1473 that devastated Barcelona.

Joan II's son, Fernando, succeeded to the Aragonese throne in 1479 and his marriage to Isabel, Queen of Castilla, united Spain's two most powerful monarchies. Just as Catalunya had been hitched to Aragón, now the combine was hitched to Castilla and Ramon Berenguer IV's clever marriage in 1137 in retrospect must have seemed like a nasty trap.

Catalunya effectively became part of the Castilian state, although it jealously guarded its own institutions and system of law as best it could. Juridically, Catalunya had never ceased to be a distinct entity within the Arago-Catalan arrangement. Rather than attack the problem head on, Fernando and Isabel sidestepped it, introducing the hated Inquisition to Barcelona. The local citizenry implored them not to do so as what was left of business life in the city lay largely in the hands of *conversos*, Jews at least nominally converted to Christianity, who were a particular target of Inquisitorial attention. The pleas were ignored and the conversos packed their bags and shipped out their money. Barcelona was reduced to penury.

To make matters worse, the Catholic Monarchs banned the Catalans from trading directly with the newly established American colonies. Everything had to go through the recently enriched Castilian ports of Sevilla and Cádiz. As Spain hit a high point under Carlos I (or Karl V of the Habsburg empire) and his successor Felipe II, Catalunya, now brought further to heel under a Viceroy from Madrid, continued to sink.

Impoverished and disaffected by growing financial demands from the crown, Catalunya revolted again in the 17th century and declared itself an independent 'republic', under French protection, in the Guerra dels Segadors (War of the Reapers; 1640-52). Countryside and towns were devastated and Barcelona was finally besieged into submission. The French protection was less than convincing (and in the end largely resented) however, and seven years later, when France and Spain concluded hostilities, Louis XIV and Felipe IV signed a peace that cost Spain chunks of Catalan territory – Roussillon, parts of Cerdanya and other districts.

War of the Spanish Succession

By now Spain itself was on the skids, and Catalunya was going down with it. When the last of the Habsburgs, Carlos II, died in 1700, he left no obvious successor. France

imposed the investiture of a Bourbon, Felipe V. Although the Catalans preferred the Austrian candidate, Archduke Carlos, they did not at first actively oppose Felipe's enthronement. Schooled in French-style absolutism and centralism, Felipe soon proved vexatious to the Catalans, who threw in their lot with England, Holland, some German states, Portugal and the House of Savoy in their decision to bat for Austria. In 1702 the War of the Spanish Succession broke out. Catalans thought they were on a winner. They were wrong, however, and in 1713 the allies signed the Treaty of Utrecht with France that left Felipe V in charge in Madrid.

Felipe had already taken control of Valencia and Aragón anyway. Barcelona had little to hope for from Felipe V and decided to resist his troops. The siege began in March 1713 and ended on 11 September 1714.

There were no half measures. Felipe V abolished the Generalitat, built a huge fort, the Ciutadella, to watch over Barcelona, and banned writing and teaching in the Catalan language. What was left of Catalunya's possessions were farmed out to the great powers: Menorca had gone to the British in 1713; Naples and Sardinia went to Austria and Sicily to the House of Savoy.

A New Boom

After getting over the initial shock of losing the status of an autonomous principality within the Spanish realm, Barcelona found the Bourbon rulers to be comparatively light-handed in their treatment of the city. Indeed, its prosperity and productivity was in the country's interests. Throughout the 18th century the Barcelonins concentrated on what they do best – industry and commerce.

The big break came in 1778 when the ban on American trade was lifted. Already some enterprising traders had sent vessels across the Atlantic to deal directly in the Americas – still technically forbidden. The early ventures were a commercial success and the lifting of the ban stimulated business. In Barcelona itself, growth was modest but sustained. Small-scale manufacturing provided employment and profit. Wages were rising and city fathers even had a stab at town planning, creating the grid-based workers' district of La Barceloneta.

But before the industrial revolution, based initially on the cotton trade with America, could really get underway, Barcelona and the rest of Spain had to go through a little more pain. A French Revolutionary army was unsuccessfully launched Spain's way in 1793, but when Napoleon turned his attentions to the country in 1808 it was another story. Barcelona and Catalunya suffered along with the rest of the country until the French were expelled in 1813.

It took some years for it to recover, but by the 1830s Barcelona was beginning to ride on a feel-good factor that would last for most of the century. Wine, cork and iron industries developed. Steamships were launched off the slipways from the mid-1830s on. In 1848, Spain's first railway line was opened between Barcelona and Mataró.

Well, not everyone was feeling so good. Creeping industrialisation and prosperity for the business class did not translate so well down the line. Wages were higher than in Madrid, but working-class families lived in increasingly putrid and cramped conditions. Poor nutrition, bad sanitation and disease were the norm in workers' districts and riots, predictably, resulted. As a rule they were put down with little ceremony – the 1840-42 rising was bombarded into submission. Some relief came in 1854 with the knocking down of the medieval walls, but the pressure remained acute. The population was increasing by up to 28% per annum.

In 1869, a revolutionary plan to expand the city was begun. Ildefons Cerdà designed l'Eixample (The Enlargement) as a grid, broken up with gardens and parks, and it was grafted on to the old town, beginning at Plaça de Catalunya. It became (and to a large extent remains) the most sought-after chunk of real estate in Barcelona – but the parks were sacrificed to an insatiable demand for filling spaces with housing. The flourishing bourgeoisie paid for lavish,

ostentatious buildings, many of them in the unique, modernista (Catalan Art Nouveau) style, the leading exponent of which was Antoni Gaudí.

There seemed to be no stopping this town. In 1888 it hosted a Universal Exhibition. It did so in spite of going almost broke in the process, partly due to lack of funding from Madrid. Little more than a year before, work on the exhibition buildings and grounds had not even begun, but they were all completed and only 10 days late. Although the Exhibition attracted more than two million curious visitors, it did not get the international attention some had hoped for.

Nevertheless, Barcelona had become something of a world centre. Changing the cityscape had by now become habitual. La Rambla de Catalunya and Avinguda del Paral.lel were both slammed through in 1888. The rather odd Monument a Colom and Arc de Triomf also saw the light of day that year. Columbus had passed through Barcelona but his Atlantic exploits had precious little to do with that city, and however triumphant the town denizens were feeling at this stage, arches were probably not the most appropriate expression of their mood.

Renaixença

Barcelona was comparatively peaceful through most of the second half of the 19th century. This is not to say that the city was politically inert. The relative peace and growing wealth that came with commercial success helped revive interest in all things Catalan.

The so-called Renaixença (Renaissance) reflected the feeling in Barcelona of renewed self-confidence which lasted into the 1890s. The mood was both backward and forward looking. Politicians and academics increasingly studied and demanded the return of former Catalan institutions and legal systems. The Catalan language was readopted by the middle and upper classes and a new Catalan literature emerged.

In 1892, the Unió Catalanista was formed and demanded the reestablishment of the Corts Catalanes in a document known as the

Bases de Manresa. In 1906 the suppression of Catalan news-sheets was greeted by the formation of Solidaritat Catalana. Led by Enric Prat de la Riba, it attracted a broad band of Catalans, not all of them nationalists.

Perhaps the most dynamic expression of this Catalan renaissance occurred in the world of art. Barcelona was the home of modernisme, the Catalan version of Art Nouveau. While the rest of Spain largely stagnated in the arts, Barcelona was a hotbed of activity. It was a centre for avant-garde art, with close links to Paris, and it was here that the young Picasso spread his artistic wings and drank in the famous artists' hang-out Els Quatre Gats.

1898

This was a very bad year. While textiles and mills formed the backbone of local industry in late 19th century Barcelona, a good chunk of the wealth was generated in Spain's remaining possessions abroad, Cuba and Puerto Rico in particular. A push for home rule that became a militant movement for independence in Cuba proved fatal to the little that was left of Spain's 'empire'.

Rather than meet the claims halfway, Madrid chose the heavy (and ham) fisted approach. The USA had had its eye on these territories for some time and it was not too hard for it to pose as guardian angels to independence movements. Trouble had also been brewing in the Philippines. Everyone but the Madrid government seems to have realised that Spain could not hope to win a naval tussle with this nascent superpower. To cut a long story short, virtually the entire, ill-equipped Spanish navy was sunk in two ignominious battles in Cuba and the Philippines and the colonies were lost to the USA. It was notable how quickly the Americans forgot about notions of independence in these territories.

For Barcelona, the news was disastrous. Many families had considerable business interests tied up in the overseas possessions and they lost everything. As the rag-tag Spanish army was slowly transported home, the most common sight on Barcelona's docks at the turn of the century was of disease-ridden and near-starving conscripts being shipped home to no prospects. The last years of the century saw storm clouds once again on the horizon.

Mayhem

Barcelona's proletariat was growing fast. The total population grew from 115,000 in 1800 to over 500,000 by 1900 and over one million by 1930, boosted, in the early 19th century, by poor immigrants from rural Catalunya and later from other regions of Spain. All this made Barcelona ripe for unrest.

The city became a swirling vortex of anarchists, Republicans, bourgeois regionalists, gangsters, police terrorists and hired gunmen (*pistoleros*). Madrid could not resist introducing a meddling hand in this dangerous cocktail. (Read Gerald Brenan's *The Spanish Labyrinth* or Eduardo Mendoza's novel *City of Marvels* for a taste of some of the unbelievable things that went on: in one episode related by Brenan, gangsters in police pay planted 2000 bombs at or near the bourgeoisie's factories to provide the police with an excuse for arresting anarchists.)

One genuine anarchist bomb at the Liceu opera house on La Rambla in the 1890s killed 20 people. Anarchists were also reckoned to be behind the Setmana Tràgica (Tragic Week) in 1909 when, following a military call-up for Spanish campaigns in Morocco, mobs wrecked 70 religious buildings and workers were shot on the streets in reprisal.

The political front was also active. In 1914, Solidaritat Catalana launched the Mancomunitat de Catalunya, a kind of shadow parliament which demanded a Catalan state within a Spanish federation.

In the post-WWI slump, unionism took hold. This movement was led by the anarchist Confederación Nacional del Trabajo (CNT) – National Confederation of Work, which embraced as many as 80% of the city's workers. During a wave of strikes in 1919-20, employers hired assassins to eliminate union leaders. The 1920s dictator

General Miguel Primo de Rivera opposed both bourgeois Catalan nationalism and working-class radicalism, banning the CNT and Mancomunitat and even closing Barcelona football club, a potent symbol of Catalanism. But he did support the staging of a second world fair in Barcelona, the Montjuïc World Exhibition of 1929.

A Taste of Nationhood

Rivera's repression only succeeded in uniting, after his fall in 1930, the pent-up fervour of Catalunya's radical elements. Within days of the formation of Spain's Second Republic in 1931, leftist Catalan nationalists (Esquerra Republicana de Catalunya – ERC) led by Francesc Macià and Lluís Companys proclaimed Catalunya a republic within an imaginary 'Iberian Federation'. Madrid quickly pressured them into accepting unitary Spanish statehood, but in 1932 Catalunya got a new regional government, with the old title of Generalitat.

Francesc Macià, its first president, died in 1933 and was succeeded by Lluís Companys who, in 1934, tried again to achieve near-independence, proclaiming that 'the Catalan State of the Spanish Federal Republic'. The Madrid government responded with an army bombardment of the Generalitat offices and Barcelona's city hall. The Generalitat was closed and its members given 35-year jail terms. They were released, and the Generalitat restored, when the leftist Popular Front won the February 1936 Spanish general election. Now, briefly, Catalunya gained genuine autonomy. Companys, its president, carried out land reforms and planned an alternative Barcelona Olympics to the official 1936 games in Nazi Berlin.

But things were racing out of control. The left and the right across Spain seemed to be shaping up for an inevitable showdown. Anarchists (and their trade union the CNT) and Socialists (embodied in the Unión General de Trabajadores – General Workers' Union) lined up on the left, the former of the two the most vocal in its support of revolt. Against them were disgruntled sectors of the armed forces, a mixed bag of royalists and conservatives routed in the 1936 polls, and the fringe Falange movement of José Antonio Primo de Rivera (the ex-dictator's dapper son) who were all moving closer to forming a single front.

The Civil War

On 17 July 1936, the day before the Barcelona games were to start, an army uprising in Morocco began the Spanish Civil War. Barcelona's army garrison attempted to take the city for Franco but was defeated by armed anarchists and police loyal to the government.

Franco's forces quickly took hold of most of southern and western Spain. Galicia and Navarra in the north were also his. Most of the east and industrialised north stood with Madrid and the Republic. Initial rapid advances on Madrid were stifled and the two sides settled in for almost three years of misery.

Most, but not all, the army backed the coup. Franco's forces soon had the upper hand economically, occupying much of the grain and grazing country. By the end of 1936 Hitler's Germany and Mussolini's Italy had recognised Franco and were supplying arms, troops, airforce units and cash.

The Republican side had most of the airforce and navy (the latter proved almost unbelievably ineffectual), and much of the country's industry. Although France was sympathetic, the west decided to keep out and even blocked military supplies in the interests of 'neutrality'. The only help came from Stalin's Soviet Union – in the form of military advisers and hardware. But this assistance was never enough and was bought at the price of the nation's entire gold reserves. The rather romantic International Brigades contributed in particular to the defence of Madrid, but were illustrative of the Republic's biggest problem – splintering. Language wasn't the main problem.

Ideology was ultimately what killed the Republicans' chances. While radical anarchists wanted to pursue social revolution at all costs, the increasingly tough and militant communists ostensibly set winning the war as their primary goal, all the while devoting considerable energy to suppressing anarchists and even moderate socialists – their own allies! Their infighting was one of Franco's greatest allies.

The War in Barcelona

The civil war broke the Catalan class alliance. For nearly a year Barcelona was run by anarchists and the POUM (Partido Obrero de Unificación Marxist – the Marxist Unification Workers' Party) Trotskyist militia, with Companys president only in name. Factory owners and rightists fled the city. Unions took over factories and public services, hotels and mansions became hospitals and schools, everyone wore workers' clothes, bars and cafés were collectivised, trams and taxis were painted red and black (the colours of the anarchists), private cars vanished from the streets, and even one-way streets were ignored as they were considered part of the old system.

The anarchists were a disparate lot ranging from gentle idealists to hardliners who drew up death lists, held kangaroo courts, shot priests, monks and nuns (over 1200 of whom were killed in Barcelona province during the civil war), and burnt and wrecked churches – which is why so many Barcelona churches are today oddly plain inside.

The revolutionary atmosphere waned as anarchists began to join the Catalan and Spanish Republican governments and, under Soviet influence, the Catalan communist party (PSUC) grew more powerful. In May 1937 Companys ordered police to take over the anarchist-held telephone exchange on Plaça de Catalunya. After three days of street fighting, chiefly between anarchists and the PSUC, in which at least 1500 died, the anarchists asked for a cease-fire. They and the POUM were soon disarmed.

Barcelona became the Republicans' national capital in autumn 1937 after the Spanish government fled Valencia. The city was first bombed from the air in March 1938. In the first three days 670 people

CATALANS!..

11 de SETEMBRE 1714-1938

Poster war: from Spanish succession to Catalan success – the struggle continued.

were killed; after that, the figures were kept secret. In the end, after the Republicans' defeat in the Battle of the Ebro – the last big set-piece clash of the war – around Tortosa in southern Catalunya in summer 1938, Barcelona was left undefended. Combatants and the Catalan and Spanish Republican governments joined the civilians who were fleeing to France – around 500,000 in all – and the city fell to the Nationalists on 25 January 1939.

Up to 35,000 people were shot in the ensuing purge, and the executions continued into the 1950s. Lluís Companys was arrested in France by the Gestapo in August 1940, handed over to Franco, and shot in secret on 15 October on Montjuïc hill. He is reputed to have died with the words *'Visca Catalunya!'* ('Long live Catalunya!') on his lips.

The Franco Era

Franco didn't hang about waiting for the war to end before he abolished the Generalitat yet again. This symbolic act was carried out in 1938.

Companys was succeeded as the head of the Catalan government-in-exile by Josep Irla, a former ERC MP who remained in charge until May 1954. Irla was succeeded by the charismatic Josep Tarradellas after the parliament-in-exile met in Mexico. Tarradellas remained at the head of the government-in-exile until after the death of Franco.

Franco, meanwhile, embarked on a program of Castilianisation in Catalunya. He banned public use of Catalan and had all town, village and street names rendered in Spanish. Book publishing in Catalan was allowed from the mid-1940s, but education, radio, TV and the daily press remained in Spanish.

In response the occasional anarchist bombing or shooting took place in the 1940s, but by the 1950s opposition had turned to peaceful mass protests and strikes. In 1960 an audience at the city's Palau de la Música Catalana concert hall sang a banned Catalan anthem in front of Franco. The ringleaders included a young Catholic banker, Jordi Pujol, who spent two years in jail as a result. Pujol was to become Catalunya's president in the post-Franco era.

The big social change under Franco was a flood of immigrants from poorer parts of Spain, chiefly Andalucía, attracted by economic growth in Catalunya. Some 750,000 came to Barcelona in the 1950s and 1960s, and almost as many to the rest of Catalunya. Many lived in appalling conditions. While some made the effort to learn Catalan and integrate as fully as possible into local society, the majority came to form great pockets of Spanish-speaking population in the poorer working-class districts of the city. In the earlier days many lived in shanty towns or even caves, worked extraordinary hours for very low pay and struggled along. Spain as a whole suffered in the postwar years, but when economic take-off began in the 1960s many of the newcomers to Barcelona reaped at least some of the benefits.

After Franco

Two years after Franco's death in 1975,

Josep Tarradellas was invited to Madrid by the newly elected Adolfo Suárez to hammer out the Catalan part of a regional autonomy policy. Shortly afterwards, Barcelonins celebrated the Diada, which marks the 1714 defeat, 11 September, with a huge pro-autonomy march across the city – some say as many as a million people marched.

Eighteen days later, King Juan Carlos I decreed the re-establishment of the Generalitat de Catalunya and recognised Josep Tarradellas as its president. When Tarradellas finally returned to Barcelona he announced: '*Ja soc aquí*' ('Here I am').

The new Spanish constitution promulgated in 1978 included a policy of autonomy not only for Catalunya but for all the regions. Catalan and Basque claims for some form of devolution were historically the strongest, but the constitution's architects wanted to leave nothing to chance. Rather than risk upsetting some regions that would inevitably claim they were getting the short end of the stick, it was decided to embark on a staggered program of devolution for the whole country.

In Catalunya, a commission of experts had already cobbled together an autonomy statute in 1977. This got the royal seal of approval in 1979. The Catalan nationalist, Jordi Pujol, was elected Tarradellas' successor in April 1980 and he has remained at the helm of the Generalitat ever since.

Pujol has waged a constant war of attrition with Madrid, eking out ever more powers. Catalunya has made considerable advances on this front, controlling a range of areas including local police, education, trade, tourism, agriculture, hospitals, social security, culture and so on.

The key to local power is taxation. In the 1996 national elections, tax was one of the trade-offs used by the nationalist groupings from Catalunya, the País Vasco (Basque Country) and elswhere, when they helped the conservative Partido Popular's José María Aznar into government. In exchange for their support, Aznar allowed the regions to collect up to a third of income tax directly (previously the limit had been 15%).

The present tax-raising regime expires in 2001, but the Catalans are already pushing for a bigger slice of the tax cake. The País Vasco has special financial arrangements with the central state and, in what is essentially a game of leapfrog, Barcelona's power-brokers can see no reason why they should not be put on at least an equal footing with the Basques (which of course in turn irritates all the other regions).

Politics aside, the big event in post-Franco Barcelona was the successful 1992 Olympics, which spurred a burst of public works and brought new life to areas like Montjuïc, where the major events were held. The once-shabby waterfront is also now transformed with promenades, beaches, marinas, restaurants, leisure attractions and new housing. The Olympics focused world attention on Barcelona's prosperity and cultural, entertainment and tourist attractions. It may come as a disappointment to Jordi Pujol that not too many people outside Spain have ever heard of Catalunya – but Barcelona needs no introduction.

GEOGRAPHY

Barcelona spreads south-west to north-east along the Catalan coast in what is known as the Pla de Barcelona (Barcelona Plain), roughly midway between the French border and the regional frontier with Valencia. The plain averages about 4m above sea level. Mont Taber, the little elevation upon which the Romans built their town, is 15m above sea level. To the south-west, Montjuïc is 173m high.

Urban sprawl tends to be channeled along the coast in either direction, as the landward side is effectively blocked off by the Serralada Litoral mountain chain, which between the Besòs and Llobregat rivers is known as the Serra de Collserola. Tibidabo is the highest point of this chain at 512m, with commanding views across the whole city. As is typical for any large and growing European metropolis, surrounding villages have tended to be swallowed up in the expanding conurbation.

Badalona to the north-east and L'Hospitalet to the south-west mark the municipal boundaries of the city – although, as you drive through them, you'd never know where any began and ended. The Riu Llobregat, which rises in the Pyrenees south of La Molina ski resort (in the Cerdanya area), empties into the Mediterranean just south of l'Hospitalet. Just over the south side of the river is El Prat de Llobregat and Barcelona's airport. To the north, the Riu Besòs in part marks the northern limits of the city.

CLIMATE

Barcelona enjoys a Mediterranean climate, with cool winters and hot summers. July is the most torrid month, with August just behind. Highs can reach 37°C. The seaside location promotes humidity, but sea breezes can bring relief (especially if you happen to be sitting in a seaward apartment room a few floors up). A hotel room with a fan or air-conditioning can make all the difference to a good night's sleep.

In the depths of winter (especially in February) it gets cold enough (average lows of 6.7°C) for you to wish you had heating in your room, but by March, with a little luck, things begin to thaw out. Oddly enough, you can get lucky with the weather in January, which has a tendency to be quite sunny if not terribly warm.

As a rule rainfall is highest in autumn and winter. In September and into October Barcelona often gets a washdown in cracking, late summer thunderstorms.

As Barcelona is downwind from the Pyrenees, cold snaps are always on the cards and

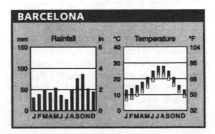

the April-May period is often very changeable. At its best, May can be the most pleasant month of the year – clear and fresh.

ECOLOGY & ENVIRONMENT

Problems of air pollution are typical of a comparatively crowded and busy Mediterranean conurbation such as Barcelona. Although some restrictions apply to parking and driving through the centre of town, the city is generally full to bursting. Cars jostle about the place and the air is none too clean. As the city is close to the sea, the smog gets shifted about a little by sea breezes.

The water down along the beaches is not the most inviting you will see on the Catalan coast but, compared with the way the beaches were prior to the Olympics, the change for the better has been remarkable. Barcelona is a busy port, however, and the water will probably always have a rather murky appearance. You can swim in it though, and plenty of people do.

The disposal of garbage remains a fairly unecological affair. True, large brightly coloured containers have been scattered about the city for the separated collection of paper, glass and cans – but use of them depends entirely on the citizens. Discouragingly, it is not unusual to see mounds of rubbish piling up around these and other general refuse containers – the stuff is eventually hauled off, but it is hard to escape the feeling that it is not a big priority. You will also no doubt notice that many Barcelonins have a love affair with canines. This is never clearer than in the narrow lanes of the Barri Gòtic, where poochy waste products can make unpleasant close encounters with your shoes.

Barcelona, like so many Spanish cities, is justly acclaimed for its nightlife. Those long summer nights are perfect for sitting at open-air cafés and bars (*terrasses/terrazas*), sipping away into the wee hours. To the general hubbub are added the dubious pleasures of impromptu street entertainment and busking. Fantastic. But spare a thought for the poor sods who live on the squares and streets where all the fun is going on. In some areas (Plaça del Pi in the Barri Gòtic, Plaça del Sol in Gràcia just to name a couple), the local residents have hung out mournful banners asking 'Where are the Police?' and pitifully stating 'We Want to Sleep'. Hard to blame them really. Noise pollution is a big problem throughout the city. Rowdy traffic, late night garbage collection, lusty use of sirens by the emergency services and trigger-happiness with car horns all help to keep nerves well jangled.

GOVERNMENT & POLITICS

The Generalitat de Catalunya is the regional parliament of Catalunya, resurrected by royal decree in 1977. Its power as an autonomous goverment is enshrined in general in the statutes of the national Spanish constitution of 1978, and by the Estatut d'Autonomia, which got the royal green light in 1979. The Govern, as the government is also known, is housed in the Palau de la Generalitat on Plaça de Sant Jaume in central Barcelona.

The Generalitat has wide powers over matters like education, health, trade, industry, tourism and agriculture. Education is now nearly all in Catalan which, at the time of Franco's death, had been in some danger, not only because of the immigration of Castilian-speakers but also because many Catalans, although they spoke Catalan, could no longer read or write it.

Since the first post-Franco regional elections in 1980, Jordi Pujol's nationalist, right-of-centre Convergència i Unió (CiU) coalition has been at the controls in the Palau de la Generalitat. CiU does not want full independence from Spain but constantly seeks to strengthen Catalan autonomy. Indeed, only a few Catalans seriously contemplate the idea of independence. The pro-independence party Esquerra Republicana de Catalunya (ERC; Republican Left of Catalonia) has won only 8% to 10% of the vote in recent elections. ERC is avowedly non-violent and there's no Catalan equivalent of the Basque ETA.

In spite of the popular Spanish image of

the whole Catalan populace as a kind of rude, Catalan-babbling separatist movement, the Ajuntament (town hall) is proof that there is more to this than meets the eye. The Ajuntament stands opposite the Palau de la Generalitat and has traditionally been a Socialist haven. Although the Partit Socialista de Catalunya (PSC) is as pro-devolution as anyone else in Catalunya, it does not have a very hardline view of how to proceed. The CiU gets a lot of its support from the Catalan provinces. Barcelona, the one-time haven of anarchist revolution, is unsurprisingly less tolerant of nationalist rigidity of any kind. The PSC, aligned with the main Spanish socialist party, the Partido Socialista Obrero Español (PSOE), has a younger leadership than the CiU, which probably also helps to explain its appeal to Barcelonese voters.

Until 1997, the highly popular Pascual Maragall was *alcalde* (mayor) at the head of the Ajuntament. Much of the go-ahead feeling of Barcelona today is attributed to his forward-looking vision. He was succeeded by Joan Clos, who is tipped to be the socialist candidate in the next municipal elections in 1999.

Pujol may have a tougher time of it at the regional level. In the 1995 elections, CiU lost its overall majority in the Generalitat for the first time since taking power in 1980. When Maragall stepped down from the Ajuntament he disappeared to Rome for a year's sabbatical. His real aim was never really in doubt – he plans to challenge Pujol for the presidency of the Generalitat next time around (elections are due by spring 1999) and, according to recent polls, he might just command enough popularity to succeed. Interestingly, the race might be so close that whoever wins may be forced to deal with to form a government – and the ERC wants to scrap the present autonomy statute and start afresh!

Elections to both the Ajuntament and Generalitat take place every four years. They are free and by direct universal suffrage. The members of each house thus elected then vote to appoint the president of the Generalitat and *alcalde*.

For administrative purposes Barcelona is divided into 10 *districtes*, each with its own ajuntament (local council).

ECONOMY

Barcelona has a reputation for being a hard-working industrial and mercantile city. The roots of its trading culture lie in the days of Mediterranean empire-building, but industry first stirred to life in the small-scale textiles factories that emerged in the 18th century. It gathered steam under the aegis of burgeoning trade between the city and the Americas but it was not until the mid-19th century that industry really took off, and even then Barcelona was far from being a world leader. Metallurgy and engineering became sources of pride to prosperous Barcelona. Steamships were launched here and the country's first trains were 'made in Barcelona'. But business relied on heavy protection, meaning that with the loss of the last American possessions in 1898, Barcelona had to rely almost exclusively on selling inside Spain. With few raw materials of its own, Barcelona in fact played second fiddle to Bilbao (País Vasco) and Oviedo (Asturias) in the mining and secondary industry fields.

In the 1950s and 60s, hundreds of thousands of immigrants in search of work converged on Barcelona from the rest of a largely impoverished Spain. The conditions they encountered were often miserable, but most were absorbed eventually into the local industrial workforce.

With all its ups and downs, Barcelona is today an economic powerhouse. An estimated 26.6% of all Spanish exports come from Catalunya and three-quarters of the region's industry is in or near the capital. Textiles remain big business, alongside leather goods, chemicals, pharmaceuticals and cosmetics. The heart of the city's metal and other heavy industries was La Barceloneta and then Poble Nou, but in the past couple of decades it has shifted farther from the city centre.

It was here in Barcelona that the national car manufacturing company, Seat, came into being. The company is still turning out cars, although it is part-owned by the German company Volkswagen, which in the mid-90s actually considered pulling the plug. Since that blip things seem to be going better and Seat cars are sold with increasing success in markets as far away as Australia.

Across Catalunya about 60% of the population is employed in the services sector, 36% in industry and 4% in agriculture. Tourism is big in Spain and that is reflected in Catalunya, which receives 27% of the country's total visitors – most of them end up in Barcelona at some point. Many of Barcelona's visitors aren't strictly tourists. In 1997, for instance, 42% were tourists, but 39.5% were business people in town to work or attend trade fairs and conferences. They all spend money though, which is what locals are interested in.

The post-Olympic effect is more than visible. As Spaniards and foreigners alike pour in looking for pleasant distractions, snack and tapas bars (not essentially a Barcelonese tradition) have mushroomed. The Bus Turístic, when it began operations in 1990, transported 24,000 people. Seven years later the estimate was 430,000. Barcelona is hot, and that means bucks. In 1998 it was estimated that the total number of visitors to Catalunya (tipped to hit 19 million, a quarter of whom chose Barcelona as their main destination) was up 7% on the previous year. Tourist authorities estimate income for the year at one billion pesetas.

By European standards, Catalunya is not doing too badly in the employment stakes. According to EU statistics, 19.8% of the entire Spanish population is out of work, but in Catalunya the figure is closer to 11%. Governments in Spain prefer to use a different measure – the number of people officially registered as unemployed. On that basis, 11% is the national rate, while in Catalunya 7.4% of the active population is out of a job. Unemployment has been falling steadily throughout the country since halfway through the 1990s, and the Catalan figure is the lowest since 1979.

POPULATION & PEOPLE

The city of Barcelona is home to 1.5 million Barcelonins, although the greater Barcelona area, which takes in villages that will sooner or later be swallowed up in the city administration, counts 2.8 million people. The population for the entire region of Catalunya is 6.09 million (Spain's is 39.5 million). The average age in Catalunya is 39½ – almost two years above that for the rest of Spain. If it weren't for a continued trickle of inwards migration, population growth would stand at zero.

Most of the growth in Barcelona came this century, particularly in the decades following the civil war when poverty in other parts of Spain spurred up to 750,000 people to migrate to Barcelona and its surrounding areas in search of work. It is estimated that at the height of this exodus in the late 1960s, a quarter of those flocking to the city were from rural Catalunya. Roughly 30% came from Andalucía, 11% from the two Castillas, 7% from Extremadura and about 6% each from Galicia and Aragón. In all, it is estimated that from 1950 to 1975, 1.4 million migrants from the rest of Spain moved to Catalunya. For this reason alone you are just as likely to hear Castilian as Catalan in Barcelona.

Officially, some 43,000 foreigners are registered as residents in Barcelona, although the floating population is likely to be considerably higher. People from Latin America (especially Peru, the Dominican Republic and Argentina) make up 36% of the figure. Residents of 'European origin' (mostly Brits, Germans, French and Italians) come in second at 34%. Asians (mostly Filipinos) make up 18.6%, followed by the equally broad category of Africans (11.4%), most of whom are Moroccans.

EDUCATION

Each region in Spain administers its own education system, although overall guidelines are similar throughout the country. In Catalunya a total of 1.29 million people are enrolled in some kind of educational institute, from pre-school to university.

What makes education in Catalunya an issue with spark is language. Until the 1980s, Catalans and non-Catalans alike largely went through school without so much as a word of tuition in the local lingo. Now Catalan gets at least equal treatment, and in some schools teaching of Spanish kicks in only after Catalan. Not everyone is happy with this, fearing that future generations will grow up with Spanish as a second and inadequately used language. Of course it may be that no such thing will happen, and Jordi Pujol's Convergència i Unió coalition claims to be convinced that Catalans will instead enjoy the privilege of true bilingualism.

University education is in some respects a more complex issue. Some classes are still held in Castilian, but ideally the Generalitat would like to change that too. Making the speaking of Catalan a prerequisite for lecturing would exclude the rest of the country's academics from teaching in Catalunya, something that ultimately might do more harm than good.

Illiteracy is still an issue in Catalunya, as it is in the rest of Spain and, contrary to popular belief, in many western countries. Some 3.3% of the Catalan population is illiterate (the national average is 3.9%). Since the bulk of these people are in older age groups, it is to be supposed that the problem will gradually diminish.

ARTS
Painting
Medieval Painting A great many anonymous artists left their work behind in medieval Catalunya, mostly in the form of frescoes, altar pieces and the like in Romanesque and later Gothic churches across the region and in Barcelona. But a few leading lights managed to get some credit. Ferrer Bassá (c1290-1348) is considered one of the region's first masters. Influenced by the Siennese school, his only surviving

works are murals with a slight touch of caricature in the Monestir de Pedralbes. The style of which he is commonly considered to be the originator is also known as Italo-Gothic.

The style soon displayed a more international flavour best expressed in the work of Bernat Martorell (?-1452), a master of chiaroscuro who worked in the mid-15th century. As the Flemish school gained influence, painters like Jaume Huguet (1415-1492) adopted its sombre realism and lightened it with Hispanic splashes of gold, as can be seen in Huguet's *Sant Jordi* in the Museu Nacional d'Art de Catalunya.

There are a few clues to enable you to distinguish between the Romanesque and the Gothic. Firstly, much Romanesque work was done al fresco on church walls and the like; by the Gothic period, such mural painting had largely ceased in Catalunya. Gothic figures are more lifelike than the naively two-dimensional didactic representations of the Romanesque period. Artists now began to inject *feeling* into their portraits – though they still aimed to transmit to the illiterate masses images of the story (1863), when Spanish arms managed a rousing victory over a ragtag Moroccan enemy in North Africa.

Modernisme As the years progressed, painters developed a greater eye for intimate detail and less for epic themes and this led painters into Anecdotisme, out of which would emerge a fresher generation of artists – the modernistas of the turn of the century. Influenced by their French counterparts (Paris was seen as Europe's artistic capital), the modernistas allowed themselves greater freedom in interpretation, producing portraits and scenes, at times of a disturbing nature, which showed more than what the 'eye' supposedly could see, which was what 'realistic' painting purported to depict. But neither Barcelona nor any other place in Spain was exactly at the forefront of innovation. Ramon Casas (1866-1932) and Santiago Rusiñol (1861-1931) were easily the most important exponents of the new forms. The former was a wealthy dilettante of some talent, the latter perhaps a more earnest soul who ran a close second. Although both were the toast of the Bohemian set in turn-of-the-century Barcelona, neither was destined for greatness.

Noucentisme From about 1910, as modernisme was fizzling out, the more conservative cultural movement, noucentisme sought, in general, to advance Catalunya. In the next 20 years, illiteracy was attacked with force, generalised education spread rapidly telecommunications were extended across the region. Artistically speaking, noucentisme claimed to be looking back to more classical models. Joaquim Sunyer (1874-1956) was one of a gaggle of noucentista painters who, just as had happened to their odernista predecessors, were eventually largely forgotten and overshadowed by true genius.

Picasso Born in Málaga, Andalucía (southern Spain), in 1881, Pablo Ruiz Picasso didn't wait long before he started to record images. By the age of nine he was sketching away and, after the family moved to La Coruña (Galicia, in far north-western Spain) in 1891, he began to attend art classes and did his first oil paintings.

In 1895 Picasso landed in Barcelona. His father had obtained a post teaching art at the Escola de Belles Artes de la Llotja (the stock exchange building) and had his son enrolled there too. It was in Barcelona and Catalunya that Picasso was formed. and he spent the following 10 years in Catalunya ceaselessly drawing and painting.

Although schooled in an academic style, he slowly gained enough confidence to go his own way. His paintings showed a diversity of style and a verve of movement in the brushstrokes that already left behind the strictures of 'schooled' art. It is little surprise that, when his father sent him down to the Escuela de Bellas Artes de San Fernando in Madrid for a year in 1897, the precocious Picasso was already bored with school and took himself to the Prado to

Precocious young Pablo Ruiz Picasso learnt to paint from life in the streets of Barcelona.

learn from the masters and to the streets to depict life as he saw it.

Back in Catalunya he spent six months with his friend Manuel Pallarès in bucolic Horta de Sant Joan – he would later claim that it was here he learned everything he knew.

In Barcelona Picasso lived and worked in the Barri Gòtic and got an introduction to the underside of life in the Barri Xinès. By 1900 he was a young regular of Els Quatre Gats, the modernistas' tavern and lair of the avant-garde in Barcelona. He exhibited here and in the same year made his first trip to Paris. His experiences in Barcelona influenced his subject matter and opened his eyes to still wider possibilities. By the time Picasso moved to France, definitively, in 1904, he had already explored his first very personal style. In this so-called Blue Period, many of his canvases have a melancholy feel heightened by the dominance of dark blues. This was followed by the Pink Period; the subjects became merrier and the colouring leaned towards light pinks and greys.

Picasso was a turbulent character and gifted not only as a painter but as a sculptor, graphic designer and ceramicist, and his work encompassed many different style changes. With *Les Demoiselles d'Avignon* (1907), Picasso broke with all forms of traditional representation, introducing a deformed perspective that would later spill over into cubism. By the mid-1920s he was dabbling with surrealism. His best-known work is *Guernica*, a complex painting portraying the horror of war and which was inspired by the German aerial bombing of the Basque town, Gernika, in 1937.

Picasso was prolific during and after WWII and he was still cranking out paintings, sculptures, ceramics and etchings until the day he died in 1973.

Joan Miró By the time the 13-year-old Picasso arrived in Barcelona, his near contemporary, Joan Miró (1893-1983), was cutting his teeth on rusk biscuits in the Barri Gòtic, where he was born and would spend all his younger years. Indeed, he passed a

Dona i Ocell, sculpture created by Joan Miró whose work dealt with symbolic figures, primary colours and the essence of shapes.

DAMIEN SIMONIS

third of his life in his home town. Later in life he divided his time between France, the Tarragona countryside and Mallorca, where he ended his days.

Like Picasso, Miró attended the Escola de Belles Artes de la Llotja, but he missed the whole modernista train. He was a shy man and initially less certain about his artistic vocation – in fact he studied commerce. Nevertheless, from 1915 he produced a series of panoramas which betrayed the influence of Cézanne and portraits which were reminiscent of the naivety of Romanesque frescos.

His first trip to Paris came in 1920, but he was still deeply drawn to the Catalan countryside and coast. From 1919 to the early 1930s Miró wintered in Paris and spent the summers at his family's farmhouse at Montroig on the southern Catalan coast. In Paris he mixed with Picasso, Hemingway, Joyce & Co and made his own mark, after several years of struggle, with an exhibition in 1925. The masterpiece from this, his so-called realist period, was *La Masia* (The Farmhouse).

In the early 1930s Miró went through an artistic crisis, temporarily rejecting painting in favour of collage and other techniques: 'Painting must be murdered' was his cry. The civil war years provoked strong reactions from the painter, particularly with a series of lithographs entitled *Barcelona*. These anguished images reflected the revulsion that war inspired in Miró.

But it was during WWII, while living in seclusion in Normandy, that his definitive leitmotivs finally emerged. Among Miró's most important images are women, birds (the link between earth and the heavens), stars (the unattainable heavenly world, source of imagination), and a sort of net entrapping all these levels of the cosmos. The Miró that most people are acquainted with emerged from this time – arrangements of lines and symbolic figures in primary colours, with shapes reduced to their essence.

In the 1960s and 70s Miró devoted more time to sculpture and textiles. From 1956 he lived in Mallorca, home of his wife Pilar Juncosa, until his death in 1983.

Dalí Salvador Dalí i Domènech (1904-1989) spent precious little of his time in Barcelona, and nothing much of his can be seen there. But it would be churlish to leave him out of the picture altogether. He was born and died in Figueres, where he left his single greatest artistic legacy, the Teatre-Museu.

m.w.

Prolific painter, showman, shameless self-promoter, or just plain weirdo, Dalí was nothing if not a character – probably a little too much for the conservative small-town folk of his home town.

From the age of 13 he was taking drawing lessons and by 1922 his name had appeared in Barcelona's press as an up-and-coming artist. His move to Madrid that year to study at the Escuela de Bellas Artes de San Fernando was important, not for what he studied (he seems to have no more liked the school than Picasso before him) but for his meetings with the poet Federico García Lorca and future film director Luis Buñuel.

Every now and then a key moment arrives that can change the course of one's life. Dalí's came in 1929 when the French poet Paul Eluard visited Cadaqués with his Russian wife Gala. The rest, as they say, is histrionics. Dalí shot off to Paris to be with Gala and plunged into the world of surrealism. He was prolific – perhaps one of the best known works of this time was *El Gran Masturbador* (1929), now in Madrid's Centro de Arte Reina Sofía.

In the 1930s, Salvador and Gala returned to live at Port Lligat on the north Catalan coast, where they played host to a long list of fashionable and art-world guests until the war years – the parties were by all accounts memorable. From the outbreak of war until his return to Port Lligat in 1948, Dalí spent time in France and the USA. Excluded by now from the surrealist movement, his painting style underwent something of an about-face, reaching back to classical roots; but it remained unmistakably Dalian. Hallucination seems always to have been its hallmark. Besides painting, Dalí collaborated in the theatre and cinema, mostly working on sets, and dabbled in writing. All he did seemed calculated to increase his prestige and income, and André Breton, poet and leading light of the surrealist movement, dubbed him Avida Dollars (an anagram of his name).

Back in Port Lligat, the international guest list again grew, as did the scope of the partying. The stories of sexual romps and Gala's appetite for young local boys are legendary. The 1960s saw Dalí painting pictures on a grand scale, including his 1962 reinterpretation of Marià Fortuny's *Batalla de Tetuán*. From 1979 things began to go rapidly downhill. Gala died and Dalí became a recluse, nearly dying in a fire at his property at Púbol. On his death in 1989 he was buried (according to his own wish) in the Teatre-Museu he had created in the old theatre in central Figueres, which houses the single greatest collection of Dalí's work (see the Excursions chapter for this 'must see').

(continued on page 49)

ARCHITECTURE
OF BARCELONA

Title Page: Gaudí's most famous building, La Sagrada Família (photograph by C Groenhout)

Top: Palau de la Música Catalana, in La Ribera, Barcelona

Bottom: Casa Battló – Gaudí's contribution to the Manzana de la Discordia

When most people think of architecture and Barcelona, it is Gaudí's name which usually springs to mind. But the genius of that architect was in a sense the fruit of all that went before his work. The Romans built a modest town here and medieval Barcelona was at first full of Romanesque monuments. But if you were to sum up the city in a word, it would be Gothic. Barcelona is one of Europe's great Gothic treasure houses and it was largely on the legacy of this artistic dish that the modernistas of the late 19th and early 20th centuries supped so keenly, adapting the old to fit the new ways of seeing and building.

Early Barcelona

The evidence for a pre-Roman town in Barcelona is, as we have seen, sparse at best. What Caesar Augustus and Co called Barcino was a fairly standard Roman rectangular job. The forum lay more or less where Plaça de Sant Jaume is today and the whole place covered little more than 10 hectares.

Today there remain some impressive leftovers of the 4th century walls which once comprised 70 towers. In the basement of the Museu d'Història de la Ciutat you can inspect parts of a tower and the wall, as well as other Roman remains. Elsewhere in the immediate vicinity stand temple columns and, a little farther north, a modest burial ground (in Plaça de la Vila de Madrid).

Romanesque

Unfortunately, little remains of Barcelona's Romanesque past – it was all torn down to make way for what were considered greater Gothic spectacles as the city moved into its golden age. If you have the opportunity, a tour through the northern reaches of Catalunya in particular should more than satisfy your curiosity as to what form the Catalan version of this first great wave of Christian European architecture took.

It was Lombard artisans from northern Italy who first introduced the style of monumental building to Catalunya. It is characterised above all by a pleasing simplicity. The exterior of most early Romanesque edifices that have not been tampered with is virtually bereft of decoration. Churches, for instance, tend to be austere, angular constructions, accompanied by tall, square-based bell-towers. There were a few notable concessions to the curve – almost always semicircular or semicylindrical. These included the barrel vaulting inside the churches, the apse (or apses – as the style was developed, up to five might be tacked on to the 'stern' of a church), and arches atop all the openings.

The main portal and windows are invariably topped with straightforward arches. When builders got a little saucy, they might adorn the main entrance with several arches within one another. From the 11th century on, stonemasons began to fill the arches with statuary.

Inset: Tile on staircase at Parc Güell (photograph by D Buckton)

DAMIEN SIMONIS

One of the more charming examples of simple Catalan Romanesque is the church of Sant Climent in Taúll, in north-western Catalunya. But it is by no means the only one – northern (or Old) Catalunya is peppered with as many as 2000 such churches. The most magnificent structure is the church of Sant Vicenç in the castle complex dominating Cardona (less than an hour by car north-west of Barcelona). As for Romanesque decoration, the main doorway to 12th century Santa Maria de Ripoll, north of Barcelona, is the most extravagant display you will see in Catalunya.

In Barcelona itself you can espy only a few Romanesque remnants. In the Catedral the 13th century Capella de Santa Llúcia survives, along with part of the cloister doors. The 12th century former Benedictine monastery of Sant Pau del Camp is also a good example, especially the cloisters. There are a few other scattered reminders, but if Romanesque is your thing and you want to see a little more without really leaving Barcelona, catch the FGC train north to Sant Cugat del Vallès. Although much was incorporated into a later Gothic construction, the 12th century cloister is fine and the Lombard bell tower is Romanesque. Here you will even find remains of pre-Romanesque Visigothic building. The counterpoint to Romanesque architecture was the art used to decorate so many of the churches and monasteries built in the style. In this respect Barcelona is *the* place to be, as the best of Romanesque art from around Catalunya has been concentrated in the Museu Nacional d'Art de Catalunya.

Above: A rare Barcelona example of Romanesque and Visigothic decoration on the Església de Sant Pau del Camp, El Raval.

Gothic

This soaring form of architecture took off in France in the 13th century and spread across Europe. In Barcelona, its emergence coincided with Jaume I's march in to Valencia and annexation of Mallorca and Ibiza, accompanied by the rise and rise of a trading class and a burgeoning mercantile empire The enormous cost of the grand new monuments could thus be covered by the steady increase in the city's wealth.

Gothic buildings did not simply pop up like mushrooms from one day to the next. The style of architecture reflected the development of building techniques. The introduction of buttresses, flying buttresses and ribbed vaulting in ceilings allowed engineers to raise edifices that were loftier and seemingly lighter than ever before. The pointed arch became a standard characteristic and the great rose windows were the source of light inside these enormous spaces. Think about the little hovels that most of the labourers on such enormous projects lived in, the precariousness of wooden scaffolding and the primitive nature of building materials available and you get some idea of the degree of awe the great cathedrals, once completed, must have inspired in the common pleb.

Catalan Gothic, however, did not follow exactly the same course. Decoration tends to be more sparing than in northern Europe and the most obvious defining characteristic is the triumph of breadth over height. While some northern European cathedrals reach for the sky, Catalan Gothic has a tendency rather to push to the sides, stretching vaulting design to the limit. The Saló del Tinell, with a parade of 15m arches (among the largest ever built without reinforcement) holding up the roof, is a perfect example of Catalan Gothic. Another is the Drassanes, Barcelona's enormous medieval shipyards (and home today to the Museu Marítim). In their churches, too, the Catalans opted for a more robust shape and lateral space – step into Santa Maria del Mar

Right: A jewel of Catalan Gothic – the Església a Santa Maria del Mar in Barcelona's La Ribera.

DAMIEN SIMONIS

SIMON BRACKEN

or Santa Maria del Pi and you'll soon get the idea. It seems that the long, narrow and high naves of many northern European Gothic churches inspired more claustrophobia than admiration in the Catalans. While on the subject of churches, a peculiarly Spanish touch that can be seen here and throughout the peninsula is the presence of a *coro*, or enclosed choir stalls, smack in the middle of the main nave – the one in the Catedral is a good specimen.

Another notable departure from what you might have come to expect of Gothic beyond the Pyrenees is the lack of spires and pinnacles. Bell-towers tend to terminate in a flat or nearly flat roof. Occasional exceptions prove the rule – the main façade of Barcelona's Catedral, with its three gnarled and knobbly spires, does vaguely resemble the outline that confronts you in Chartres or Cologne.

Perhaps the single greatest building spurt came under Pere III. Odd in a sense because, as Dickens might have observed, it was not only the best of times, but also the worst. As the Mediterranean empire had spread, Barcelona's coffers had been filled, but by the mid-14th century, when Pere III was in command, the city had been pushed to

Above: The Gothic exception that proves the rule – the Catedral in the Barri Gòtic.

the ropes by a series of disasters: famine, repeated plagues, and pogroms.

Maybe the king didn't notice. He built, or began to build, much of the Catedral, the Drassanes shipyards, the Llotja stock exchange, the Saló del Tinell, the Casa de la Ciutat (which houses the Ajuntament) and numerous lesser buildings, not to mention part of the city walls. Along with the Catedral, the churches of Santa Maria del Pi and Santa Maria del Mar were completed by the end of the century. The last of these is considered by many to be the finest of Barcelona's great Gothic monuments on account of the harmony of its proportion.

Gothic had a longer use-by date in Barcelona than in many other European centres. It seemed that with this style the city had found the expression of its soul. Even several centuries later, architects still felt subject to this style. By the early 15th century the Generalitat still didn't have a home worthy of the name and the architect Marc Safont set to work on the present building on Plaça de Sant Jaume. Even renovations carried out a century later were largely in the Gothic tradition, although some Renaissance elements eventually snuck in – the façade on Plaça de Sant Jaume is a rather disappointing result.

Carrer de Montcada, in La Ribera, was the result of a late medieval act of town planning – a street laid out by design rather than simply 'evolving'. Eventually, mansions belonging to the moneyed classes of 15th and 16th century Barcelona were erected along this street. Many now house museums, art galleries and the like. Though these former mansions appear austere and forbidding on the outside, their interiors

Right: The Monestir de Pedralbes, one of the few examples of Gothic buildings outside Barcelona's old city.

DAMIEN SIMONIS

often reveal another world altogether, of pleasing courtyards and decorated stairs.

The great bulk of Barcelona's Gothic heritage lies, predictably enough, within the boundaries of the Ciutat Vella, but a few examples can be found beyond it, notably the Monestir de Pedralbes in the barrio of Sarrià, which until 1921 was a separate village.

Renaissance & Baroque

The strong Barcelonese affection for the Gothic style, coupled with a decline in the city's fortunes which led to a decrease in urban development, seems to have largely closed Barcelona to the extravagances that elsewhere in Europe accompanied the Renaissance and baroque. Such modest examples of baroque as can be found in Barcelona are generally decorative rather than structural, and are usually additions to pre-existing Gothic structures.

Among the more important but restrained baroque constructions in Barcelona are the Església de la Mercè, home to the medieval sculpture of Our Lady of Mercy (Barcelona's co-patron with Sant Eulàlia), the Església de Sant Felip Neri and the Jesuits' Església de Betlem (largely destroyed in the civil war and since rebuilt). Also worth a look is the courtyard of the Palau Dalmases, in Carrer de Montcada, reworked from the original Gothic structure.

The Modernistas

Say Barcelona and most people respond Gaudí (often pronouncing it 'gawdy', in some cases an expression of artistic judgement).

Antoni Gaudí (1852-1926; pronounced Gowdy, with the emphasis on the y) was born in Reus and initially trained in metalwork. He obtained his architecture degree in 1878. He personifies, and in large measure transcends, a movement in architecture that brought a thunderclap of innovative greatness to an otherwise middle-ranking (artistically speaking) European city. But this startling wave of creativity subsided just as quickly – the bulk of the modernistas' work was done from the 1880s to about 1910.

What the Catalans call modernisme emerged as a trend in all the arts in Barcelona in the 1880s. The avowed aims (especially in literature) of its followers were perhaps outlandish and pretentious, but the urge to seek innovation in expression coincided with a period of generalised optimism in Barcelona and throughout much of western Europe. In spite of the loss of Cuba and the Philippines in 1898 and the spread of violence in the city in the first decade of this century, Barcelona experienced a *belle époque* to equal to those which occurred elsewhere.

Modernisme did not appear in isolation in Barcelona. To the British and French the style was called *Art Nouveau*; to the Italians it was *lo stile Liberty*; the Germans called it *Jugendstil* (Youth Style) and their Austrian confrères *Sezession* (Secession).

There is something misleading about the name modernisme. It suggests the adoption of new means of construction and/or decoration and the rejection of the old. In a sense, nothing could be further from the truth. From Gaudí down, modernista architects looked to the past for inspiration. Gothic, Islamic and Renaissance all had something to offer. At its most playful, modernisme was able to intelligently flout the rulebooks on all these styles and create new and exciting cocktails. Even many of the materials used by the modernistas were traditional – but their application was utterly innovative.

The search for a source or spirit was complemented by a desire to renew and transform those sources into a new expression, or re-expression, of timeless values in a contemporary universe. Those roots and their transformation are of course more readily observed in some modernista constructions than in others.

As many as 2000 buildings in Barcelona and throughout Catalunya display at least some modernista traces and Gaudí also undertook a handful of projects beyond Catalunya. It is one thing to have at hand an architect of genius. It is still more remarkable that several others of considerable talent should have been working at the same time. But the proliferation of their work was due, above all, to the availability of dosh – as with most great artists down the centuries, genius required both a muse *and* a patron. Gaudí & Co had no shortage of orders. By happy coincidence modernisme picked up pace at the same time as Barcelona's urban expansion project, the area known as l'Eixample, was gathering steam. The money for building was available and so was the space.

Modernisme also emerged within the context of the Catalan Renaixença, a rebirth or rediscovery of Catalan heritage by a certain intellectual elite. This rebirth expressed itself in many ways, from the

Modernista masterpieces: **(right)** Casa Vicenç, designed by Antoni Gaudí, (see Things to See & Do chapter); **(far right)** the Arc de Triomf, designed by Josep Vilaseca as an entrance to the 1888 Universal Exhibition.

DAMIEN SIMONIS

DAMIEN SIMONIS

ARCHITECTURE OF BARCELONA

founding of avowedly Catalan nationalist political pressure groups that sought the re-establishment of autonomous rights for the region through to the (self)conscious resurrection of Catalan as an active literary language. The good and the great of Barcelona felt too that their town was emerging on the world stage. After all, it had staged the 1888 Universal Exhibition, the first city in Spain to have done so.

Three Geniuses

Gaudí does not appear to have held overly strong views on Catalanism, but the two architects who most closely followed him in talent, Lluís Domènech i Montaner (1850-1923) and Josep Puig i Cadafalch (1867-1957), were prominent nationalists. Puig i Cadafalch, in fact, was a prominent politician and president of the Catalan Mancomunitat (see Mayhem, History in Facts about Barcelona) from 1916 to 1923.

A quick comparison of some of the work by these three architects is enough to illustrate the difficulty in defining closely what is modernisme. As Gaudí became more adventurous he increasingly appeared as a lone wolf in the modernista panorama. With age he became

D BUCKTON

Left & facing page:
Gaudí found his inspiration in the curved forms of nature, as evidenced in these details of his Casa Milà (La Pedrera).

DAMIEN SIMONIS

DAMIEN SIMONIS

DAMIEN SIMONIS

Top: Mosaic magic at Domènech i Montaner's Palau de la Música Catalana in La Ribera

Middle: Hospital de la Santa Creu i Sant Pau, designed by modernista architect Domenech i Montaner

Bottom: Tilework on the Hospital de la Santa Creu i Sant Pau

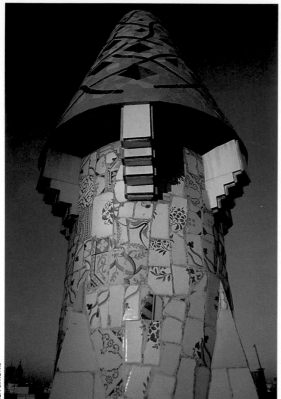

DAMIEN SIMONIS

DAMIEN SIMONIS

DAMIEN SIMONIS

C GROENHOUT

Parc Güell (details **top left, right & middle**) one of Gaudí's most ambitious projects and still not completed when he died, is a place where the artificial seems more natural than the natural.

DAMIEN SIMONIS

DAMIEN SIMONIS

DAMIEN SIMONIS

C GROENHOUT

Top left, right & middle: More details from Parc Güell. **Bottom & facing page:** The wave effect of the uneven grey stone façade of Gaudí's Casa Milà is emphasised by the elaborate balconies.

DAMIEN SIMONIS

DAMIEN SIMONIS

Top: Tiles from the Palau de la Música, a high-point of modernista architecture

Bottom: Spires of La Sagrada Família, Gaudí's homage to the holy family, which drew on Gothic roots but incorporated the modern architect's own view of the world.

almost exclusively motivated by stark religious conviction and devoted much of the latter part of his life to what remains Barcelona's call sign – the Sagrada Família church. His inspiration in the first instance here is clearly Gothic. But you don't have to take too close a look at the parts built in his lifetime to see that he is right out there by himself. Gaudí sought the perfection of harmony and perspective he observed in nature. Straight lines were out. Man was hard-pressed to emulate the works of nature, but he could try. Gaudí found his inspiration in the forms of plants and stones and used complex string models weighted with plumb drops to make his calculations (you can see an example in the upstairs mini-museum in La Pedrera). The architect's work is at once a sublime reaching out to the heavens and yet an earthy appeal to the sinewy movement – even in stillness – of nature's own constructs.

Others of his key works show a similar preoccupation with the forms of nature such as the Casa Milà (La Pedrera) and Casa Batlló (for more on which see the Things to See & Do chapter), where not a single straight line appears anywhere.

ARCHITECTURE OF BARCELONA

DAMIEN SIMONIS

For real contrast, just look from Casa Batlló to Puig i Cadafalch's Casa Amatller next door, where the straight line is all too much in evidence. This architect has also looked to the past, and to foreign influence (the gables are borrowed from the Dutch), and still managed to create a house of startling beauty and invention. Domènech i Montaner, too, clearly looks into the Gothic past, but never simply copies, as evidenced by the Castell dels Tres Dragons (built as a café-restaurant for the Universal Exhibition in 1888 and now home to the Museu de Zoologia) or the Hospital de la Santa Creu i Sant Pau. In these buildings, Domènech i Montaner has put his own spin on the past, in both decoration and in structure. In the case of the Castell dels Tres Dragons, the main windows are more of a neo-classical borrowing, and Islamic touches can be made out in the detail. Domènech i Montaner seems to come closest to Gaudí's ideas in the Palau de la Musica Catalana. The structure may be largely linear, but the decor is anything but.

DAMIEN SIMONIS

Top: Domènech i Montaner's Hospital de la Santa Creu i Sant Pau

Bottom: detail of tilework on the Hospital

DAMIEN SIMONIS

The curve implies movement and hence vitality and this idea informed a great deal of Art Nouveau thinking across Europe, in part inspired by long-standing tenets of Japanese art.

Materials & Decoration

All three of the 'greats', and a whole gaggle of lesser known figures of the modernista style, relied heavily on artisanal skills which, by now, had been all but relegated to history. There were no concrete pours for these guys. Unclad brick, exposed iron and steel frames, copious use of glass and tiles in decoration were all features of the new style – and indeed it is often in the décor that modernisme is at its most flamboyant and identifiable. The kinds of craftsmen required to execute these tasks were the heirs of the guild masters, and had absorbed centuries of know-how about just what could and could not be done with these materials. Forged iron and steel were newcomers, but the approach in learning how they could be used was not dissimilar to that adopted for more traditional materials. Gaudí, in particular, relied on these old skills and even

Top: Casa Amattler, designed by Puig i Cadafalch, who played it straight to great effect.

ARCHITECTURE OF BARCELONA

DAMIEN SIMONIS

ran schools in the Sagrada Família workshops to keep them alive.

Iron came into its own in this period. Nowhere is this more evident than in Barcelona's great covered markets: Mercat de la Boqueria, Mercat del Born (now empty and destined for conversion into a library) and Mercat de Sant Antoni, just to name the main ones. Their grand metallic vaults not only provided shade over the produce for sale but were a proclamation both of Barcelona's dynamism and the success of 'ignoble' materials in grand building.

The Rome-trained sculptor Eusebi Arnau (1864-1934) was one of the most constant figures called up to decorate Barcelona's great modernista buildings, both inside and out. The appearance of the Hospital de la Santa Creu i Sant Pau is one of his legacies and he was heavily involved in the design and embellishment of monuments in the Parc de la Ciutadella. He also had a hand in the Palau de la Música Catalana, the Fonda Espanya restaurant in El Raval, the Casa Amatller and others.

Decorators of several less grand establishments were quick to jump on to the modernista bandwagon. Casa Quadros on La Rambla, with

DAMIEN SIMONIS

Top: A dreamy example of modernista design on the shopfront at Casa Quadros.

Bottom: Detail of tile-work at Gaudí's rather ambitious Parc Guell.

its Chinese dragon and impossible cladding of umbrellas, remains a dreamy example of daring shopfront design. Less obvious but just as clearly modernista on a closer look are the many surviving shop fronts of, above all, pharmacies (eg Carrer de València 256 and Carrer de Mallorca 312) and bakeries (eg Antiga Casa Figueras, La Rambla 83).

Where to Look
Barcelona is full of modernista traces. A separate guide book would be needed to detail all of them. In the Things to See & Do chapter there is a walking tour of the main modernista sights (largely concentrated in l'Eixample or nearby, although there are some important exceptions). A number of lesser sights are also briefly mentioned in passing. The main ones are discussed in more detail later in that chapter. Tourist offices can also provide pamphlets and other material with detailed maps covering a greater range of modernista sights. Remember that, as many of these modernista buildings are still private houses and/or offices, it is often difficult to see inside them.

Noucentisme & After
Even before Gaudí died, modernisme had been swept aside. In the aftermath of WWI especially, it seemed already stale, decadent and somehow unwholesome. Even before the war, *noucentisme* (literally, '19th-centuryism') had shunted aside modernisme in the arts. This new style represented a return to classic Mediterranean forms and was as unimaginative as it must have been comforting to some. Between the two world wars a host of neoclassical and neo-baroque edifices went up (around Plaça de Catalunya, along the newly created Via Laietana and on Montjuïc for the World Exhibition of 1929).

The chaos and civil war of the 1930s, followed by the penury of the 1940s and 1950s, left little room for architectural fancy work. Apartment blocks and offices, designed with a realism and utilitarianism that to most mortals seem deadly dull, were now erected.

Barcelona Today
The title of Llàtzer Moix's study of architecture and design in modern Barcelona, *La Ciudad de los Arquitectos*, (The City of Architects) could just as well serve as an epithet for the city.

In the run-up to the 1992 Olympics, more than 150 architects were beavering away at almost 300 building and design projects! Things have slackened off a little since then, but that doesn't mean Barcelona has lost its taste for building.

The World Trade Centre, due for completion by 1999, is touted as the biggest commercial centre in any European port and a building of the 'latest generation'.

Ricard Bofill's team designed the recently finished Teatre Nacional de Catalunya – a mix of neoclassicism and the modern – just off

(continued on page 48)

Gaudí – God's Architect

The idea for La Sagrada Família came from a rich publisher, Josep Marià Bocabella i Verdaguer, the man behind the emergence of an arch conservative society dedicated to Sant Josep (St Joseph). The society came together in part as a response to calls from Pope Pius IX for a renewal of the Catholic faith, which he saw threatened in a Europe flooded with ideas of liberalism, democracy, modernity and other such iniquitous nonsense.

The Pope had concrete cause for concern. Garibaldi's victories in Italy had left the Vatican virtually bereft of secular power. Liberalism in Spain seemed equally pernicious.

Among the Pope's exhortations was a renewal of devotion to Jesus, Mary and Joseph, the Holy Family, or *Sagrada Família*. And so Bocabella had an inspired idea. What decadent, liberal Barcelona needed was a great church raised to the Holy Family, where contrite citizens could expiate their sins. The society raised the cash and the first stone of a neo-Gothic structure was laid in 1882. The original architect soon quit, and into the breech stepped Antoni Gaudí in 1884.

He was given a free hand. He conceived a structure that drew on Gothic roots, and embellished it with his own very particular spin.

Gaudí, born into an artisan family in Reus, southern Catalunya, and trained as a metalsmith, was already a successful architect. Up to 1910 he worked on numerous buildings in Barcelona and elsewhere – beyond Catalunya he left three monuments, one each in Comillas (Cantabria), Astorga and León. After abandoning the more or less finished Pedrera on Passeig de Gràcia for the Milà family, he began to narrow his efforts.

True, he continued to work for Eusebi Güell, his chief patron and wealthy industrialist, on two ambitious projects that never reached completion: the Parc Güell and Colònia Güell (see Things to See and Do for more on both – the crypt of the church in the latter provides many clues as to how Gaudí aimed to approach technical challenges in his masterwork). Funds for both projects had petered out by 1916, by which time his only interest seemed to be La Sagrada Família.

SIMON BRACKEN

South-west (Passion) façade of La Sagrada Família, completed between 1954 and 1976

A conservative and moderate Catalanist, Gaudí became increasingly religious and came to view his great church, into which he poured all the architectural and design knowledge he had accumulated, as a sacred mission. As Bocabella's Josephine society and Barcelona's wealthy tired of the project and having to cough up money for what seemed a bottomless pit, Gaudí resigned himself, with suitably religious stoicism, to a long struggle. He invested everything he had into it, and ran craft workshops on site to nurture a skilled workforce to carry out the kind of decoration he wanted. He was probably deep in thought about how to proceed next when he was run over by a tram on the corner of Gran Via de les Corts Catalanes and Carrer de Bailén in 1926. He was so ragged and poor that at first no one recognised him. He died three days later and the whole city turned out for his funeral.

Gaudí – God's Architect

As he worked on La Sagrada Família, Gaudí evolved steadily grander and more original ideas for it. He stuck to the basic Gothic cross-shaped ground plan with an apse, but eventually devised a temple 95m long and 60m wide, able to seat 13,000 people, with a central tower 170m high and another 17 of 100m or more. With his characteristic dislike for straight lines (there were none in nature, he said), Gaudí gave his towers swelling outlines inspired by the weird peaks of the holy mountain Montserrat outside Barcelona, and encrusted them with a tangle of sculpture that seems an outgrowth of the stone.

At Gaudí's death only the crypt, the apse walls, one portal and one tower had been finished. Three more towers were added by 1930 – completing the north-east (Nativity) façade – but in 1936 anarchists burned and smashed everything they could in La Sagrada Família, including the workshops, models and plans.

Work restarted in 1952 using restored models and photographs of drawings, with only limited guidance on how Gaudí had thought of solving the huge technical problems of the building. Between 1954 and 1976 the south-west (Passion) façade, with four more towers, was completed, with only some decorative detail work outstanding. The nave, started in 1978, is coming along nicely.

Constant controversy has dogged the building program. Some say the quality of the new work and its materials – concrete instead of stone – are inferior to the earlier parts; others claim that, in the absence of detailed plans, the shell should have been left as a monument to Gaudí; yet others simply oppose all the expenditure (although the funding is private). The chief architect, Jordi Bonet, and his supporters, aside from their desire to see Gaudí's mighty vision made real, argue that their task is a sacred one – this is a church intended to atone for sin and appeal for God's mercy on Catalunya. The way things are going, it might be finished by 2020 – a truly medieval construction timetable.

Gaudí's own story is far from over. The rector of La Sagrada Família, Lluís Bonet Armengol, is promoting Gaudí's beatification. Although more than 70 years have passed since his death, the rector is convinced that sufficient proof of Gaudí's saintliness can be found to eventually move the Pope to canonise him. Says Bonet Armengol, Gaudí's contemporaries 'knew he was God's Architect'.

DAMIEN SIMONIS

The swelling outline of the towers of La Sagrada Família was inspired by the holy mountain of Montserrat.

SIMON BRACKEN

Left: The Olympic Stadium, one of 300 buildings designed by more than 150 architects in the run-up to the 1992 Games.

Plaça de les Glòries Catalanes. Across the road, Rafael Moneo's Auditori Municipal is destined to become the city's main venue for classical music.

As these projects wind up, Barcelona looks further ahead to the next big event – the World Cultural Forum in 2004. Exactly what this will be is a little hazy, but in the meantime it provides an excuse to further spruce up the city. The area from Port Olímpic to the Riu Besós is set to be revamped as a new waterfront residential haven, and the so-called Front Marítim along the shore has been earmarked for gardens and hotels. The Avinguda Diagonal will now finally get the look originally intended for it and will stretch uninterrupted from Pedralbes to the sea just short of the Riu Besòs. The riverbanks along the Besòs are being turned into a 'green space'.

Shopping centres are always popular and right on Plaça de Catalunya a new one (which will include some of the most expensive office space in the city), El Triangle, is nearing completion. Not only is the airport due for a third runway, the nearby Riu Llobregat will be diverted too in what is claimed will be an environmentally friendly redevelopment of the whole area.

D BUCKTON

BETHUNE CARMICHAEL

Top: Gaudi was an artisan as well as an architect and gloried in details such as these mosaics at his garden city, Parc Güell.

Bottom: A mosaic-roofed fantasy near the entrance to Parc Güell

Gaudí's Casa Batlló, one of three distinctive buildings which constitute the Manzana de la Discordia

(continued from page 32)
Contemporary After such a trio, all other artists and their work seem a little dull by comparison. But Antoni Tàpies (1923-) is one important contemporary artist who has often been overlooked in all the commotion over the big three. Much of his work can now be seen in the Fundació Antoni Tàpies (see the Things to See & Do chapter).

To get an idea of what is happening in Catalan art today, you should make for the MACBA art gallery (see Things to See & Do). There is no shortage of Barcelona-born artists beavering away at all sorts of things. Among them are Susana Solano (1946-), Xavier Grau (1951-), Sergi Aguilar (1946-), Joan Hernàndez Pijuan (1931-), Ignasi Aballí (1958-) and Jordi Colomer (1962-).

Avant-Garde in the Streets Barcelona hosts quite an array of street sculpture, from Miró's *Dona I Ocell*, which stands in the park dedicated to the artist, to the *Peix* by contemporary architect Frank Gehry, on the Vila Olímpica waterfront

Others you may want to keep an eye out for are *Barcelona's Head* by Roy Lichtenstein (on Moll de la Fusta, the waterfront area by Maremàgnum) and Fernando Botero's characteristically tumescent *El Gat* at Carrer del Portal de Santa Madrona, behind the Drassanes.

Perhaps the weirdest monument is what looks like a pile of square containers with windows leaning precariously, like so many dice, on La Barceloneta beach. Made in 1992 by Rebecca Horn, it is called *Homenatge a la Barceloneta* (Hommage to La Barceloneta).

Literature
Beginnings The earliest surviving documents written in Catalan date to the 12th century. Most of them are legal, economic, historical and religious texts. The oldest of them is a portion of the Visigothic law code, the *Liber Iudicorum,* rendered in the vernacular. The oldest original texts in Catalan are the *Homilies d'Organyà*, which constitute a religious work.

Catalunya's first great writer was Ramon Llull (1235-1315), who eschewed the use of either Latin or Provençal in literature. His two best known works are perhaps *El Llibre de les Bèsties* and *El Llibre d'Amic i Amat*, the former an allegorical attack on feudal corruption and the latter a series of short pieces aimed at daily meditation – both inspired in part by Islamic works.

The count-king Jaume I was a bit of a scribbler himself and penned a rare autobiographical work, the *Llibre dels Feyts* (Book of Deeds), in the late 13th century. Ramon Muntaner (1265-1336), more of a propagandist than anything else, spent a good deal of his life eulogising various Catalan leaders and their deeds of derring-do in his *Crónica.*

Segle d'Or Everyone seems to have a 'golden century', and for Catalan writers it was the 15th. Ausiàs March (actually a Valenciano), announcing he had abandoned the style of the troubadors, forged a Catalan poetic tradition. His style is tormented and highly personal and continues to inspire Catalan poets to this day.

Most European peoples seem to feel it necessary to claim to have produced the first European novel. The Catalans claim it was Joanot Martorell's *Tirant lo Blanc.* Cervantes himself thought it the best book in the world. Martorell was also a busy fighting knight and his writing tells of bloody battles, war, politics and sex. Some things don't change. More obscure names of the epoque include Bernat Metge (who saw out the 14th century), Roís de Corella and Jaume Roig.

Renaixença Catalan literature declined rapidly after the 15th century and suffered a seemingly mortal blow in the wake of the defeat in 1714. The Bourbon king Felipe V banned the language and forced it so far underground that to many it must have seemed doomed to extinction.

As Catalunya began to enjoy a burgeoning economy in the 19th century, there was sufficient leisure time for intellectuals, writers and artists to take a renewed interest in all things Catalan.

The revival of Catalan literature is commonly dated to 1833 when the rather saccharine poem *A la Pàtria* was written in Madrid by Carles Aribau.

From 1859, when high-minded Catalan intellectuals reintroduced the Catalan language poetry competitions, Jocs Florals, a steady stream of material that was generally fit to be ignored started to dribble out of the tap. True quality in poetry came only with the appearance in 1877 of country pastor, Jacint Verdaguer (1845-1902), whose *L'Atlantida* is an epic that defies easy description. To the writer's contemporaries, however, the poem confirmed Catalan's arrival as a 'great' language. Verdaguer inspired others, above all the novelist Narcís Oller (1846-1930) and playwright Àngel Guimerà (1845-1924). The former's *La Febre d'Or* (1893) describes the shaky world of speculative finance that dominated much of boomtime Barcelona.

Modernisme & Noucentisme Modernisme's main literary voice of worth was the poet Joan Maragall (1860-1911). Also noteworthy is the work of Víctor Català (1873-1966) (a pseudonym of Caterina Albert – why did women have to pretend to be men in order to get anywhere?). Her principal work is *Solitud*, a mysterious novel charting the awakening of a young woman whose husband has taken her to live in the Pyrenees.

Eugeni d'Ors (1881-1954), more of a journalist, critic and social commentator than writer, was one of the leading figures of noucentisme, which aimed in part to rid the cultural scene of what many saw as the decadence of modernisme. Carles Riba (1893-1959), was the period's most outstanding poet, although that is not saying an awful lot.

To the Present Mercé Rodoreda (1909-83) was one of the major writers in Catalan of the 20th century. Her first successful novel was *Paloma (1938)* which tells the story of a young girl seduced by her brother-in-law. After the civil war Rodoreda went into exile and in 1962 published one of her best known works, *Plaça del Diamant*, which recounts life in Barcelona in the war years seen through the eyes of a working-class woman. The book has been translated into English and several other languages.

Josep Pla (1897-1981) was a prolific writer who, after the victory of Franco in 1939, spent many years abroad. He wrote in Catalan and Castilian and his work ranged from travel writing to histories and fiction. His complete works total 46 volumes.

Since the demise of Franco, the amount of literature being produced in Catalan has increased greatly, but not a few of the region's more noteworthy scribblers write in Spanish too, and in some cases prefer to do so.

Juan Goytisolo (1931-) started off in the neorealist vein but his more recent works, such as *Señas de Identidad* and *Juan sin Tierra*, are decidedly more experimental.

A highly accessible writer is Barcelona-born José Luis Sampedro (1917-). A professor of structural economics(!) and one-time senator, his novels are wide-ranging and thought-provoking. He considers *Octubre, Octubre* his life testament. *La Sonrisa Etrusca* is a touching account of the loves and death of a Calabrian peasant in Milan – other works take Sampedro from the Baltic to the South Seas.

Jorge Semprún (1923-), who lost his home and family in the civil war, ended up in a Nazi concentration camp for his activities with the French Resistance in WWII. He writes mostly in French. His first novel, *Le Grand Voyage*, is one of his best.

Eduardo Mendoza (1943-) is a fine Barcelona writer, whose *La Ciudad de los Prodigios* (also published in English as *The City of Marvels*) is an absorbing novel set in the city in the period between the Universal Exhbition of 1888 and the World Exhibition in 1929. Together with his sister, Cristina, Mendoza has also written *Barcelona Modernista*.

Terenci Moix is a successful columnist and writer who also tends to write in Castilian (although not exclusively). His books are fairly lightweight, but highly popular, literature exploring Spanish society and often involving a lot of self-discovery. A big hit was *Lleonard o el Sexo de los Ángeles*, and he has also written a couple of historical novels.

Montserrat Roig (1946-1991) crammed a lot of writing (largely in Catalan), journalistic and fiction, into her short life. Her novels include *Ramon Adéu, El Temps de les Cireres* and *L'Hora Violeta*.

Quim Monzó (1952-) has more than a dozen volumes (in Catalan) of essays and columns. His wide-ranging work is marked always by his mordant wit and a lingering interest in pornography.

Ana María Moix (1947-) gained considerable acclaim in 1970 with her prize-winning *Julia*, but then fell silent until 1985 when she resurfaced with a collection of short stories, *Las Virtudes Peligrosas*, that take a caustic look at society.

Theatre

Barcelona is possibly the most dynamic centre of theatre in Spain, although Madrileños (citizens of Madrid) might contest this. Purely Catalan theatre was revived, amid the rhetoric of the Renaixença, in the late 19th century, with playwright and all-round Catalan nationalist Àngel Guimerà its principal driving force.

Possibly one of the whackiest theatre companies is La Fura dels Baus. These guys turn theatre spaces (often warehouses) into a kind of participatory apocalypse – 60 minutes of, at times, spine-chilling performance. The audience becomes an integral part of the 'act', prodded and cajoled to contribute its own two cents' worth. The company grew out of Barcelona's street theatre culture in the late 1970s and although it has grown in technical prowess, it has not abandoned the rough-and-ready edge of the street.

Tricicle is another big Barcelona name. It's a three-man mime team easily enjoyed by anyone – no need to understand Catalan. Els Comediants and La Cubana are two highly successful groups that also owe a lot to the impromptu world of street theatre.

A big name in Catalan theatre is Josep Maria Flotats, who, after a long career in Paris, took control of the Teatre Nacional de Catalunya. Flotats, whose directing skills have been acclaimed all over Europe, fell out with the Generalitat in 1997 and bowed out of the Teatre Nacional. He has not, however, walked away from theatre – productions with his name on them are worth keeping an eye out for, but you will be more likely to see them in Madrid than in Barcelona!

Music

Traditional It is hard to know into what category to put the medieval troubadors. In many respects the verses they sang (largely the plaintive cries of courtly love inspired by French traditions) represent some of the earliest medieval literature in Mediterranean Europe. Provençal and not Catalan, however, remained the universal language for a long time.

The strongest musical tradition to have survived to some degree in popular form in Catalunya is that of the *havaneres*, nostalgic songs and sea shanties brought back from Cuba by Catalans who lived, sailed and traded there. Even after Spain lost Cuba in 1898, the havanera tradition continued, especially in Barcelona and along the Catalan coast, as a melancholy memory of good times past (although they had not always been so great for the Cubans). Today the havaneres are enjoying something of a revival, and in some coastal towns you can turn up to listen to an evening's *cantada de havaneres*. Calella on the Costa Brava is particularly well known for this, and occasionally you can hear the songs in Barcelona too.

Baroque The Catalan Jordi Savall (1941-) has assumed the task of rediscovering a Europe-wide heritage in music which predates the era of the classical greats. Born in Igualada, Savall studied at the conservatorium in Barcelona. He and his wife, the soprano Montserrat Figueras, have been largely responsible, with musicians from other countries, for resuscitating the beauties of medieval, Renaissance and, above all, baroque music. In 1987 Savall founded La Capella Reial de Catalunya and two years later he formed the baroque orchestra, Le Concert des Nations. He was awarded the Creu de Sant Jordi in 1990 and continues to teach, perform and record. Anyone who has seen the film *Tous Les Matins du Monde* (1991) starring Gérard Depardieu will know his work.

Classical Spain's contribution to the world of classical music has been comparatively marginal, but Catalunya did produce a few exceptional composers to prove the rule.

Perhaps best known is Isaac Albéniz (1860-1909), who was born in Camprodon and was a gifted pianist who later turned his hand to composition. Among his best remembered works is the *Iberia* cycle.

The Lleida-born Enric Granados i Campina (1867-1916) came onto the scene early this century. Another fine pianist, he established Barcelona's conservatorium in 1901 and composed a great many pieces for piano, including *Danzas Españolas*, *Cantos de la Juventud* and *Goyescas*.

Other Catalan composer/musicians of some note include Eduard Toldrà and Frederic Mompou.

Opera Monsterrat Caballé is, without doubt, Barcelona's most successful voice. Born in Gràcia in 1933, the soprano made her debut in 1956 in Basle (Switzerland). Her hometown launch came four years later in the Gran Teatre del Liceu. In 1965 she performed at New York's Carnegie Hall to wild acclaim. She hasn't looked back and remains one of the world's top sopranos. Catalunya's other world opera star is the renowned tenor Josep (José) Carreras (1946-).

Contemporary A good deal of Spain's most representative modern music has grown out of the lively Barcelona *movida*, that post-Franco outburst of activity and

nightlife that filled the streets of Spain in the early 1980s).

For years a big rock drawcard was El Último de la Fila, a fine Barcelona duo that finally decided to pack it in in 1997. Milder and poppier are Los Fresones Rebeldes, a fresh-faced sextet and light-hearted departure from the trend towards indie groups and techno blare. Their first album, *Es Que No Hay Manera*, is a bouncy punk pop offering that should ensure their continued popularity.

If techno is your thing, the Barcelonese trio Vanguard and compatriot An Der Beat are both riding high – more to be danced to than listened to.

Mojinos Escozíos tout themselves as 'fat, ugly and heavy to the death'. Although three of the five members are from Sevilla, the other two are Catalans and all live near Barcelona. They are the latest flavour in heavy rock, a genre that gets quite a following throughout Spain.

Rock Catalá (Catalan rock) is not essentially different from rock anywhere else, except that it is sung in Catalan by local bands that appeal to local tastes. Among the most popular bands at the moment are Sau (their latest CD is *La Lluna a l'Esquena*) Els Pets (look out for their CD, *Bondia*), The Mad Makers, Ja T'ho Diré, Sopa de Cabra, Lax'n'Busto, Whiskin's, Les Pellofes Radioactives, Psiconautes and Fes-te Fotre. All of these got together in August 1998 for the first Catalan rock festival, Senglar Rock, in the southern Catalan town of Prades. Organisers hope it will become an annual event.

Dance
Sardana The Catalan dance, par excellence, is the *sardana*, although its roots lie in the far northern l'Empordà region of Catalunya. Compared with flamenco it is a sobre sight indeed, but is not unlike a lot of folk dances seen in various parts of the Mediterranean. The dancers hold hands in a circle and wait for the 10 or so musicians to begin. The performance starts with the piping of the *flabiol*, a little wooden flute. When the other musicians join in, the dancers begin – a series of steps to the right, one back and then the same to the left. As

the music 'heats up' the steps become more complex, the leaps are higher and the dancers lift their arms. Then they return to the initial steps and continue. If newcomers wish to join in, space is made for them as the dance continues and the whole thing proceeds in a more or less seamless fashion.

In Barcelona you can see people doing the sardana at noon on Sundays, 6.30 pm on Saturdays and 7 pm on Wednesdays in front of the Catedral. Another option is at 6 pm on Sundays in Plaça de Sant Jaume. In summer these times tend to change and, in August, about your only chance will be during one of the local festes (such as la Festa Major de Gràcia).

Contemporary Barcelona is the capital of contemporary dance in Spain. This is not necessarily saying much, as dance does not thrive here as in other European capitals like Paris, Brussels and even London.

Ramon Oller is, with little doubt, the city's leading choreographer, working with one of the country's most solidly established companies, Metros. Its dance is rooted in comparatively formal technique. Four other prominent companies worth keeping an eye out for are: Cesc Gelabert (run by the choreographer of the same name), Mudanzas (Àngels Margarit), Lanonima Imperial (Juan Carlos García) and Mal Pelo (Maria Muñoz and Pep Ramis). All four tend to work from a base of 'release technique', which favours 'natural' movement, working from the skeleton, over reliance on muscular power.

Cinema

In December 1896, the Cinématographe Lumière was installed in the Salón Fotográfico Napoleón and the first brief movies were shown to an appreciative audience. The French brothers Lumière were roundly congratulated in the Barcelona press for their success – the Catalan city was present at the earliest stages in the life of the 'seventh art'. Two years later, the first film theatre was opened on La Rambla.

In 1932, Francesc Macià, president of the Generalitat, opened Spain's first studios for

making 'talkies' and a year later Metro Goldwyn Mayer had a dubbing studio in Barcelona. Prior to the civil war, *El Fava d'en Ramonet* was about the only cinematic hit in Catalan to make it to the screen.

In the wake of Franco's victory, pretty much all cinematic production happened in Madrid and was, in any case, a mix of propaganda and schmaltz. In 1952 a small group of Catalans made a film called *El Judes*, in Catalan, but it was banned.

In 1956, the so-called Escola de Barcelona began to produce experimental stuff, some of which did see the light of day. Film-makers like Vicente Aranda, cut their teeth here. Aranda later gained fame for *Amantes* (1991). Pere Portabella is another producer who emerged from the 'Barcelona school' (which was a financial flop). He worked on Buñuel's *Viridiana* in the 1960s.

All in all, it has been slow going in the Catalan film world. Since Franco's death any sign of restrictions on theme or use of Catalan has disappeared, but the centre of Spanish cinema remains Madrid. Since even the European cinema heavyweights – Britain, France and Italy, have trouble keeping national cinema afloat in the face of Hollywood, it is hardly surprising that the Catalan industry has even greater problems, in spite of subsidies from the Generalitat.

Possibly the biggest name in Catalan film directing is Bigas Luna, whose *Angoixa* (Anxiety) was a worldwide success. He also produced the popular comedy *Jamón, Jamón*.

Ventura Pons is another name worth watching. His latest film, *Caricias* (Caresses; 1997), slides through a loveless urban jungle (Barcelona), only allowing a glimmer of humanity to poke through the gloom towards the end. Francesc Bellmunt, Antoni Verdaguer and Rosa Vergès are other directors who have had some success.

SOCIETY & CULTURE

Catalans have a bit of a reputation for being reserved. That may or may not be true, but as a rule Barcelonins are tolerant and courteous.

No-one really expects you to speak Catalan, but if you can stumble along good-humouredly in Castilian in shops and other situations you'll generally meet with a friendly response.

Codes of good manners differ the world over, and what can sometimes seem brusque treatment to Anglos is not intended as anything of the sort. While the latter may be obsessed with 'please' and 'thank you', you'll find your average Barcelonins not overly fussed. Profusions of 'por favors' are not part of the local mindset. In bars and the like you are likely to hear the most respectable people simply say 'give me...' whatever it might be. But Catalans stand on ceremony in other ways. It is common to wish all and sundry '*bon dia/buenos días*' when entering a shop or bar and to say '*adéu/adiós*' on the way out. Not mandatory, but common.

Spaniards, in general, are individualistic and Catalans are not much of an exception to that rule. That is not to say they are lone wolves. Although not as party conscious as some of their more southern neighbours, Barcelonins love to hang out in bars and open-air cafés. Invitations to people's homes are more of an exception than the rule.

Dos & Don'ts

The standard form of greeting between men and women (even when meeting for the first time) and between women is a kiss on each cheek, right then left. Now we're not talking about big sloppy ones, a light brushing of cheeks is perfectly sufficient. Men seem to be able to take or leave handshakes on informal occasions, but they are pretty much standard in a business context.

In many bars it is quite the norm to chuck your rubbish – paper, toothpicks, cigarette butts etc – onto the floor. At the end of the day it will all be swept up. This does not apply everywhere, so don't start indulging your deeply buried urges to be a litterbug unless you are quite sure you are in a sufficiently grungy bar. A quick inspection of the floor and of other customers' behaviour should clue you in.

RELIGION

Barcelona, like the rest of Spain, is largely Catholic, at least in name. But a strong anarchist and socialist tradition, which historically has almost always meant anticlericalism, has left an indelible mark here, and many Barcelonins pay little more than lip service to their faith.

From the end of the 19th century through to the end of the Civil War, church-burning was a popular pastime. The two worst waves came in 1909 during the Setmana Tràgica and again at the outbreak of the Civil War in 1936. Under Franco, Catholicism was again made a state religion and the Church played a preponderant role in society, although less markedly so in Barcelona, where vast sections of the populace remained essentially 'red'.

In September 1998, a nationwide debate on whether or not to liberalise existing abortion laws brought a stinging counterattack from the church, felt in Barcelona as much as anywhere. The effect was that the motion put to the Cortes (national parliament) failed to pass – by one vote. Many Spanish theologians, much as their counterparts elsewhere in Europe and the USA have done, have criticised the Church for its conservatism on issues of sex, abortion, divorce and the like, warning that it will lose even further ground with Spaniards if it does not 'modernise'.

Facts for the Visitor

WHEN TO GO

Spring and early summer is the best time to be in Barcelona. The weather is usually pleasantly warm, the number of other tourists manageable and the city humming. High summer (particularly mid-July to late August) is probably one of the worst times to be there, although it appears to be the choice of many Europeans. All sensible locals abandon town for their annual holidays (this *is* a good time of year for finding parking spaces!), leaving it to swarms of uncomfortably sweaty foreigners.

September is not a bad month either, when the city recovers its normal rhythms, the heat eases off and tourist numbers drop but it can be a strange time weatherwise, hot one day and pouring rain the next. For *real* rain, hang about in October.

Winter is not especially distressing in Barcelona. True, things are more subdued than in the hotter months, but at least you can get around the place in peace. It can get quite nippy (you will want a room with heating), so come prepared.

ORIENTATION

Barcelona's coastline runs roughly from north-east to south-west and many streets are parallel or perpendicular to this.

Major arteries include: Gran Via de les Corts Catalanes, running parallel to the coast right across the city Avinguda Meridiana, which cuts a (nearly) straight path north out of the city; Avinguda del Paral.lel (according to tradition, the road was built along parallel 41°, 44') and its continuation under other names. which would run perpendicular to the Meridiana if two actually met; and Avinguda Diagonal, which cuts a swathe across the city from Pedralbes towards the coast. Roadworks now underway will finally see Avinguda Diagonal hit the sea sometime in 1999.

The city is officially divided into 10 municipalities. The Ciutat Vella (Old City) takes in the Barri Gòtic, El Raval, La Ribera, Port Vell and La Barceloneta. Spreading away from it to the north-west is the 19th century l'Eixample (Enlargement). L'Eixample and the Ciutat Vella are surrounded (from south to north) by Sants Montjuïc (which stretches from the coast and the Montjuïc hill as far inland as the Sants train station), Les Corts (split in two by Avinguda Diagonal, the main thoroughfare heading west out of town), Sarrià Sant Gervasi, Gràcia, Horta Guinado and Sant Martí (which spreads north-east away from Parc de la Ciutadella). Farther out again to the north and west are the dormitory areas of Nou Barris and Sant Andreu.

These main areas are themselves subdivided into *barris/barrios* (as exemplified by the Ciutat Vella). The areas of most interest to visitors can be broken down thus:

La Rambla & Plaça de Catalunya

The focal axis is La Rambla, a 1.25km boulevard running north-west and slightly uphill from Port Vell (the Old Harbour) to Plaça de Catalunya. The latter marks the boundary between the Ciutat Vella and the more recent parts farther inland.

Montjuïc & Tibidabo

Two good pointers to indicate which way you're facing are the hills of Montjuïc and Tibidabo. Montjuïc, the lower of the two, begins about 700m south-west of the bottom of La Rambla. Tibidabo, with its landmark TV tower and golden Christ statue, is 6km north-west of the top of La Rambla. It's the high point of the range of wooded hills forming a backdrop to the whole city.

Ciutat Vella

The Ciutat Vella, a warren of narrow streets, centuries-old buildings and a lot of bottom-end and mid-range accommodation, spreads either side of La Rambla. Its heart is the lower half of the section east of La Rambla called the Barri Gòtic (Gothic quarter), which is where the medieval core of the city grew on the site of the old Roman settlement. West of La Rambla is El Raval (from Arabic for 'the suburb'), whose lower half is the seedy Barri Xinès (Chinese quarter, a strange expression which actually means red-light zone).

The Ciutat Vella continues north-east of the Barri Gòtic, across Via Laietana, to the area called La Ribera, east of which lies the pretty Parc de la Ciutadella.

Waterfront

Port Vell has an excellent modern aquarium and two marinas. At its north-eastern end is La Barceloneta, the old sailors' and fishermen's quarter, from where beaches and a pedestrian promenade stretch 1km north-east to the Port Olímpic, a harbour built for the 1992 Olympics and now surrounded by lively bars and restaurants.

L'Eixample

Plaça de Catalunya at the top of La Rambla marks the beginning of l'Eixample (el Ensanche in Spanish), the grid of straight streets into which Barcelona spread in the 19th century. This is where you'll find most of Barcelona's *modernista* architecture – including La Sagrada Família – as well as its glossiest shops and many expensive hotels. The main avenues are Passeig de Gràcia and Rambla de Catalunya, running parallel to the north-west from Plaça de Catalunya. The part to the west of Passeig de Grácia is known as L'Esquerra (the Left) de l'Eixample, while to the east it's La Dreta (the Right) de l'Eixample.

Gràcia

Beyond l'Eixample you're in the suburbs – some of which have plenty of character as they began life as villages outside the city. Gràcia, beyond the wide Avinguda Diagonal on the north edge of central l'Eixample, is a net of narrow streets and small squares with a varied population and can be a lively

place to spend a Friday or Saturday night. Just north of Gràcia is Gaudí's Parc Güell.

Main Transport Terminals

The airport is 14km south-west of the centre at El Prat de Llobregat. The main terminus for domestic trains is Estació Sants (metro: Sants-Estació), 2.5km west of La Rambla, on the western fringe of l'Eixample. International trains usually terminate at Estació de França, 1km east of La Rambla, near Barceloneta metro station. The main bus station, Estació del Nord (metro: Arc de Triomf), is 1.5km north-east of La Rambla. (See the Getting Around chapter also.)

Getting Located

Many addresses in this book are accompanied by references to the nearest metro station. Where FGC is indicated instead, it refers to the two-line suburban train system that operates along with the metro.

MAPS

Tourist offices hand out free city and transport maps that are OK, but better is the Michelin No 40 *Barcelona* map (825 ptas), which comes with a comprehensive street index (Michelin No 41). Plenty of stalls on La Rambla sell maps – but prices vary considerably.

If you intend to hang about for a while and want a handy map book, Editorial Pamias' *Guía Urbana Barcelona* (1960 ptas) is a compact and complete guide to city streets and is packed with other information including phone numbers for everything from the vet to emergencies.

TOURIST OFFICES
Local Tourist Offices

The main tourist office is the Centre d'Informació Turisme de Barcelona (☎ 906-30 12 82 from within the country and ☎ 93 304 34 21 from abroad) at Plaça de Catalunya 17-S (actually underground), which concentrates on city information. It opens daily from 9 am to 9 pm. Staff also sell the Barcelona Card which entitles the holder to discounts on many sights, transport and some shops and restaurants (see the Things to See & Do chapter for more details).

The regional office (☎ 93 238 40 00) is located in the Palau Robert, Passeig de Gràcia 107. It opens Monday to Saturday from 10 am to 7 pm and Sundays from 10 am to 2 pm. In the Ajuntament (town hall) on Plaça de Sant Jaume there is another information office with similar hours. It has more information on Catalunya.

Turisme de Barcelona in Estació Sants covers Barcelona only. It's open Monday to Friday from 8 am to 8 pm, and Saturday, Sunday and holidays from 8 am to 2 pm (8 am to 8 pm daily in summer). There's also a tourist office (☎ 93 478 05 65) in the EU airport arrivals hall, open Monday to Saturday from 9.30 am to 8 pm, Sunday from 9.30 am to 3 pm (about a half-hour later in summer). They have information on all Catalunya. The office (☎ 93 478 47 04) at the international arrivals hall is open Monday to Saturday from 9.30 am to 3 pm.

Another useful office for information on events (and tickets) is the Palau de la Virreina arts information office at La Rambla de Sant Josep 99.

You can find out about accommodation on ☎ 93 304 32 32 or you can check out www.deinfo.es/barcelona-on-line.

Tourist Offices Abroad

Information on Barcelona is available from the following branches of the Oficina Española de Turismo abroad:

Belgium
(☎ 02-280 1926), Avenue des Arts 21, 1040 Brussels
Canada
(☎ 416-961 3131), 2 Bloor St West, 34th Floor, Toronto, Ontario M4W 3E2
Denmark
(☎ 33 15 11 65), Store Kongensgade 1-3, 1264 Copenhagen
France
(☎ 01 45 03 82 50), 43 rue Decamps, 75784 Paris, Cedex 16
Italy
(☎ 06-678 3106), Via del Mortaro 19 interno 5, 00187 Rome

(☎ 02-72 00 46 17), Piazza del Carmine 4, 20121 Milan
Germany
(☎ 030-8 82 65 43), Kurfürstendamm 180, 10707 Berlin
(☎ 0211-6 80 39 80), Grafenberger Allee 100 – 'Kutscherhaus', 40237 Düsseldorf
(☎ 069-72 50 33), Myliusstrasse 14, 60325 Frankfurt/Main
(☎ 089-5 38 90 75), Schubertstrasse 10, 80336 Munich
Netherlands
(☎ 070-346 59 00), Laan Van Meerdervoort 8-8a, 2517 The Hague
Portugal
(☎ 01-354 1992), Edificio Monumental, Avenida Fontes Pereira de Melo 51-4° andar D, 1000 Lisbon
UK
(☎ 0171-486 8077; from 22 April 2000 ☎ 020-7486 8077, brochure request ☎ 0891-669920 at 50p a minute), 22-23 Manchester Square, London W1M 5AP
USA
(☎ 212-265 8822), 666 Fifth Ave, 35th Floor, New York, NY 10103
(☎ 213-658 7188), 8383 Wilshire Blvd, Suite 960, Beverly Hills, Los Angeles, CA 90211
(☎ 312-642 1992), 845 North Michigan Ave, Chicago, IL 60611
(☎ 305-358 1992), 1221 Brickell Ave, Suite 1850, Miami, FL 33131

DOCUMENTS
Visas

For tourist visits of up to 90 days, nationals of many countries – including the EU states, Australia, Canada, Israel, Japan, New Zealand, Norway, Switzerland and the USA – require no visa. They must carry a valid passport or (in the case of those EU countries that issue them) an ID card.

South Africans are among those who *do* need a visa – unless they are resident in a 'Schengen country' (see next section). Options include 30-day and 90-day single-entry visas (in London these cost UK£17.75 and UK£21.30 respectively), 90-day multiple-entry visas (UK£24.85), and various transit visas.

You usually have to supply four passport-size photos with your visa application form.

If you are resident in the country where

you apply for a visa, and you do so in person, the process should take 24 to 48 hours.

If you apply for the visa in a country where you are *not* resident, your request may be forwarded to Madrid and a reply could take weeks. In addition, you may be asked to present tickets for onward or return flights, to provide evidence of hotel accommodation and solvency or even of an invitation from someone in Spain. Finally, you may not be allowed the option of the 90-day three-entry visa.

The Schengen System Spain is one of the 'Schengen countries' which have theoretically done away with passport control on travel between them. (The others are Portugal, France, Germany, Italy, the Netherlands, Belgium, Luxembourg and Austria. Greece, Sweden, Denmark, Finland, Norway and Iceland are expected to join up before long.) In fact, the Schengen countries reserve the right to make spot passport checks. These occur fairly regularly at Spanish airports and have been known to occur on trains.

If you need a visa but don't have one you might still gamble on not being caught. Travelling from the UK by boat or train there is a chance your passport will not be checked on entering France or Belgium. From there you could travel overland with some hope (but no certainty) of not having your passport checked. Travelling by air, however, you have no chance. Take this seriously, as travellers have been bundled on to planes and sent back to the country they flew from.

One saving grace of the system is that a visa for one Schengen country is valid for all other Schengen countries too – so, for instance, a French visa is good for Spain, and vice-versa. Compare validity periods, prices and the number of permitted entries from the respective embassies before you apply. Schengen visas are free for spouses and children of EU nationals.

If you are going to visit more than one Schengen country that requires you to obtain a visa, you should apply for the visa at an embassy of your main destination country.

Legal residents of one Schengen country do *not* require a visa for another Schengen country.

Visa Extensions & Residence Nationals of EU countries, Norway and Iceland can virtually (if not technically) enter and leave Spain at will. Those wanting to stay in Spain longer than 90 days are supposed to apply during their first month for a resident's card *(tarjeta de residencia)*. This is a lengthy bureaucratic procedure: if you intend to subject yourself to it, consult a Spanish consulate before you go to Spain as you will need to take certain documents with you.

People of other nationalities who want to stay in Spain longer than 90 days are also supposed to get a resident's card, and for them it's a truly nightmarish process, starting with a residence visa issued by a Spanish consulate in your country of residence. Start the process light years in advance.

Non-EU spouses of EU citizens resident in Spain can apply for residence too. The process is lengthy and those needing to travel in and out of the country in the meantime could ask for an *exención de visado* – a visa exemption. In most cases, the spouse is obliged to make the formal application in his/her country of residence. A real pain.

Travel Insurance
Medical costs might already be covered through reciprocal health care agreements (see Health later in this chapter) but you'll still need cover for theft or loss and for unexpected changes in travel plans (ticket cancellation etc). Check what's already covered by your local insurance policies and credit card: you might not need separate travel insurance. In most cases, however, this secondary type of cover is limited and its small print is laced with loopholes. For peace of mind, nothing beats straight travel

insurance at the highest level you can afford.

Driving Licence & Permits

For information on driving licences, International Driving Permits and vehicle papers and insurance see the Car & Motorcycle section in the Getting There & Away chapter.

Hostel Cards

A valid HI (Hostelling International) card or youth hostel card from your home country is required at most HI youth hostels in Spain, including those in Barcelona. If you don't have one, you can get an HI Card, valid until 31 December of the year you buy it, at most HI hostels in Spain. You pay in instalments of 300 ptas for each night you spend in a hostel, up to 1800 ptas. The cards are also available from USIT Unlimited (☎ 93 423 33 60 & 93 426 57 00) at Carrer de Rocafort 116-122 (metro: Rocafort). They act as Catalunya's equivalent of TIVE, the Spanish youth travel organisation.

Student, Teacher & Youth Cards

These cards can get you worthwhile discounts on travel, and reduced prices at some museums, sights and entertainments.

The International Student Identity Card (ISIC), for full-time students, and the International Teacher Identity Card (ITIC), for full-time teachers and academics, are issued by more than 5000 organisations around the world – mainly student travel-related and often selling student air, train and bus tickets too. They include:

Australia
  (☎ 03-93492411) STA Travel, 222 Faraday St, Carlton, Victoria 3053
  (☎ 02-9360 1822) STA Travel, 9 Oxford Street, Paddington, Sydney, NSW 2021
Canada
  (☎ 416-979 2406), Travel CUTS, 187 College St, Toronto
  (☎ 514-398 0647), Voyages Campus, Université McGill, 3480 rue McTavish, Montreal
UK
  Cards are best obtained from STA Travel and

Usit Campus Travel offices (see under Air in the Getting There & Away chapter)
USA
  (☎ 212-822 2700), Council Travel, 205 East 42nd St, New York, NY 10017
  (☎ 310-208 3551), Council Travel, 10904 Lindbrook Drive, Los Angeles, CA 90024
  (☎ 415-421 3473), Council Travel, 530 Bush St, San Francisco, CA 94108

The fake student card business is alive and well and some travel agents will even issue cards with certain discounted air tickets without asking to see any proof of student status.

Anyone under 26 can get a GO25 card or a >Euro26 card. Both these give similar discounts to the ISIC and are issued by most of the same organisations. The >Euro26 has a variety of names including the Under 26 Card in England and Wales and the Carnet Joven Europeo in Spain. For information you can contact Under 26, 52 Grosvenor Gardens, London SW1W OAG, UK (☎ 0171-730 7285, from 22 April 2000 ☎ 020-7730 7285). In Spain, the >Euro26 is issued by various youth organisations, including Barcelona's USIT Unlimited (see Hostel Cards above).

As an example of the sort of discounts you can expect in Spain, the better things on offer for >Euro26 card holders include 20% or 25% off most 2nd-class train fares; 10% or 20% off many Trasmediterránea ferries and some bus fares; good discounts at some museums; and discounts of up to 20% at some youth hostels.

Other Documents

If you intend to look for work in Barcelona (see also Visas above and Work towards the end of this chapter), you should bring along any paperwork that might help. English teachers, for instance, will need certificates demonstrating qualifications and references from previous employers. Increasingly there is cross-recognition of degrees and other tertiary qualifications, so it may be worthwhile bringing these as well. Translations validated by the Spanish embassy in your country wouldn't hurt either.

Photocopies

Keep photocopies of the data pages of your passport and other identity cards, and even your birth certificate if you can manage it. This will help speed up replacement if the originals go missing. If your passport is stolen or lost, notify the police and obtain a statement, then contact your embassy or consulate as soon as possible.

Other worthwhile things to photocopy include airline tickets, travel insurance documents with emergency numbers, credit cards (and phone numbers to contact in case of card loss), driving licence and vehicle documentation. Keep all of these, and a list of your travellers' cheque numbers, separate from the originals. Leave extra copies with someone reliable at home.

EMBASSIES & CONSULATES
Spanish Embassies & Consulates

Here is a list of Spanish embassies in a selection of countries throughout the world:

Andorra
   (☎ 82 00 13), Carrer del Prat de la Creu 34, Andorra la Vella
Australia
   (☎ 02-6273 3555), 15 Arkana St, Yarralumla, Canberra, ACT 2600
   Consulates: Brisbane (☎ 07-3221 8571), Melbourne (☎ 03-9347 1966), Perth (☎ 09-9322 4522), Sydney (☎ 02-9261 2433)
Canada
   (☎ 613-747 2252), 74 Stanley Ave, Ottawa, Ontario K1M 1P4
   Consulates: Toronto (☎ 416-977 1661), Montreal (☎ 514-935 5235)
France
   (☎ 01-44 43 18 00), 22 avenue Marceau, 75008 Paris Cedex 08
Germany
   (☎ 0228-21 70 94), Schlossstrasse 4, 53115 Bonn
   Consulates: Berlin (☎ 030-261 60 81), Düsseldorf (☎ 0211-43 90 80), Frankfurt/Main (☎ 069-96 10 41), Munich (☎ 089-98 50 27) and other cities
Ireland
   (☎ 01-269 1640), 17A Merlyn Park, Balls Bridge, Dublin 4
Morocco
   (☎ 07-707600, 07-707980), 105 Ave Allal ben Abdellah, 3 Zankat Madnine, Rabat

New Zealand
   Spain has no diplomatic representation in New Zealand
Netherlands
   (☎ 070-364 38 14), Lange Voorhout 50, 2514 EG The Hague
Portugal
   (☎ 01-347 2381), Rua do Salitre 1, 1200 Lisbon
Tunisia
   (☎ 01-280613), 22 Ave Dr Ernest Conseil, Cité Jardin, 2001 Tunis
UK
   (☎ 0171-235 5555, from 22 April 2000 ☎ 020-7235 5555), 39 Chesham Place, London SW1X 8SB
   Consulates: (☎ 0171-581 7888, 0171-589 8989, from 22 April 2000 ☎ 020-7581 7888, 020 7589 8989), 20 Draycott Place, London SW3 2RZ
   (☎ 0161-236 1233), Suite 1A, Brook House, 70 Spring Gardens, Manchester M2 2BQ
   (☎ 0131-226 4568, 0131-220 1843), 63 North Castle St, Edinburgh EH2 3LJ
USA
   (☎ 202-728 2330), 2375 Pennsylvania Ave NW, Washington, DC 20037
   Consulates: Boston (☎ 617-536 2506), Chicago (☎ 312-782 4588), Houston (☎ 713-783 6200), Los Angeles (☎ 213-938 0158), Miami (☎ 305-446 5511), New Orleans (☎ 504-525 4951), New York (☎ 212-355 4080), San Francisco (☎ 415-922 2995)

Consulates in Barcelona

Most countries have diplomatic representation in Spain, but all the embassies are in the capital, Madrid. Consulates in Barcelona, including the following, are generally open Monday to Friday from 9 or 10 am to 1 or 2 pm. You can find them listed in the phone book under Consulat/Consulado.

Australia
   (☎ 93 330 94 96), Gran Via de Carles III
Belgium
   (☎ 93 487 81 40), Carrer de la Diputació 303
Canada
   (☎ 93 215 07 04), Passeig de Gràcia 77
Denmark
   (☎ 93 488 02 22), Rambla de Catalunya 33
France
   (☎ 93 317 81 50), Ronda de l'Universitat 22B 4rt

Germany
  (☎ 93 292 10 00), Passeig de Gràcia 111
Ireland
  (☎ 93 491 50 21), Gran Via de Carles III 94
Italy
  (☎ 93 467 73 05), Carrer de Mallorca 270
Japan
  (☎ 93 280 34 33), Avinguda Diagonal 662-664
Netherlands
  (☎ 93 410 62 10), Avinguda Diagonal 601
Sweden
  (☎ 93 488 25 01), Carrer de Mallorca 279
Switzerland
  (☎ 93 330 92 11), Gran Via de Carles III 94
UK
  (☎ 93 419 90 44), Avinguda Diagonal 477
USA
  (☎ 93 280 22 27), Passeig de la Reina Elisenda de Montcada 23-25

Embassies (*embajadas* in the phone book) in Madrid include:

Australia
  (☎ 91 441 93 00), Plaza del Descubridor Diego de Ordás 3-2, Edificio Santa Engracia 120
Canada
  (☎ 91 431 43 00), Calle de Núñez de Balboa 35
France
  (☎ 91 435 55 60), Calle de Salustiano Olózaga 9
  Consulate: (☎ 91 597 32 67), Paseo de la Castellana 79
Germany
  (☎ 91 557 90 00), Calle de Fortuny 8
Ireland
  (☎ 91 576 35 00, 91 435 16 77), Calle de Claudio Coello 73
Morocco
  (☎ 91 563 79 28, 91 563 10 90), Calle de Serrano 179
  Consulate: (☎ 91 561 89 12, 91 561 21 45), Calle de Leizaran 31
Netherlands
  (☎ 91 359 09 14), Avenida del Comandante Franco 32
New Zealand
  (☎ 91 523 02 26, 91 531 09 97), Plaza de la Lealtad 2
Portugal
  (☎ 91 561 78 00), Calle del Castillo 128
  Consulate: (☎ 91 445 46 00), Paseo de General Martínez Campos 11
Tunisia
  (☎ 91 447 35 08), Plaza de Alonso Martínez 3

UK
  (☎ 91 319 02 00), Calle de Fernando el Santo 16
  Consulate: (☎ 91 308 52 01), Calle del Marqués Ensenada 16
USA
  (☎ 91 587 22 00), Calle de Serrano 75

CUSTOMS

People entering Spain from outside the EU are allowed to bring in, duty-free, one bottle of spirits, one bottle of wine, 50 ml of perfume and 200 cigarettes. If you are travelling from one EU country to another, for the moment you can bring 2L of wine *and* 1L of spirits, with the same limits applying on other goods. But duty-free allowances for travel between EU countries are due to be abolished on 30 June 1999. For duty-paid items bought at normal shops in one EU country and taken into another, the allowances are 90L of wine, 10L of spirits, unlimited quantities of perfume and 800 cigarettes.

MONEY

A combination of travellers cheques and credit or cash cards is the best way to carry your money.

Currency

Spain's currency, the peseta (pta), comes in coins of one, five, 10, 25, 50, 100, 200 and 500 ptas, and notes of 1000, 2000, 5000 and 10,000 ptas.

A five ptas coin is widely known as a *duro* and it's fairly common for small sums to be quoted in duros: *dos duros* for 10 ptas, *cinco duros* for 25 ptas, even *veinte duros* for 100 ptas.

The Euro The new common currency for most EU countries, the euro, was launched on 1 January 1999 with Spain among the first wave of countries to adopt it. However, use of the euro will at first be restricted to things like share prices and inter-bank transfers. Euro coins and notes will not appear until 1 January 2002, although euro equivalents for some shop prices, exchange rates etc may be quoted before that time to get people used to the idea. The euro will then circulate alongside the peseta for a few months. By 1 July 2002 the peseta will cease to be legal tender.The euro will have a fixed peseta value (about 165 ptas) and will be divided into 100 cents.

Exchange Rates

Country	unit		peseta
Australia	A$1	=	87 ptas
Canada	C$1	=	91 ptas
euro	€1	=	167 ptas
France	1FF	=	25 ptas
Germany	DM1	=	85 ptas
Japan	¥100	=	110 ptas
New Zealand	NZ$1	=	73 ptas
Portugal	100$00	=	83 ptas
UK	UK£1	=	235 ptas
USA	US$1	=	142 ptas

Exchanging Money

You can change cash or travellers cheques at virtually any bank or exchange office, at bus and railway stations and at the airport. The main-road border crossings also usually have exchange facilities. Banks tend to offer the best rates, with minor differences between them. They're mostly open Monday to Friday from 8.30 am to 2 pm, and Saturday from 9 am to 1 pm – although some don't bother with Saturday opening in summer. A great many banks have ATMs (automated teller machines). Barcelona has numerous banks, including several around Plaça de Catalunya and more on La Rambla.

Exchange offices (you'll see many along La Rambla and elsewhere in central Barcelona), usually indicated by the word *cambio* (exchange), generally offer longer opening hours and quicker service than banks but have poorer exchange rates (American Express exchange offices are an honourable exception).

Travellers cheques usually bring a slightly better exchange rate than cash but often attract higher commissions than cash exchange.

Wherever you change your money, ask about commissions first and confirm that exchange rates are as posted (in other words, that they haven't changed since the sign was last updated). Also, make sure that the exchange rate posted is for buying pesetas, not for selling them. Commissions vary from bank to bank, may be different for travellers cheques and cash, and may depend on how many cheques, or how much in total, you're cashing. A typical commission is 3%, with a minimum of 300 to 500 ptas, but there are places with a minimum commission of 1000 or even 2000 ptas. Places that advertise 'no commission' may offer poor exchange rates to start with (American Express is again an honourable exception).

American Express (☎ 93 415 23 71 or 93 217 00 70; fax 93 217 19 50) at Passeig de Gràcia 101 (the entrance is on Carrer del Rosselló) has a machine giving cash on American Express cards. The office is open Monday to Friday from 9.30 am to 6 pm, and Saturday from 10 am to noon. There is another branch on La Rambla dels Caputxins 74.

Cash Don't bring wads of cash from home (travellers cheques and plastic are much safer – see below). If you wander around with pounds and dollars in your pockets you are just inviting rubber fingers to make you instantly poor. It is, however, an idea to keep an emergency stash separate from other valuables in case you should lose your travellers cheques and credit cards.

You will, of course, need pesetas in cash for many day-to-day transactions (many small pensiones, eateries and shops take cash only). Try not to carry around more than you need at any one time – in much the same way as you try to avoid doing so at home!

Travellers Cheques & Eurocheques
These protect your money because they can be replaced if they are lost or stolen. They can be cashed at most banks and exchange offices. American Express and Thomas Cook are widely accepted brands. For

American Express travellers cheque refunds you can call ☎ 900-99 44 26 from anywhere in Spain.

It doesn't really matter whether your cheques are denominated in pesetas or in the currency of the country you buy them in: Spanish exchange outlets will change most non-obscure currencies. Get most of your cheques in fairly large denominations (the equivalent of 10,000 ptas or more) to save on any per-cheque commission charges. American Express exchange offices charge no commission to change travellers cheques (even other brands).

It's vital to keep your initial receipt and a record of your cheque numbers and the ones you have used, separate from the cheques themselves.

Eurocheques (with guarantee card) are widely accepted. You write the amount in pesetas, which will be charged to your account at the more favourable interbank rate.

Take along your passport when you go to cash travellers cheques.

Credit/Debit Cards You can use plastic to pay for many purchases (including meals and rooms at many establishments, especially from the middle price range up, and long-distance trains), and you can use it to withdraw cash pesetas from banks and ATMs. Among the most widely usable cards are Visa, MasterCard, Eurocard, Eurocheque, American Express, Cirrus, Plus, Diners Club and JCB.

On the exchange rate front you also generally get a better deal than with cash and cheques, even taking into account any charges levied on foreign transactions and cash advances (usually 1.5%). Some foreign cash cards, for accessing money in personal bank accounts, can also be used in Spain and do not attract any cash-advance fee.

A high proportion of Spanish banks, even in small towns and villages, have an ATM *(caixer automàtic/cajero automático)* that will dispense cash pesetas at any time (and no queues!) if you have the right piece of

plastic to slot into it. Some stop accepting foreign cards at midnight.

Check with your card's issuer before leaving home on how widely usable your card will be, on how to report and replace a lost card, on withdrawal/spending limits, and on whether your personal identification number (PIN) will be acceptable (some European ATMs don't accept PINs of more than four digits).

American Express cardholders can get cash or at least travellers' cheques – up to various maximums depending on the type of card – from American Express offices by writing a personal cheque drawn on their home bank account.

American Express cards are among the easiest to replace – you can call ☎ 91 572 03 03 or ☎ 91 572 03 20 (in Madrid) at any time. Always report a lost card straight away. You can ring the following numbers to do so: Visa, MasterCard or Access ☎ 93 315 25 12 in Barcelona or ☎ 91 519 21 00 in Madrid, Eurocard ☎ 91 519 60 00 (Madrid) Diners Club ☎ 91 547 40 00 (Madrid).

TravelMoney A recently introduced option worth considering, for travellers from Britain at least, is Visa TravelMoney, a prepaid disposable credit card which you can buy from selected banks or travel agencies for amounts from UK£100 to UK£5000. It works for ATM withdrawals wherever the Visa sign is displayed. Inquire at Thomas Cook or call Visa before you travel.

International Transfers To have money transferred from another country, you need to organise someone to send it to you (through a bank there or a money-transfer service such as Western Union or Money-Gram) and a bank (or Western Union or MoneyGram office) in Barcelona at which to collect it. If there's money in your bank account back at home, you may be able to instruct the bank yourself.

For information on Western Union services and branches, call ☎ 900-63 36 33 free from anywhere in Spain. For Money-Gram call ☎ 900-20 10 10.

A bank-to-bank telegraphic transfer typically costs the equivalent of about 3000 or 4000 ptas and should take about a week. For sums up to US$400, MoneyGram charges the *sender* US$20; the money can supposedly be handed over to the recipient within 10 minutes of being sent. Western Union provides a similar service.

It's also possible to have money sent by American Express.

Security

Keep only a limited amount of cash and the bulk of your money in more easily replaceable forms such as travellers cheques or plastic. If your accommodation has a safe, use it. If you have to leave money in your room, divide it into several stashes and hide them in different places.

For carrying money on the street the safest thing is a shoulder wallet or under-the-clothes money belt. An external money belt attracts rather than deflects attention from your valuables. Watch out for people who touch you or seem to be getting unwarrantedly close, in any situation.

Barcelona has been ranked Europe's worst city for credit card theft (the writer is one of the unhappy victims!), so pay attention!

Costs

As Spain's second city, Barcelona is expensive by local standards, but northern Europeans generally find it quite reasonable. Travellers from beyond the EU (such as the USA and Australia) tend to find anywhere in Europe pricey. Costs of accommodation, eating out and transport are considerably lower than in Britain or France. If you are particularly frugal, it's just about possible to scrape by on 3500 to 4000 ptas a day; this would involve staying in the cheapest possible accommodation, not eating in restaurants or going to museums or bars, and not moving around too much.

A more comfortable budget would be 6000 ptas a day. This could allow you around 2500 ptas for accommodation; 600 ptas for breakfast (coffee, juice and a pastry); 900 to 1200 ptas for a set lunch; 280 ptas for public transport (two metro or bus rides); 1000 ptas a day for museums; and 800 ptas for a simple dinner, with a bit over for a drink or two.

With 20,000 ptas a day you can stay in excellent accommodation, splurge in Barcelona's better restaurants and even hire a car for a few days' touring outside town.

Ways to Save Two people can travel more cheaply (per person) than one by sharing rooms. You'll also save money by avoiding the peak tourist seasons (Christmas, Easter, summer), when most room prices go up. A student or youth card, or a document such as a passport proving you're at least over 60, brings worthwhile savings on some travel costs and entry to some museums and sights (see Visas & Documents in this chapter). Occasional museums and sights have free days now and then, and a few are cheaper for EU passport holders.

Prolific letter-writers can save a few pesetas on long-distance mail by sending aerograms instead of standard letters or postcards (this does not apply to letters under 20g posted to European countries).

Tipping & Bargaining

In restaurants, the law requires that menu prices include service charges, and tipping is a matter of personal choice – most people leave some small change if they're satisfied and 5% is usually plenty. It's common to leave small change at bar and café tables. Hotel porters will generally be happy with 200 ptas and most won't turn their noses up at 100 ptas.

In some pensiones and hotels it is worth asking about discounts for prolonged stays.

Taxes & Refunds

Value-added tax (VAT) is known as IVA (`EE-ba', *impuesto sobre el valor añadido*). On accommodation and restaurant prices, IVA is 7% and is usually – but not always – included in quoted prices. On retail goods IVA is 16%. On vehicle hire it seems to fluctuate between 7% and 16%. To check whether a price includes IVA, you can ask *'¿Está incluido el IVA?'* ('Is IVA included?').

Visitors are entitled to a refund of the 16% IVA on purchases costing more than 15,000 ptas, from any shop, if they take the goods out of the EU within three months. Ask the shop for an invoice showing the price and IVA paid for each item and identifying the vendor and purchaser. Then present the invoice to the customs booth for IVA refunds when you leave Spain. The officer will stamp the invoice and you hand it in at a bank at the departure point for the reimbursement.

POST & COMMUNICATIONS
Post

Stamps are sold at most *estancos* (tobacconist shops with 'Tabacs/Tabacos' in yellow letters on a maroon background), as well as post offices (Correus i Telègrafs/ Correos y Telégrafos).

The main post office (☎ 902-19 71 97) is on Plaça d'Antoni López opposite the north-east end of Port Vell. It's open for stamp sales, poste restante (window No 36) and information Monday to Friday from 8 am to 10 pm (Saturdays to 8 pm). The post code for poste restante is 08080.

The post office also has a public fax service, as do many shops and offices around the city.

Another useful post office is at Carrer d'Aragó 282, just off Passeig de Gràcia, open Monday to Friday from 8.30 am to 9 pm, and Saturday from 9 am to 2 pm. Other district offices tend to open Monday to Friday from 8 am to 2 pm only.

Rates A postcard or letter weighing up to 20g costs 70 ptas to other European countries, 115 ptas to North America, and 185 ptas to Australasia or Asia. Three A4 sheets in an air-mail envelope weigh between 15g and 20g. An aerogram costs 85 ptas to anywhere in the world.

Certificado (registered mail) costs an extra 175 ptas for international mail. *Urgente* service, which means your letter may arrive two or three days quicker, costs an extra 230 ptas for international mail. You can send mail both urgente and certificado.

A day or two quicker than urgente service – but a lot more expensive – is Postal Exprés, sometimes called Express Mail Service (EMS). This uses courier companies for international deliveries. Packages weighing up to 1kg cost 3780 ptas to the EU or Norway, 6300 ptas to North America, and 8015 ptas to Australia or New Zealand.

Sending Mail It's quite safe to post your mail in the yellow street postboxes (*bústies/buzones*) as well as at post offices. Ordinary mail to other western European countries normally takes up to a week; to North America up to 10 days; to Australia or New Zealand up to two weeks.

Receiving Mail Delivery times are similar to those for outbound mail. Using the Spanish five-digit postcode (which goes *before* the name of the city) will help speed up the process.

Poste restante mail can be addressed to you at *lista de correos*. It will be delivered to the main post office unless another one is specified. Take your passport when you go to pick up mail. A letter addressed to poste restante in central Barcelona should look like this:

> Jenny JONES
> Lista de Correos
> 08080 Barcelona
> Spain

American Express card or travellers cheque holders can use the free client mail-holding service at its main office in Barcelona (see Money above).

Couriers Most international courier services have reps in Barcelona. United Parcel Service (UPS, ☎ 900-10 24 10), for instance, has an office on the corner of Avinguda Diagonal and Carrer de Fra Luis de Granada. DHL (☎ 902-12 24 24) has an office out at Hospitalet de Llobregat.

Getting Addressed

Just because you have an address in your hot sweaty palm doesn't mean you will have no trouble finding what you are after. If the pensión you are looking for is at C/ de Montcada 23, 3°D Int, just off Av Marqués, you could be forgiven for scratching your head a little. Abbreviations contain a lot of information, and in Barcelona things are made worse by the fact that some people may give you the Catalan version of an address while others may give you the Castilian version. Here are some common abbreviations:

Av or Avda	Avinguda/Avenida
Bda	Baixada/Bajada
C/	Carrer/Calle
Cí or C°	Camí/Camino
Ctra, Ca or C^a	Carretera
Cró/Cjón	Carreró/Callejón
Gta	Glorieta (major roundabout)
Pg or P°	Passeig/Paseo
Ptge/Pje	Passatge/Pasaje
Plc/Plz	Placeta/Plazuela
Pl, Pza or P^a	Plaça/Plaza
Pt or Pte	Pont/Puente
Rbla	Rambla
Rda	Ronda
s/n	*sense numeració/*
	sin número (without number)
Tr or Trav	Travessera
Trv	Travessia/Travesía
Urb	Urbanització/Urbanización

The following are used where there are several flats, *hostales*, offices etc in one building. They're often used in conjunction, eg 2°C or 3°I Int:

Ent	Entresuelo (ground floor)
Pr	Principal (what Brits & Co would consider the 1st floor)
1°	1st floor (2nd floor to Brits & Co)
2°	2nd floor (3rd floor to Brits & Co)
C	*centre/centro* (middle)
D	*dreta/derecha* (right-hand side)
Esq, I or Izq	*esquerra/izquierda* (left-hand side)
Int	*interior* (a flat or office too far inside the building to look on to any street – usually has windows onto an interior patio or shaft – the opposite is Ext, *exterior*)

If someone's address is Apartado de Correos 206 (which can be shortened to Apda de Correos 206 or even Apdo 206), don't bother tramping the streets in search of it – it is a post office box.

Street names often get short shrift too. Carrer de Madrid (literally Street of Madrid) will often appear simply as Carrer Madrid. In spoken exchanges the word Carrer is often dropped. Thus Carrer del Comte d'Urgell will be referred to simply as Comte d'Urgell.

Telephone

The ubiquitous blue payphones are easy to use for international and domestic calls. They accept coins, phonecards issued by the national phone company Telefónica *(tarjetas telefónicas)* and, in some cases, various credit cards. Tarjetas telefónicas come in 1000 and 2000 ptas denominations (the latter usually have 2100 ptas worth of call time as an enticement) and, like postage stamps, are sold at post offices and *estancos*.

Public phones inside bars and cafés, and phones in hotel rooms, are nearly always a good deal more expensive than street pay phones.

There are telephone and fax offices at Estació Sants (open daily except Sunday from 8.30 am to 9 pm) and the Estació del Nord bus station.

Costs Domestic and international calls from pay phones cost 35% more than from private phones. A three-minute pay-phone call using coins or a tarjeta telefónica costs around 20 ptas within your local area, 75 ptas to other places in the same province, 180 ptas to other Spanish provinces, 260 ptas to other EU countries, 350 ptas to North America and 600 ptas to Australia. All these calls are cheaper (around 15% cheaper for international calls) between 10 pm and 8 am and on Sundays and holidays. As the pressure of private competition grows, prices will almost certainly drop. Domestic calls are also cheaper after 2 pm on Saturday.

Calls to Spanish numbers starting ☎ 900 are free. Calls to numbers starting ☎ 902 cost around 140 ptas for three minutes. Calls to mobile phones – numbers starting ☎ 607, ☎ 608, ☎ 609, ☎ 629, ☎ 639 or ☎ 670 – cost about 200 ptas for three minutes.

If you're arriving from the USA or the UK, you are probably already acquainted with the idea of buying cut-price phone cards. You buy the card, dial a toll-free number and then follow the instructions – they can bring big savings on international calls. This sort of thing seems to come and go in Spain. At the time of writing you could buy Fon-Olé cards from the BCN

Original shop at the main tourist office on Plaça de Catalunya.

Domestic Calls There are no area codes in Spain. All numbers have nine digits and you just dial that nine-digit number. Older signs still give the first two digits as an area code (the 93 with which all Barcelona numbers start was, until early 1998, a two-digit area code).

Dial ☎ 1009 to speak to a domestic operator, including for a domestic reverse-charge (collect) call *(una llamada por cobro revertido)*. For directory inquiries dial ☎ 1003; calls cost about 60 ptas.

International Calls The access code for international calls is ☎ 00. To make an international call dial the access code, wait for a new dialling tone, then dial the country code, area code and number you want.

International collect calls are simple: dial ☎ 900 99 followed by a code for the country you're calling: Australia (00 61); Belgium (00 32); Canada (00 15); Denmark (00 45); France (00 33); Germany (00 49); Ireland (03 53); Israel (09 72); Italy (00 91); Japan (09 81); Netherlands (00 31); New Zealand (00 64); Portugal (03 51); UK (00 44); USA (00 11 for AT&T; 00 13 for Sprint or 00 14 for MCI); codes for other countries are sometimes posted up in pay phones. You'll get straight through to an operator in the country you're calling. The same numbers can be used with direct-dial calling cards.

If for some reason the above information doesn't work for you, in most places you can get an English-speaking Spanish international operator on ☎ 1008 (for calls within Europe) or ☎ 1005 (rest of the world).

For international directory inquiries dial ☎ 025.

Retevisión Some phone users subscribe to a private-enterprise competitor called Retevisión, which offers lower costs on inter-provincial and international calls. To make a Retevisión inter-provincial or international call you dial ☎ 050 then continue as with a normal call. Another competitor service, Lince, is expected to begin operating along similar lines by the end of 1998.

Calling Barcelona from Abroad Spain's country code is ☎ 34. Follow this with the full nine-digit number you are calling.

Voicemail Voicemail could be an efficient way to keep in touch with friends and family. In London, Travellers' Connections (0181-286 3065; from 22 April 2000 ☎ 020-8286 3065, www.netcomuk.co.uk/~travcons) offers such a service. It works rather like an answer phone. You are allotted a London phone number and a PIN. Whenever you call that number you can leave a greeting – the message can be as long as you like – and you can also retrieve messages.

Fax

Most main post offices have a fax service: sending one page costs about 350 ptas within Spain, 920 ptas for elsewhere in Europe, and 1700 to 2000 ptas to other countries. However, you'll often find cheaper rates at shops or offices with 'Fax Público' signs.

Email & Internet Access

Those travelling with their own computers will need access to a phone. The phone jacks in Barcelona are the standard American-style RJ-11 variety, making modem connection easy. Be wary of plugging into hotel room phone outlets though, as hotel PABX phone systems can fry your modem and computer. Unless you have access to an international provider, you will need to call long distance to your provider's node at home or consider joining a local service during your stay – for most people probably too much hassle.

CompuServe's node in Barcelona is ☎ 93 487 38 88. It has direct nodes in Madrid and Valencia too. Since late 1998, CompuServe has imposed an extra hourly phone line charge for hooking up to the net on its Spain nodes – prompting many locals to abandon the service.

Cybercafés You can use the Internet for 600 ptas a half-hour (or 800 ptas an hour for students) upstairs at El Café de Internet (☎ 93 412 19 15; cafe@cafeinternet.es), Gran Via de les Corts Catalanes 656 (see Places to Eat – L'Eixample). Other options include:

Café Insòlit
  (☎ 93 225 81 78; bar.internet@insolit.es); in the waterfront Maremàgnum shopping complex
Café Interlight
  (☎ 93 301 11 80) Carrer de Pau Claris 106
Internet kiosk (self-service)
  Main concourse, Estació Sants railway station
Pere Noguera
  (☎ 93 442 11 04; pere noguera@cambrabcn.es) Carrer de Sant Pau 124
E
  (☎ 93 481 75 75) La Rambla 42 (map 5), actually in Passatge de Bacardí 1; another email service is: www.emailfromspain.es

INTERNET RESOURCES

Scouring the Net for a few hours can lead you to some interesting tips about most aspects of the city, including a lot of practical information like event listings and public transport details. Many of the sites are multilingual (eg Catalan, Castilian, English and French). Some initial sites you might like to surf include:

www.deinfo.es/barcelona-on-line
  This is the single most useful Web site on Barcelona, with numerous links to wider Catalan and Spanish topics and loads of busy pages covering restaurants, bars, places to stay (including homestays), bars and discos, shops, tourist information, museums, weather information, Spanish and Catalan newpaper and magazine Web site links, transport information and so on. You can also plug into lots of chat forums.
www.infobarna.es/
  Turisme de Barcelona's official site, with information on sights, eateries and other aspects of Barcelona interest, along with up-to-date details on what's on in the city. You can contact them by email on central@infobarna.com.
www.bcn.es/
  This general Web site is administered by the

Ajuntament and offers a wide variety of information on the city's services and events.

www.gencat.es
The Generalitat's Web site contains some curious pages dealing with various aspects of Catalunya's history and culture. It's in Spanish, Catalan and English.

www.gpd.org/
Another general start that provides good links to specific Barcelona topics

www.gencat.es/jov
For information on official Xarxa d'Albergs de la Generalitat – which covers most of the HI youth hostels in Barcelona and Catalunya

http://barcelona.de/
A German-language information site on Barcelona, with forum for message exchange

http://city.net/countries/spain/barcelona
Excite's travel Web pages, with farefinder and bookings and links to metro maps, restaurant tips and the like

www.netcafeguide.com/spain1.html
At this site you can get a list of Internet cafés in Barcelona (and around Spain). It's not as up-to-date as you might expect, but it is a start (see also Cybercafés above).

www.tmb.net
For everything you wanted to know, and probably plenty you didn't, on Barcelona's public transport system

http://vilaweb.com
For those curious about what is going on farther afield in Catalunya, this is a series of linked sites, usually produced from individual towns and communities. Its avowed aim is to link up Catalans wherever they may be.

BOOKS

Most books are published in different editions by different publishers in different countries. As a result, a book might be a hard-cover rarity in one country and readily available in paperback in another. Fortunately, bookshops and libraries search by title or author, so your local bookshop or library is best placed to advise you on the availability of the following recommendations.

Bookshops Abroad In London several good bookshops specialise in the business of travel. For guidebooks and maps, Stanfords bookshop (☎ 0171-836-2121, from 22 April 2000 ☎ 020-7836-2121), 12-14 Long

Acre (WC2E 9LP), is acknowledged as one of the better first ports of call. A well-stocked source of travel literature is Daunts Books for Travellers (☎ 0171-224 2295, from 22 April 2000 ☎ 020-7224 2295), 83 Marylebone High Street (W1M 4AL).

Books on Spain (☎ /fax 0181-898 7789, from 22 April 2000 ☎ 020-8898 7789), PO Box 207, Twickenham TW2 5BQ, England, can send you a catalogue of hundreds of old and new titles available by mail order. For books in Spanish, one of the best options is Grant & Cutler (☎ 0171-734 2012, from 22 April 2000 ☎ 020-7734 2012) 55-57 Great Marlborough St, London W1V 2AY.

In Australia, the Travel Bookshop (☎ 02-9241 3554), 20 Bridge Street, Sydney, is worth a browse. In the US, try Book Passage (☎ 415-927 0960), 51 Tamal Vista Boulevard, Corte Madera, California, and the Complete Traveler Bookstore (☎ 212-685 9007), 199 Madison Ave, New York. In France, L'Astrolabe rive gauche (☎ 01-46 33 80 06), 14 rue Serpente, Paris, is recommended.

Lonely Planet

If you're planning to travel extensively from Barcelona, check out Lonely Planet's companion titles, including *Spain*, *Walking in Spain*, *Andalucía* and *France*.

Guidebooks

The *Blue Guide Barcelona* is full of intriguing detail about the city's churches and museums, while the *Time Out* guide to the city is strong on obscure listings details. An interesting walking guide to the city is *Dotze Passejades per la Història de Barcelona*, published by the Fundació de la Caixa. The only extant versions seem to be in Catalan, but given that two of its co-authors were Anglos, you might get lucky and strike an English-language version kicking around.

A still more comprehensive street by street guide to the city is *50 Vegades Barcelona* (50 Times Barcelona), published by the Ajuntament.

History & People

Homage to Barcelona by Colm Tóibín (1990) is an excellent personal introduction to the city's modern life and artistic and political history, by an Irish journalist who has lived there.

Homage to Catalonia is George Orwell's account of the 1936-39 civil war in Catalunya, moving from the euphoria of the early days in Barcelona to disillusionment with the disastrous infighting on the Republican side. If you want a good general history of the war, get *The Spanish Civil War* by Hugh Thomas.

The Usatges of Barcelona, translated by Donald J Kagay, is the Catalan equivalent of the Magna Carta. The document, and Kagay's commentary, gives a fascinating insight into the historical backdrop for Catalunya's separateness from the rest of Spain.

A guidebook with a difference leads you on strolls around Barcelona while recounting the histories and stories of its women. Called *Guia de Dones de Barcelona*, it is by Isabel Segura and also available in Castilian.

Arts

It is no easy task to categorise Robert Hughes' *Barcelona*, a witty and passionate study of the art and architecture of the city through history. It is neither flouncy artistic criticism nor dry history, rather a distillation of the life of the city and people and an assessment of its expression.

Architecture

A useful building-by-building account of architecture in the city is *Passejant per Barcelona – Art i Espais Urbans*, by Núria Casas and Lourdes Mateo. If your Spanish is good you shouldn't have too much trouble deciphering at least some of the Catalan.

If you prefer English, *Barcelona Architecture Guide*, by Antoni González Moreno-Navarro and Raquel Lacuesta Contreras, adopts a more technical approach to the same subject, but only covers the years 1929 to 1996. The same authors have also put out the *Guía de Arquitectura Modernista de Cataluña*.

Xavier Güell's *Gaudí Guide* (available in several languages) is poor in text but rich in black and white photography. In the handy Thames & Hudson series on artistic movements, *Romanesque Art* by Meyer Schapiro covers the pre-Gothic era that so sharply marked early Catalan architecture.

Cuisine

Several books have been published locally on Catalan cuisine. If you really want to test yourself you could try *Cuina Catalana* by Pere Sans – in Catalan. If English is more your thing, take a look at *Catalan Cuisine* by Colman Andrews.

General

To put things in context, you may want to read a little more widely about Spain. The two best overall introductions to modern Spain are *The New Spaniards* by John Hooper, a former Madrid correspondent for *The Guardian*, and the more controversial and personal *Fire in the Blood* by Ian Gibson, based on a British TV series. Gibson has also written a weighty biography of Salvador Dalí.

If you can, grab a copy of Eduardo Mendoza's *La Ciudad de los Prodigios* (City of Marvels), a novel set in Barcelona from the Universal Exposition of 1888 to the World expo of 1929.

Long-termers who have acquired a reading knowledge of Catalan and want to explore the more arcane sidelights of the city's story, or, more exactly, the outer conurbation, might get a kick out of the anecdotal *Off Barcelona*, by Ignasi Riera.

CD-ROMS

Only a handful of CD-Roms are available on subjects specifically related to Barcelona. The multilingual *Around Barcelona* is basically a guide to the city's architecture (5900 ptas). More general is *Barcelona – Ciudad Mediterránea* (3995 ptas), which contains more than 1000 illustrations and allows access to key Web sites on the Internet.

NEWSPAPERS & MAGAZINES

You can easily find a wide selection of national daily newspapers from around Europe and the UK at newsstands all over central Barcelona and especially along La Rambla. The *International Herald Tribune*, *Time*, *The Economist*, *Le Monde*, *Der Spiegel* and a host of other international magazines are also available.

DAMIEN SIMONIS

Spanish National Press

The main Spanish dailies can be identified along roughly political lines, with the old-fashioned paper *ABC* representing the conservative right, *El País* identified with the PSOE (Spain's centre-left socialist party) and *El Mundo*, a more radicalised left-wing paper that prides itself on breaking political scandals. For a good spread of national and international news, *El País* is the pick. One of the best-selling dailies is *Marca*, devoted exclusively to sport.

Local Press

El País includes a daily supplement devoted to Catalunya, but Barcelona is home to a lively home-grown press too. *La Vanguardia* and *El Periódico* are the main local Castilian-language dailies. The latter also publishes an award-winning Catalan version. The more Catalan-nationalist oriented daily is *Avui*. In 1998, *Diari de Barcelona*, which has come and gone with almost monotonous regularity since it was founded in 1792, reappeared as an online paper only (www.diariodebarcelona.com), heavily sponsored by the Ajuntament.

Useful Publications

Barcelona's entertainment bible is the weekly Castilian-language magazine *Guía del Ocio* (125 ptas), which comes out on Thursday and lists almost everything that's on in the way of music, film, exhibitions, theatre and more. You can pick it up at most newsstands. An alternative is *La Agenda de Barcelona* (225 ptas).

The free monthly English-language *Barcelona Metropolitan* is a handy magazine with articles on the local scene and classifieds that will lead you to English-speaking doctors, dentists, baby-sitters and other useful information. It's aimed at long-term residents. You can pick it up at various bars, restaurants and shops all over town as well as at several consulates, schools and occasionally at the tourist offices (such as International House). Once you have a copy, keep the page at the back, which has a list of places where you can find next month's magazine.

RADIO

You can pick up BBC World Service broadcasts on a variety of frequencies. Broadcasts are directed at western Europe on, among others, 648, 9410 and 12,095 kHz (short wave). Or you may get broadcasts aimed at southern Spain and North Africa, mainly on 15,485 kHz. Voice of America can be found on various short-wave frequencies, including on 9700, 15,205 and 15,255 kHz, depending on the time of day. The BBC and

VOA broadcast for much of the day from about 5 am to after 9 pm, but the quality of reception varies considerably.

The Spanish national network Radio Nacional de España (RNE) has several stations: RNE 1 (738 AM; 88.3 FM in Barcelona) has general interest and current affairs programs; RNE 5 (576 AM) concentrates on sport and entertainment; RNE 3 (98.7 FM) presents a decent range of pop and rock music. For classical music you can tune into Sinfo Radio (104.2 FM). Among the most listened to rock and pop stations are 40 Principales (93.9 FM), Onda Cero (89.1 FM) and Cadena 100 (100 FM).

Those wanting to get into Catalan can tune into Catalunya Ràdio (102.8 FM), Ràdio Espanya Catalunya (94.9 FM). There are also a host of small local broadcasters.

A few local radio stations broadcast the odd program in English. Ràdio Contrabanda (91.3 FM) is one and Ràdio Gràcia (107.6 FM) is another.

TV

Most TVs receive seven channels – two from Spain's state-run Televisión Española (TVE1 and La 2), three independent (Antena 3, Tele 5 and Canal Plus), the Catalunya regional government station, TV-3, and another Catalan station, Canal 33. Most TV sets will also get the local city station, Barcelona TV.

News programs are generally decent and you can occasionally catch an interesting documentary or film (look out for the occasional English-language classic late at night on La 2). Otherwise, the main fare is a rather nauseating diet of soaps (many from Latin America), endless talk shows and almost vaudevillian variety shows (with plenty of glitz and tits). Canal Plus is a pay channel dedicated mainly to movies: you need a decoder and subscription to see the movies, but anyone can watch the other programs.

Many private homes and better hotels have satellite TV. Foreign channels you may come across include BBC World (mainly news and travel), BBC Prime (other BBC programs), CNN, Eurosport, Sky News, Sky Sports, Sky Sports 2, Sky Movies and the German SAT 1.

VIDEO SYSTEMS

If you want to record or buy video tapes to play back home, you won't get a picture if the image registration systems are different. TVs and nearly all pre-recorded videos on sale in Spain use the PAL (phase alternation line) system common to most of western Europe and Australia, incompatible with France's SECAM system or the NTSC system used in North America and Japan. PAL videos can't be played back on a machine that lacks PAL capability.

Buying Videos

If you can't be bothered shooting your own videos on Barcelona, a few local products are available (try the bookshops in the tourist offices). *Barcelona* (2995 ptas) is a general introduction to the city, available in several languages. *La Ruta del Modernisme* (1995 ptas), takes you on a tour around the city's modernista monuments. Finally, the Fundació Joan Miró has put out a video (with the same name) on its work and exhibits (2995 ptas). Some of these are available in several formats.

PHOTOGRAPHY & VIDEO
Film & Equipment

Most main brands of film are widely available and processing is fast and generally efficient. A roll of print film (36 exposures, ISO 100) costs around 650 ptas and can be processed for around 1700 ptas – although there are often better deals if you have two or three rolls developed together. The equivalent in slide *(diapositiva)* film is around 850 ptas plus 850 ptas for processing.

There are plenty of places to have films developed. Panorama Foto, which has seven branches around town, including Passeig de Gràcia 2 (map 5), will develop most photos, including slides, in an hour. They also sell standard blank video cassettes.

Technical Tips

Bright middle-of-the-day sun tends to

bleach out your shots. You get more colour and contrast earlier and later in the day, whether you are using still or video film.

Restrictions
Some museums and galleries ban photography, or at least flash, and soldiers can be touchy about it. Video is also often not allowed.

Photographing People
It's common courtesy to ask – at least by gesture – when you want to photograph people unless, perhaps, they're in some kind of public event like a procession. Even some of the 'artists' operating in La Rambla get pissed off by people taking shots without asking first.

Airport Security
Your camera and film will be passed routinely through airport X-ray machines. These shouldn't damage film but you can ask for inspection by hand if you're worried. Lead pouches for film, available in some specialised camera stores, are another solution

TIME
Spain (and hence Barcelona) is on GMT/UTC plus one hour during winter, and GMT/UTC plus two hours during the daylight-saving period from the last Sunday in March to the last Sunday in October. Most other western European countries have the same time as Spain year round, the major exceptions being Britain, Ireland and Portugal, which are an hour behind.

When it's noon in Barcelona, it's 11 am in London, 6 am in New York and Toronto, 3 am in San Francisco, 9 pm in Sydney and 11 pm in Auckland. Note that the changeover to/from daylight usually differs from the European setup by a couple of weeks in North America and Australasia.

ELECTRICITY
Electric current in Barcelona is 220V, 50Hz, as in the rest of Continental Europe. Several countries outside Europe (such as the USA and Canada) have 60Hz, which means that appliances that have electric motors, (such as some CD and tape players) from those countries may perform poorly. It is always safest to use a transformer.

Plugs have two round pins, again as in the rest of Continental Europe.

WEIGHTS & MEASURES
The metric system is used in Spain. Like other Continental Europeans, the Spanish indicate decimals with commas and thousands with points. You will sometimes see years written thus: 1.998.

LAUNDRY
Self-service laundries are a rarity indeed. One is the Bugaderia on Carrer del Consolat de Mar. A 7kg load costs 575 ptas and drying costs 105 ptas for five minutes.

Lavandería Tigre at Carrer d'En Rauric 20 in the Barri Gòtic will wash, dry and fold 3kg in a couple of hours for 820 ptas (7kg for 1265 ptas). Doing it yourself costs 495 ptas/745 ptas to wash, plus extra to dry. The laundry is open daily except Sunday from 8 am to 6.30 pm.

TOILETS
Public toilets are not particularly common in Spain but it's OK to wander into most bars and cafés to use their toilet, even if you're not a customer. It's worth carrying some loo paper with you, though, as many toilets don't have it. If there's a bin beside the loo, it's there because the local sewerage system couldn't cope otherwise, so put paper etc in it.

HEALTH
You should encounter no particular health problems in Barcelona. Your main risks are likely to be sunburn, dehydration or mild gut problems at first if you're not used to a lot of olive oil. Most travellers experience no problems.

Spain has reciprocal health agreements with other EU countries. Citizens of those countries need to get hold of an E111 form

Medical Kit Check List

Following is a list of items you should consider including in your medical kit – consult
your pharmacist for brands available in
your country.

☐ **Aspirin** or **paracetamol** (acetamin-
ophen in the US) – for pain or fever.

☐ **Antihistamine** – for allergies, eg hay
fever; to ease the itch from insect bites
or stings; and to prevent motion sick-
ness.

☐ **Antibiotics** – consider including these
if you're travelling well off the beaten
track; see your doctor, as they must be
prescribed, and carry the prescription
with you.

☐ **Loperamide** or **diphenoxylate** –
'blockers' for diarrhoea; **prochlorper-
azine** or **metaclopramide** for nausea
and vomiting.

☐ **Rehydration mixture** – to prevent dehydration, eg due to severe diarrhoea;
particularly important when travelling
with children.

☐ **Insect repellent, sunscreen, lip balm**
and **eye drops.**

☐ **Calamine lotion, sting relief spray** or
aloe vera – to ease irritation from
sunburn and insect bites or stings.

☐ **Antifungal cream** or **powder** – for
fungal skin infections and thrush.

☐ **Antiseptic** (such as povidone-iodine)
– for cuts and grazes.

☐ **Bandages, Band-Aids (plasters)** and
other wound dressings.

☐ **Water purification tablets** or **iodine.**

☐ **Scissors, tweezers** and a **thermometer**
(note that mercury thermometers are
prohibited by airlines).

☐ **Syringes** and **needles** – in case you
need injections in a country with
medical hygine problems. Ask your
doctor for a note explaining why you
have them.

☐ **Cold** and **flu tablets, throat lozenges**
and **nasal decongestant.**

☐ **Multivitamins** – consider for long
trips, when dietary vitamin intake may
be inadequate.

from their national health bodies (in the
case of the UK and Ireland, get one at the
local post office). If you should require
medical help you will need to present this,
plus photocopies and your national health
card. This is only valid for Spanish public
health care.

Travel insurance is still a good idea,
however. You should really get it to cover
you for theft, loss and unexpected travel cancellations anyway, so you will be covered for
the cost of private health care as well.

No vaccinations are required for Spain
unless you are coming from an infected area
(this generally relates to yellow fever – you
may be asked for proof of vaccination).

For minor health problems you can head
to your local *farmàcia* where pharmaceuticals tend to be sold more freely without
prescription than in places like the USA,
Australia or UK.

Medical Services & Emergency

Hospitals with emergency service include
the Hospital Creu Roja (☎ 93 433 15 51),
Carrer del Dos de Maig 301 (metro: Hospital de Sant Pau), and Hospital de la Santa
Creu i de Sant Pau (☎ 93 291 90 00), Carrer
de Sant Antoni Maria Claret 167 (metro:
Hospital de Sant Pau – which is also the
name by which the hospital is more commonly known).

For an ambulance, call ☎ 061, ☎ 93 329
97 01 or ☎ 93 300 20 20; for emergency
dental help, try ☎ 93 415 99 22.

There's a 24-hour pharmacy at Carrer
d'Aribau 62 and another on the corner of
Passeig de Gràcia and Carrer de Provença.
Otherwise, for information on duty
chemists call ☎ 010. Note that at some late-
night pharmacies you have to knock at a
small shutter for service; often they will
only fill prescriptions or deal with urgent
problems outside normal business hours –
this is not the time to buy your shampoo.

STDs & AIDS

Although the spread of AIDS/HIV
(SIDA/VIH in Castilian Spanish) has
slowed in the past couple of years, it

remains a big problem in Spain. Barcelona is no exception.

The Hospital del Mar (☎ 93 221 10 10; map 6) has a special AIDS-testing clinic, but it is entirely probable that you will be first asked to visit your local public GP, or CAP (Centre d'Assistència Primària) to fill in forms. As most foreign visitors won't have a CAP, they may be obliged to go to a private clinic for a test (which in turn may well *not* be covered by insurance).

For AIDS-related information you can call the service run by the Generalitat on ☎ 93 339 87 56. It operates Monday to Friday from 8 am to 3.15 pm.

WOMEN TRAVELLERS

As visitors have flooded into Barcelona, the fascination of the local boys with foreign women has tended to diminish. In general terms, therefore, harassment is unlikely to be much more apparent here than in any other European metropole, and in some cases probably less so.

Since the death of Franco, women have surged into the workforce and become far more assertive, but the truisms which apply elsewhere in the world apply here too. More often than not women are paid less than their male counterparts. Household duties still tend to fall onto the shoulders of women (even among younger people) and in many cases working women find themselves doing most of the family raising too.

These days, on the beaches and in the swimming pools you'll see just as many women with bikini tops on as off.

Organisations

The first stop for anyone seeking information on women's issues should be the Institut Català de la Dona (☎ 93 317 92 91), Carrer de Portaferrissa 1-3 (map 5). They can point you in the right direction for: information on rape/assault counselling; marriage, divorce and related issues for longtermers; social activities, women's clubs and so on.

Ca la Dona (☎ 93 412 71 61), Carrer de Casp 38, is the nerve centre of Barcelona's feminist movement. It includes about 25 diverse women's groups and has been going since 1988.

The Centre Municipal d'Informació i Recursos per a les Dones (☎ 93 291 84 92), Carrer de la Llacuna 161, is a local government-run information service. Among other things it publishes the *Guia de Grups i Entitats de Dones de Barcelona*, which is a comprehensive guide to all associations and groups connected with women and women's issues in the city.

On the subject of assault, the nationwide Comisión de Investigación de Malos Tratos a Mujeres (Commission of Investigation into the Abuse of Women) has a free 24-hour national emergency line for victims of physical abuse: ☎ 900-10 00 09. English may be in short supply, however.

GAY & LESBIAN TRAVELLERS

Gay and lesbian sex are both legal in Spain and the age of consent is 16 years, the same as for heterosexuals. Catalunya went a step further in October 1998 by introducing a law recognising de facto gay and lesbian couples. A similar law at national level has been stalled in the Cortes by the ruling conservative PP and it is unlikely to move while that party remains in power. The Catalan law does not yet sanction marriage of such couples nor the adoption of children by them but nevertheless it marks the region out as one of the most gay-friendly in the world.

Guia Gay Visado is a guide to gay and lesbian bars, discos, contacts etc in Spain. You can find it, along with one or two similar publications, at some of the newsstands on La Rambla in Barcelona and in lesbian/gay bookshops. *Entiendes*, a gay magazine, is on sale at some newsstands for 500 ptas.

International gay and lesbian guides worth tracking down are the *Spartacus Guide for Gay Men* (the Spartacus list also includes the comprehensive *Spartacus National Edition España*, in English and German), published by Bruno Gmünder Verlag, Mail Order, PO Box 11 07 29, D-1000 Berlin 11; *Places for Women*, published by Ferrari Publications, Phoenix,

AZ, USA; and *Women Going Places*, published in London by Women Going Places.

There are a few Spanish queer sites on the World Wide Web. One of the best is *Gay Spain* (http://www.gayspain.com). It has city and regional listings of bars, clubs and accommodation and includes options in Barcelona. The information is in Spanish.

Organisations

Casal Lambda (☎ 93 412 72 72) at Carrer Ample 5 in the Barri Gòtic is a gay and lesbian social, cultural and information centre. Coordinadora Gai-Lesbiana (☎ 93 309 79 97; fax 93 309 78 40; cogailes@ pangea.org), Carrer de Buenaventura Muñoz 4, is the city's main coordinating body for gay and lesbian groups. Some of the latter, such as Grup de Lesbianes Feministes, are to be found at Ca la Dona (see Women Travellers above). There is a free gay help-line on ☎ 900-60 16 01.

Sextienda, a gay sex shop at Carrer d'En Rauric 11 in the Barri Gòtic, has a giveaway map of gay Barcelona showing lesbian and gay bars, discos and restaurants.

DISABLED TRAVELLERS

The British-based Royal Association for Disability & Rehabilitation (RADAR) publishes a useful guide, *Holidays & Travel Abroad: A Guide for Disabled People*, with a section on Spain covering contact addresses, transport, services and accommodation. Contact RADAR (☎ 0171-250 3222, from 22 April 2000 ☎ 020-7250 3222) at 12 City Forum, 250 City Rd, London EC1 8AF. Mobility International (☎ 02-410 6274, fax 02-410 6297), Rue de Manchester 25, Brussels B1070, Belgium, has researched facilities for disabled tourists in Spain. Another organisation worth calling is Holiday Care Service (☎ 01293-774535).

Organisations

In Barcelona itself ECOM (☎/fax 93-451 69 04), Spain's federation of private organisations for the disabled, is at Gran Via de les Corts Catalanes 562, 08011 Barcelona. They can provide information on accommodation with disabled people's facilities, public and private transport options (eg bus lines and taxis that are wheel-chair equipped) as well as leisure time and holiday possibilities in and around Barcelona.

For more city information you could also try the Institut Municipal para Personas amb Disminució (☎ 93 291 84 00), Carrer de Llacuna 161.

SENIOR TRAVELLERS

Those over 65 are generally entitled to discounts on entry to some museums and other sights, usually on provision of some form of ID. It is always worth asking.

BARCELONA FOR CHILDREN

Although in general it can be said that Spain is a child-friendly country, Barcelona is, after all, a busy city. That said, you will generally have no problem in restaurants, hotels, cafés and the like, although few locals are inclined to take their *peques* (little ones) out for a night on the tiles.

Kids can nevertheless open doors where adults alone never would. This is especially so where a language barrier impedes communication – cute kids doing the cute things that cute kids sometimes do can be a great ice-breaker.

Catalans have fewer qualms about keeping their children up late than people from more northerly climes. In summer especially, you'll see them at the local festes until the wee hours. Taking children to cafés or snack bars which have outdoor tables (preferably in pedestrian zones) is no problem at all. Of course your wee bairn's body clock may not quite be up to it.

What to Do with Anklebiters

Some of the museums appear to have been thought out for kids as much as for adults. The Museu Marítim and the Museu d'Història de Catalunya fall into that category, the former with its audio-visual trek through time and the latter with its various hands-on gadgets.

The Parc d'Atraccions up on Tibidabo is perfect for the kids and few young ones will turn up their noses at the beach or outdoor pools in summer. If you've been cruel enough to subject them to the Museu d'Art Modern in the Parc de la Ciutadella, why not compensate with an ice-cream and a stroll through the park, a trip to the zoo and/or a bit of a row on the little artificial lake? Still not satisfied? The high-level *funicular aereo* (cable car) between Montjuïc and La Barceloneta might be the go, as indeed could be a harbour excursion on one of the Golondrina boats.

The watery tunnels of L'Aquàrium, Europe's biggest fish 'zoo', should be a winner and you could also try the nearby Imax cinema.

For some, the best thing in life is a game hall with all that electronic wizardry can provide. If you think that might mollify the disgruntled darlings for a while, one such option is the New Park games parlour on La Rambla

Finally, even the most adventurous of children will at times feel nostalgia for toys back home. Bring a couple of favourites along to keep them occupied in dull moments or when you're just trying to kick back yourself.

Before You Go

There are no particular health precautions you need to take, though kids tend to be more affected than adults by unaccustomed heat, changes in diet and sleeping patterns, and just being in a strange place. Nappies, creams, lotions, baby foods and so on are all easily available in Barcelona, but if there's some particular brand you swear by it's best to bring it with you. Calpol, for instance, isn't easily found.

Lonely Planet's *Travel with Children* has lots of practical advice on the subject and first-hand stories from many Lonely Planet authors, and others, who have done it.

USEFUL ORGANISATIONS

The Instituto Cervantes, with branches in over 30 cities around the world, exists to promote the Spanish language (but not Catalan) and the cultures of Spain and other Spanish-speaking countries. It's mainly involved in Spanish teaching and library and information services. The library at the London branch (☎ 0171-486 4350, from 22 April 2000 ☎ 020-7486 4350), 102 Eaton Square, London SW1 W9AN, has a wide range of reference books, literature, books on history and the arts, periodicals, more than 1000 videos (including feature films), language-teaching material, electronic databases and music CDs. In New York, the institute (☎ 212-689 4232) is at 122 East 42nd St, Suite 807, New York, NY 10168.

UNIVERSITIES

Barcelona has five universities spread about the city. Teaching is predominantly in Catalan, meaning that even Castilian speakers may have difficulties at first. European students in Barcelona are mostly on one-year programs as part of the Erasmus scheme. They do this as part of their undergraduate studies. You need to approach the Socrates and Erasmus council in your country for more information.

Of the universities, the oldest and biggest is the Universitat de Barcelona (☎ 93 403 54 17), with campuses at Gran Via de les Corts Catalanes 585 and the Zona Universitària (metro: Zona Universitària).

The remaining institutions are:

Universitat Politècnica de Catalunya
(☎ 93 401 73 96), Avinguda de Marañon 42 (metro: Zona Universitària). As the name suggests, it is a technical and engineering university.
Universitat Pompeu Fabra
(☎ 93 542 22 28), Pla de la Mercè 10-12. Based in the old city, this university concentrates on social sciences.
Universitat Autònoma de Barcelona
(☎ 93 581 11 11), Bellaterra. This place is outside the city near Sabadell and an unlikely choice for foreigners.
Universitat Ramon Llull
(☎ 93 253 04 50), Carrer de Sant Joan de la Salle. A private institute for students with fat wallets. The faculty buildings are spread across town.

Foreign students in Barcelona can get help on a range of information from lodgings to language tuition, how to organise work experience in local companies, cultural activities and so on, at Barcelona Centre Universitari (☎ 93 483 83 83), Carrer de Calàbria 147

CULTURAL CENTRES

British Council
    (☎ 93 209 63 88), Carrer d'Amigó 83 (FGC: Muntaner). English classes, library services, film seasons and other cultural events.
Institute for North American Studies
    (☎ 93 200 75 51), Via Augusta 123 (FGC: Muntaner). Library material is also available here. The institute serves mainly as a place for locals doing language and other study with a view to spending time in the USA.
Institut Français de Barcelona
    (☎ 93 209 59 11), Carrer de Moià 8 (map 1; metro: Diagonal). Puts on films, concerts and exhibitions.
Goethe Institut
    (☎ 93 292 22 26), Carrer de Manso 24-28 (map 4). Apart from German classes and library services, the institute organises lectures, exhibits, film seasons and the like.
Istituto Italiano di Cultura
    (☎ 93 487 53 06), Passatge de Méndez Vigo 5 (map 2; metro: Passeig de Gràcia). The institute's main aim is to teach Italian. It also has a library and puts on lectures and film seasons.

DANGERS & ANNOYANCES

Barcelona is a fairly secure city, although petty crime (in particular theft) is a problem and its victims are often newcomers in town.

Before You Leave Home

You can take a few precautions before you even arrive in Barcelona. Inscribe your name, address and telephone number *inside* your luggage and take photocopies of the important pages of your passport, travel tickets and other important documents. Keep the copies separate from the originals and ideally leave one set of copies at home. These steps will make things easier if you do suffer a loss or theft. Travel insurance against theft and loss is another very good idea.

Prevention

... is better than a cure! Only walk around with the amount of cash you intend to spend that day or evening. Hidden money belts or pouches are a good idea. The popular 'bum bags' and external belt pouches people wear around their tummies are like shining beacons to hawks looking for targets. You may as well wear a neon sign saying: 'Pick Me: I'm a Tourist'.

Theft & Loss

You need to keep an eye out for pickpockets and bagsnatchers in the most heavily touristed parts of town, especially La Rambla and the Ciutat Vella. The Barri Xinès, the lower end of La Rambla and the area around Plaça Reial, although much cleaned up in recent years, remain dodgy. As a rule, dark, empty streets are to be avoided. They may be perfectly OK, but who wants to be the one to find out that they are not? Luckily, Barcelona's most lively nocturnal areas are generally busy with crowds having a good time – and there is definitely safety in numbers.

In summer, the beach is a particularly popular playground for thieves – always keep your belongings within reach and in view. If alone, you may want to invest in a waterproof neckpouch so that when you go swimming your documents, money etc can go with you. The beach theft problem is bad enough for local police to mount a special anti-theft operation on the beach in summer (in July and August 1998 about 150 thieves were caught in the act).

Never leave anything visible in your car and preferably leave nothing at all. Temptation usually leads at least to smashed windows. Foreign and hire cars are especially vulnerable.

In hotels, hostels etc, use the safe if there is one. Try not to leave valuables in your room. If you must, then bury them deep in your luggage.

If anything does get lost or stolen, you need to report it to police and get a written statement from them if you intend to claim on insurance. If your ID or passport disappears, you must also contact your nearest consulate, as early as possible, to arrange for a replacement.

Emergency

The Guàrdia Urbana (City Police; ☎ 092) has a station at La Rambla 43, opposite Plaça Reial, to help tourists who are victims of crime. It's open from 7 am to midnight (to 2 am on Friday and Saturday nights). There's always an English speaker on duty, and usually a French speaker. Asistencia al Turista (☎ 93 482 05 26) may also be able to help distressed visitors.

Lost & Found

The city's main lost-and-found *(objetos perdidos)* office is on ☎ 93 402 31 61. If you leave anything in a taxi, you can call ☎ 93 223 40 02 to see if it's been handed in.

LEGAL MATTERS

If you're arrested you will be allotted the free services of a duty solicitor *(abogado de oficio)*, who may speak only Catalan and/or Spanish. You're also entitled to make a phone call. If you phone your embassy or consulate, it will probably be able to do no more than refer you to a lawyer who speaks your language. If you end up in court, the authorities are obliged to provide a translator.

Drugs

Spain's liberal drug laws were severely tightened in 1992. The only legal drug is cannabis, and then only if it's for personal use – which means very small amounts.

Public consumption of any drug is apparently illegal, yet you may still come across the occasional bar where people smoke joints openly. Most, however, will ask you to step outside if you light up. In short, be discreet if you use cannabis. There is a reasonable degree of tolerance when it comes to people having a smoke in their own home, but it would be unwise to do so in hotel rooms or guesthouses, and could be risky in even the coolest of public places.

Travellers entering Spain from Morocco should be ready for intensive drug searches, especially if they have a vehicle.

BUSINESS HOURS

Generally, people work Monday to Friday from about 9 am to 2 pm and then again from 4.30 or 5 pm for another three hours. Shops and travel agencies are usually open these hours on Saturday too, although some may skip the evening session. Big supermarkets and department stores such as El Corte Inglés often stay open all day Monday to Saturday, from about 9 am to 9 pm. A handful of shops are open on Sunday. Many government offices don't bother with afternoon opening any day of the year.

Museums all have their own unique opening hours: major ones tend to open for something like normal Spanish business hours (with or without the afternoon break), but often have their weekly closing day on Monday, not Sunday.

See earlier sections of this chapter for bank and post office hours.

PUBLIC HOLIDAYS & SPECIAL EVENTS
Vacation Periods

The two main periods when Barcelonins go on holiday are Setmana Santa (the week leading up to Easter Sunday) and, more noticeably, the month of August. In Easter, incoming tourists make up in numbers for the leaving locals (accommodation is at a premium this week), but in August the city is like a ghost town, even though in recent years the tendency has been to stagger departures and returns in two-week chunks over July and August.

Public Holidays

In Barcelona, as in the rest of Spain, there are 14 official holidays a year – some observed nationwide, some local. When a holiday falls close to a weekend, people like to make a puente (bridge) – meaning they take the intervening day off too. On the odd occasion when a couple of holidays fall close, they make an acueducto (aqueduct)!

The seven national holidays are:

Any Nou/Año Nuevo (New Year's Day)
1 January – plenty of parties in the discos and clubs on New Year's Eve (Cap d'Any/Noche Vieja) – expect to pay higher than usual prices.

As the clock strikes midnight you are expected to eat a grape for each chime.

Divendres Sant/Viernes Santo (Good Friday)
March/April – Setmana Santa (Holy Week) is not, in general, celebrated with either the verve or the almost sinister pageantry which it is accorded farther south in Spain, but you get a taste of it on Good Friday with the procession from the Església de Sant Agustí in El Raval in the early afternoon of Good Friday. Accompanying the huge image of the Virgin that is the centrepiece of the march (which then proceeds up La Rambla and on to Plaça de Catalunya) are solemn bands, members of various religious fraternities (*cofradías*) dressed in robes and the conical hoods evocative of, for some, Andalucía and, for others, the Ku Klux Klan (with which, it should be stressed, they have nothing to do whatsoever). Most striking perhaps are the barefoot women penitents dressed in black and dragging heavy crosses and chains around their ankles. Look closely at the men and women in the parade and at the onlookers – almost certainly you will see the occasional tear. It is easy to assert that the whole spectacle is show, but perhaps the participants feel and see more than the detached observer?

Dia del Treball/Fiesta del Trabajo (Labour Day)
1 May – in this one-time anarchist stronghold where nowadays the Socialists always win the municipal elections, Labour Day once attracted big demonstrations. That is all but a memory nowadays – you'll probably hardly notice it's a holiday except for all the closed offices, banks and shops.

L'Assumpció/La Asunción (Feast of the Assumption)
15 August

Festa de la Hispanitat/Día de la Hispanidad (Spanish National Day)
12 October – the day off is appreciated, but no special celebrations mark this occasion

La Immaculada Concepció/La Inmaculada Concepción (Feast of the Immaculate Conception)
8 December

Nadal/Navidad (Christmas)
25 December – this is a family time. Many celebrate with a big midday meal, although some prefer to eat on Christmas Eve (*nit de Nadal/nochebuena*). One of the oddest things about Christmas is the nativity scenes that families traditionally set up at home (a giant one goes up in Plaça de Sant Jaume too). The cribs themselves are common throughout the Catholic world, and particularly in the Mediterranean. What makes these ones different is the presence, along with the Baby Jesus, Mary,

Joseph and the Three Kings, of a chap who has dropped his pants and is doing number twos. The Catalans proudly claim the *caganer* (the crapper) as their own but if, indeed, he is a Catalan invention, he has wide appeal – similar figures can be seen in the family cribs as far away as the Canary Islands.

In addition to these national holidays, the Generalitat and Ajuntament add the following holidays during the year:

Epifanía (Epiphany) or El Dia dels Reis/Día de los Reyes Magos (Three Kings' Day)
6 January – when children traditionally receive presents (generally they get little or nothing at Christmas).

Dilluns de Pasqua Florida (Easter Monday)
April

Dilluns de Pasqua Granada
May/June – the day after Pentecost Sunday.

Dia de Sant Joan/Día de San Juan Bautista (Feast of St John the Baptist)
24 June – The saint's day of King Juan Carlos – the night before the people of Barcelona hit the streets or hold parties at home to celebrate the *berbena de Sant Joan*, an evening of drinking, dancing and fireworks. The latter can be seen in districts all over town (and indeed across Catalunya), for which reason the evening is also known as La Nit del Foc, or Fire Night. The traditional pastry to eat on this summer solstice is a kind of dense candied cake known as *coca de Sant Joan.*

Diada Nacional de Catalunya
11 September – Catalunya's national day commemorates Barcelona's surrender to the Spaniards at the conclusion of the War of the Spanish Succession. It is a relatively sobre occasion, when small independence groups demand the predictable without anyone paying too much attention.

Festes de la Mercè
24 September – this week of festivities begins shortly after the official close of summer and acts as a final burst of pre-winter madness all over Barcelona, although the bulk of the activities take place in the centre of town. Nostra Senyora de la Mercè (whose image lies in the church of the same name on Pla de la Mercè in La Ribera) was elevated to co-patron of the city after she single-handedly beat off a plague of locusts in 1637.

In 1714, as Barcelona faced defeat in the War of the Spanish Succession, light-headed town elders at one point appointed Our Lady commander-in-chief of the city's defences (an eloquent expression of hopelessness if ever there was one).

This is the city's *festa major* or Big Party. There's a swimming race across the harbour, a fun run, an outstanding series of free music concerts organised under the auspices of BAM (Barcelona Acció Musical; see Festivals below), and a bewildering program of cultural events all over town and in many of the museums and galleries. There's also all the predictable stuff that usually accompanies a major Catalan festa: *castellers* (human castle builders), *sardanes* (traditional folk dancing), parades of *gegants* and *capgrossos* (giants and big heads) and a huge *correfoc* (fire race). The latter is a pyromaniac's dream. It's held on the last night (a Sunday), and crowds hurl themselves through the streets before fire-spurting demons (not to mention kids armed with high-calibre firecrackers) who have been released from the Porta de l'Infern (Gate of Hell), located before the Catedral.

The fire race can be dangerous and you are advised to wear old cotton clothes (long sleeves and trousers) and a hood to cover up your head, earplugs and running shoes if you intend to participate in all the madness. The heat can be intense, but an old habit of tipping water from balconies above over participants has been banned – apparently mixing water with gun powder can have unpredictable consequences.

El Dia de Sant Esteve
26 December – the local equivalent of Boxing Day, it is a family occasion, much like Christmas Day, with festive lunches.

Festivals

Barcelona is perhaps not as addicted to partying as some more southerly Spanish cities, but it puts in a fair effort with some wild occasions dotting the calendar in between the official holidays. Several *barris* celebrate their own *festes majors*.

5 January
Cavalcada dels Reis
The day preceding Epiphany (a public holiday) sees the Three Kings 'arrive' in Barcelona at Moll de la Fusta and then parade up into town (the route tends to change). As the Kings parade around with floats, they hurl sweets to the kids in the crowd.

17 January
Festes dels Tres Tombs
A key part of the district festival of Sant Antoni, the festa of the Three Circuits involves a parade of horsemen who march around Ronda de Sant Antoni to Plaça de Catalunya, down La Rambla and back up Carrer Nou de la Rambla. Sant Antoni Abat (St Anthony the Abbot) is apparently the patron saint of muleteers. It was once one of the more important of Barcelona's celebrations, but is fairly muted nowadays.

February
Festes de Santa Eulàlia
Coinciding with Carnaval (see next entry), this is the feast of Barcelona's first patron saint. The Ajuntament organises all sorts of cultural events, from concerts through to performances by castellers and the appearance of *mulasses* (dragons) in the main parade.

February/March
Carnestoltes/Carnaval *(Carnival)*
Several days of fancy-dress parades and merrymaking in many places, usually ending on the Tuesday 47 days before Easter Sunday. For about 10 days there are parades and dancing, and parties in the discos and clubs. It is not as riotous as the Canary Islands version of Carnaval, but busy enough to keep most punters happy. As it does elsewhere in Spain, the carnival culminates in the Enterrament de la Sardina (burial of the fish), often on Montjuïc. The whole affair is a dramatic celebration of the end of winter.

23 April
Dia de Sant Jordi
The day of Catalunya's patron saint and also the Day of the Book – men give women a rose, women give men a book; publishers launch new titles, La Rambla and Plaça de Sant Jaume (where the Generalitat building is open to the public) are filled with book and flower stalls.

May/June
L'Ou com Balla
A curious tradition with several centuries of history, the 'Dancing Egg' is an empty shell which bobs on top of the flower-festooned fountain in the cloister of the Catedral. This spectacle is Barcelona's way of celebrating Corpus Christi (the Thursday after the eighth Sunday after Easter Sunday). Other dancing eggs can be seen on the same day in the courtyard of the Casa de l'Ardiaca and various other fountains in the Barri Gòtic.

28 June
Dia per l'Alliberament Lesbià i Gai
Gay and lesbian festival and parade.

Around 15 August
Festa Major de Gràcia
Apart from the Festes de la Mercè, this is one of the biggest local festivals in Barcelona. More than a dozen streets in Gràcia are decorated by their inhabitants according to a certain theme as part of a competition for the most imaginative street of the year. Locals set up tables and benches to enjoy local feasts, but people from all over the city pour in to participate. In squares (particularly Plaça del Sol) and intersections all over the *barri*, bands compete for attention. Snack stands abound and there are numerous bars open onto the streets to sell rivers of drink to the thirsty crowds. Local residents who hope to get any sleep in this week tend to move to friends' places or leave town!

Around August 24
Festa Major de Sants
This barri launches its own version of decorated mayhem, hard on Gràcia's heels. Although the festival has neither the history nor the grandeur of the Gràcia festival, locals have in recent years injected an increasing amount of life into it and here you'll experience the true flavour of the barri.

September/October
Festa Major de la Barceloneta
Barcelona's partiers barely get a chance to relax before the next opportunity for merry-making comes along. Although on a small scale, La Barceloneta's gig still involves plenty of dancing and drinking (especially down on the beach).

Arts & Music Festivals Barcelona plays host to several arts-oriented festivals in the course of the year. Among the more important are:

June
Sonar
Barcelona's celebration of electronic music. It is claimed to be Europe's biggest such event and you can get into the latest house, hiphop, triphop, eurobeat and anything else they have come up with in the meantime.

Late June to August
Festival del Grec
Many theatres shut down for the summer but into the breach steps this eclectic program of theatre, dance and music. Performances are held all over the city, not just at the amphitheatre on Montjuïc (map 7) from which the festival takes its name. Programs and tickets are available from the Palau de la Virreina on La Rambla (see under Tourist Offices) and at a temporary booth set up on Avinguda del Portal de l'Àngel (just off Plaça de Catalunya).

Around 24 September
BAM
All the great free music put on for the Festes de la Mercè (see above) is organised as Barcelona Acció Musical. Most of the performances take place on squares in the centre of town and/or on the waterfront. The hot guest for 1998 was Lou Reed.

Late October to late November
Festival Internacional de Jazz de Barcelona
Jazz and blues around the city.

DOING BUSINESS

The Barcelonins are often viewed by their counterparts in Madrid as rather dull workaholics and tightwads. The image is not without foundation and, especially since manufacturing took off here in the 19th century, the city has had (and indeed cultivated) an image of industriousness which is viewed with a mix of envy and scorn by much of the rest of Spain.

This has been in Barcelona's favour as Spain has integrated into the EU and the global market in the past 20 years. The city is now viewed enthusiastically by both the foreign business community and tourists.

Business Services

Business people who need to work in Barcelona temporarily or long term, and people hoping to set up new businesses here, should first contact the trade department of the Spanish embassy or consulate in their own country. Next port of call should be the Cambra Oficial de Comerç, Indústria i Navegació (☎ 93 416 93 00; fax 93 416 93 01), Avinguda Diagonal 452. It has a documentation centre (centredoc@ mail.cambrabcn.es) and business-oriented bookshop, the Llibreria de la Cambra. It also has a services centre, or Centre de Relacions Empresarials (☎ 93 478 67 99; fax 93 478 67 05), at the airport on the first floor of Terminal B, with an information desk and several office spaces (with phone, basic office equipment and screens for presentations). In general, only member-companies of the Cambra can organise use of the office space, so contact them beforehand to confirm that you can set up meetings here.

The Fira de Barcelona's information office (see next entry) offers business services (communications etc), meeting rooms and other facilities for people working at trade fairs.

Have you brought your portable computer along? It's malfunctioning? You could try the English-speaking PC Assistance on ☎ 93 446 50 23 (you can find several ads for English-speaking computer technicians in the free English-language magazine, *Barcelona Metropolitan* – see Newspapers & Magazines above).

Exhibitions & Conferences

With more than 60 trade fairs a year and a growing number of congresses of all types, Barcelona is becoming an important centre of international business in Europe. It claims to rank fifth worldwide for the organisation of congresses, in part due to the lower costs involved – the Fira de Barcelona, the city's trade fair, claims that organising congresses costs as little as 20% less here than in other major European cities.

The nature of the fairs ranges from fashion to technology, from furniture to recycling, jewellery to books.

The main trade fair is located between the base of Montjuïc and Plaça d'Espanya, with 250,000 sq m of exhibition space. To cope with expansion in the past years, the Fira 2 (Fair No 2) south-west of Montjuïc, with another 110,000 sq m, has been added.

The Palau de Congressos at Fira 1 can host up to 1650 people.

The Fira has an information centre (☎ 93 233 22 22) right on Plaça d'Espanya. It can

provide limited communications facilities for business people and professionals involved in the fairs. Usually, additional facilities are provided by individual fair organisers too.

WORK

Although unemployment has fallen over the past couple of years, and Catalunya has one of the lowest levels in Spain, unemployment in the region still outstrips the EU averages and this is hardly the ideal place to look for work. But there are a few ways of earning your keep (or almost) while you're here.

Bureaucracy

Nationals of EU countries, Norway and Iceland may work in Spain without a visa, but for stays of more than three months they are supposed to apply within the first month for a *tarjeta de residencia* (residence card); for information on this laborious process, see Visas & Documents earlier in this chapter. If you are offered a contract, your employer will usually steer you through the labyrinth.

Virtually everyone else is supposed to obtain, from a Spanish consulate in their country of residence, a work permit and, if they plan to stay more than 90 days, a residence visa. These procedures are well-nigh impossible unless you have a job contract lined up before you begin them; in any case you should start the process a long time before you aim to arrive in Barcelona. That said, quite a few people do work, discreetly, without bothering to tangle with the bureaucracy.

Opportunities

Language Teaching This is the obvious option, for which language-teaching qualifications are a big help (often indispensable). Barcelona is loaded with language schools, although many fall into the 'cowboy outfit' category – they tend to pay badly and often aren't overly concerned about quality. Still, the only way you'll find out is by hunting around. Schools are listed under Acadèmias de Idiomas' in the yellow pages.

Getting a job in a school is harder if

you're not an EU citizen. Some schools do employ people without work papers, usually at lower than normal rates. Giving private lessons is another worthwhile avenue, but unlikely to bring you a living wage straight away.

Sources of information on possible teaching work – school or private – include foreign cultural centres (the British Council, Alliance Française etc), foreign-language bookshops (such as Come In), universities and language schools. Many of

these have notice boards where you may find work opportunities, or where you can advertise your own services.

Busking La Rambla is one of the great busking stages of Europe, so you could try your luck here. It's no easy road though. Competition is tight and the quality of some acts is surprisingly high, but if you have an original and well-rehearsed act to present, this could be the place to try it out.

Getting There & Away

After Madrid, Barcelona is Spain's biggest international transport hub. It's easy to reach by air from anywhere in Europe and North America. Regular rail and bus links and a smooth super highway plug Barcelona into France and the rest of Europe and there are plenty of air and land connections to destinations all over Spain.

AIR

A phalanx of airlines fly direct to Barcelona from the rest of Europe. It pays to shop around for flight deals and, for short stays, it is sometimes more convenient to book a flight/hotel package. From North America the cheaper flights may entail a stopover en route (either Madrid or another European centre). Travellers coming from more distant locales, such as Asia and Australasia, have fewer choices.

Barcelona is not one of the world's great discount ticket centres, although for short European hops to the main capitals you can occasionally dig up cheap deals. See also Travel Agents towards the end of this chapter.

For more detailed information on airport facilities, see the next chapter.

Departure Tax

There are departure taxes when you are leaving Spain by air (fluctuating around 1000 ptas for European flights and rising to as much as 8500 ptas to the USA), but these are included in the price of the ticket at purchase. For European flights they are generally only charged if you are taking a *return* flight.

Other Parts of Spain

Flying within Spain is generally not an economical affair. Iberia (☎ 902-40 05 00) and the small subsidiary Binter Mediterráneo cover all destinations, with a range of fares. Ask about discounts and special rates. You get 25% off on flights departing after 11 pm

(admittedly there are few of these). People under 22 or over 63 get 25% off *return* flights, another 20% off night flights.

A standard one-way fare between Madrid and Barcelona ranges from 11,700 (night flights) to 15,550 ptas.

Competing with Iberia are Spanair (☎ 902-13 14 15) and Air Europa (☎ 902-24 00 42). Air Europa is the bigger of the two, with regular flights from Barcelona to Madrid, Palma de Mallorca, Málaga and a host of mainland Spanish destinations.

Six Air Europa flights connect Madrid with Barcelona daily (four on weekends). The one-way economy (*turista*) fare is 12,600 ptas. The return fare ranges from 25,100 ptas *down* to 13,700 ptas (this latter is for a minimum stay of four days and maximum of 14 days).

Canary Islands

From Barcelona, Iberia, Air Europa, Spanair and charters all fly to Tenerife and Las Palmas (Gran Canaria). Tourist-class return flights between Santa Cruz de Tenerife and Barcelona average around 34,000 ptas, although return charter fares can be as low as 18,900 ptas.

The UK

Most British travel agents are registered with ABTA (Association of British Travel Agents). If you have paid for your flight with an ABTA-registered agent who then goes bust, ABTA will guarantee a refund or an alternative. Unregistered bucket shops are riskier but sometimes cheaper.

One of the more reliable, but not necessarily cheapest, agencies is STA (☎ 0171-361 6161, from 22 April 2000 ☎ 020-7361 6161, for European flights; www.sta-travel.com). STA has several offices in London, as well as branches on many university campuses and in cities such as Bristol, Cambridge, Leeds, Manchester (☎ 0161-834 0668) and Oxford.

Air Travel Glossary

Baggage Allowance This will be written on your ticket and usually includes one 20kg item to go in the hold, plus one item of hand luggage.

Bucket Shops These are unbonded travel agencies specialising in discounted airline tickets.

Bumped Just because you have a confirmed seat doesn't mean you're going to get on the plane (see Overbooking).

Cancellation Penalties If you have to cancel or change a discounted ticket, there are often heavy penalties involved; insurance can sometimes be taken out against these penalties. Some airlines impose penalties on regular tickets as well, particularly against 'no-show' passengers.

Check-In Airlines ask you to check in a certain time ahead of the flight departure (usually one to two hours on international flights). If you fail to check in on time and the flight is over-booked, the airline can cancel your booking and give your seat to somebody else.

Confirmation Having a ticket written out with the flight and date you want doesn't mean you have a seat until the agent has checked with the airline that your status is 'OK' or confirmed. Meanwhile you could just be 'on request'.

Courier Fares Businesses often need to send urgent documents or freight securely and quickly. Courier companies hire people to accompany the package through customs and, in return, offer a discount ticket which is sometimes a phenomenal bargain. In effect, what the companies do is ship their freight as your luggage on regular commercial flights. This is a legitimate operation, but there are two shortcomings – the short turnaround time of the ticket (usually not longer than a month) and the limitation on your luggage allowance. You may have to surrender all your allowance and take only carry-on luggage.

Full Fares Airlines traditionally offer 1st-class (coded F), business class (coded J) and economy class (coded Y) tickets. These days there are so many promotional and discounted fares available that few passengers pay full economy fare.

ITX An ITX, or 'independent inclusive tour excursion', is often available on tickets to popular holiday destinations. Officially it's a package deal combined with hotel accommodation, but many agents will sell you one of these for the flight only and give you phoney hotel vouchers in the unlikely event that you're challenged at the airport.

Lost Tickets If you lose your airline ticket an airline will usually treat it like a travellers cheque and, after inquiries, issue you with another one. Legally, however, an airline is entitled to treat it like cash and if you lose it then it's gone forever. Take good care of your tickets.

MCO An MCO, or 'miscellaneous charge order', is a voucher that looks like an airline ticket but carries no destination or date. It can be exchanged through any International Association of Travel Agents (IATA) airline for a ticket on a specific flight. It's a useful alternative to an onward ticket in those countries that demand one, and is more flexible than an ordinary ticket if you're unsure of your route.

No-Shows No-shows are passengers who fail to show up for their flight. Full-fare passengers who fail to turn up are sometimes entitled to travel on a later flight. The rest are penalised (see Cancellation Penalties).

On Request This is an unconfirmed booking for a flight.

Air Travel Glossary

Onward Tickets An entry requirement for many countries is that you have a ticket out of the country. If you're unsure of your next move, the easiest solution is to buy the cheapest onward ticket to a neighbouring country or a ticket from a reliable airline which can later be refunded if you do not use it.

Open Jaw Tickets These are return tickets where you fly out to one place but return from another. If available, this can save you backtracking to your arrival point.

Overbooking Airlines hate to fly empty seats and since every flight has some passengers who fail to show up, airlines often book more passengers than they have seats. Usually excess passengers make up for the no-shows, but occasionally somebody gets bumped. Guess who it is most likely to be? The passengers who check in late.

Point-to-Point Tickets These are discount tickets that can be bought on some routes in return for passengers waiving their rights to a stopover.

Promotional Fares These are officially discounted fares, available from travel agencies or direct from the airline.

Reconfirmation At least 72 hours prior to departure time of an onward or return flight, you must contact the airline and 'reconfirm' that you intend to be on the flight. If you don't do this the airline can delete your name from the passenger list and you could lose your seat.

Restrictions Discounted tickets often have various restrictions on them – such as needing to be paid for in advance and incurring a penalty to be altered. Others are restrictions on the minimum and maximum period you must be away, such as a minimum of 14 days or a maximum of one year.

Round-the-World Tickets RTW tickets give you a limited period (usually a year) in which to circumnavigate the globe. You can go anywhere the carrying airlines go, as long as you don't backtrack. The number of stopovers or total number of separate flights is decided before you set off and they usually cost a bit more than a basic return flight.

Stand-by This is a discounted ticket where you only fly if there is a seat free at the last moment. Stand-by fares are usually available only on domestic routes.

Transferred Tickets Airline tickets cannot be transferred from one person to another. Travellers sometimes try to sell the return half of their ticket, but officials can ask you to prove that you are the person named on the ticket. This is less likely to happen on domestic flights, but on an international flight tickets are compared with passports.

Travel Agencies Travel agencies vary widely and you should choose one that suits your needs. Some simply handle tours, while full-services agencies handle everything from tours and tickets to car rental and hotel bookings. If all you want is a ticket at the lowest possible price, then go to an agency specialising in discounted tickets.

Travel Periods Ticket prices vary with the time of year. There is a low (off-peak) season and a high (peak) season, and often a low-shoulder season and a high-shoulder season as well. Usually the fare depends on your outward flight – if you depart in the high season and return in the low season, you pay the high-season fare.

A similar place is Trailfinders (☎ 0171-937 5400, from 22 April 2000 ☎ 020-7937 5400, for European flights). Its short haul booking centre is at 215 Kensington High St, London W8 7RG They also have agencies in Bristol, Birmingham, Glasgow and Manchester.

Usit Campus (European flights on ☎ 0171-730 3402, from 22 April 2000 ☎ 020-7730 3402), 52 Grosvenor Gardens, London SW1W 0AG, is in much the same league and has four other branches in London.

The two flag airlines linking the UK and Spain are British Airways (☎ 0345-222111), 156 Regent St, London W1R, and Spain's Iberia (☎ 0171-830 0011, from 22 April 2000 ☎ 020-7830 0011), 11 Haymarket, London SW1Y 4BP. Of the two, BA is more likely to have special deals which are lower than the standard scheduled fares.

If you are over 26 and have no student card, you will be looking at UK£234 with BA for a low-season return to Barcelona from London for a maximum of two months (fixed dates). From Barcelona you would be looking at around 52,000 ptas return.

EasyJet (☎ 0870-6000 000) has tickets from London's Luton airport to Barcelona for as little as UK£49 each way, plus UK£10 tax. It is an odd system in which prices rise as tickets are sold – the earlier you book a particular flight, the better your chances of the cheapest deal. The highest fare is UK£99 each way (at which point you should look elsewhere). From Barcelona (☎ 902-29 99 92), a return flight could cost as little as 28,000 ptas.

Next best is usually Debonair, which also uses Luton airport. At the time of writing it charged 38,000 ptas return for stays of up to a month. Contact Debonair on ☎ 902-14 62 00 in Spain and ☎ 0541-500300 in the UK.

The Charter Flight Centre (☎ 0171-565 6755, from 22 April 2000 ☎ 020-7565 6755), 15 Gillingham St, London SW1 V1HN, has return flights, which are valid for up to four weeks in low season, costing UK£127 (including taxes).

Spanish Travel Services (☎ 0171-387 5337, from 22 April 2000 ☎ 020-7387 5337), 138 Eversholt St, London NW1 1BL, has charter flights from as low as UK£118 return (including taxes) to Barcelona in the low season.

Remember that if you miss a charter flight, you have lost your money.

For more information on bucket shops dealing in flights to Barcelona, call the Air Travel Advisory Bureau (☎ 0171-636 5000, from 22 April 2000 ☎ 020-7636 5000). You need to tell them your destination and they will then provide a list of relevant ticket sellers.

Several times a year, usually around Easter and again in autumn (any time from September to November), various charter companies put on four and five-day long-weekend fares to Barcelona and/or other Spanish destinations for silly prices: UK£49 return is not unheard of.

Open-jaw tickets are also a possibility. At the time of writing STS had one going with Debonair into Barcelona and out of Madrid, or the other way around, for UK£129 in low season.

You can also hunt for fares on Teletext and the Internet.

Continental Europe

Short hops can be expensive, but for longer journeys you can often find air fares that beat overland alternatives on cost.

France Sometimes good deals float around. It is possible to find return flights for as little as 900FF to Barcelona (plus airport taxes of around 200FF). A more likely fare is 1450FF, and there are no charters.

From Barcelona the choices are generally less attractive – at the time of writing a standard return fare was 44,000 ptas (31,000 ptas for students).

Regional Airlines (☎ 93 318 76 48) links Barcelona (and Madrid) with several regional centres in France, including Marseille, Nice, Lyon and Toulouse. It is aimed mainly at business travellers.

Germany Munich is a haven of bucket shops and more mainstream budget travel outlets. Council Travel (☎ 089-39 50 22), Adalbertstr 32, near the university, is one of the best. STA Travel (☎ 089-39 90 96), Königstr 49, is also good.

In Berlin, Kilroy Travel-ARTU Reisen (☎ 030-310 00 40), at Hardenbergstr 9, near Berlin Zoo (with five branches around the city), is a good travel agent. In Frankfurt a/M, you could try STA Travel (☎ 069-70 30 35), Bockenheimer Landstr 133.

The Netherlands Amsterdam is a popular departure point. The student travel agency NBBS Reiswinkels, Rokin 38 (☎ 020-624 09 89), offers reliable and reasonably low fares. Compare them with the pickings in the bucket shops along Rokin before deciding. NBBS has several branches throughout the city as well as in Brussels, Belgium.

Other Countries Virgin Express (☎ 900-99 32 76) links Barcelona with Brussels (Belgium), Copenhagen (Denmark) and Rome (Italy). The service often undercuts the opposition airlines, but check first.

The USA
Several airlines fly to Barcelona (usually with a layover), including Iberia, BA and KLM.

Discount and rock-bottom options from the USA include charter flights, stand-by and courier flights. Stand-by fares are often sold at 60% of the normal price for one-way tickets. Airhitch (☎ 212-864 2000; www .airhitch.org), 2641 Broadway, New York, NY 10025, specialises in this sort of thing. Airhitch has several other offices in the USA, including Los Angeles (☎ 310-726 5000). You can contact its Madrid representative on ☎ 91 366 79 27, or check out its Spain website (www.collegeclub .com/~AHValencia) if you prefer.

Reliable travel agents specialising in budget travel (especially for students) include STA (www.sta-travel.com) and Council Travel (www.ciee.org/travel.htm), both of which have offices in major cities.

Another travel agent specialising in budget air fares is Discount Tickets in New York (☎ 212-391 2313).

Sometimes you can get a courier flight if you accompany a parcel to its destination. You're unlikely to get one to Barcelona, but you could consider Madrid (which can cost under US$300 from New York, more from the west coast), where you can connect by air, train or bus. Most flights depart from New York. A good source of information on courier flights is Now Voyager (☎ 212-431 1616), Suite 307, 74 Varrick St, New York, NY 10013. The Denver-based Air Courier Association (☎ 303-278 8810) also does this kind of thing.

At the time of writing no one airline leaving from Barcelona could claim to offer unbeatable value. Shoulder season flights hover around the 73,000 ptas mark (taxes included). From Barcelona for example, the best offer was with Lufthansa via Frankfurt. In high season (15 June to 15 September), about the best you could hope for was 86,000 ptas return.

With Iberia or Delta you are looking at US$620 to US$680 return from New York, Miami, Atlanta or Chicago. Fares from the west coast hover around US$750. In high season (mid-June to mid-September) expect high prices and low availability.

If you can't find a good deal, consider taking a cheap transatlantic hop to London and then stalking the bucket shops there. Again, Teletext and the Internet are further sources of fare information.

Canada
Iberia has direct flights to Barcelona from Toronto and Montreal. Other major European airlines offer competitive fares to Barcelona via other European capitals. Travel CUTS (☎ 800-777 0112; www.travelcuts.com), which specialises in discount fares for students, has offices in all major cities.

For courier flights, contact FB On Board Courier Services (☎ 514-633 0740 in Toronto or Montreal, or ☎ 604-338 1366 in Vancouver).

Australia
STA Travel (Australia-wide fast fares on ☎ 1300 660 960) and Flight Centres

International (Australia-wide ☎ 131600) are major dealers in cheap air fares, although heavily discounted fares can often be found at your travel agent.

As a rule there are no direct flights from Australia to Spain. You will have to fly to Europe via Asia or America and change flights (and possibly airlines).

Discounted return air fares on mainstream airlines through reputable agents can be surprisingly cheap, with low-season fares around A$1800 return with Garuda.

On some flights between Australia and destinations like London, Paris and Frankfurt, a return ticket between that destination and another major European city such as Barcelona is thrown in.

For courier flights try Jupiter (☎ 02-9317 2230), Unit 3, 55 Kent Rd, Mascot, Sydney 2020.

New Zealand

As with Australia, STA Travel and Flight Centres International are popular agents. A RTW (round-the-world) ticket may be cheaper than a normal return. Otherwise, you can fly from Auckland to pick up a connecting flight in Melbourne or Sydney. Return fares from NZ to London are around NZ$2700. But shop around as a number of airlines may offer cheaper deals.

Asia

Although most Asian countries are now offering fairly competitive air fare deals, Bangkok, Singapore and Hong Kong are still the best places to shop around for discount tickets. Hong Kong's travel market can be unpredictable, but some excellent bargains are available if you are lucky.

A one-way fare to Europe can cost about US$660 but shop around. Bucket shops in Bangkok can get you a one-way fare for about US$460.

STA has branches in Hong Kong, Tokyo, Singapore, Bangkok and Kuala Lumpur.

Airline Offices in Barcelona

You can find airlines listed under Línias Aèries/Líneas Aéreas in the phone book.

They include:

Air Europa
   Airport (☎ 902-24 00 42)
Alitalia
   Avinguda Diagonal 403 (☎ 902-10 03 23)
British Airways
   Airport (☎ 93 487 21 12)
Delta Airlines
   Passeig de Gràcia 16 (☎ 93 412 43 33)
EasyJet
   Airport (☎ 902-29 99 92)
Iberia
   Passeig de Gràcia 30 (☎ 93 412 56 67)
KLM
   Airport (☎ 93 379 54 58)
Lufthansa
   Passeig de Gràcia 55-57 (☎ 93 487 03 52)
Spanair
   Airport (☎ 902-13 14 15)
TWA
   Carrer del Consell de Cent 360 (☎ 93 215 84 86)
Virgin Express
   Airport (☎ 900-99 32 76)

TRAIN

The two main stations are Estació Sants, on Plaça dels Països Catalans, 2.5km west of La Rambla (metro: Sants-Estació) and Estació de França on Avinguda del Marquès de l'Argentera, 1km east of La Rambla (metro: Barceloneta).

All trains within Spain (except some Barcelona suburban services) use Estació Sants. Most trains to/from France or beyond use Estació de França. Some trains stop at both stations.

Other useful stations for long-distance and regional trains are Catalunya on Plaça de Catalunya (metro: Catalunya), and Passeig de Gràcia, on the corner of Passeig de Gràcia and Carrer d'Aragó, 700 metres north of Plaça de Catalunya (metro: Passeig de Gràcia).

Eurail, InterRail, Europass and Flexipass tickets are valid on the national rail network RENFE (Red Nacional de los Ferrocarriles Españoles) throughout Spain.

Information & Tickets

It's advisable to book at least a day or two ahead for most long-distance trains, domestic or international. There's a RENFE information and booking office in Passeig de Gràcia station, open daily from 7 am to 10 pm (9 pm on Sunday). At Estació Sants, the Informació Largo Recorrido windows give information on all except suburban trains.

The station has a *consigna* (lockers) open from 5.30 am to 10 pm (400 or 600 ptas for 24 hours), a tourist office, a telephone and fax office, a hotel reservations office, currency exchange booths open from 8 am to 10 pm daily, and ATMs. Estació de França has a train information office and consigna.

For information on international trains you can call ☎ 93 490 11 22, for domestic trains ☎ 93 490 02 02.

Train timetables are posted at the main stations. Impending arrivals (*arribades/llegadas*) and departures (*sortides/salidas*) appear on big electronic boards and TV screens. Timetables for specific lines are generally available free of charge.

The UK

Your choices from London are limited by the options in Paris, where you must change trains.

Trains run from Charing Cross or Victoria station to Paris (via ferry or hovercraft from Dover to Calais or Folkestone to Boulogne), or from Waterloo (Eurostar). You arrive at the Gare du Nord and then you must get to the Gare d'Austerlitz (take the RER B to St Michel and change there for the RER C to Austerlitz), Gare de Montparnasse (Metro 4) or Gare de Lyon (RER B to Châtelet and then RER A for Gare de Lyon). See also the following section on France.

The one-way/return fares to Barcelona are UK£97/153 (more if you take the Eurostar), and tickets are valid for two months. Under-26s can get Wasteels or BIJ (Billet International de Jeunesse) tickets for UK£81/139.

Children qualify for discounts and those over 60 can get a Rail Europe Senior Railcard (valid only for trips that cross at least one border). UK citizens pay UK£5 for the card but must already have a British Rail card (UK£16). The pass entitles you to roughly 30% off standard fares.

Information can be had from European Rail (☎ 0171-387 0444, from 22 April 2000 ☎ 020-7387 0444) or, for trips involving the Eurostar leg to Paris, from the International Rail Centre (☎ 0990-848848).

France

The only truly direct train to Barcelona is the *trenhotel* sleeper-only job. It leaves Gare d'Austerlitz at 8.47 pm daily and arrives between 9.13 and 9.30 am (stopping at Dijon, Figueres, Girona and Barcelona França). The standard one-way fare in a couchette is 780FF. Going the other way, the trenhotel leaves Barcelona França at 8.15 pm and arrives 12 hours later in Paris. A bed costs 27,800 ptas, or you can get a couchette for 16,500 ptas.

Otherwise, the cheapest and most convenient option to Barcelona is the 10.02 pm from Gare d'Austerlitz, changing at Latour-de-Carol and arriving in Barcelona Sants at 11.27 am. A reclining seat costs 485FF one way, or 555FF in a 2nd-class couchette. There is an alternative train with a change at Portbou (on the coast). Under-26s get a 25% reduction. Note also that fares rise in July and August.

There are several other possibilities. Up to three TGVs (high speed Trains de Grande Vitesse) also put you on the road to Barcelona (leaving from Paris Gare de Lyon), with a change of train at Montpellier or Narbonne. Prices and timetables vary, so check the latest details.

A direct service also connects Montpellier with Barcelona (4½ hours; 252FF or 5305 ptas in 2nd class). A couple of other slower services (with change of train at Portbou) also make this run. All these trains stop in Perpignan.

When appropriate track is eventually laid, Barcelona will be linked to the French TGV network.

From Estació Sants, six to 10 trains a day run to Cerbère (2½ hours) and one to three to Latour-de-Carol (3½ hours). From these stations you have several onwards connections to Montpellier and Toulouse respectively.

Other International Services

Direct overnight trains from Estació de França also run to Zürich (13 hours) and

Milan (12¾ hours), from three to seven days a week, depending on the season. These trains meet connections for numerous other cities. The cheapest beds cost 30,000 ptas (Zürich) and 29,000 ptas (Milan). Or you can get seats for 22,400 and 22,000 ptas respectively.

Other Parts of Spain

Trains run from Barcelona to most large Spanish cities. These trains offer a huge range of seat and sleeper accommodation; there are day and night trains and a mind-boggling array of fares. Most trains depart daily from Estació Sants (some also stopping at Estació de França and/or Passeig de Gràcia).

The trip to Madrid can take 6½ to 9½ hours and a basic 2nd-class fare is 4900 ptas. Other examples include:

from	to	one way	hours
Barcelona	Granada	6200 ptas	12¾
	Pamplona	3900 ptas	6½ to 10
	San Sebastián	4600 ptas	8¼ to 10
	Zaragoza	2900 ptas	3½ to 4½

Euromed A high speed AVE train on standard Spanish narrow-gauge track connects Barcelona with Valencia (three hours) five times a day, and twice a day with Alicante (4¾ hours). The respective *turista/preferente* (equivalent to 2nd/1st class) fares are 4600/6500 ptas to Valencia and 6300/8800 ptas to Alicante.

Catalunya Services Three types of local trains fan out from Barcelona across the autonomous region of Catalunya. The slowest all-stops ones are called Regionals. Making fewer stops are the Deltas, while Catalunya Exprès trains are the fastest (and about 15% dearer than the others). They are run by the national RENFE company. Long- distance mainline trains also stop at several Catalunya destinations, but fares are often more expensive still. Regional trains within Catalunya depart from Estació Sants; many

also stop at Catalunya and/or Passeig de Gràcia.

Rodalies (*Cercanías* in Castilian), a cross between regional and suburban trains, are a more reliable way to get to some destinations not too far out from Barcelona (such as Sitges). They run on a fixed-fare six-zone system, with prices rising marginally on weekends. Line 1 connects the centre of town with the airport – with piped classical music in the background, this is a highly civilised introduction to Barcelona (see the Getting Around chapter for more details)! These trains often stop at several stations with metro connections, including Estació Sants, Catalunya, Passeig de Gràcia, Arc de Triomf and Clot.

See individual destination sections in the Excursions chapter for how to get about Catalunya.

BUS

The bus is generally cheaper than the train, but less comfortable for the long haul.

The main intercity bus station is the modern Estació del Nord at Carrer d'Alí Bei 80, 1.5km north-east of La Rambla and 1½ blocks from Arc de Triomf metro. Its information desk (☎ 93 265 65 08) opens daily from 7 am to 9 pm.

A few services – most importantly some international buses and the few buses to Montserrat – use Estació d'Autobusos de Sants beside Estació Sants train station.

The main international services are run by Eurolines/Julià Via (☎ 93 490 40 00) from Estació d'Autobusos de Sants, and by Eurolines/Linebús and Starbus (both ☎ 93 265 07 00) from Estació del Nord.

Other Parts of Spain

You can ride buses to most large Spanish cities. A plethora of companies operate to different parts of the country, although many come under the umbrella of Enatcar. For schedule information call ☎ 93 265 65 08.

Departures from Estació del Nord include the following, with journey time and fare (where frequencies vary, the lowest figure is usually for Sunday):

departure	daily	hours	cost
Almería	2	13½	7045 ptas
Burgos	2 to 4	8	4960 ptas
Granada	4	13 to 15	7830 ptas
Madrid	<16	7 or 8	2940 ptas
Salamanca	3	11½	6425 ptas
Sevilla	1	16	8820 ptas
Valencia	5 to 10	4½	2900 ptas
Vigo	2	15	6710 ptas
Zaragoza	9	4½	1640 ptas

The UK

Eurolines (☎ 0990-143219), 52 Grosvenor Gardens, Victoria, London SW1 (the terminal is a couple of blocks away), runs buses to Barcelona on Saturday, Monday (leaving at 11 am; connection to Alicante) and Thursday (9.30 pm). The trip takes 23-25 hours. The one-way and return fares are, respectively, UK£77 and UK£119 (UK£71 and UK£109 for those under 26 and senior citizens). The standard adult one-way fare going the other way is 13,450 ptas.

France

Eurolines has offices in several French cities, including the Paris bus station (☎ 01 49 72 51 51), 28 Ave du Générale de Gaulle, and on the left bank at rue St Jacques 55 (☎ 01 43 54 11 99), off Blvd St Germain. UK passengers may have to change buses here. The standard fare from Barcelona is 11,450 ptas. To Marseille you pay 6700 ptas.

Other International Services

Eurolines/Julià Via also has services at least three times weekly to Amsterdam, Brussels, Florence, Geneva, Milan, Montpellier, Nice, Perpignan, Rome, Toulouse, Venice and Zürich, and twice a week to several cities in Morocco.

CAR & MOTORCYCLE

To give you an idea of how many clicks you'll put behind you if travelling with your own wheels, Barcelona is 1932km from Berlin, 1555km from London, 1146km from Paris, 1300km from Lisbon, 1199km from Milan, 780km from Geneva and 690km from Madrid – quite central in its own way when you think about it!

Paperwork & Preparations

Vehicles must be roadworthy, registered and insured for third party at least. The Green Card, an internationally recognised proof of insurance, is compulsory.

A European breakdown assistance policy such as the AA Five Star Service or the RAC Eurocover Motoring Assistance is a good investment.

All EU member states' driving licences are fully recognised throughout the Union.

In the UK, further information can be obtained from the RAC (☎ 0990-722722) or the AA (☎ 0990-500600).

For details of driving conditions in Barcelona and renting or purchase, see Car & Motorcycle in the Getting Around chapter.

Access Roads

The A-7 autopista is the main toll road from France (via Girona and Figueres) in the north. It skirts inland around the city before proceeding south to Valencia and Alicante. About 40km south-west of Barcelona, the A-2, also a toll road, branches westwards off the A-7 towards Zaragoza. From there it links up with the dual carriageway N-II for Madrid (no tolls) and feeds the A-68 toll road north-west to the País Vasco. Other tollways include: the A-19, which follows the coast north-east as far as the south end of the Costa Brava; the A-18, which winds north to Manresa and peters out in the foothills of the Pyrenees at Sallent; and the A-16, which follows the coast south-west of Barcelona to Sitges and links up with the A-7 26km short of Tarragona.

As a rule alternative toll-free routes are busy (if not clogged). The N-II is the most important. From the French border it follows the A-7, branches off to the coast and then follows the A-19 into Barcelona, from where it heads west to Lleida. From there it follows the A-2 to Zaragoza and becomes the main highway to Madrid. It is interesting to note that drivers in Catalunya are the most heavily penalised – a third of the entire country's tollways are in this region.

Road Rules

In general, standard European road rules apply. In built-up areas the speed limit is usually 50km/h, rising to 100km/h on major roads and 120km/h on *autopistas* and *autovías* (toll and toll-free motorways).

Motorcyclists must use headlights at all times. Crash helmets are obligatory on bikes of 125 cc or more.

Vehicles already in roundabouts have right of way.

The blood-alcohol limit is 0.05%. Fines for many traffic offences range from 50,000 to 100,000 ptas. Nonresident foreigners can be fined up to 50,000 ptas on the spot. Pleading linguistic ignorance will not help – your traffic cop will produce a list of infringements and fines in as many languages as you like.

Petrol

Prices vary (up to four pesetas a litre) between service stations (*gasolineres/gasolineras*) and fluctuate with oil tariffs and tax policy. Super costs 119.5 ptas/litre and the increasingly popular diesel (or *gasóleo*) 90.9 ptas/litre. Lead-free *(sense plom/sin plomo*; 95 octane) costs 113.9 ptas/litre and a 98 octane variant (also lead free) that goes by various names, up to 125.9 ptas a litre.

Road Assistance

The Real Automóvil Club de España's head office (RACE; ☎ 91 447 32 00) is at Calle de José Abascal 10 in Madrid. For RACE's 24-hour, country-wide emergency breakdown assistance, call ☎ 900-11 81 18. The Catalunyan version of the RACE is the RACC (Reial Automòbil Club de Catalunya) with headquarters at Avinguda Diagonal 687 (☎ 902-30 73 07). Their assistance number is ☎ 900-36 55 05. As a rule, holders of motoring insurance with foreign organisations such as the RAC, AA (UK) or AAA (USA) will be provided with an emergency assistance number to use while travelling in Spain, so in general you should not require the above numbers. Whichever numbers

you use, in Catalunya you will usually be assisted by the RACC. If you plan on a long stay in Barcelona, you may want to take out local insurance with the RACC, which is quite possible for foreign registered cars.

BICYCLE

If you plan to bring your own bike, check with the airline about any hidden costs. It will have to be disassembled and packed for the journey. Bicycle (especially mountain bike) touring is growing in popularity in Catalunya. UK-based cyclists planning to do some of this during their time in Barcelona might want to contact the Cyclists' Touring Club (☎ 01483-417217), Cotterell House, 69 Meadrow, Godalming, Surrey GU7 3HS, UK. It can supply information to members on cycling conditions, itineraries and cheap insurance. Membership costs UK£25 per annum.

HITCHING

Hitching is never entirely safe and we don't recommend it. Travellers who decide to hitch should understand that they are taking a small but potentially serious risk. To get out of Barcelona you need to start well out of the city centre. The chances of anyone stopping for you on autopistas are low – try the more congested national highways (such as the N-II described above).

BOAT
Italy

After a 15-year absence, the so-called *canguro* (kangaroo) shipping run between Barcelona and Genova was relaunched in September 1998. The Italian company Grimaldi is running the operation. Their vessel, the *Fantastic* (sic), can carry 1900 passengers, 760 cars and a hefty goods load. It went down the slipways in 1996.

At the moment, there are three weekly departures planned from Barcelona on Tuesday, Thursday (both 10 pm) and Sunday (3 am). Going the other way, departures are Mondays, Wednesdays and Fridays. An airline style seat costs 8300 ptas one way, while a car costs 12,700 ptas to 14,300 ptas depending on size. Luxury suites for two cost 25,100 ptas. The trip lasts about 17 hours. Book tickets with any travel agent. The boat docks at Moll de Ponent.

Grimaldi must think it's on a winner, because it plans to add a second vessel and so allow daily departures each way.

Islas Baleares

Passenger and vehicular ferries to the Islas Baleares, operated by the Trasmediterránea line, dock close to its new office near the Moll de Barcelona wharf in Port Vell. Information and tickets are available from Trasmediterránea (☎ 93 295 90 00; fax 93 295 91 34) there, or from travel agents.

Scheduled services are: Barcelona-Palma (eight hours; seven to nine services weekly); Barcelona-Maó (nine hours; two to six services weekly); Barcelona-Ibiza city (9½ hours, or 14½ hours via Palma; three to six services weekly). Fares to any of the islands are 6660 ptas for a 'Butaca Turista' (seat). You can also get sleeping berths and transport vehicles. In summer, Trasmediterránea also operates a 'Fast Ferry' service to Palma (4¼ hours; 8150 ptas; up to three services a week).

Buquebús (☎ 902-41 42 42) is a sleek high-speed ferry that rockets from Barcelona to Palma de Mallorca and back at 80km h daily (twice a day in summer) in just 3¼ hours. The catamaran can carry up to 900 passengers and 240 cars. One-way tickets start at 8150 ptas (double return). Airlines can often undercut the return fare (the same goes for Trasmediterránea's Fast Ferries).

Cruises

Barcelona has become a major port of call for cruise ships. Trips tend to take a couple of weeks and typically include a stop of a night or two in Barcelona. To give you some idea, the number of cruise ships that docked here in 1992, the Olympic year, was already a record 220. In 1997 the total was 417 – and 1998 looked set to top even that figure!

Several companies can be approached. Fares start at about UK£1000. One company

is Fred. Olsen Cruise Lines (☎ 01473-29 22 22), Fred. Olsen House, White House Rd, Ipswich, Suffolk IP1 5LL, UK. More expensive still is the Holland America Line (☎ 0171-613 3300, from 22 April 2000 ☎ 020-7613 3300), 77-79 Great Eastern St, London EC2A 3HU.

TRAVEL AGENTS

Barcelona is hardly one of Europe's discount flight capitals. That said, you can still find reasonable deals to main western European destinations, and occasionally to the USA. You could start with the following agents, but there is no substitute for shopping around.

USIT Unlimited (☎ 93 423 33 60 & 93 426 57 00) at Carrer de Rocafort 116-122 (metro: Rocafort) is Catalunya's equivalent of TIVE, the Spanish youth travel organisation, and sells youth and student air, train and bus tickets. It has another branch (☎ 902-32 52 75) at Ronda de l'Universitat 16.

Viajes Wasteels at Catalunya metro station has similar youth and student fares.

Halcón Viatges is a reliable chain of travel agents that sometimes has good deals. Its branch at Carrer de Pau Claris 108 (☎ 93 412 44 11) is one of 25 around town.

WARNING

The information in this chapter is particularly vulnerable to change: prices for international travel are volatile, special deals come and go and routes, schedules and visa requirements change. Airlines and governments seem to take a perverse pleasure in making price structures and regulations as complicated as possible. You should check with the airline or a travel agent to make sure you understand how a fare (and ticket you may buy) works. The travel industry is highly competitive and there are many lurks and perks.

Get quotes and advice from as many airlines and travel agents as possible before you part with your hard-earned cash. The pointers in this chapter are no substitute for your own careful research.

Getting Around

EL PRAT DE LLOBREGAT AIRPORT

Barcelona's airport lies 14km south-west of the city centre at El Prat de Llobregat. The airport building contains three terminals. Terminal A handles non-EU international arrivals and all departures by non-Spanish airlines. Terminal B handles EU arrivals and international and domestic departures with Spanish airlines. Terminal C is for the Pont Aeri (Puente Aereo), the Barcelona-Madrid shuttle.

The arrivals halls are all on the ground floor; departures are on the 1st floor.

The main tourist office at the airport is on the ground floor of Terminal B (☎ 93 478 05 65). It opens Monday to Saturday from 9.30 am to 8 pm, Sunday from 9.30 am to 3 pm (about a half-hour later in summer) and has information on all Catalunya. Another office on the ground floor of Terminal A (☎ 93 478 4704) opens Monday to Saturday from 9.30 am to 3 pm. ATMs are scattered about all three terminals and currency exchange facilities are available at terminals A and B. You'll find a *correus* (post office) at these two terminals too. Newspaper stands and bookshops, a smattering of bars and restaurants and duty-free gift shops provide all the essentials for airport survival.

When you arrive inside the terminals building, follow the *Recollida d'Equipatges/Recogida de Equipajes* (Baggage Claim) signs that will take you through passport control (there is usually no passport control for arrivals from other Schengen countries (see also the Facts for the Visitor chapter).

For flight information call ☎ 93 478 50 00.

Left Luggage

The left luggage (*consigna*) is on the ground floor at the end of Terminal B closest to Terminal C. It is open 24 hours a day and charges 635 ptas per item and per 24-hour period or fraction thereof. See the

Facts for the Visitor chapter for other left luggage options around town.

To/From the Airport

Train The airport is the terminus for Rodalies (Cercanías) train line 1 (which heads for Mataró and beyond on the north-eastern edge of Barcelona). You are in zone 4 here and the trip into the centre of town (zone 1) costs 305 ptas (350 ptas on weekends and holidays). Main stops include Estació Sants, Plaça de Catalunya, Arc de Triomf and El Clot-Aragó. Trains run every 30 minutes from 6.10 am to 10.40 pm daily. It takes 16 minutes to Sants and 21 minutes to Catalunya. Departures from Sants to the airport are from 5.45 am to 10.15 pm; from Catalunya they're five minutes earlier.

The only drawback with the train is that it's a five-minute hike (eased by moving walkways when they work) to/from the terminal buildings – a bit of a pain if you're heavily loaded up. The station lies between terminals A and B. You get tickets either at the booth or from the automatic machines if you have coins; you then stamp them in the turnstyle slot as you pass to the platform.

Bus The A1 Aerobús service runs from the airport to Plaça de Catalunya via Estació Sants Monday to Friday every 15 minutes from 6 am to 11 pm, and Saturday, Sunday and holidays every 30 minutes from 6.45 am to 10.45 pm. Departures from Plaça de Catalunya are Monday to Friday from 5.30 am to 10 pm, and Saturday, Sunday and holidays from 6 am to 10 pm. The trip is about 40 minutes – depending on traffic – for 475 ptas.

Cheaper suburban buses (Buses EA and EN) leave every 80 minutes for Plaça d'Espanya and cost 140 ptas. They take about 50 minutes.

In both cases you pay on the bus (unless, on the suburban bus, you have some kind of multi-trip ticket or pass – see Public Transport below).

Taxi A taxi to/from the centre – a half-hour ride – is about 2500 ptas. There is generally no shortage of them.

Parking The short term car parks in front of the main terminal buildings charge 210 ptas an hour for the first two hours, then 180 ptas an hour. If you leave the car for eight hours or more, the daily charge becomes 1480 ptas. You pay at the machines (coins or credit cards) before going to your car – once you have paid, you have 20 minutes to get your car out of there.

If you intend to leave your car for any lengthy period at the airport, you may wish to avail yourself of the Parking VIP service. You drive to the terminal and a driver takes your car to a covered parking area that offers permanent surveillance. When you return, you call ahead to have your car delivered to you at your arrival terminal. The daily parking fee is 1700 ptas, the driver is a once-off 800-ptas fee and you have to add 16% IVA. For information and to book ahead, call ☎ 93 478 66 71.

PUBLIC TRANSPORT

The metro is the easiest way of getting around and reaches most places you're likely to visit (but not the airport). The metro is supplemented by a few train lines run by Ferrocarrils de la Generalitat de Catalunya (FGC). The main tourist office gives out the comprehensive *Guia d'Autobusos Urbans de Barcelona*, with a metro map and all bus routes. For public transport information you can call ☎ 010 or ☎ 93 412 00 00, or ☎ 93 205 15 15 for FGC trains only. For information on disabled facilities call ☎ 93 412 44 44.

Targetas

Targetas are multiple-trip city transport tickets and offer worthwhile savings. They are sold at most city-centre metro stations. Targeta T-1 (775 ptas) gives you 10 rides on the metro, buses and FGC trains; Targeta

T-2 (760 ptas) gives 10 rides on the metro and FGC trains; Targeta T-DIA (575 ptas) gives unlimited metro, bus and FGC train travel in one day.

A plethora of other options exists, including monthly passes for unlimited use of all public transport at 3810 ptas (you need to get a Targetren ID card, available at the Centre d'Atenció al Client in the Plaça de Catalunya and Plaça d'Espanya stations), Targeta T-50/30 (for 50 trips within 30 days) and discounted tickets/passes for pensioners and students.

If you only want to use buses and the metro (not FGC trains) and intend to move around town a lot, the three and five-day Abonament tickets are good value at 1300/2000 ptas.

If you take the Aerobús from the airport, you can get an all-in ticket for the bus and unlimited use of Barcelona's buses and metro for three days (1800 ptas) or five days (2300 ptas).

Bus

Buses run along most city routes every few minutes from 5 or 6 am to 10 or 11 pm. Many routes pass through Plaça de Catalunya and/or Plaça de la Universitat. After 11 pm, a reduced network of yellow *nitbusos* (night buses) run until 3 to 5 am. All nitbus routes pass through Plaça de Catalunya and most run every 30 to 45 minutes. A single fare on any bus is 140 ptas.

Bus Turístic

This bus service covers two circuits (24 stops) linking virtually all the major tourist sights. Tourist offices and many hotels have leaflets explaining the system, or you can call ☎ 93 423 18 00. Tickets, available on the bus, are 1700 ptas for one day's unlimited rides, or 2300 ptas for two consecutive days. Service is about every 20 minutes from 9 am to 9.30 pm. Tickets entitle you to discounts of up to 300 ptas on entry fees and tickets to more than 20 sights along the route, as well as shopping discounts and a meal at Kentucky Fried Chicken and Pizza Hut (oh great!). The discounts don't *have* to be used on the day(s) you use the bus.

Tombbus

The T1 Tombbus route has been thought out for shoppers and runs regularly from Plaça de Catalunya up to Avinguda Diagonal, along which it proceeds west to Plaça de Pius XII, where it turns around again. On the way you pass such landmarks as El Corte Inglés (several of them), Bulevard Rosa, FNAC and Marks & Spencer. Tickets are 160 ptas per trip.

Metro

The metro has five lines, numbered and colour-coded, and is efficient and easy to use. A single ride is 140 ptas and tickets are easily available from machines at most stations. At interchange stations, you just need to work out which line and which direction you want. The metro runs Monday to Thursday from 5 am to 11 pm; Friday, Saturday and the day before public holidays from 5 am to 2 am; Sunday from 6 am to midnight. Line 2 has access for the disabled. See the colour metro map at the front of the book.

FGC Suburban Trains

Suburban trains run by the Ferrocarrils de la Generalitat de Catalunya include a couple of useful city lines. One heads north from Plaça de Catalunya. A branch of it will get you to Tibidabo and another within spitting distance of the Monestir de Pedralbes. Some trains along this line continue beyond Barcelona to Sant Cugat, Sabadell and Terrassa.

The other FGC line heads to Manresa from Plaça d'Espanya and is less likely to be of use. These trains run Monday to Thursday from 5 am to 11 pm, and Friday to Sunday from 5 am to 1 am. Rides within the city are 130 ptas.

Rodalies/Cercanías

These RENFE-run local trains serve towns around Barcelona, as well as the airport. For more details see the Getting There & Away chapter.

Fines

The fine for being caught without a ticket on public transport is 5000 ptas.

CAR & MOTORCYCLE

An effective one-way system makes traffic flow fairly smoothly, but you'll often find yourself flowing the way you don't want to go – unless you happen to have an adept navigator and the Michelin *Barcelona* map (825 ptas), which comes with a comprehensive street index and shows one-way streets (as do more expensive map guides to the city). Parking can also be tricky and expensive if you choose a parking garage. It's better to leave your car alone while you're here and use Barcelona's public transport.

Parking

As you will soon discover, parking is no easy task in Barcelona (except in August, when half the city departs on annual vacation). Parking in the Ciutat Vella is virtually impossible and frankly not worth trying for all the stress it will cause. The narrow streets of Gràcia are almost worse.

The broad boulevards of L'Eixample offer possibilities, but you need to watch out for a lot of things. On some streets you may not park at all. In other cases you will see parts of streets marked in red – also no go. Blue markings mean you must stick money in the meter (a maximum of 510 ptas for two hours) and leave the ticket on the dash. Obviously you can't park in driveways and the like, and anything marked in yellow usually means you are permitted to stop for up to 30 minutes for loading and unloading (*càrrega*) and (*descàrrega*). Many people take their chances and leave cars in such zones for longer – eventually you'll get a ticket, and towing is common.

As a general rule, many of the zones marked in yellow are only problematic on weekdays from 8 am to 8 pm. This includes most of the handy, chopped-off angles at intersections in L'Eixample, which seem to have been designed especially for parking – although presumably it was not much of an issue in the late 19th century. Meter parking is enforced during similar hours (with a break for a couple of hours around lunch time) from Monday to Saturday.

There are streets in L'Eixample where – if you can find a space – you can park without worry. If the only road markings you see are white and there are no parking restriction signs, you should be OK.

The same rules apply elsewhere in the centre. Other tricks abound though. In some roads you can only park on one side, and this is swapped around every two weeks – this should be signposted (usually a round no-parking symbol with '1-15' or '16-31', meaning the first and second fortnight of the month). If you leave your car for any length of time and find it has been shifted days later, it's probable that some kind of road works had to be done and your car was moved.

A personal tip for parking if you are getting nowhere fast is Carrer de Wellington on the far side of the Parc de la Ciutadella. It's a little far off but you can almost be guaranteed of finding a space there or in the streets off it, and there are no restrictions. It's a good idea to check on your car and move it around every few days as 'abandoned' cars can be a target for the authorities and thieves. Two words of caution – at night Carrer de Wellington is a fairly sad hookers' strip – perhaps not the greatest time to be wandering around there. And hire cars left sitting around here for days are a tempting target.

Parking motorbikes and scooters is obviously easier. On occasion you'll see spaces marked out especially for bikes.

If you get towed, call the Guàrdia Urbana on ☎ 092 for directions to the *depósito de vehículos* (car pound). Expect to pay up to 15,000 ptas to free your beastie.

Car Rental

You obviously wouldn't want to rent a car to slope around Barcelona, but one could come in handy for touring the surrounding countryside. It won't pay if you only intend to make a few simple day trips however.

If you haven't organised a rental car from abroad, local firms such as Julià Car, Ronicar and Vanguard are generally cheaper than the big international names. From these

a typical small car like a Ford Fiesta or Renault Twingo, with minimum compulsory insurance, should cost around 2500 ptas a day plus 25 ptas a km, plus IVA. For unlimited kilometres, they're around 20,000 ptas for three days or 35,000 ptas a week, plus IVA. Special low weekend rates (from Friday lunchtime or afternoon to Monday morning) are worth looking into. Rental firms include:

Avis (☎ 93 487 87 45), Carrer d'Aragó 235, l'Eixample
Europcar (☎ 93 488 23 98), Carrer del Consell de Cent 363, l'Eixample
Hertz (☎ 93 217 32 48), Carrer d'Aragó 382-384, l'Eixample
Julià Car (☎ 93 317 64 54), Ronda de la Universitat 5, l'Eixample
Ronicar (☎ 93 405 09 51), Carrer d'Europa 34-36, Les Corts
Vanguard (☎ 93 439 38 80), Carrer de Londres 31, l'Eixample

Vanguard also rents out motorcycles. If you want something decent for touring outside Barcelona, you'll be looking at around 12,000 ptas a day (plus 7% IVA).

Purchase

Only people legally resident in Spain may buy vehicles here. One way around this is to have a friend who is a resident put the ownership papers in their name.

Car-hunters need a reasonable knowledge of Spanish to get through paperwork and understand dealers' patter. Trawling around showrooms or looking through classifieds can turn up second-hand Seats and Renaults (4 or 5) in good condition from around 300,000 ptas. The annual cost of third party insurance on such a car, with theft and fire cover and national breakdown assistance, comes in at between 40,000 and 50,000 ptas (with annual reductions if you make no claims).

Vehicles of five years and older must be submitted for roadworthiness checks, known as Inspección Técnica de Vehículos (ITV). If you pass, you get a sticker for two years. Check that this has been done when buying: the test costs about 4000 ptas.

You can get second-hand 50 cc *motos* for anything from 40,000 to 100,000 ptas.

TAXI
Taxis are black-and-yellow (with the exception of the black-and-cream taxis in Palma de Mallorca, Barcelona's taxis are the only ones in Spain which are different from the standard all-white jobbies around the rest of the country) and cost 295 ptas flagfall plus meter charges. These work out to about 100 ptas per kilometre (slightly more from 10 pm to 6 am and all day Saturday, Sunday and holidays). A further 300 ptas is added for all trips to/from the airport, and 100 ptas for luggage bigger than 55 by 35 by 35cm. The trip from Estació Sants to Plaça de Catalunya, about 3km, is about 700 ptas. You can call a taxi on ☎ 93 225 00 00, 93 481 10 85 or 93 490 22 22. General information on taxis is available on ☎ 010 and ☎ 93 428 10 85.

Barnataxis (☎ 93 358 11 11) has disabled-adapted taxis, as does Radio Taxi Móvil (☎ 93 357 77 55). Another number you can try is ☎ 908-89 16 06.

A green light on the roof means the taxi is free (*lliure/libre* in the Catalan or Castilian sign usually placed in the lower passenger side of the windscreen).

BICYCLE & MOPED
The *moto* (moped) rules in Barcelona, although plenty of people zip around on bicycles.

Bike lanes have been laid out along quite a few main roads (for instance along Gran Via de les Corts Catalanes, Avinguda Diagonal, Carrer d'Aragò, Avinguda de la Meridiana and Carrer de la Marina), and most of the town is pretty flat. Otherwise, dodging around in the traffic can be a little hairy, but by and large bicycle is not a bad option for getting around town. A bicycle path has also been traced out along much of the waterfront from Port Olímpic towards the Riu Besòs. New routes are being planned all the time, and there are several scenic itineraries mapped out for bike-riders in the Collserola parkland.

Bike on Public Transport
You can transport your bicycle on the metro except during rush hours on weekdays (ie, not between 6.30 to 9.30 am and 4.30 to 8.30 pm). In July and August there are no restrictions. You can also use FGC trains (except the Plaça d'Espanya-Igualada line), except from opening time until 9.30 am on weekends. Finally you can transport your bike on rodalies trains (belonging to RENFE) from 10 am to 3 pm on weekdays and all day on weekdays and holidays.

Bicycle Rental
Several outlets rent out bicycles. Un Menys (☎ 93 268 21 05), Carrer de l'Esparteria 3, charges 2000 ptas for a whole day, 1500 ptas for half a day or 600 ptas an hour. Escenic (☎ 93 221 16 66), Avinguda de la Marina 22, charges 750 pts an hour.

Moped Rental
For tooling about town, you could make your own two-stroke contribution to the city's noise pollution by renting out a motor scooter. On average it will cost you from 3300 ptas to 4000 ptas a day (plus 7% IVA), depending on where you rent and for how long. You are not supposed to take scooters beyond Barcelona's city limits.

You can rent them at Vanguard (☎ 93 439 38 80), Carrer de Londres 31, and Piaggio Center (☎ 93 202 07 78), Carrer de Balmes 303.

WALKING

The Barri Gòtic and surrounding areas are ideal for walking, but you'll need to use public transport to get more efficiently to farther-flung sights (such as the Sagrada Família, the Monestir de Pedralbes, Montjuïc and Tibidabo).

Although drivers here are generally more considerate than drivers in, say, Madrid, do not take it for granted that cars will stop at crossings. In fact, play it safe and assume they won't. Red lights, however, in general are respected by everyone.

One of the great rules of wandering around cities is 'look up' – you never know what you may see. Unfortunately, 'look down' is in some respects a safer bet in Barcelona, especially in the centre. The reason is that there are large clumps of dog-do liberally spread out all over the place.

ORGANISED TOURS
Gaudí

If you want to approach the work of Gaudí and the modernistas in a systematic fashion, a couple of options present themselves.

The Agència del Paisatge Urbà (Urban Landscapes Agency; ☎ 93 488 01 39) offers four tours (of eight buildings, including the Palau Güell, Sagrada Família, Manzana de la Discordia and Palau de la Música Catalana), and gives you a written description of 50 modernista buildings throughout the city (and the *Ruta del Modernisme* map, which you can pick up free at the tourist office). Of the three buildings which make up the Manzana de la Discordia, only the Casa Lleo Morera can be entered. The whole lot costs 1600 ptas and you get the ticket (valid for a month) at the Palau Güell, La Pedrera or Casa Morera.

The Centre Cultural Caixa Catalunya (☎ 93 484 89 09) organises two four-hour Gaudí tours. The first covers his work in Barcelona, including the Casa Batlló (but not inside), Sagrada Família and Parc Güell (departures from La Pedrera at 9 am and 3 pm). The second covers the Finca Güell at Pedralbes and Colònia Güell at Santa Coloma de Cervelló (outside town near the Riu Llobregat), which was intended as a kind of Utopian working families' colony. Its main interest lies in the crypt of the unfinished church (departures from La Pedrera at 9 am on Sundays only). Tickets cost 5000 ptas and places are limited. See also the Things to See & Do chapter.

Bicycle Tours

Un Menys bicycle store (☎ 93 268 21 05), Carrer de la Espartería 3, organises bicycle tours around the old centre of town, La Barceloneta and Port Olímpic. Daytime tours take place on Saturdays and Sundays, starting at the store at 10 am and finishing at 12.30 pm. The 2000 ptas price includes a stop for a drink in Port Vell. The night version is on Tuesdays and Saturdays, starting at 8.30 pm and finishing at midnight. The 5000 ptas price tag includes a drink stop and a meal along the Barceloneta waterfront.

Other Tours

The Bus Turístic (see Public Transport in this chapter) is better value than conventional tours for getting around the sights, but if you want a guided trip, Julià Tours (☎ 93 317 64 54) at Ronda de la Universitat 5 (metro: Universitat) and Pullmantur (☎ 93 318 02 41) at Gran Via de les Corts Catalanes 635 (metro: Girona) both do daily city tours by coach, plus out-of-town trips to Montserrat, Vilafranca del Penedès, the Costa Brava and Andorra. Their city tours are about 4000 ptas for a half-day, 10,000 ptas a full day.

A walking tour of the Ciutat Vella on Saturday mornings departs from the Centre d'Informació Turisme de Barcelona on Plaça de Catalunya (English at 10 am; Spanish & Catalan at noon). The price is 950 ptas. A similar tour for 1½ hours (1000 ptas) starts at Plaça de l'Àngel – look for the guide in the yellow BCN T-shirt. Tours in English go daily, except Monday, at 10.30 am and 4 pm.

For other guide services and tailor-made options, get in touch with the Barcelona Guide Bureau (☎ 93 310 77 78; fax 93 268 22 11).

Things to See & Do

Barcelona offers a rich palette of sights with something to interest everyone – from Picasso to history, from the grand seafaring museum to the waxworks, from the aquarium to the monuments of the Modernistas.

Weekends are obviously the busiest time. Museum and art gallery opening hours vary considerably, but as a rule of thumb you should be OK between about 10 am and 6 pm in most places (although many do shut for lunch from 2 to 4 pm). Most museums and galleries close all day Monday and Sunday afternoon from 2 pm. Some are toying with the idea of opening at night (in summer at any rate); check with the tourist office. Admission prices also vary, but 500 to 700 ptas is the average. Students generally pay a little over half, as do senior citizens (65 and over) with appropriate proof, and children under 12.

Explanations tend to be in Catalan, although English gets a fairly good run. Sometimes both appear with no Castilian!

Possession of a Bus Turístic ticket (see the Getting Around chapter) entitles you to discounts to some museums.

If you intend to get around Barcelona fast and visit lots of museums in the blink of an eye, the Barcelona Card might come in handy. It costs 2500/3000/3500 ptas for 24/48/72 hours. You get free transport and up to 50% off the entry to many museums and other sights, as well as minor discounts on purchases at a limited number of shops and restaurants. The card is available at the main tourist office, where you should have a look at the pamphlet first to see whether discounted museums and the like are what you were hoping to see.

WALKING TOURS

To see a decent chunk of Barcelona and give it any justice you will need a good week and plenty of energy. As quite a few attractions are well dispersed throughout the city, you'd be wise to use public trans-

HIGHLIGHTS

- La Sagrada Família
- Festa de la Mercè madness in September
- Fine seafood in one of Barcelona's quality restaurants
- The Museu Marítim
- Ferreting out hidden bars in the Ciutat Vella
- The tram to Tibidabo and the views there
- Sipping cava on the roof of La Pedrera in summer
- Museu d'Història de la Ciutat and its Roman excavations
- A stroll down La Rambla
- A drink or three at a summertime terrassa on Gràcia's Plaça del Sol

port to save some shoe leather. We suggest two thematic walks. One takes you around the Ciutat Vella (the Old Town), stopping off at main points of interest spanning Roman times to the 18th century. The second is devoted to modernisme. You will notice a few overlaps – so you may want to combine elements of the two tours, or come up with your own. The walks are to get you oriented and they thread together a lot of the sights of old and modernista Barcelona. They are not meant to be done in a day. Break them up to suit your own pace.

Quite a few sights beyond the thematic and/or geographical scope of these tours are mentioned only in passing or not at all – you can read more about them later under their individual entries. Conversely, several minor sites get a quick mention and are not referred to again in the chapter. Happy yomping!

Ciutat Vella (Old Town)

A walking tour of the medieval rabbit warren that is Old Barcelona will necessarily weave and wind and bend back on itself. If you intend stopping at any of the sights along the way, you'll need to allow at least two long hard days.

Sights preceded by an asterisk are dealt with in greater detail later in this chapter.

Plaça de Sant Jaume This square is the heart of Barcelona so it seems a reasonable place to start.

The north-west and south-east sides of the square are lined by the *Palau de la Generalitat and *Ajuntament, the seats of regional and city government respectively. Close your eyes for a second and imagine low, columned buildings and lots of togas. This was the forum of Roman Barcino and the temple was just back a bit to the north on the modest rise of Mont Taber. Together these two buildings formed the centre of civic and religious life. The town's two main roads crossed through the forum. From roughly north to south ran the *decumanus* (now Carrer del Bisbe Irurita), intersected by the *cardo* – a classic plan for a Roman settlement, as seen right across the empire. It was a military camp turned into a town – you can learn about it in the Museu d'Història de la Ciutat (see under Barri Gòtic).

Jewish Quarter & Around From Plaça de Sant Jaume, head west along Carrer del Call, the main street in the former Jewish quarter (*Call*) in medieval Barcelona (Carrer de Ferran, the straight street just below it, also leading off towards La Rambla, was only rammed through in 1823). At No 5, the jewellery shop, just past Carrer de Ramon del Call, you can see remnants of the Roman walls and south-western gate A block north up here you reach Carrer de Marlet. At No 1 is a Hebrew inscription in the wall, one of the few overt reminders of the area's former identity. According to the Castilian translation underneath (1820), a holy rabbi, Samuel Hasareri, must have lived or died here. What is truly intriguing is the date (692 AD) – of his death?

The next junction is with Carrer dels Banys Nous, where the Jewish community was permitted to build new public baths just beyond the then city walls (before Jaume I raised new walls along the present day Rambla). From here the street changes name to Carrer de la Boqueria. Take the next right and follow it into Plaça de Sant Josep Oriol. The Gothic church in front of you is *Santa Maria del Pi (entrance in the adjoining square). Opposite it, at No 4, stands the **Palau de Fiveller**, a one-time private mansion dating to 1571.

Wend your way back east down Carrer de l'Ave Maria, dogleg left up Carrer dels Banys Nous and first right up Baixada de Santa Eulàlia (we are heading back into the Call). Where the street name changes to Carrer de Sant Sever, you'll see a tiny lane to your left. Head down this into a quiet, leafy, but rather neglected square, which boasts the rather obscure **Museu del Calçat**, or footwear museum. It is open Tuesday to Sunday from 11 am to 2 pm (200 ptas). The church before you is the baroque **Església de Sant Felip Neri**, completed in 1752. It adjoins the Palau del Bisbat (Episcopal Palace). Follow Carrer de Montjuïc del Bisbe, surely one of the narrowest lanes in Barcelona, into Carrer del Bisbe Irurita.

The Catedral You are facing the entrance into the shady cloister of the *Catedral. You could turn right and head back to Plaça de Sant Jaume, passing first the modest Església de Sant Sever and then the main Gothic façade of the Palau de la Generalitat.

Roman Route Turn left (north-west) and head out through old city gates (parts of the Roman originals are still extant) where Carrer del Bisbe Irurita leads into Plaça Nova. (For the record, the south-western gates stood on Carrer del Call, just beyond Carrer de Ramon del Call. To the south-east, the entrance to Barcino was on what is now Carrer del Regomir, while the north-eastern exit was about where Carrer de la Llibreteria runs into Baixada de la Llibreteria.)

THINGS TO SEE & DO

CIUTAT VELLA WALKING TOUR

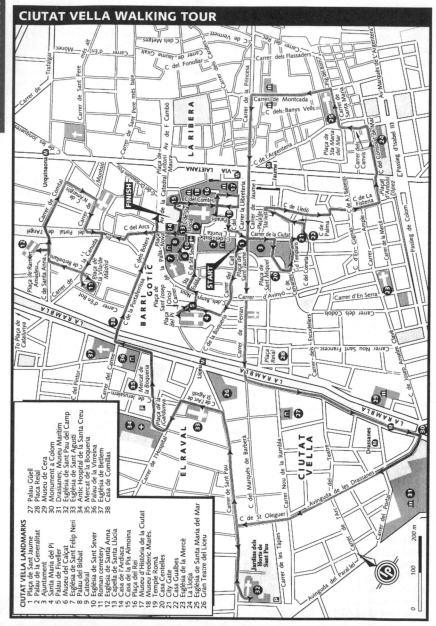

CIUTAT VELLA LANDMARKS
1 Plaça de Sant Jaume
2 Palau de la Generalitat
3 Ajuntament
4 Santa Maria del Pi
5 Palau de Fiveller
6 Museu del Calçat
7 Església de Sant Felip Neri
8 Palau del Bisbat
9 Catedral
10 Església de Sant Sever
11 Roman cemetery
12 Capella de Santa Llúcia
13 Casa de l'Ardiaca
14 Casa de la Pia Almoina
15 Museu d'Història de la Ciutat
16 Palau del Rei
17 Temple Romà
18 Casa Centelles
19 Casa Gualbes
20 City Gate
21 Casa de la Mercè
22 Casa Gualbes
23 La Llotja
24 Església de la Mercè
25 Església de Santa Maria del Mar
26 Gran Teatre del Liceu
27 Palau Güell
28 Plaça Reial
29 Museu de Cera
30 Monument a Colom
31 Drassanes; Museu Marítim
32 Església de Sant Pau del Camp
33 Antic Hospital de la Santa Creu
34 Mercat de la Boqueria
35 Palau de la Virreina
36 Església de Betlem
37 Casa de Comillas

Rough Justice

At the junction of Baixada de Santa Eulàlia and Carrer de Sant Sever you may notice a devotional niche and a ceramic plaque quoting a passage from one of the works of the 19th century Catalan cleric and writer Jacint Verdaguer. He talks of one of the many tortures of Santa Eulàlia, joint patron saint of Barcelona. Supposedly born into the pagan world of Roman Barcino before Christianity became the official religion of the empire, Eulàlia was so appalled by the licentious living of her contemporaries that she became a Christian.

This apparently was not considered good form, and the locals took time off to demonstrate the extent of their disapproval. Flung into a tower in the Call, she subsequently underwent a series of highly unpleasant trials – apparently one of them was to be stuffed into a barrel (some versions say with nails hammered into it) which was rolled down the hill of what is now Baixada de Santa Eulàlia. She eventually died at the stake (no-one can agree where) and her purported remains lie buried in the crypt of the Catedral (see under Catedral). At least that's what we think. Many experts actually identify her with a like-named saint from Mérida (Extremadura, western Spain) and there is no shortage of doubting Thomases who claim the whole story is a load of old tosh.

The martyrdom of Saint Eulàlia, as depicted in a sculpture in Barcelona's Catedral

Proceed up Carrer dels Arcs and a short way along Avinguda del Portal de l'Àngel before hanging a left into Carrer de la Canuda. It is speculated that this was part of the old Roman branch road of the Via Augusta (that linked Rome to Cádiz) into Barcelona. Proceed along it until you hit Plaça de la Vila de Madrid. Here you will see a small **Roman cemetery** with a few sad looking tombs.

In Search of Guifré El Pelós Take Carrer de Bertrellans north a block to Carrer de Santa Anna. Turn right and you'll find almost immediately to your left a lane leads into a surprisingly tranquil square backed by the unassuming **Església de Santa Anna**. It originally dates to the 12th century, but little remains of the original Romanesque structure. The Gothic cloister is a shady haven – if you can get in.

Back on Carrer de Santa Anna, cross Avinguda del Portal de l'Àngel and continue down Carrer de Comtal. Taking a right down Carrer de N'Amargòs is interesting if only to see the plaque at No 8. This claims that the palace garden walls of the first Count of Barcelona, Guifré el Pelós (Willy the Hairy – see History in the Facts about Barcelona chapter) stood here. Carrer de N'Amargòs was also the first in the city to get gas lighting.

Back to the Catedral Turn right at Carrer de Montsió and at Avinguda del Portal de l'Àngel take a left and retrace your steps to Plaça Nova and the Catedral. The narrow old streets around the cathedral are beautifully traffic free and dotted with buskers playing classical guitar or Catalan folk songs.

Re-enter the Roman gates (note on your left the remnants of the aqueducts that supplied Roman Barcino with water) and take the first left. You are on Carrer de Santa Llúcia. On your right is the Romanesque *Capella de Santa Llúcia dedicated to the saint of the same name (wedged onto the Catedral). On your left is *Casa de l'Ardiaca. Farther ahead on your right is the main entrance to the Catedral. The building under partial restoration ahead of you is the *Casa de la Pia Almoina.

The lane leading south down the east flank of the Catedral, Carrer dels Comtes, will lead you to the complex of buildings making up the former Palau Reial Major. The courtyard is known as *Plaça del Rei and access to the complex (which includes an underground tour of this sector of Roman Barcino) is through the *Museu d'Història de la Ciutat and the *Museu Frederic Marès. When you're through, dogleg your way down Carrer del Paradis for a quick look at what's left of the

*Temple Romà, Barcino's Roman temple. This brings you back to Plaça de Sant Jaume, and this might be a jolly good moment to give it a rest for the day.

Southern Barri Gòtic From Plaça de Sant Jaume, head south-east down Carrer de la Ciutat along the only remaining Gothic façade of the Ajuntament. Turn right around the building and you end up in the rather nondescript Plaça de Sant Miquel. The one-time Roman baths here have long since been covered up. Still in one piece, however, is the charming 15th century **Casa Centelles**, on the corner of Baixada de Sant Miquel. You can wander into the fine Gothic-Renaissance courtyard if the gates are open, but that's as far as you'll get.

Head east again along Carrer dels Templaris and make a right down Carrer de la Ciutat. Where it becomes Carrer del Regomir you will notice the site of Roman Barcino's southernmost **city gate**. The area is undergoing some restoration. Just beyond the gate at No 13 is another 15th century mansion, **Casa Gualbes**. Just for fun, backtrack a little and turn into Carrer del Cometa and then left into Carrer de Palma. Follow this into the charming little Plaça de Sant Just, flanked by the Gothic church of the same name and a lovely spot for a rest and coffee.

From the square you can now take another street back down towards the waterfront, Carrer de Lledo. It's a rundown old lane, but once was a fine medieval residential street. Follow it (don't mind the changes of name en route) all the way down to **Carrer de la Mercè**. The Baroque church of the same name, **Església de la Mercè** (home to Barcelona's most celebrated patron saint), lies three blocks west.

La Ribera You are going to head east, cross Via Laietana into La Ribera, stroll along Carrer del Consolat de Mar past **La Llotja**, the city's medieval stock exchange. The fine Gothic interior built in the 14th century is encased in a neoclassical façade. Picasso and Miró both attended art school in this building. it is now the seat of Barcelona's

Chamber of Commerce and you can visit it on Fridays from 10 am to 2 pm. Groups (maximum 15) will need to call ahead on ☎ 93 416 93 00.

When you see Carrer dels Canvis on your left, take this to reach Plaça de Santa Maria del Mar. The area is sprinkled with appealing little bars and places to eat and dominated by the Gothic *Església de Santa Maria del Mar. Wander along its eastern flank and around the apse you'll find yourself in *Carrer de Montcada, a fine medieval street bursting with mansions, museums, shops and a couple of choice watering holes. This street alone may well do you for the day. In any case, this is a good place to break the walk, as the next stage takes us back across the Barri Gòtic to El Raval, west beyond La Rambla.

To pursue the walk there, head west along Carrer de la Princesa from the top end of Carrer de Montcada. Cross Via Laietana and slice across the Barri Gòtic along Carrer de Jaume I, Plaça de Sant Jaume and Carrer de Ferran until you end up on La Rambla.

El Raval In front of you is the *Gran Teatre del Liceu (see the Entertainment chapter). Our objective is to reach the waterfront. As you wander down La Rambla you can duck to the right down Carrer Nou de la Rambla (carved through El Raval at the end of the 18th century to give quicker access to Montjuïc from the centre) to see Gaudí's *Palau Güell (see the next walk and under El Raval) or to the left for *Plaça Reial. Farther down La Rambla on the left is the *Museu de Cera (wax museum) and right on the waterfront traffic circle the 19th century *Monument a Colom (known to Anglos as Columbus). Over to your right are the great Gothic shipyards, the *Drassanes, which house the fine *Museu Marítim.

From here each sight requires a bit of legwork. Head west along Avinguda de les Drassanes and on to Carrer de Sant Pau. A few blocks towards Avinguda del Paral.lel is the Romanesque *Església de Sant Pau del Camp. You then backtrack most of the

way along Carrer de Sant Pau to La Rambla, turning left up Carrer de l'Arc de Sant Agusti. **Església de Sant Agusti** is where the city's main Good Friday procession begins. At Carrer de l'Hospital head west for the *Antic Hospital de la Santa Creu. For a change of scene and a departure from the medieval side of Barcelona's life, you can wander from the hospital across Plaça de la Cardunya into the back end of the bustling *Mercat de la Boqueria before re-emerging on La Rambla. To the left (heading towards Plaça de Catalunya) are, firstly, the 18th century *Palau de la Virreina and then, across Carrer del Carme, the baroque *Església de Betlem. Cross the road to No 118 – the Llibreria & Informaciò Cultural de la Generalitat de Catalunya, housed in a former mansion, the **Casa de Comillas**, built in 1774. It was one of many such houses of the well-to-do that went up along La Rambla in the late 18th and early 19th centuries.

Should you want to return to the centre of the Barri Gòtic, simply head down Carrer de la Portaferrissa – you'll emerge in front of the Catedral.

For a walking tour of Modernista buildings see colour insert, page 112

LA RAMBLA

Spain's most famous street is the place to head for a first taste of Barcelona's atmosphere. Flanked by narrow traffic lanes, the middle of La Rambla is a broad, tree-lined pedestrian boulevard, crowded every day until the wee hours with a cross-section of Barcelona's varied populace and out-of-towners.

Dotted with cafés, restaurants, kiosks and news-stands, sporting reams of international newspapers and magazines as well as pornography; and enlivened by buskers, pavement artists, mimes and living statues, La Rambla rarely allows a dull moment.

La Rambla gets its name from a seasonal stream (raml in Arabic) that once ran here. It was outside the city walls until the 14th century, and built up with monastic buildings and subsequently mansions of the well to do in the 16th to the early 19th centuries. Unofficially, it's divided into five sections, with their own names, although street numbers are in a single sequence, going up from the bottom (south-east) end. This explains why to many people the boulevard also goes by the name of Las Ramblas.

Rambla de Canaletes
A block to the east of this first stretch of La Rambla along Carrer de la Canuda is Plaça de la Vila de Madrid, with a sunken garden where some Roman tombs have been exposed (see also Walking Tours above). Also on this part of La Rambla is a turn-of-the-century fountain, the water of which supposedly emerges from what were once known as the springs of Canaletes. It used to be said of anyone who lived in Barcelona that s/he 'drank the waters of Les Canaletes'. Nowadays they say that anyone who drinks from the fountain will return to Barcelona, which is not such a bad prospect really.

Rambla dels Estudis
This second stretch of La Rambla, from below Carrer de Santa Anna to Carrer de la Portaferrissa, is also called Rambla dels Ocells (birds) because of its twittering bird market.

Rambla de Sant Josep
This section, from Carrer de la Portaferrissa to Pla de la Boqueria, is lined with verdant flower stalls, which give it the alternative name Rambla de les Flors (flowers).

The Palau de la Virreina, La Rambla de Sant Josep 99, is a grand 18th century rococo mansion housing an arts/entertainment information and ticket office run by the *Ajuntament* (Town Hall). Just across Carrer del Carme, the Església de Betlem was constructed in baroque style for the Jesuits in the late 17th and early 18th centuries to replace an earlier church destroyed by fire in 1671. Fire was a bit of a theme for this site. The church was once considered the most splendid of Barcelona's few baroque offerings, but leftist arsonists torched it in 1936. Continuing towards the waterfront from Palau de la Virreina, you are confronted by the bustling sound, smell and taste-fest of the Mercat de la Boqueria. It is possibly La Rambla's most interesting building, not so much for its modernista-influenced design as for the action of the food market.

Barcelona seems to take pride in being a pleasure centre and in the Museu de l'Eròtica, at No 96, you can observe how people have been enjoying themselves since ancient times – lots of Karma Sutra and flimmering porn flicks from the 1920s. The centre opens daily from 10 am to 10 pm (975 ptas).

Plaça de la Boqueria, where four side streets meet just north of Liceu metro station, is your chance to walk all over a Miró – the colourful Mosaïc de Miró in the pavement, with one tile signed by the artist.

Rambla dels Caputxins
Also called Rambla del Centre, this stretch runs from Plaça de la Boqueria to Carrer dels Escudellers – named after the potters' guild, founded in the 13th century, whose members lived and worked here (their raw materials came principally from Sicily). On the west side is the intact façade of the Gran Teatre del Liceu, Barcelona's famous 19th century opera house, gutted by fire in 1994. The Liceu, which launched such famous Catalan singers as Josep (aka José) Carreras and Montserrat Caballé, was one of the most beautiful opera houses in the world and the town fathers promise it will be better still in its repaired state when the curtain goes up again in October 1999.

On the east side of Rambla dels Caputxins, farther south, is the entrance to the large Plaça Reial (see the Barri Gòtic section). Just below Plaça Reial, La Rambla gets seedier, with a few strip clubs and peep shows.

Rambla de Santa Mònica
This final stretch of La Rambla widens out to approach the Columbus monument overlooking Port Vell. On the east side, at the end of narrow Passatge de la Banca, is the Museu de Cera (Wax Museum), which has tableaux of a Gitano (gypsy) cave, a bullring medical room and a hall of horror as

well as wax figures of Cleopatra, Franco etc – not bad as wax museums go. It's open Monday to Friday from 10 am to 2 pm and 4 to 8 pm; weekends and holidays from 4.30 to 8.30 pm. In September it opens daily from 10 am to 8 pm (900 ptas).

Monument a Colom

The goings on around the bottom of La Rambla, and the harbour beyond it, are supervised by the tall Columbus monument, built for the Universal Exhibition in 1888. It was in Barcelona that Columbus gave the delighted Catholic Monarchs a report of his first discoveries in the Americas, but that's about the extent of his involvement with the place. Or is it? It was popularly believed in the 19th century that Columbus was one of Barcelona's most illustrious sons, although it is commonly accepted that he was born and raised in Genoa (that town's senior officials attended the inauguration of the monument). Then, in 1998, a Catalan historian was insisting he had evidence to prove Columbus was in fact a Catalan, which would have put the mockers on the claims that a little cottage preserved in downtown Genoa was his birthplace. At any rate, Columbus died penniless and forgotten in 1506 in Valladolid, central Spain. Regardless of his birthplace you have to ask just *why* he is pointing to the Mediterranean, one-time source of Barcelona's medieval splendour and prosperity, when his great deeds took him to the Atlantic? There are no prizes for guessing the explanation for his white hair and the bad case of dandruff.

You can ascend by lift (250 ptas) daily from 10 am to 7.30 pm, except for a 1.30 to 3.30 pm break on Monday to Friday.

Museu Marítim

West of the Monument a Colom on Avinguda de les Drassanes stand the Reials Drassanes (Royal Shipyards), a rare work of non-religious monumental Gothic architecture that now houses the Museu Marítim – a fascinating tribute to the seafaring exploits that shaped much of Barcelona's history.

The shipyards were, in their heyday, among the greatest in all Europe. Begun in the 13th century and completed by 1378, the buildings demonstrate that the Catalan Gothic penchant for broad, stout construction had some useful applications. Look up at the ceilings and you feel you are looking at the upturned hulls of so many galleys. The long arched (the arches reach 13m at their highest) bays sloped off as slipways directly into the water – which lapped the seaward side of the Drassanes until at least the end of the 18th century.

By then, shipbuilding here had ceased and the buildings were being used for artillery production and as a training ground, ammunition dump and barracks. Only in 1935 were the shipyards handed over to the Ajuntament, which had already decided to convert them into a maritime museum. This finally happened in 1941 after civil war had returned them briefly to the role of arms factory.

Much of the building remained neglected, however, and only in 1987 was an ambitious plan put into effect to restore the shipyards to their medieval glory and install what is without doubt one of the city's most imaginative and captivating museums.

The first few sections include models, charts and a collection of *mascarons* (figureheads) from sailing ships. Sailors hoped these figures would help steer their vessels clear of unwanted nastiness. Also here is material devoted to one of the world's first successful submariners, Narcis Monturiol i Estarriol.

From these first rooms you enter the main bays of the shipyards, dominated by a full size replica (made in the 1970s) of Don John of Austria's flagship, which he took into battle against the Turks off Lepanto (Italy) in 1571. The result of this, the last great sea struggle between fleets of galleys (under sail or otherwise), was a famous victory for the Christians. This part of the museum is full of vessels (some real but mostly models) of all types and epoques, from coastal fishing skips to giants of the steam age. You can wander through lifesize dioramas on board a sailing ship, read captains' logs and watch videos (in Catalan) on different aspects of sailing history.

Taking A Dive

Would the real Captain Nemo please stand up? Narcis Monturiol i Estarriol (1819-85) was a curious character with, from all appearances, a generous heart. His interests were wide-ranging. As an editor of publications defending workers' and women's rights he ran into trouble with the authorities and their censor's scissors. He also followed closely attempts to set up some (rather pitiful in retrospect) utopian societies in the Americas.

His optimism reached its high point in a rather different field – scientific invention. The bee in his bonnet was the submarine. By the beginning of the 19th century several attempts had been made to take vessels below the sea, some of them successful. But these projects did not attract funds and generally ended where they had started, on the drawing board.

In 1856 Monturiol got to work on his first wooden, fish-shaped sub, the *Ictíneo*. It was about six metres long – a cramped little underwater beast – but it worked. The screws were driven by the crew's muscle power and a shortage of air made the dives fairly brief affairs, but Monturiol made more than 50 dives in the couple of years after he launched the sub in 1859.

He became an overnight celebrity but got no money from the navy. Undeterred, Monturiol sank himself further into debt by designing *Ictíneo II*. This time he really did come up with a first. Seventeen metres long, its screws were steam driven and Monturiol had worked out a system for renewing the oxygen inside the vessel. Nothing like it had been built before. It trialed in 1864 but again attracted no money, either from the navy or from private industry. Everyone had something nice to say about it, but Monturiol owed a huge sum of money on it. In 1868, his creditors lost patience and had it broken up for scrap, a blow from which Monturiol never really recovered.

Best of all, head for Àmbit (Area) 12, pick up the audio phones and follow the red lights. This wonderful little tour takes you amidships of Don Juan's galley, where audiovisuals help you to imagine the ghastly life of the slaves, prisoners and volunteers (!) who at full steam could haul this vessel along at 9 knots. They remained chained to their seats, four to an oar, at all times. Here they worked, drank lots (fresh water was stored below decks, where the infirmary was also located),

ate, slept and went to the loo. It seems unlikely they could have greatly enjoyed their maritime adventures. The tour takes you on to a dockside scene in Havana at the time Barcelona's merchants were doing a brisk business in late 19th century Cuba; you also board a steam liner and join Narcis Monturiol on his underwater experiments.

The museum is open Tuesday to Saturday from 10 am to 6 pm; Sundays from 10 am to 2 pm (800 ptas, 600 for students and seniors). Many of the explanations are in Catalan only, but scattered about the various sections are sheets in several languages explaining key points.

BARRI GÒTIC

The 'Gothic quarter' is the nucleus of old Barcelona. The medieval city was elevated on the Roman core, which in succeeding centuries slowly spread north, south and west. The Barri Gòtic is a classic warren of narrow, winding streets and unexpected little squares, and home to a dense concentration of budget hotels, bars, cafés and restaurants. Few of its great buildings date from after the early 15th century – the decline Barcelona went into at that time curtailed grand projects for several centuries.

The Barri Gòtic stretches from La Rambla in the west to Via Laietana in the east, and roughly from Carrer de la Portaferrissa in the north to Carrer de la Mercè in the south. Carrer de Jaume I and Carrer de Ferran (the latter, which was named after king Fernando VII, was sliced through the city in 1823) form a kind of halfway line: these streets and those to their north tend to be dotted with chic little shops and feel 100% safe; those to their south become darker and a little seedier – albeit still full of perfectly respectable places to eat, drink and stay.

Plaça de Sant Jaume

In the 2000 or so years since the Romans settled in here, this square (oft remodelled) has been the focus of Barcelona's civic life.

Facing each other across it are the Palau de la Generalitat (the seat of Catalunya's government) on the north side and the Ajuntament (Town Hall) on the south. Both have fine Gothic interiors which, unhappily, the general public can only enter at limited times.

Palau de la Generalitat Founded in the early 15th century to house Catalunya's parliament, the Palau was extended over the centuries as its importance (and bu-

reaucracy) grew. It is open to the public only on 23 April, the Dia de Sant Jordi (St George, Catalunya's patron saint), and on 24 September (Festes de la Mercè). At any time, however, you can admire the original Gothic main entrance on Carrer del Bisbe Irurita (designed by medieval architect Marc Saffont and now part-hidden by restorers' scaffolding). Of lesser interest are the façades around the back on Carrer de Sant Sever and on Carrer de Sant Honorat, but at least they too preserve something of the feeling of the building's ancient roots. The modern main entrance on Plaça de Sant Jaume is a late Renaissance job with neoclassical leanings – nothing to write home about. If you wander by in the evening, squint up through the windows into the Saló de Sant Jordi and you will get some idea of the sumptuousness of the interior.

If you *do* get inside, you're in for a treat. Normally you will have to enter from the rear (Carrer de Sant Sever). The first rooms you pass through are characterised by low vaulted ceilings. From here you pass upstairs to the raised courtyard known as the **Patio dels Tarongers**, a modest Gothic orangerie. .The 16th century Sala Daurada i de Sessions, one of the rooms leading off the patio, is a splendid meeting hall lit up by huge chandeliers. Still more imposing is the Renaissance Saló de Sant Jordi, whose murals were added this century – many an occasion of pomp and circumstance takes place here. Finally you descend the staircase of the Gothic Patio Central to leave by what was, in the beginning, the building's main entrance.

Ajuntament Otherwise known as the Casa de la Ciutat, across the square from the Generalitat, this has been the seat of city power, for centuries. The Consell de Cent, from medieval times the ruling council of the city, first sat here in the 14th century, but the building has lamentably undergone many changes since the days of Barcelona's Gothic-era splendour.

Only the original, now disused, entrance on Carrer de la Ciutat retains its

Gothic ornament. The main 19th century neoclassical façade on the square is a charmless riposte to the Palau de la Generalitat and the remaining sides of the building are recent and utterly depressing. Inside, however, it is quite another story. To *get* inside, you have to turn up on Saturday or Sunday between 10 am and 2 pm (free). You enter a courtyard and will probably be directed to the right (pick up a brochure on the way) to the **Escala d'Honor**, a majestic staircase that leads you up to the Gothic gallery.

From here you enter directly the **Saló de Cent**, the hall in which the town council once held its plenary sessions. The broad vaulting is pure Catalan Gothic and the wooden artesonado ceiling demonstrates fine work. In fact, however, much of what you see is comparatively recent. The building was badly damaged in a bombardment in 1842 and has been repaired and tampered with repeatedly. The wooden neo-Gothic seating was added at the beginning of the 20th century, as was the grand alabaster retablo at the back. To the right you enter the small **Saló de la Reina Regente**, built in 1860, where the Ajuntament now sits. To the left of the Saló de Cent you reach the Saló de les Croniques – the murals recount Catalan exploits in Greece and the Near East in Catalunya's merchant empire-building days.

As you head down the other set of stairs to the courtyard, you may notice several statues of women – the least recognisable as such is Joan Miró's *Dona*.

Catedral & Around

Approached from Avinguda de la Catedral, Barcelona's central place of worship presents a magnificent image. The richly decorated main (north-west) façade, laced with gargoyles and all the stone intricacies you would expect of northern European Gothic, sets it quite apart from other churches in Barcelona. The facade was added in 1870, although based on a 1408 design. The rest of the building was built between 1298 to 1460. The remaining façades are spare in decoration and the oc-

tagonal, flat-roofed towers are a clear reminder that, even here, Catalan Gothic architectural principles prevailed.

The interior – open from 8.30 am to 1.30 pm and 4 to 7.30 pm (5 to 7.30 pm on Saturday and Sunday) – is a broad, soaringly high space divided into a central nave and two aisles by lines of elegant, slim pillars. The cathedral was one of the few churches in Barcelona spared by the anarchists in the civil war, so its ornamentation, never overlavish, is intact.

In the first chapel on the right from the north-west entrance, the main Crucifixion figure above the altar is the **Sant Crist de Lepant**. The figure is said to have been carried on the prow of the Spanish flagship at the battle of Lepanto. Farther along this same wall, past the south-west transept, are the wooden **coffins of Count Ramon Berenguer I and** his wife **Almodis**, founders of the 11th century Romanesque predecessor of the present cathedral.

Smack in the middle of the central nave is the late 14th century **coro**, or choirstalls. This central position is a singularly Spanish ingredient in churches

A broad staircase before the main altar leads to the **crypt**. It contains the tomb of Santa Eulàlia, one of Barcelona's two patron saints. The carving on the alabaster sarcophagus, executed by Pisan artisans, recounts some of her tortures and, along the top strip, the removal of her body to its present resting place.

You can visit the cathedral's **roof and tower** by an *ascensor* (lift), which rises every half hour from 10.30 am to 12.30 pm and 4.30 to 6.30 pm from the Capella de les Animes del Purgatori near the north-east transept. Tickets (200 ptas) are sold in the coro.

From the south-west transept, exit to the lovely **claustre** (cloister), with its trees, fountains and flock of geese (there have been geese here for centuries, and nobody has yet come up with a convincing reason why). One of the cloister chapels commemorates 930 priests, monks and nuns martyred in the civil war.

I f you wanted to see every vaguely modernista building or façade in Barcelona, you'd need several days. The itinerary that follows is by no means exhaustive but would definitely be exhausting if you tried to do it in a day, so you may want to spread things out or be selective.

Casa Lleó Morera

On the assumption that you are feeling methodical, chronologically inclined and have nosed around the Ciutat Vella, we'll start this meander there too. Where possible, completion dates of buildings are given.

Palau Güell (1) (1886), Carrer Nou de la Rambla in El Raval, is our starting point. It is an early job done by Gaudí for his main patron, the industrialist Eusebi Güell. Walk a few paces east on to La Rambla and turn left (north). Within a couple of blocks you pass the **Antiga Casa Figueras (2)** at No 83, with its elaborate tilework and, virtually across the road, **Casa Quadros (3)**, lavishly decorated in oriental style with outward-jutting dragon and umbrellas (which tell you what this place once sold). Make a quick detour down Carrer de Sant Pau and peer inside the restaurant of the **Fonda Espanya (4)** (1903, now part of the Hotel España – see the Places to Stay chapter). Ramon Casas had a hand in the decoration.

Casa Amattler

Mercat de la Boqueria (5) is on your left as you proceed up La Rambla. It is one of several covered markets that can be considered modernista constructions, although it was built over a long period – 1840 to 1914. Cross the boulevard and head east along Carrer de Santa Anna, dogleg across Avinguda del Portal del Àngel and go into Carrer de Montsió. Here you can admire **Els Quatre Gats (6)** restaurant which, along with being *the* hangout for modernista artists and other hip souls from 1897 to 1903, was in fact one of Puig i Cadafalch's first creations – **Casa Martí (6)** (1896).

Take the first left (Passatge del Patriarca), then make a right turn down Carrer de Comtal. This takes you into the busy boulevard Via Laietana. Head north a few paces and cross to the little laneway called Carrer de Ramon Mas. Spare a moment to admire the **Caixa de Pensions (7)**, Via Laietena 56. This largely neo-Gothic fantasy was headquarters to the bank of the same name from 1914 to 1917. Follow Carrer de Ramon Mas (it turns right down Carrer de Francesc de Paula into Carrer de Sant Pere més alt), to stand before Domènech i Montaner's **Palau de la Música Catalana (8)**. Now backtrack to Via Laietana and cruise north along Carrer de les Jonqueres and cross Plaça d'Urquinaona. As you head up Carrer de Roger de Llúria you will pass the **Cases Cabot (9)** (1905) at Nos 8-14, designed by Josep Vilaseca. The first doorway has fine decoration. Around the corner is Gaudí's **Casa Calvet (10)** (1900), Carrer de Casp 48. Inspired by the baroque, the main attraction is the staircase inside.

Fundació Antoni Tàpies

We continue up to Gran Via de les Corts Catalanes where, at No 654, we pass Enric Sagnier's **Casa Mulleras (11)** (1904), the best feature of which is the gallery on the façade. Farther west, Josep Vilaseca's **Casa Pia Batlló (12)** (1906), Rambla de Catalunya 17, is most interesting for its use of ironwork.

Cross Gran Via and head north-west a couple of blocks, turn right into Carrer del Consell de Cent and on a block to the corner of Passeig de Gràcia. Here is **Casa Lleó Morera (13)** (1905), first of the Manzana de la Discordia buildings. The other two, **Casa Amattler (14)** and **Casa Batlló (15)**, are around the corner to your left.

The next left into Carrer d'Aragó takes you to the **Fundació de Tapies (16)**, originally built by Domènech i Montaner for Editorial Montaner i Simon (1885). Head up Passeig de Gràcia – you will probably have noticed

MODERNISTAS WALKING TOUR

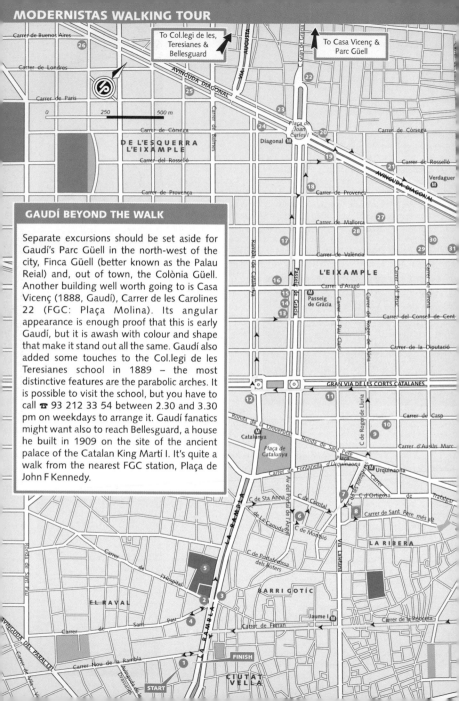

To Col.legi de les, Teresianes & Bellesguard

To Casa Vicenç & Parc Güell

Carrer de Buenos Aires

Carrer de Londres

Carrer de Paris

0   250   500 m

DE L'ESQUERRA L'EIXAMPLE

Carrer de Còrsega

Carrer del Rosselló

Carrer de Provença

AVINGUDA DIAGONAL

VIA AUGUSTA

Plaça de Joan Carles

Diagonal Ⓜ

Carrer de Còrsega

Carrer de Rosselló

Verdaguer Ⓜ

AVINGUDA DIAGONAL

Carrer de Provença

Carrer de Mallorca

Carrer de València

L'EIXAMPLE

Carrer d'Aragó

Passeig de Gràcia Ⓜ

Carrer del Consell de Cent

Carrer de la Diputació

GRAN VIA DE LES CORTS CATALANES

Carrer de Casp

Ronda de la Universitat

Ronda de Sant Pere

Carrer d'Ausiàs Marc

Catalunya Ⓜ

Plaça de Catalunya

Carrer de Fontanella d'Urquinaona

Urquinaona Ⓜ

Trafalgar

C de Sta Anna

C de Cúcal

C d'Ortigosa

Carrer de Sant Pere més alt

LA RIBERA

C de La Canuda

C de Montsió

C de Portaferrissa dels Boters

BARRI GOTIC

EL RAVAL

C de l'Hospital

Jaume I Ⓜ

Carrer de la Princesa

Ronda de Sant Pau

Carrer de Sant Pau

Carrer de Ferran

AVINGUDA DEL PARAL·LEL

Carrer Nou de la Rambla

START

FINISH

CIUTAT VELLA

GAUDÍ BEYOND THE WALK

Separate excursions should be set aside for Gaudí's Parc Güell in the north-west of the city, Finca Güell (better known as the Palau Reial) and, out of town, the Colònia Güell. Another building well worth going to is Casa Vicenç (1888, Gaudí), Carrer de les Carolines 22 (FGC: Plaça Molina). Its angular appearance is enough proof that this is early Gaudí, but it is awash with colour and shape that make it stand out all the same. Gaudí also added some touches to the Col.legi de les Teresianes school in 1889 – the most distinctive features are the parabolic arches. It is possible to visit the school, but you have to call ☎ 93 212 33 54 between 2.30 and 3.30 pm on weekdays to arrange it. Gaudí fanatics might want also to reach Bellesguard, a house he built in 1909 on the site of the ancient palace of the Catalan King Martí I. It's quite a walk from the nearest FGC station, Plaça de John F Kennedy.

MODERNISTAS LANDMARKS

1 Palau Güell
2 Antiga Casa Figueras
3 Casa Quadros
4 Fonda Espanya
5 Mercat de la Boqueria
6 Casa Martí (Els Quatre Gats)
7 Caixa de Pensions
8 Palau de la Música Catalana
9 Cases Cabot
10 Casa Calvet
11 Casa Mulleras
12 Casa Pia Batlló
13 Casa Lleo Morera
14 Casa Amatller
15 Casa Batlló
16 Fundació de Tapies
17 Casa Enric Batlló
18 Casa Milà
19 Palau Quadras
20 Casa Comalat
21 Casa de les Punxes
22 Casa Fuster
23 Església de Pompeia
24 Casa Serra
25 Casa Sayrach
26 Casa Company
27 Casa Thomas
28 Palau Montaner
29 Casa Lamadrid
30 Casa
31 Casa Llopis i Bofill
32 Casa Macaya
33 La Sagrada Família
34 Hospital de la Santa Creu i de Sant Pau
35 Plaça de Braus Monumental
36 Arc de Triomf
37 Palau de la Justicia
38 Castell dels Tres Dragons

Casa Milà (La Pedrera)

C GROENHOUT

the modernista street lamps along it. You will pass **Casa Enric Batlló (17)** at No 75, another apartment building by Vilaseca. Cross at Carrer de Provença for Gaudí's masterpiece, **Casa Milà (18)** (aka La Pedrera) before turning right at the next block into Carrer de Rosselló. On the corner of Carrer de Pau Claris is Puig i Cadafalch's **Palau Quadras (19)**.

North across Avinguda Diagonal is the **Casa Comalat (20)** (1911) by Salvador Valeri. The Gaudí influence on this modernista late-comer is obvious. Head around the back to Carrer de Còrsega to see a lighter, more playful façade. If you can sneak in you can admire the fine mosaics and stained glass inside. Heading east a couple of blocks down Avinguda Diagonal you reach **Casa de les Punxes (21)**.

At this point you've probably had more than enough for one day. If you are a diehard, another half dozen or so buildings can be seen around here and farther west up the Diagonal. On the walking tour map they are Nos 22-26: **Casa Fuster (22)** (1910, Domènech i Montaner); **Església de Pompeia (23)** (1915, Sagnier); **Casa Serra (24)** (1903, Puig i Cadafalch); **Casa Sayrach (25)** (1918, Manuel Sayrach); and **Casa Company (25)** (1911, Puig i Cadafalch).

A further cluster of about a dozen minor modernista creations lies sprinkled south of Diagonal between Carrer de Roger de Llúria and Passeig de Sant Joan. However, you still have some major modernista sights to deal with, and it is preferable to see them, so you might be better off leaving this lot for another day or forgetting about them altogether.

Should you get around to them, from Casa de les Punxes drop two blocks south down Carrer del Bruc. **Casa Thomas (27)** (1898), by Domènech i Montaner, Carrer de Mallorca 291, is your first port of call. It is one of his earlier efforts – the ceramic details are a trademark. Less than a block west, **Palau Montaner (28)** was finished off by the same architect in 1893. Similar to Casa Thomas is Domènech i Montaner's **Casa Lamadrid (29)** (1902), Carrer de Girona 113. Virtually across the road at No 122, Jeroni Granell's **Casa (30)** (1903) is a colourful offsider. **Casa Llopis i Bofill (31)** (1902), Carrer de València 339, is an interesting block of flats by Antoni Gallissà – the façade is particularly striking. Puig i Cadafalch's **Casa Macaya (32)** (1901), Passeig de Sant Joan 108, has a wonderful courtyard, if you can get a look inside.

However, let's assume you don't want to run around here yet. You have reached Casa de les Punxes, and those who don't want to head straight for a footbath will probably have their hearts set on Gaudí's **Sagrada Família (33)**. To save on toe power you could jump on the metro at Verdaguer station and travel one stop on line 5.

Another stop on line 5 takes you to the **Hospital de la Santa Creu i de Sant Pau (34)**. Or you could walk up along Avinguda de Gaudí, which sports some fine modernista street lamps.

Even if you are not interested in bullfighting, you might want to cast your eye briefly over the **Plaça de Braus Monumental (35)** (1915), five blocks or one metro stop south of the Sagrada Família (metro: Monumental), on the corner of Gran Via de les Corts Catalanes and Carrer de la Marina. It was built by Ignasi Mas and is the larger of the city's two bullfighting rings. The other, Les Arenes, on Plaça d'Espanya, was built around the same time but is no longer in use. Both edifices play with Islamic themes, but you could swear that Mas had a dash of Dalí's blood in his veins – the arena is topped by ceramic-clad eggs!

From here, the Plaça de Braus Monumental, walk two blocks south to Carrer de Ribers, where you swing south-west towards the **Arc de Triomf (36)**, built by Vilaseca for the Universal Exhibition in 1888. Heading south along Passeig de Lluís Companys towards the Parc de la Ciutadella you pass on your left the **Palau de Justicia (37)** (1915), a rather austere, modern building done largely by Sagnier. At Passeig de Pujades you swing right and then left into Passeig de Picasso. On your left is Domènech i Montaner's **Castell dels Tres Dragons (38)**, now the Museu de Zoologia.

Castells dels Tres Dragons

Measure for Measure

Have a close look at the external wall of the Romanesque Capella de Santa Llúcia. At about waist level you can make out the inscription 'A 2 Canas lo Pou'. The *cana* was a unit of measurement (eight palms or 1.55m) once in common use by tailors. Apparently a well (*pou*) was situated about 3m from where you stand. If you inspect the corner of the same building, you'll notice two vertical grooves etched into the stone – they measure 2 canas. The story goes that if, after having bought some material, you discovered you had been cheated by the tailor, you could search for the local gendarmes who in turn would have the good salesman accompany them to this spot to verify whether the cana he was using gave the full measure. Of course, the tailor may have kept a proper cana hidden away for just such occasions.

At the north-west end of the cloister is the **Capella de Santa Llúcia**, one of the few bits of Romanesque Barcelona still in one piece. Walk out the door onto Carrer de Santa Llúcia and turn around to look at the exterior – you can see that, although incorporated into the Catedral, it is in fact a separate building.

Now turn on your heels and you are facing the 16th century **Casa de l'Ardiaca** (archdeacon's house), which now serves as an archive. In office hours you may wander into the supremely serene courtyard, cooled by trees and a fountain. Climb the stairs to the next level. Here you can look down into the courtyard and across to the Catedral.

Across Carrer del Bisbe Irurita is the 17th century **Palau Episcopal** or Palau del Bisbat (bishop's palace). Virtually nothing remains of the original 13th century structure. As noted in the walking tour above, the Roman city's north-west gate stood here, and you can see the lower segments of the Roman towers that stood on either side of the gate at the base of the Palau Episcopal and Casa de l'Ardiaca. In fact, the lower part of the entire north-west wall of the Casa de l'Ardiaca is of Roman origin – you can also make out part of the first arch of the one-time Roman aqueducts – which supplied the ancient town with water.

Casa de la Pia Almoina The Roman walls continued across present day Pla de la Seu into what subsequently became the Casa de la Pia Almoina. In the 11th century the city's main centre of charity was located here, although the much crumbled remains of the present building (undergoing restoration) date to the 15th century. It houses the Museu Diocesà (Diocesan Museum) and for 300 ptas you can see temporary exhibitions along with a sparse collection of medieval religious art. Otherwise there's little there. It opens Tuesday to Saturday from 10 am to 2 pm and 4 to 7 pm, Sunday from 10 am to 2 pm.

Temple Romà d'Augusti Opposite the south-east end of the cathedral, narrow Carrer del Paradis leads towards Plaça de Sant Jaume. Inside No 10 are four columns of Barcelona's main Roman temple, dedicated to Caesar Augustus and built to worship his imperial highness in the 1st century AD. You are now standing on the highest point of Roman Barcino – Mont Taber. Though it is generally said that this mound is 15m high, a plaque outside No 10 says it is 16.9m. You can visit (free) Monday to Saturday from 10 am to 2 pm and 4 to 8 pm, and Sunday from 10 am to 2 pm (take the official times with a pinch of salt – if the door's open, wander in).

Plaça del Rei & Around

Plaça del Rei is the courtyard of what was the Palau Reial Major, the palace of the counts of Barcelona and monarchs of Aragón. It's surrounded by tall, centuries-old buildings, most of which are now open to visitors as the Museu d'Història de la Ciutat (City History Museum).

Museu d'Història de la Ciutat You enter this museum, one of the most intriguing in Barcelona, in **Casa Padellàs** on Carrer del Veguer. It's open Tuesday to Saturday from 10 am to 2 pm and 4 to 8 pm, and Sunday from 10 am to 2 pm (500 ptas, free on the first Wednesday of the month and Wednesday afternoons). You can pay an extra 200 ptas to see a 3D video tracing, in entertaining fashion, the history of the city, before you commence your visit proper. Since most of the explanations in the museum are in Catalan and/or Castilian (and very occasionally in English), it is worth asking for the pamphlet in your language to give you some clues as to what you will be looking at.

When you enter Casa Padellàs, built for a 15th century noble family, you find yourself in a courtyard typical of Barcelona's Gothic mansions, with an external staircase up to the 1st floor.

Buy your tickets inside on the ground floor, then pass through a few small rooms housing a handful of ancient artefacts from Roman and pre-Roman days. Enter the video room (the show takes 28 minutes), then get the elevator down to a remarkable piece of Barcelona – a whole stretch of the excavated Roman town. The elevator is cute. Instead of the floor number it has the year 1996. You get out at –12 in Barcino.

As you wander around the ruins of the Roman town you can inspect part of the *cardo* or main cross-road, a defensive tower, shops, houses (a few with floor mosaics intact), public baths and storage areas for wine and *garum* (a kind of fish sauce that was a staple throughout the Roman empire). The walk takes you right under the Catedral so you can see what little remains of its Romanesque and Visigothic predecessors (the latter consists of a baptismal font).

Once you are through, you will emerge on Plaça del Rei. Head directly for the fan-shaped stairway in the north corner. Inside on the left is the **Saló del Tinell**, the banqueting hall of the royal palace and a fine example of Catalan Gothic (built in 1359-70). Its broad arches and bare walls give a sense of solidity and solemnity that would have made an appropriate setting for Fernando and Isabel to hear Columbus' first reports of the New World – as it is claimed to have been.

As you back out of the Saló you end up in the **Capella Reial de Santa Àgata**, the palace chapel also built in the 14th century. Outside, a spindly bell tower rises from the north-east side of Plaça del Rei, while inside, all is bare except for the 15th century altarpiece and the magnificent *techumbre* (wooden ceiling). The stained glass is a recent addition.

Follow the series of staircases and you will end up in the gallery overlooking the square and then inside the multi-tiered **Mirador del Rei Martí** (Lookout Tower of King Martin), built in 1555. You can climb to the top of the tower, which dominates Plaça del Rei and affords excellent views over the city.

Casa del Lloctinent The south-west side of Plaça del Rei is taken up by this viceroy's palace, built in the 1550s as the residence of the Spanish viceroy of Catalunya. It is worth wandering in (from Carrer dels Comtes) and heading upstairs – the building is somewhat rundown but boasts a fine wooden ceiling and pleasing courtyard.

Until 1993 it housed the Arxiu de la Corona d'Aragón, a unique collection documenting the history of the kingdom prior to unity under Fernando and Isabel. The archive is now at Carrer dels Almogàvers 77.

When you walk back outside, have a look at the walls of the Catedral. See all the grooves cut into the stone? It appears the viceroy's soldiers who were housed here used the church walls to sharpen their weapons.

Museu Frederic Marès A short distance up Carrer dels Comtes, this museum is housed in yet another building of the Palau Reial Major. Marès was a rich 20th century Catalan sculptor, traveller and obsessive collector. He specialised in medieval Spanish sculpture, huge quantities of which are displayed on the ground and 1st floors – including some lovely coloured wood sculptures of the Crucifixion and the Virgin.

The top two floors, known as the Museu Sentimental, hold a mind-boggling array of other Marès knick-knacks, from toy soldiers and cribs to scissors and tarot cards. All but the cool patio and café were closed for refurbishment at the time of writing.

Roman Walls

From Plaça del Rei it's worth a little detour to see the two best surviving stretches of Barcelona's Roman walls. One is on the south-west side of Plaça de Berenguer Gran, with the Capella Reial de Santa Àgata atop them. The other is a little further south, by the north end of Carrer del Sots-tinent Navarro. They date from the 3rd and 4th centuries, when the Romans rebuilt their walls after the first attacks by Germanic tribes from the north.

Plaça de Sant Josep Oriol & Around

This small plaza, not far off La Rambla, is the prettiest in the Barri Gòtic. Its bars and cafés attract buskers and artists and make it a lively place to hang out for a while. But spare a thought for the long-suffering locals who live in apartments on the square – the signs they have hanging on their balconies suggest they are sick of all-night drummers who pee at their doorsteps and keep them awake – hard to blame them really!

The square is surrounded by some of the Barri Gòtic's quaintest little streets, many of them dotted with other appealing cafés, restaurants and shops. The plaza is dominated by the **Església de Santa Maria del Pi**, a Gothic church built in the 14th to 16th centuries, open daily from 8.30 am to 1 pm and 4.30 to 9 pm. The beautiful rose window above its entrance on Plaça del Pi is claimed to be the world's biggest. The inside of the church was gutted by fire in 1936 and most of the stained glass is modern. The third chapel on the left is dedicated to Sant Josep Oriol, with a map showing spots in the church where he worked numerous miracles.

The area between Carrer dels Banys Nous and Plaça de Sant Jaume is known as the **Call**, Barcelona's former Jewish quarter and centre of learning, from at least the 11th century until anti-Semitism saw Jews expelled in 1424 (see also Walking Tours earlier). Even before the expulsion, Jews were not exactly privileged citizens. As in many medieval centres they were obliged to wear a special identifying mark on their garments and had trouble getting permission to expand their ghetto as the Call's population increased.

Plaça Reial & Around

Just south of Carrer de Ferran, near its La Rambla end, is Plaça Reial, a large, traffic-free plaza whose 19th century neoclassical façades hide numerous eateries, bars, nightspots and budget places to stay.

Residents here have an even worse time than those in Plaça de Sant Josep Oriol, but perhaps they should be grateful for a lesser evil. Until the area was cleaned up in the 1980s, it had a fearsome reputation for poverty, crime and drugs. Indeed, the whole area between Carrer d'Avinyó and La Rambla was once a red-light zone and a notorious den of low life. The plaza retains a restless atmosphere, where respectable tourists, ragged buskers and down and outs come face to face. Don't be put off, but watch your bags and pockets. The lampposts by the central fountain are Antoni Gaudí's first known works.

This southern half of the Barri Gòtic is imbued with the memory of Picasso, who lived as a teenager with his family in Carrer de la Mercè, had his first studio in Carrer de la Plata (see also the Places to Eat chapter), and was a regular visitor to a brothel at Carrer d'Avinyó 27, which may have inspired his 1907 painting *Les Demoiselles d'Avignon*.

EL RAVAL

West of La Rambla, the Ciutat Vella spreads to Ronda de Sant Antoni, Ronda de Sant Pau and Avinguda del Paral.lel, which together trace the line of Barcelona's 14th century walls. Known as El Raval, from an Arabic word that denoted the one-time suburban sprawl *extra muros*, the area contains one of the city's most dispiriting slums, the seedy red-light zone of the Barri Xinès.

For centuries the Barri has been home to whores, louche lads and, at times, a bohemian collection of interlopers. In the 1920s and 30s especially, it was a popular playground with Barcelonins of many classes; busy at night with the activity in taverns, *cafés concerts*, cabarets and brothels. In the harsh light of day the tawdriness and poverty is more evident, hardly surprising given the concentration of people living in often less than ideal circumstances. Carrer Nou de la Rambla, where Picasso lived for a while, was particularly lively. By the 1950s brothels had been outlawed and many of the bars had shut down. In later years drug abuse became an increasing problem, and the physiognomy of the area changed with the waves of impecunious migrants, mainly from North Africa and the Indian sub-continent, who moved in to cheap and often dank lodgings.

Past and present lend the Barri Xinès, which occupies the southern half of El Raval, a certain fascination, but this is not the place to bring your Rolex. It's not overly dangerous, but among the mixed bag of whores and pimps, transvestites and transsexuals, drug abusers of all persuasions and a picaresque assortment of local low life, the percentage of dodgy characters with a keen eye for prosperous pockets is quite high – so take care.

El Raval has not been completely abandoned to its fate. Various projects, including one to create a huge new shady square north of Carrer de Sant Pau, are signs that some day the area may yet be turned around (although town planners have been scratching their heads about just how to achieve this since late in the last century). Still the northern half of El Raval is already notably less seedy, and an increasingly bohemian set is moving in to take advantage of low rents. From an outsider's point of view, it would in some respects be a shame to sanitise it all – but local residents probably feel differently!

Església de Sant Pau del Camp

Back in the 9th century, when monks founded the monastery and church of Sant Pau del Camp (Saint Paul in the Fields), it was a good walk from the city gates amid fields and gardens. Today you see only the church and cloister erected in the 12th century. Sadly neglected amid the worst squalor El Raval has to offer, this is one of the best of Barcelona's few Romanesque remnants. The doorway to the church in fact bears some rare Visigothic decoration, predating the Muslim invasion of Spain. The cloister is open only from 5 to 8 pm (closed Tuesday and Sunday).

Antic Hospital de la Santa Creu

Almost directly north from the Església de Sant Pau del Camp stands what was, in the 15th century, the city's main hospital. The Antic Hospital de la Santa Creu today houses the Biblioteca de Catalunya (Catalunya's national library) and the Institut d'Estudis Catalans. The library is the single most complete collection of documents tracing the region's long history. In its medieval heyday, the hospital was deemed one of the great hospitals of Europe, where the sick got comparatively (for the times) good care and abandoned children and lunatics were also taken in – presumably they were housed in separate wards. Parts of what you see today were added in the 16th and 17th centuries. The hospital lies on what was the main entrance to the city from the imperial road from Madrid.

As you enter the main courtyard, you can't help being reminded you are in El Raval. Dilapidated, it serves as a kind of park to all and sundry – round old ladies gossiping and walking their little dogs, the occasional drunk taking a snooze, outmoded young punks having a snack. Earnest students and academics from other parts of town head for the library, which opens Monday to Friday from 9 am to 8 pm and Saturday from 9 am to 2 pm. Head in too, and you can see (in good shape) some fine Catalan Gothic vaulting in the ceilings. The **capella** (chapel) of the former hospital is sometimes used for temporary exhibitions.

Palau Güell

A few steps off La Rambla at Carrer Nou de

la Rambla 3-5, the Palau Güell is one of the few modernista buildings in the Ciutat Vella. Gaudí built it in the late 1880s for his most important patron, the industrialist Eusebi Güell. It was intended as a guest wing and social annexe to Güell's main mansion on La Rambla. The Palau Güell lacks some of Gaudí's later playfulness but is still a characteristic riot of styles – Gothic, Islamic, Art Nouveau – and materials. After the civil war it was in police hands and political prisoners were tortured in its basement.

You will be taken on a compulsory guided tour of the place, which is a compendium of Gaudí's earlier architectural ideas. When you enter the building, turn back around to face the entrance – it is a parabolic arch, the predominant form throughout the building, and characteristic of other Gaudí constructions.

You will first be taken downstairs to the low-vaulted brick stables. Even the solid upwards-fanning pillars are of slim brick – at the time considered by more conventional designers an ignoble material best hidden from view. *Au contraire*, said Gaudí and the modernistas – just look at the great works of Islamic and mudéjar architecture spread across Spain, all in brick.

From the ground floor you are led up dark grey marble stairs to the next floor, whose main feature is backlit mirrors posing as windows to increase the impression of space. Up another floor and you reach the main hall and its annexes. The hall is like a four-sided empty parabolic pyramid – each wall an arch stretching up three floors and coming together to form a dome that reaches the roof. The chapel that once filled one of the walls was partly destroyed in the civil war.

The adjoining rooms boast varying themes on artesonado ceilings – finely carved wood, drawing on a long tradition with its roots in Islamic design. The liberal use of wrought iron in decoration, for example in the one-time gas lamps and roof ornamentation, is another reaffirmation of the value of 'ignoble materials'. The whole effect, while a masterful insight into mod-ernista ideas and in particular those of Gaudí, is a little gloomy until you emerge on to the flat roof to be confronted by a riot of tiled colour and fanciful design in the building's chimney pots.

The Palau Güell is open Monday to Saturday from 10 am to 2 pm and 4 to 8 pm (400 ptas, 200 for students) and tours usually start on the hour. This is also where you can pick up Ruta del Modernisme tickets, which allow you to see other modernista efforts around the city (see also the Getting Around chapter).

Picasso – who hated Gaudí's work – began his Blue Period in 1902 in a studio across the street at Carrer Nou de la Rambla 6.

Museu d'Art Contemporàni & Around

One thing that gave the northern half of El Raval a fillip was the opening, in 1995, on Plaça dels Àngels of the vast, white Museu d'Art Contemporàni de Barcelona (MACBA).

The ground and first floors are given over to exhibitions from the gallery's own collections. First things last, so head to the first floor to approach the collection in a vaguely chronological fashion. Here, the emphasis is on fairly modern times – from the 1940s to the 80s. You will find works by, among others, Joan Miró, Antoni Tàpies, Paul Klee and Alexander Calder. So-called conceptual art in the 1970s had its expression in Catalunya in the Grup de Treball, among whose adherents were Francesc Abad, Fina Miralles and Àngels Ribé. Such artists as Miquel Barceló and Ferran García Sevilla, protagonists of neo-expressionism emerged in the 1980s.

Downstairs you will see work of the past 10 years or so, represented above all by contemporary Catalan artists. Names to look for include Susana Solano, Juan Muñoz and Carlos Pazos.

The gallery also presents temporary exhibitions and boasts a good art bookshop.

Opening hours are Monday to Friday (closed Tuesday) from noon to 8 pm, Saturday from 10 am to 8 pm, and Sunday and holidays from 10 am to 3 pm (700 ptas, 350 ptas on non-holiday Wednesdays).

On Carrer de Montalegre behind the museum you will find the **Centre de Cultura Contemporània de Barcelona**, or CCCB, a complex of auditoriums and exhibition and conference halls opened in 1994 in what had been an 18th century hospice. The big courtyard, with a vast glass wall on one side, is spectacular. With 4500 sq metres of exposition space in four display areas, the centre plays host to a constantly changing program of exhibitions with 'the city' as their core theme. Often staged in conjunction with other European museums and galleries, the exhibition ranges broadly from architectural studies to photo exhibits. For instance, at the time of writing the main exhibition, *Un Paese Unico, Italia*, was a fascinating photo exhibition spanning the 20th century in Italy. The centre organises all sorts of other activities too, ranging from folk music performances to art lectures.

LA RIBERA

La Ribera is the area of the Ciutat Vella north-east of the Barri Gòtic, from which it's divided by noisy Via Laietana, which was driven through this part of the city in 1907. La Ribera has intriguing, narrow streets, some major sights, good bars and restaurants, and lacks the seedy character of some parts of the Barri Gòtic.

Palau de la Música Catalana

This concert hall at Carrer de Sant Pere més alt 11 is one of the high points of modernista architecture. It's not exactly a symphony, more a series of crescendos in tile, brick, sculptured stone and stained glass. Built between 1905 and 1908 by Lluis Domènech i Montaner for the Orfeo Català musical society, with the help of some of the best Catalan artisans of the time, it was conceived as a temple for the Catalan Renaixença.

You can see some of its splendours, such as the main façade with its mosaics, floral capitals and the sculpture cluster representing Catalan popular music – from outside, and you can glimpse lovely tiled pillars inside the ticket office entrance on Carrer de

Sant Francesc de Paula. Best, however, is the richly colourful auditorium upstairs, with its ceiling of blue and gold stained glass and, above a bust of Beethoven, a towering sculpture of Wagner's Valkyries (Wagner was No 1 in the Renaixença charts). To see this, you need to attend a concert, book yourself on one of the regular free building tours (☎ 93 268 10 00) or get the Ruta del Modernisme ticket from Palau Güell (see Organised Tours in the Getting Around chapter).

Carrer de Montcada

Possibly an early example of deliberate town planning, this medieval high street was driven down towards the sea from the road that in the 12th century led north from the city walls. It would, in time, become the best address in town for the city's emerging merchant class, and the bulk of the great mansions that remain intact today date back to the 14th century.

Capella d'En Marcús On the little square of the same name that caps the top (north-western) end of Carrer de Montcada lies the often unnoticed chapel of this 12th century alms house. Erected on land which was at that time outside the city walls and on the road north-east from Barcelona, the complex was a halfway house for poor wayfarers and also served as a small hospital. Construction was financed as a private work of charity by a wealthy businessman, Bernat Marcús. Although its original Romanesque elements are recognisable, the tiny chapel has been much meddled with over the centuries.

Museu Picasso Barcelona's most visited museum, the Museu Picasso occupies three of the many fine medieval stone mansions on Carrer de Montcada, at Nos 15-19. It is worth wandering in just to admire the courtyard and internal staircase of the first of these, but few people do so without subsequently devoting a couple of hours to the collection.

Although Picasso never visited Spain during the Franco years, he always had a soft spot for Catalunya and in 1962 agreed to the idea of his old Barcelona friend and secretary Jaume Sabartés that a Picasso museum be founded here. Sabartés' collection was combined with works already owned by the city. Later, Picasso himself made large donations (including many early works and a bequest of graphics) to the museum, and in 1981 his widow, Jacqueline Roque, gave 141 ceramics.

The collection is strongest on Picasso's earliest years, up until 1904, but there is enough material from subsequent periods to give you a deep impression of the man's versatility and genius. Above all, you feel that Picasso is always one step ahead of himself, let alone anyone else, in his search for new forms of expression.

The collection starts, naturally enough, at the beginning, with sketches, oils and doodling from Picasso's earliest years in Málaga and La Coruña – most of it done in 1893-95. Some of his self-portraits and the portraits of his father, which date from 1896, are evidence enough of his precocious talent. *Retrato de la Tía Pepa* (Portrait of Aunt Pepa), done in Málaga in 1897, is a key painting

On the second floor you are in a pivotal year of the master's life – 1900. By now he is gaining confidence and abandoning the strictures of academic painting. This was the year of his first exhibition in Els Quatre Gats and his first trip to Paris. The lines are fluid and alive, and soon he embarks on his first conscious thematic adventure, the Blue Period. From this point he distanced himself increasingly from simply depicting scenes of Barcelonese or Parisian life, from the streets to the cabarets, to interpreting them more symbolically. The blue-tinted glasses through which he regards the world lend to many of his paintings in this period a melancholy air – some of the titles, such as *The Defenceless*, confirm the tendency.

From here on the collection is less comprehensive. There are a handful of examples from his subsequent Pink Period (Paris) and a modest selection of Cubist paintings.

More significant is the section from rooms 22 to 26. From 1954 to 1962 Picasso was obsessed by the idea of researching and 'rediscovering' the greats, in particular Velázquez. In 1957 he executed a series of renditions of the latter's masterpiece, *Las Meninas* (which hangs in El Prado in Madrid). It seems as though Picasso has looked at the original Velázquez painting through a prism that reflected all the artistic styles the later painter had worked through. The series includes studies of single characters from the original work through to depictions of the work as a whole. Room 24 contains eight appealing treatments of *Pichones* (Pigeons).

Finally, on the top floor (rooms 28-36) is a series of lithographs done in Picasso's last years, the so-called Suite 156.

The museum is open Tuesday to Saturday from 10 am to 8 pm, and Sunday from 10 am to 3 pm (600 ptas, 250 ptas on non-holiday Wednesdays, free on the first Sunday of each month). There are additional charges for special exhibitions.

Museu Tèxtil i d'Indumentària This Textile & Costume Museum occupies the 13th century Palau dels Marquesos de Lliò at Carrer de Montcada 12, and part of the Palau Nadal next door (both buildings underwent repeated alterations into the 18th century). Its 4000 items range from 4th century Coptic textiles to 20th century local embroidery, but best is the big collection of clothing from the 16th century to the 1930s. The items in the museum were collected over a period of more than 100 years. Opening hours are Tuesday to Saturday, 10 am to 5 pm, Sunday and holidays 10 am to 2 pm (400 ptas, 700 if you combine it with the Museu Barbier-Mueller d'Art Precolombí next door). There's a nice café in the old courtyard.

Museu Barbier-Muellerd'Art Precolombí Occupying the rest of the Palau Nadal at No 14, this museum holds part of one of the most prestigious collections of pre-Colombian art in the world. The artefacts from South American 'primitive' cultures come from the collections of the Swiss businessman Josef Mueller (who died in 1977) and his son-in-law Jean-Paul Barbier, who directs the Musée Barbier-Mueller in Geneva.

All the rooms have been blacked out, with only the artefacts on display eerily lit up in the gloom. The first room you enter is given over to South American gold jewellery. From then on you pass through a series of rooms containing ceramics, jewellery, statues, textiles and other objects. Explanations are in several languages including English.

It is open Tuesday to Saturday from 10 am to 8 pm and Sundays from 10 am to 3 pm (500 ptas, 700 ptas combined with the Museu Tèxtil i d'Indumentària).

Along Carrer de Montcada Several other mansions on the street are now commercial art galleries where you're welcome to browse (they often stage exhibitions). The biggest is the **Galeria Maeght** at No 25 in the 16th century Palau dels Cervelló. For more tips on art galleries, turn to the Shopping chapter. If you can get a peek into the baroque courtyard of the originally medieval Palau de Dalmases at No 20 (now a hideously expensive place to sip wine; see the Entertainment chapter), do so – it is one of the finest on the strip.

Església de Santa Maria del Mar Carrer de Montcada opens at its south-east end into **Passeig del Born**, a plaza where jousting tournaments took place in the Middle Ages and which was Barcelona's main square from the 13th to 18th centuries. At the south-west end of Passeig del Born stands one of Barcelona's finest Catalan Gothic churches, Santa Maria del Mar. Built in the 14th century, Santa Maria was lacking in superfluous decoration even before anarchists gutted it in 1909 and 1936. This only serves to highlight its fine proportions, purity of line and sense of space. The apse features a beautiful slim arcade, and there's some lovely 15th to 18th century stained glass. The church is open daily from 9 am to 1.30 pm and 4.30 to 8 pm.

PARC DE LA CIUTADELLA

East of La Ribera and north of La Barceloneta, Parc de la Ciutadella is perfect if you just need a bit of space and greenery, but also has a couple of more specific attractions.

After the War of the Spanish Succession, Felipe V built a huge fort (La Ciutadella) to keep watch over Barcelona. It became a much loathed symbol of everything Catalans hated about Madrid and was later used as a political prison. Only in 1869 did the central government allow its demolition. The site was turned into a park and used as the main site for the Universal Exhibition of 1888. It's open daily from 8 am to 8 pm (to 9 pm from April to September). Arc de Triomf and Barceloneta, both about half a kilometre away, are the nearest metro stations.

The single most impressive thing in the park is the monumental **Cascada** near the Passeig de Pujades entrance, created in 1875-81 by Josep Fontsère with the help of the young Gaudí. It's a dramatic combination of classical statuary, rugged rocks, greenery and thundering water. Nearby, you can hire little rowboats to paddle about the small lake – a potential diversion for the kids.

Museu Nacional d'Art Modern de Catalunya In the south-east of the park, next door to the **Parlament de Catalunya**, where the regional parliament meets, this art gallery is housed in the fort's former arsenal.

The art gallery is devoted to Catalan art from the mid-19th century to the mid-20th century. Most of the paintings are of comparatively little interest, spanning Catalan Realisme, Anecdotisme, Modernisme (Ramon Casas and Santiago Rusiñol are each represented by about a dozen paintings, among the most interesting Casas' depiction of himself and Pere Romeu on a tandem bicycle. Romeu was the director of Els Quatre Gats, the Barcelona tavern where modernista artists and hangers on hung out) and into Noucentisme, a kind of retrograde reaction to Modernisme that sought a new outlet in recycled classicism and a concentration on 'Mediterranean' light and vision.

More interesting are the many items of modernista interior and, in the case of iron grills designed by Gaudí for the Casa Vicenç, exterior design. They include furniture, lampshades, doors and so on.

Among the noucentistes, perhaps the work of Joaquim Sunyer (1874-1956) is the most striking on show. Three fairly minor works by Dalí have managed to find their way in here too.

The museum is open Tuesday to Sunday from 10 am to 7 pm (300 ptas, 200 ptas for students).

Zoo The south end of the park is occupied by a large Parc Zoològic (zoo), which is best known for its albino gorilla Copito de Nieve (Snowflake), orphaned by poachers in Guinea (Africa) in the 1960s. Copito is claimed to be the only albino gorilla in the world and is something of a symbol for the zoo. It's open daily from 10 am to 7 pm, to 5 pm in winter (1400 ptas).

Around the Park Along the Passeig de Picasso side of the park are several buildings constructed for, or just before, the Universal Exhibition. The one at the top end is the most interesting. Known as the Castell dels Tres Dragons, it is a product of the medieval imagination of modernista architect Domènech i Montaner, who put the castle trimmings on a pioneering steel frame. The coats of arms are all invented and the whole building exudes a rather playful air. It was used as a café-restaurant during the life of the exhibition. Nowadays it houses the **Museu de Zoologia** (open Tuesday to Sunday from 10 am to 2 pm; 300 ptas).

If you like stuffed animals, model elephants and the inevitable skeletons of huge ex-living things, this rather fusty old institution is the place for you.

Then comes L'Umbracle, one of two arboretums, a mini botanical garden with a pleasant café in its midst. Next is the **Museu de Geologia**. Most people would have to have rocks in their heads to spend too much time in here, but then again, budding geologists may well want to examine the stones, minerals and fossils on display in this old-time museum. It opens daily except Monday from 10 am to 2 pm (300 ptas). The museum

is followed by L'Hivernacle, another arboretum (*sans* café).

North-west of the park along Passeig de Lluís Companys is the imposing modernista **Arc de Triomf**, designed by Josep Vilaseca as an entrance to the Universal Exhibition, with unusual, almost Islamic-style brickwork. Just what the triumph was is a little hard to guess. It is difficult to put yourself back into the clothes and feelings of Barcelonins in the late 1880s. The exhibition was an (at times farcical and certainly very expensive) attempt to put this middle-ranking and much-ignored city on the world map. The wheels of industry were turning (albeit not at the pace of great European centres further north) and the loss of Cuba, (see History section in Facts about Barcelona) which would have a devastating impact on Barcelona's trade and manufacturing, was another 10 years off. The town fathers were obviously feeling in good spirits, even if no particular 'victory' offered itself as cause for erecting triumphal arches!

PORT VELL

Barcelona's old port at the bottom of La Rambla, once such an eyesore that it caused public protests, has been transformed beyond recognition since the 1980s. Instead of warehouses, railyards and dumps, you are confronted by chic shopping, harbourside munching, movies on-sea, discos and Irish pubs, parking for yachts, a huge aquarium – all these elements and more have left the 'old port' looking brand spanking new.

For a view of the harbour from the water, you can take a **golondrina** excursion boat (☎ 93 442 31 06) from Moll de les Drassanes in front of the Monument a Colom. A 35- minute trip to the breakwater *(rompeolas)* and lighthouse *(faro)* on the seaward side of the harbour is 465 ptas; a one-hour and 20-minute trip to Port Olímpic is 1250 ptas (less for under 19s). This latter trip is on a glass-bottom catamaran. The number of departures depends largely on season and demand. Breakwater trips normally go at least hourly in the daytime, Port Olímpic trips at least three times daily. North-east from the Golondrina quay stretches the palm-lined promenade **Moll de la Fusta**.

At the centre of the redeveloped harbour is the **Moll d'Espanya**, a former wharf linked to Moll de la Fusta by a wave-shaped footbridge, the **Rambla de Mar**, which rotates to let boats enter the marina behind it. At the end of Moll d'Espanya is the glossy Maremàgnum shopping and eating complex, but the major attraction is **L'Aquàrium** (☎ 93 221 74 74) behind it – an ultra modern aquarium that opened in 1995. It's claimed to be Europe's biggest and to have the world's best Mediterranean collection. The place is actually divided into 21 aquariums, of which the 80m-long shark tunnel is a highlight. All up, some 8000 fish (including 11 sharks) have taken up residence here. Entry is a steep 1400 ptas (950 ptas for four to 12-year-olds and pensioners). It's open daily, all year, from 9.30 am to 9 pm (until 11 pm in July and August). You can also buy the *Guide Book – L'Aquàrium* for 600 ptas – it is a colourful handbook explaining all the fishies on show. Beyond L'Aquàrium is the Imax Port Vell big-screen cinema.

The **cable car** *(telefèric* or *funicular aereo)* strung across the harbour to Montjuïc provides another view of the city. You can get tickets at Miramar (Montjuïc), the Torre de Jaume I and the Torre de Sant Sebastià (in La Barceloneta). A return ticket from Miramar to Sant Sebastià will cost 1200 ptas. A return between the central Torre de Jaume I and either Miramar or Torre de Sant Sebastià is 1000 ptas, while a one-way on either run is 800 ptas. The cable car operates daily from midday to 7 pm.

LA BARCELONETA & PORT OLÍMPIC

It used to be said that Barcelona had 'turned its back on the sea', but an ambitious Olympics-inspired redevelopment program has returned to life a long stretch of coast north-east of Port Vell.

La Barceloneta is a mid-18th century sailors' and fishermen's quarter laid out by the French engineer Prosper Verboom to replace housing destroyed to make way for the Ciutadella. The narrow grid system was quite an innovation in its time, although dreary five or six-storey apartment blocks that make up the area today are hardly enticing. By the 19th century it was a pretty squalid spot, especially in hard times (read the first few chapters of Eduardo Mendoza's *City of Marvels* to get an idea of what it must have been like). La Barceloneta is still known for its seafood restaurants, of which several good ones survive (see also the Places to Eat chapter), although many disappeared in the coastal redevelopment programs that came with the Olympics.

Museu d'Història de Catalunya

The Palau de Mar building facing the harbour once served as warehouses, but was transformed in the 1990s into something quite different. Below the seaward arcades is a string of good restaurants. Inside is the Museum of Catalonian History, a 4.5 billion ptas affair, which was opened in 1996.

The permanent display covers the 2nd and 3rd floors, taking you, as the bumph says, on a 'voyage through history' from the Stone Age through to the early 1980s. The museum is a busy hodgepodge of dioramas, artefacts, videos, models, documents and interactive bits. It is an entertaining and informative exploration of 2000 years of Catalan history. See how the Romans lived, listen to Arab poetry from the time of the Muslim occupation of the city, peer into the dwelling of a Dark Ages family in the Pyrenees, mount a knight's horse and try to lift a suit of armour, or descend into an air-raid shelter from the civil war.

Labelling is in Catalan, but you can ask for a brochure (returnable) with some explanations in your own language (quite a few tongues are catered for). The museum is open Tuesday to Thursday from 10 am to 7 pm, Friday and Saturday from 10 am to 8 pm, and Sunday and holidays from 10 am to 2.30 pm (500 ptas).

Beach & Port Olímpic

Barcelona's fishing fleet ties up along the

Moll del Rellotge, south of the museum. On La Barceloneta's seaward side are the first of Barcelona's **beaches**, once dirty and unused, but now cleaned up and popular on summer weekends. **Passeig Marítim**, a 1.25km promenade from La Barceloneta to Port Olímpic – through an area formerly full of railway sidings and warehouses – makes for a pleasant stroll if you manage to dodge all the rollerbladers.

Port Olímpic was built for the Olympic sailing events and is now a classy marina surrounded by bars and restaurants. An eye-catcher on the approach from La Barcelon-eta is the giant copper *Peix* (Fish) sculpture by Frank Gehry, one of a series of modern sculptures dotted around this part of town. The area behind Port Olímpic – dominated by Barcelona's two tallest skyscrapers, the luxury Hotel Arts Barcelona and Torre Mapfre office block – is the Vila Olímpica, formerly the living quarters for the Olympic

participants, now mostly sold off as expensive apartments.

To the north-east, more beaches stretch towards the Riu Besòs (which marks the city's north-eastern boundary). City planners aim to turn this entire stretch of coast, the Front Marítim, into a luxury residential district with hotels, gardens and pricey apartments.

L'EIXAMPLE

L'Eixample (El Ensanche in Spanish, meaning the Enlargement), stretching one to 1.5km north, east and west of Plaça de Catalunya, was the city's 19th century answer to overcrowding in the confines of the medieval city.

Work on l'Eixample began in 1869 to a design by the architect Ildefons Cerdà, who specified a grid of wide streets with plazas formed by their cut-off corners. Cerdà also planned numerous green spaces but these didn't survive the intense demand for l'Eixample real estate.

Buffalo Barna

Back in December 1889, a curious crowd moved into what was vacant ground on the block bounded by Carrer de Muntaner, Corsega, Rosselló and Aribau.

Sioux, Cheyennes and Arapahoes, accompanied by Mexican bandits and cowboys, who had arrived in Barcelona by steamship from Marseille, erected tents and tepees. Buffalo Bill had arrived in town with his Wild West Show, bringing 184 people, 159 horses and 20 buffaloes.

William Frederick Cody (1846-1917), explorer, guide and tracker for General Custer, had quite a record. An expert shot, he had been a sheriff, member of the Pony Express, was obsessed by buffalo hunting and was reputedly a freemason. He came to Europe to try to make a buck out of his Exhibition of American Indian and Frontier Life.

Barcelona had recently put itself on the map with the Universal Exhibition of 1888, so it seemed only natural to pay a visit. The show stayed there for five weeks, but not everything went according to plan. In between displays of Indian attacks on wagon trains and cowboys whooping it up, torrential rains forced numerous cancellations, a tepee was destroyed by fire and a 'flu epidemic killed one of the showmasters and left several Indians under the weather.

When Bill and his circus headed off for Naples, two of this crew were left behind in the Hospital de la Santa Creu. One of them is reputed to have died here and ended up buried on Montjuïc, but nobody knows for certain. Cody & Co never returned to Spain. Bill's boast that with 30,000 Indians he could expel the Spanish army from Cuba probably didn't go down well. (The US Navy took care of the problem 10 years later in any case).

L'Eixample has been inhabited from the start by the city's middle classes, many of whom still think it's the best thing about Barcelona. Along its grid of straight streets are the majority of the city's most expensive shops and hotels, a range of eateries and several nightspots. The main sightseeing objective is modernisme architecture, the best of which – apart from La Sagrada Família – is clustered on or near l'Eixample's main avenue, Passeig de Gràcia.

Manzana de la Discordia

The so-called 'Apple (read Block) of Discord' on the west side of Passeig de Gràcia, between Carrer del Consell de Cent and Carrer d'Aragó, gets its name from three houses remodelled in highly contrasting manner between 1898 and 1906 – each house designed by one of the three leading modernista architects.

At No 35, on the corner of Carrer del Consell de Cent, is **Casa Lleo Morera**, Domènech i Montaner's contribution, with Art Nouveau carving outside and a bright, flower-tiled lobby. You can get up to the 1st floor, which houses offices of the Patronat de Turisme. Swirling sculptures interplay with rich mosaics and whimsical decoration. To see all of it properly you need to be here on the hour for the brief guided tour (usually in Catalan or Spanish).

Casa Amatller at No 41, by Puig i Cadafalch, combines Gothic window frames with a stepped gable borrowed (deliberately) from urban architecture of the Netherlands. The pillared entrance hall and the staircase lit by stained glass are like the inside of some romantic castle. The building is in private hands and you can't generally go inside, but you may get lucky and be able to poke around the foyer.

Casa Batlló, next door at No 43, is one of Barcelona's gems. Of course it's by Gaudí. The façade, sprinkled with bits of blue, mauve and green tile and studded with wave-shaped window frames and balconies, rises to an uneven blue tiled roof with a solitary tower. The roof represents Sant Jordi (St George) and the dragon, and if you stare long enough at the building, it seems

How do you like them Apples?

Despite the Catalanisation of most Barcelona names in recent decades, the Manzana de la Discordia has kept its Spanish name to preserve a pun on *manzana*, which means both 'block' and 'apple'. According to Greek myth, the original Apple of Discord was tossed on to Mt Olympus by Eris (Discord), with orders that it be given to the most beautiful goddess, sparking jealousies that helped start the Trojan War. The pun won't transfer into Catalan, whose word for block is *illa*, and for apple *poma*.

almost to be a living being. As far as getting in is concerned, the same story applies as next door, although once again you might fluke your way inside if it's open – which hardly ever seems to be the case.

Fundació Antoni Tàpies

Round the corner from the Manzana de la Discordia, at Carrer d'Aragó 255, this is both a pioneering modernista building (completed in 1885) and the major collection of a leading 20th century Catalan artist.

The building, designed by Domènech i Montaner for the publishing house Editor ial Montaner i Simón, combines a brick-covered iron frame with Islamic inspired decoration. Tàpies saw fit to crown the building with the meanderings of his own mind – to some it looks like a pile of coiled barbed wire, to others … well.

Antoni Tàpies, whose experimental art has often carried political messages – he opposed Francoism in the 1960s and 1970s – launched the Fundació in 1984 to promote contemporary art, donating a large part of his own work. The core collection spans the whole arc of Tàpies' creation, and also includes some contributions from other contemporary artists. The Fundació also houses an important research library devoted principally to Tàpies, but again embracing a wider range of contemporary art.

The Fundació is open Tuesday to Sunday from 11 am to 8 pm (500 ptas, 300 for students, free for pensioners and under-12s).

La Pedrera

Back on Passeig de Gràcia, at No 92, is another Gaudí masterpiece, built between 1905 and 1910 as a combined apartment and office block. Formally called the Casa Milà after the businessman who commissioned it, it's better known as La Pedrera (the quarry) because of its uneven grey stone façade, which ripples round the corner of Carrer de Provença. The wave effect is emphasised by elaborate wrought-iron balconies.

The Fundació Caixa Catalunya office (☎ 93 484 59 95) has opened the place up to visitors, organising it as the Espai Gaudí (Gaudí Space) and guiding visitors through the building and up on to the roof, with its giant chimney pots looking like multicoloured medieval knights. Gaudí wanted to put a tall statue of the Virgin up here too: when the Milà family said no, fearing it might make the building a target for anarchists, Gaudí resigned from the project in disgust. One floor below the roof, where you can appreciate Gaudí's taste for McDonald's M-style arches (if McDonald's had existed in those days, would he have come up with something else?), is a modest museum dedicated to his work. You can see models and videos dealing with each of his buildings. The lower floors of the building often host temporary expositions.

La Pedrera is open daily from 10 am to 8 pm (500 ptas, 300 for students). Guided visits take place at 6 pm; 11 am on weekends and holidays.

From July to September, the place is opened up on Friday and Saturday evenings (9 pm to midnight). The roof is lit up in an eerie fashion and, while you are taking in the night views of Barcelona, you also get to sip a flute of cava (1000 ptas).

You can also visit La Pedrera on the Ruta del Modernisme ticket. The Caixa Catalunya organises its own tours of other Gaudí landmarks – for more on both options, see Organised Tours in the Getting Around chapter.

Palau Quadras & Casa de les Punxes

Within a few blocks north and east of La Pedrera are two of Puig i Cadafalch's major buildings. The nearer is the Palau del Baró de Quadras at Avinguda Diagonal 373, created between 1902 and 1904 with detailed neo-Gothic carvings on the façade and fine stained glass. It houses the Museu de la Música, with an international collection of instruments. The displays include one of the most important collections of guitars in the world, as well as a series of organs dating as far back as the 16th century. Also housed here is a research library and a *fonoteca*, or library of music recordings. Plans are afoot to transfer the collection to the *Auditori* (the new auditorium under construction near Plaça de les Glóries Catalanes) in 2000. Until then, it's open Tuesday to Sunday from 10 am to 2 pm, Wednesdays until 8 pm (300 ptas).

The Casa Terrades is on the other side of Avinguda Diagonal, 1½ blocks east at No 420. This apartment block of 1903-05, like a castle in a fairy tale, is better known as the Casa de les Punxes (House of the Spikes) because of its pointed turrets.

La Sagrada Família

If you only have time for one sightseeing outing in Barcelona, this should probably be it. La Sagrada Família inspires awe by its sheer verticality, and in the true manner of the great medieval cathedrals it emulates, it's still not half built, after more than 100 years. If it's ever finished, the topmost tower will be more than half as high again as those standing today.

The Temple Expiatori de la Sagrada Família (Expiatory Temple of the Holy Family) was the project to which Antoni Gaudí dedicated the latter part of his life. It stands in the east of l'Eixample (metro: Sagrada Família) and opens to visitors daily – April to the end of August from 9 am to 8 pm; March, September and

LA SAGRADA FAMÍLIA

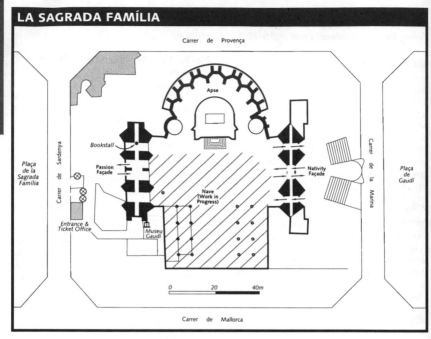

Carrer de Provença

Apse

Bookstall

Passion Façade

Plaça de la Sagrada Família

Carrer de Sardenya

Nave (Work in Progress)

Nativity Façade

Carrer de la Marina

Plaça de Gaudí

Entrance & Ticket Office

Museu Gaudí

0   20   40m

Carrer de Mallorca

October from 9 am to 7 pm; November to February from 9 am to 6 pm. The entry charge of 800 ptas for everybody – the money goes towards the building program – includes a good museum in the crypt. What you're visiting is a building site, but the completed sections and the museum can be explored at leisure. Up to four times a day 50-minute guided tours are offered at 500 ptas a head.

The entrance is by the south-west façade fronting Carrer de Sardenya and Plaça de la Sagrada Família. Inside is a bookstall where you should invest 500 ptas in the *Official Guide* if you want a detailed account of the church's sculpture and symbolism. Once inside, you can spend a further 200 ptas on a ride on lifts to take you up inside one of the towers on each side of the church.

To get your bearings, you need to realise that this façade, and the opposite one facing

Plaça de Gaudí, each with four sky-scraping towers, are at the *sides* of the church. The main façade, as yet unbuilt, will be at the south-east end, on Carrer de Mallorca.

Nativity Façade This, the north-east façade, is the building's artistic pinnacle, mostly done under Gaudí's personal supervision and much of it with his own hands. You can climb high up inside some of the four towers by a combination of lifts (when they're working) and narrow spiral staircases – a vertiginous experience. The towers are destined to hold tubular bells capable of playing complicated music at great volume. Their upper parts are decorated with mosaics spelling out 'Sanctus, Sanctus, Sanctus, Hosanna in Excelsis, Amen, Alleluia'. When asked why he lavished so much care on the tops of the spires, which no one would see from close up, Gaudí answered, 'The angels will see them'.

Beneath the towers is a tall, three-part portal on the theme of Christ's birth and childhood. It seems to lean outward as you stand beneath looking up. Gaudí used real people and animals as models for many of the sculptures.

The three sections of the portal represent, from left to right, Hope, Charity and Faith. Among the forest of sculpture on the Charity portal, you can make out, low down, the manger surrounded by an ox, an ass, the shepherds and kings, with angel musicians above. Directly above the blue stained-glass window is the Archangel Gabriel's Annunciation to Mary. At the top is a green cypress tree, symbolic refuge in a storm for the white doves of peace dotted over it.

Lower sculptures on the Hope portal show the flight into Egypt and the massacre of the innocents, with Jesus and Joseph in their carpenters' workshop just above. Sculpture on the Faith portal includes, in the centre of the lower group, the child Jesus explaining the Scriptures to the temple priests.

Interior The semicircular apse wall at the north-west end of the church was the first part to be finished (in 1894). From the altar steps you can look down the nave at work in progress, with the walls and columns near completion and the roofs begun. The main Glory Façade on the south-eastern end will, like the north-eastern and south-western façades, be crowned by four towers – the total of 12 representing the 12 apostles. Further symbolism will make the whole building a microcosmic symbol of the Christian church, with Christ represented by the massive 170m central tower above the transept and the five remaining planned towers symbolising the Virgin Mary and the four evangelists.

Passion Façade This south-western façade, on the theme of Christ's last days and death, has been constructed since the 1950s with, like the Nativity Façade, four needling towers and a large, sculpture-bedecked portal. The sculptor, Josep Subirachs, has not attempted to imitate Gaudí's work but has produced strong images of his own. The sculptures, on three levels, are in an S-shaped sequence starting with the Last Supper at bottom left and ending with Christ's burial at top right.

Museu Gaudí Open the same times as the church, the museum includes interesting material on Gaudí's life and other work, as well as models, photos and other material on La Sagrada Família. You can see a good example of his plumb line models which showed him the stresses and strains he could get away with in construction.

Hospital de la Santa Creu i de Sant Pau
The hospital is Domènech i Montaner's modernista masterpiece – a huge construction that today still serves as one of the city's most important hospitals. The architect wanted to create a unique environment that would hopefully cheer up the patients. The whole complex, made up of 48 pavilions, is lavishly decorated and no pavilion is the same as another. Among the many artists who contributed statuary, ceramics and artwork was the prolific Eusebi Arnau. You can wander around the grounds at any time, and it is well worth the stroll up Passeig de Gaudí from La Sagrada Família.

Museu Taurino
Housed in the Plaça de Braus Monumental bullring on Gran Via de les Corts Catalanes, this bullfighting museum displays bulls' heads, old posters, *trajes de luces* (bullfighters' gear) and other memorabilia. You also get to wander around the ring and corrals. It's open daily from 10.30 am to 2 pm and 4 to 7 pm; on fight days from 10.30 am to 1 pm only (350 ptas).

Museu Egipci
Only the most avid of budding Egyptologists will find it worthwhile forking out the 700 ptas entry price for this private museum, with its 300 modest items spread out over three rather small floors. True, you

are unlikely to see stuff like this elsewhere in Barcelona, but this is pretty minor material. If you do want to go, the museum is in the offices of the Fundació Arqueològica Clos at Rambla de Catalunya 55-57. It's open Monday to Saturday from 10 am to 2 pm and 4 to 8 pm, Sundays from 10 am to 2 pm.

GRÀCIA

Gràcia is the area north of the middle of l'Eixample. Once a separate village, then in the 19th century an industrial barri famous for its republican and liberal ideas, it was incorporated into the city of Barcelona in 1897. In the 1960s and 70s it became fashionable among radical and bohemian types, and even today retains some of that flavour – plenty of hip local luminaries make sure they get around the bars and cafés of Gràcia. The district's interest lies in the atmosphere of its narrow streets (don't even think about trying to park a car here!), small plazas and the bars and restaurants on them. An evening or night-time wander is the best way to savour these. Diagonal and Fontana are the nearest metro stations to central Gràcia.

The liveliest plazas are **Plaça del Sol**, **Plaça de Rius i Taulet** with its clock tower (thus also known as Plaça del Rellotge – a popular meeting point), and the tree-lined **Plaça de la Virreina** with the 17th century Església de Sant Josep. The local council at one point looked set to get rid of the trees, but thankfully the neighbours took up arms and put a stop to such ideas. Gràcia isn't exactly going to win any green awards as it is! On **Plaça de Rovira i Trias** you can sit on a bench next to a statue of Antoni Rovira, Ildefons Cerdà's rival in the competition to design l'Eixample in the late 19th century. In the pavement, Rovira's design has been laid out so you can see what you think of it.

Three blocks east of Plaça de Rius i Taulet there's a big covered market. West of Gràcia's main street, Carrer Gran de Gràcia, there's an early Gaudí house, the turreted, vaguely *mudéjar* **Casa Vicenç** at Carrer de les Carolines 22.

MONTJUÏC

Montjuïc, the hill overlooking the city centre from the south-west, is home to some fine art galleries and leisure attractions, soothing parks and the main group of 1992 Olympic sites. It's well worth a day or two of your time.

The name Montjuïc (Jewish Mountain) indicates there was once a Jewish settlement here. Before Montjuïc was turned into parks in the 1890s, its woodlands had provided food-growing and breathing space for the people of the cramped Ciutat Vella. Montjuïc also has a darker history: its castle was used by the Madrid government to bombard the city after political disturbances in 1842, and as a political prison up to the Franco era. The first main burst of building on Montjuïc came in the 1920s when it was chosen as the stage for Barcelona's 1929 World Exhibition. The Estadi Olímpic, the Poble Espanyol and some museums all date from this time. Montjuïc got a face-lift and more new buildings for the 1992 Olympics.

Abundant roads and paths, with occasional escalators, plus buses and even a chair lift allow you to visit Montjuïc's sights in any order you choose. Probably the five main attractions – which would make up a full day – are the Poble Espanyol, the Museu Nacional d'Art de Catalunya, the Estadi Olímpic, the Fundació Joan Miró and the views from the castle.

Getting There & Away

You *could* walk from the Ciutat Vella (the foot of La Rambla is 700m from the east end of Montjuïc).

More comfortable is bus No 61, which runs every 15 to 30 minutes until 8.30 pm (later on Sunday and holidays) from Avinguda de la Reina Maria Cristina, just off Plaça d'Espanya at the northern foot of the hill (metro: Espanya). This goes to the Estació Parc Montjuïc funicular and chairlift station via the Poble Espanyol, the Estadi Olímpic and the Fundació Joan Miró. The Bus Turístic (see Getting Around), also makes several stops on Montjuïc. Or you could hop on one of those silly

ags (left to right, Catalunya, Spain, Barcelona), at the Ajuntament, Plaça de Sant Jaume, Barri Gòtic

iving statue on the famous street, La Rambla.

The eagle, spirit of Barcelona

treet smart: Barcelona displays a zest for life, artistic genius and style that few other cities can rival.

Cupola, Palau de la Generalitat, Plaça de Sant Jaume

little road trains, which leave from the same spot as the bus and create havoc for normal traffic trying to get up the same hill!

Another way of saving your legs is the funicular railway up from Paral.lel metro station to Estació Parc Montjuïc. From mid-June to mid-September this goes daily from 11 am to 10 pm; from mid-March to mid-June and mid-September to the end of October (and during the Christmas holiday period), daily from 10.45 am to 8 pm; the rest of the year, only on Saturday, Sunday and holidays from 10.45 am to 8 pm (215/375 ptas one way/return).

From Estació Parc Montjuïc, the Telefèric de Montjuïc chair lift will carry you yet higher, to an upper entrance of the now closed Parc d'Atraccions (Mirador stop) and then the castle (Castell stop). From mid-June to the end of September this operates daily from 11.30 am to 9.30 pm; in October and the Christmas and Setmana Santa periods, daily from 11 am to 2.45 pm and 4 to 7.30 pm; the rest of the year, only on Saturday, Sunday and holidays, from 11 am to 2.45 pm and 4 to 7.30 pm (425/625 ptas adult one way/return).

Another option is the *funicular aereo* or cable car that runs between Miramar and Sant Sebastià (La Barceloneta). See Port Vell earlier in this chapter.

Around Plaça d'Espanya

The approach to Montjuïc from Plaça d'Espanya gives you the full benefit of the landscaping on the hill's north side and allows Montjuïc to unfold before you from the bottom up. On Plaça d'Espanya's north side is the big **Plaça de Braus Les Arenes** bullring, built in 1900 but no longer used for bullfights. The Beatles played here in 1966. Behind the bullring is the **Parc Joan Miró**, created in the 1980s – worth a quick detour mainly for Miró's giant, highly phallic sculpture *Dona i Ocell* (*Woman and Bird*) in the north-west corner. Actually, locals know the park as the Parc de l'Escorxador (Abattoir Park), as that's what once stood here – not surprising given the proximity to the bullring.

Fountains

Avinguda de la Reina Maria Cristina, lined with modern exhibition and congress halls, leads from Plaça d'Espanya towards Montjuïc. On the hill ahead of you is the Palau Nacional de Montjuïc, and stretching up a series of terraces below it are Montjuïc's fountains, starting with the biggest, La Font Màgica. This comes alive with a lights and music show on summer evenings – a unique performance in which the water at times looks like seething fireworks or a mystical cauldron of colour and, depending on the music they choose, it can be quite moving. And it's free! Well worth the effort of getting here. On the last evening of the Festes de la Mercè in September they put on a particularly spectacular display including fireworks. The regular show lasts about 15 minutes and happens from late June to late September, Thursday to Sunday, every half hour from 10 to 11.30 pm.

Museu Nacional d'Art de Catalunya

The Palau Nacional, built in the 1920s for displays in the World Exhibition, today houses the Museu Nacional d'Art de Catalunya. The building itself is quite overwhelming and, although designed by Catalan architects, is interpreted by some as an expression of central Castilian dominance over all Spain, including Catalunya (the World Exhibition was held in 1929, under the dictatorship of Miguel Primo de Rivera).

The museum's two main permanent expositions cover Romanesque and Gothic art. The former is by far the most interesting, and one of the most important concentrations of early medieval art in the world. It consists of frescoes, woodcarvings and painted altar frontals (painted, low-relief wooden panels that were forerunners of the elaborate *retablos* adorning later churches) transferred from country churches across northern Catalunya early in the 20th century. The insides of several churches have been recreated and the frescoes – in some cases fragmentary, in others extraordinarily complete and alive with colour –

have been placed as they were when *in situ*. The Gothic collection includes art from outside Catalunya and is less extensive. Most of the explanations are in Catalan, but you can pick up a catalogue style booklet that at least gives you an idea of what you are looking at.

The first thing you see as you enter the Romanesque section is a remake of the apse of the church of Sant Pere de la Seu d'Urgell, dominated by a beautiful fresco from the early 12th century. In this first hall (Àmbit I) there are coins from the early days of the Comtes de Barcelona, capitals from columns used in Muslim monuments and some finely decorated altar frontals.

In Àmbit III, the frescoes from the church of Sant Pere d'Àger stand out (item No 31). The depiction of Christ on wood from the church of Sant Martí de Tost (No 47 in Àmbit IV) is in a near perfect state of preservation – the vividness of the colours can only make you wonder what some of the more faded, grander frescos must once have looked like. Another good piece is No 49, an altar frontal depicting Christ and the Apostles.

One of the star attractions is the fresco of Mary and the Christ Child from the apse of the church of Santa Maria de Taüll (No 102 in Àmbit VII). In Àmbit X, have a look at No 116, an altar frontal in which the martyrdom of several saints figures among the main themes – here you can see the medieval mind at work, depicting holy individuals who apparently contemplate their own slow deaths with supreme indifference – whether boiling in water, having nails slammed into the head, being sliced up by sword stroke or, my personal favourite, being sawn in half from head to toe!

Moving right along, the Gothic art section reveals clearly the development of painting – from two dimensional and in many respects lifeless didactic painting to a more impassioned depiction of religious figures and events. In these halls you can see Catalan Gothic painting (look out especially for the work of Bernat Martorell in Àmbit XI and Jaume Huguet in Àmbit XII), and that of other Spanish and Mediter-

ranean regions. If the saintly martyrdom theme appeals to you, look out for the depiction of the martyrdom of Santa Llúcia and Sant Vicenç in Àmbit III.

The museum is open Tuesday to Saturday from 10 am to 7 pm (Thursday to 9 pm), Sunday and holidays from 10 am to 2.30 pm. It's closed Monday and on 1 January, 1 May and 25 December (500 ptas, extra for temporary exhibitions).

Poble Espanyol

This 'Spanish Village' in the north-west of Montjuïc – 10 minutes walk from Plaça d'Espanya or the Museu Nacional d'Art de Catalunya – is both a tacky tourist trap and an intriguing scrapbook of Spanish architecture. Built for the Spanish crafts section of the 1929 exhibition, it's composed of plazas and streets lined with surprisingly good copies of characteristic buildings from all the country's regions.

You enter from Avinguda del Marquès de Comillas, beneath a towered medieval gate from Ávila. Inside, to the right, is an information office with free maps. Straight ahead from the gate is a Plaza Mayor, or town square, surrounded with mainly Castilian and Aragonese buildings. Elsewhere you'll find an Andalucían *barrio*, a Basque street, Galician and Catalan quarters and even – at the east end – a Dominican monastery. The buildings house dozens of moderate to expensive restaurants, cafés, bars, craft shops and workshops, and a few souvenir shops.

The Poble Espanyol is open from 9 am daily (Monday to 8 pm; Tuesday to Thursday to 2 am; Friday and Saturday to 4 am; Sunday to midnight). Entry is 950 ptas (1200 combined with Galería Olímpica – see later). Students and children aged seven to 14 pay 525 ptas. After 9 pm on days other than Friday and Saturday, it's free. At night, the restaurants, bars and discos become a lively corner of Barcelona nightlife.

Museu Etnològic & Museu d'Arqueologia

Down the hill east of the Museu Nacional d'Art, these are worth a visit if their subjects interest you, although neither is very excitingly presented and most explanatory material is in Catalan.

The Museu Etnològic (Ethnology Museum) on Passeig de Santa Madrona has extensive displays covering a range of cultures from other continents, and puts on some interesting temporary exhibitions. It's open Tuesday to Sunday from 10 am to 3 pm; Tuesday and Thursday to 7 pm, except in summer (300 ptas).

The Museu d'Arqueologia (Archeology Museum), at the corner of Passeig de Santa Madrona and Passeig de l'Exposició, covers Catalunya and related cultures elsewhere in Spain. Items range from copies of pre-Neanderthal skulls to lovely Carthaginian necklaces and jewel-studded Visigothic crosses. There's good material on the Islas Baleares (rooms X to XIV) and Empúries (Emporion), the Greek and Roman city on the Costa Brava (rooms XV and XVI). Hours are Tuesday to Saturday from 9.30 am to 7 pm, Sunday from 10 am to 2.30 pm (200 ptas, free on Sunday).

Anella Olímpica

The 'Olympic Ring' is the group of sports installations where the main events of the 1992 Olympics were held, on the ridge above the Museu Nacional d'Art de Catalunya. Westernmost is the **Institut Nacional d'Educació Física de Catalunya** (INEFC), a kind of sports university, designed by Ricard Bofill. Past a circular arena, the Plaça d'Europa, with the **Torre Calatrava** communications tower behind it, is the **Piscines Bernat Picornell** building, where the swimming events were held (now open to the public – see the Swimming & Gym section later). Next comes a pleasant little park, the Jardí d'Aclimatació.

Estadi Olímpic The main stadium of the games is open daily, free, from 10 am to 6 pm; enter at the north end. If you saw some of the Olympics on TV, the 65,000 capacity stadium may seem surprisingly small.

So may the Olympic flame-holder rising at the north end, into which a long-range

archer spectacularly deposited a flaming arrow in the opening ceremony. (Well, nearly. The archer actually missed, but the clever organisers had foreseen this possibility. The flame-holder was alive with gas, so the arrow only had to pass within *two metres* of it to set the thing on fire. A gleeful Barcelona TV crew was waiting on the other side for just such a 'failure'.)

The stadium was opened in 1929 but completely restored for 1992. At the south end of the stadium (enter from outside) is the **Galería Olímpica**, which has an exhibition, including videos, on the 1992 games – open Tuesday to Saturday from 10 am to 2 pm and 4 to 6 pm (to 8 pm in summer), Sunday and holidays from 10 am to 2 pm (390 ptas).

West of the stadium is the 17,000 capacity **Palau Sant Jordi**, an indoor sports, concert and exhibition hall opened in 1990 and designed by the Japanese architect Arata Isozaki.

Cementiri del Sud-Ouest

On the hill top south of the Anella Olímpica you can see the top of a huge cemetery, the Cementiri del Sud-Ouest or Cementiri Nou, which extends right down the south side of the hill. Opened in 1883, it's an odd combination of elaborate architect-designed tombs for rich families and small niches for the rest. It includes the graves of numerous Catalan artists and politicians.

Fundació Joan Miró

Barcelona's gallery for the greatest Catalan artist of the 20th century, Joan Miró (1893-1983), is 400m east, downhill, from the Estadi Olímpic. Miró himself established the foundation in 1971. Its light-filled buildings were designed by his close friend and architect Josep Lluís Sert, who also built Miró's Mallorca studios.

This, the greatest single collection of the artist's work, comprises around 300 of his paintings, 153 sculptures, some textiles and more than 7000 drawings spanning his entire life, of which only a part is ever on display. The exhibits tend to concentrate on

Miró's more settled last 20 years, but there are some important exceptions. The ground floor Sala (room) Joan Prats shows the younger Miró moving away, under surrealist influence, from his *relative* realism (for instance his 1917 painting of the *Ermita de Sant Joan d'Horta*), then starting to work toward his own recognisable style. This section also includes the 1939-44 Barcelona series of tortured lithographs, Miró's comment on the Spanish Civil War.

The Sala Pilar Juncosa (named after his wife), upstairs, also displays works from the 1930s and 40s. After this room, the bulk of what you see is from his latter years – mostly paintings, but some sculpture (especially some playful items on the outdoor terrace). While some of the paintings are classics of the style for which he is best known, with an almost childlike delight in primary colours, in the 1970s he seems to have opted for an exploration of more muted greens, browns and black.

Another interesting section is devoted to the 'Miró Papers', which include many preparatory drawings and sketches, some on bits of newspaper or cigarette packets. *A Joan Miró* is a collection of work by other contemporary artists, donated in tribute to Miró.

The Fundació also has a contemporary art library open to the public, a good specialist art bookshop and a café; and it stages exhibitions and recitals of contemporary art and music. It's open Tuesday to Saturday from 10 am to 7 pm (an hour longer in summer); Thursday to 9.30 pm; Sunday and holidays from 10 am to 2.30 pm (700 ptas, 400 for students).

Castell de Montjuïc & Around

The south-east of Montjuïc is dominated by the big former Parc d'Atraccions funfair (closed in 1998) and the Castell (castle) de Montjuïc on the hilltop above it. Near the bottom of the Parc d'Atraccions are the Estació Parc Montjuïc funicular/telefèric station and the ornamental **Jardins de Mossèn Cinto**. What will become of the funfair is not yet clear, although some suggest it will be added to a planned botanic

garden project aimed at returning some of the green to Montjuïc that has slowly been stripped away over the years (especially for the Olympics).

From the **Jardins del Mirador** opposite the Mirador telefèric station there are fine views over the port of Barcelona.

The Castell de Montjuïc dates in its present form from the late 17th and 18th centuries. For most of its existence it has been used to watch over the city and as a political prison and killing ground. Anarchists were executed here around the turn of the century, fascists during the civil war and Republicans after it – most notoriously Lluís Companys in 1940. The army finally handed it over to the city in 1960. The castle is surrounded by a network of ditches and walls, and today houses the **Museu Militar** with a section on Catalan military history, plus old weapons, uniforms, maps, castle models and so on (open daily except Monday from 9.30 am to 8 pm). Entry to the museum is 200 ptas. Best of all are the excellent views from the castle area of the port and city below.

Towards the foot of this part of Montjuïc, above the thundering traffic of the main road to Tarragona, the **Jardins de Costa i Llobera** have a good collection of tropical and desert plants; the gardens are open from 10 am to sunset.

PARC GÜELL

North of Gràcia and about 4km from Plaça de Catalunya, Parc Güell is where Gaudí turned his hand to landscape gardening. It's a strange, enchanting place where his passion for natural forms really took flight – to the point where the artificial almost seems more natural than the natural.

The simplest way to Parc Güell is to take the metro to Lesseps, then walk 10 to 15 minutes: follow the signs north-east along Travessera de Dalt then left up Carrer de Larrard, which brings you out almost at the park's two Hansel and Gretel-style gatehouses on Carrer d'Olot. The park is open daily from 9 am: in June to September to 9 pm, April, May and October to 8 pm,

March and November to 7 pm, other months to 6 pm (free). It's extremely popular, and its quaint nooks and crannies are irresistible to photographers – who on busy days have trouble keeping out of each other's pictures.

Parc Güell originated in 1900 when Count Eusebi Güell bought a tree-covered hillside (then outside Barcelona) and hired Gaudí to create a miniature garden city of houses for the wealthy, in landscaped grounds. The project was a commercial flop and was abandoned in 1914 – but not before Gaudí had created 3km of roads and walks, steps and a plaza in his inimitable manner, plus the two gatehouses. In 1922 the city bought the estate for use as a public park.

The steps up from the entrance, guarded by a mosaic dragon/lizard, lead to the **Sala Hipóstila**, a forest of 84 stone columns (some of them leaning), intended as a market. To the left from here curves a gallery whose twisted stonework columns and roof give the effect of a cloister beneath tree roots – a motif repeated in several places in the park. On top of the Sala Hipóstila is a broad open space whose centrepiece is the **Banc de Trenadís**, a tiled bench curving sinuously round its entire perimeter.

The spired house to the right is the **Casa Museu Gaudí**, where Gaudí lived for most of his last 20 years (1906-26). It contains furniture by him and other memorabilia. It's open April to August daily 10 am to 8 pm; the rest of the year Sunday to Friday from 10 am to 2 pm and 4 to 6 pm (300 ptas).

Much of the park is still wooded but full of pathways. The best views are from the cross-topped **Turo del Calvari** in the southwest corner.

TIBIDABO

Tibidabo (542m) is the highest hill in the wooded range that forms the backdrop to Barcelona. It's a good place for some fresh air (it's often a few degrees cooler than down in the city) and, if the air's clear, views over the city and inland as far as Montserrat. Tibidabo gets its name from the devil, who, trying to tempt Christ, took him to a high place and said, in the Latin version: *'Haec omnia tibi dabo si cadens adoraberis me'* ('All this I will give you if you will fall down and worship me').

Getting There & Away

You'll have lots of fun if you go to Tibidabo the traditional way. First, get an FGC train to Avinguda de Tibidabo from Catalunya station on Plaça de Catalunya – a 10 minute ride for 140 ptas. Outside Avinguda de Tibidabo station, hop on the *tramvia blau*, Barcelona's last surviving tram, which runs up between fancy turn-of-the century mansions to Plaça del Doctor Andreu (225 ptas, 350 return). The tram runs daily in summer, and on Saturday, Sunday and holidays the rest of the year, every 15 or 30 minutes from 10 am to 9.30 pm.On other days a bus (140 ptas) serves the route at similar times. From Plaça del Doctor Andreu the Tibidabo funicular railway climbs through the woods to Plaça de Tibidabo at the top of the hill (300 ptas, 400 return), every 15 to 30 minutes from 7.15 am to 9.45 pm, daily. If you're feeling active, you can walk up or down through the woods instead. The funicular only operates when the Parc d'Atraccions is open.

The cheaper alternative is bus No T2, the 'Tibibús', from Plaça de Catalunya to Plaça de Tibidabo (225 ptas). This runs on Saturday, Sunday and holidays year-round, every 30 minutes from 10.30 am. From late June to early September it runs Monday to Friday too, every hour from 10.30 am. The last bus down leaves Tibidabo 30 minutes after the Parc d'Atraccions closes.

Temple del Sagrat Cor

The Church of the Sacred Heart, looming above the top funicular station, is meant to be Barcelona's answer to Paris' Sacré Coeur. It's certainly equally visible, and even more vilified by aesthetes (perhaps with good reason). It's actually two churches, one on top of the other. The top one is surmounted by a giant Christ and has a lift to the roof (100 ptas). Visiting times to the church are 8 am to 7 pm daily.

Parc d'Atraccions

The reason most Barcelonins come up to Tibidabo (☎ 93 211 79 42) is for some thrills (but hopefully no spills) in this funfair, close to the top funicular station. Entry is 700 ptas plus extra for each ride, or 2400 ptas with access to all rides – including seven minutes in the Hotel Krueger, an *hospedaje* of horrors inhabited by actors playing out their Dracula, Hannibal Lecter and other fantasies. The funfair's opening times change with the season, so check with a tourist office: in summer it's usually open daily until late at night; in winter it may open on Saturday, Sunday and holidays only, from about noon to 7 pm.

Torre de Collserola

From the top of the funicular it's a few minutes walk west to the 288m Torre de Collserola telecommunications tower, built in 1990-92. The external glass lift to the visitors' observation area, 115m up, is as hair-raising as anything at the Parc d'Atraccions. From the top they say you can see for 70km on a clear day. It re-opened in the summer of 1998 for the first time in many years and it was not clear how long this might last (call ☎ 93 406 93 54 for info). At the time of writing it was open Wednesday to Friday from 11 am to 2.30 pm and 3.30 to 8 pm; weekends from 11 am to 8 pm (500 ptas).

Museu de la Ciencia

This is one of those interactive science museums where you get to twiddle knobs and press buttons and so discover how the world around you works. There is also a planetarium. This could be a good one for young kids, but it's awkwardly placed at Carrer de Teodor Roviralta 55 near the Ronda de Dalt. Opening times are Tuesday to Sunday from 10 am to 8 pm (500 ptas, free on the first Sunday of the month). Bus No 60 stops close by.

CAMP NOU

Among Barcelona's most visited museums – hard on the heels of the Museu Picasso – comes the Museu del Futbol Club Barcelona at the club's giant Camp Nou (sometimes also known as Nou Camp) stadium, 3.5km west of Plaça de Catalunya (metro: Collblanc). Barça, as it's known, is one of Europe's top football clubs, having carried off the Spanish championship 15 times and the European Cup more than once. Barça has also been described as Catalunya's unarmed army: the club was banned for a while in the 1920s because the Spanish government feared its potential for focusing Catalan nationalism, and today its annual matches with Real Madrid act as a modern safety valve for the age old rivalry between Catalunya and Castilla. The many world greats who have worn Barça's blue and red stripes include Johann Cruyff and Diego Maradona.

Camp Nou, built in the 1950s and enlarged for the 1982 World Cup, is one of the world's biggest stadiums, holding 120,000 people, and the club has a world record membership of 110,000. Soccer fans who can't get to a game (see Entertainment) should find the museum – on the Carrer d'Aristides Maillol side of the stadium – worthwhile. The best bits are the photo section, the goal videos, and the views out over the stadium. Among the quirkier paraphernalia are old sports board games, a 19th century leather football, the life-size diorama of old time dressing rooms, posters and magazines from down the century and the *futbolín* (table soccer) collection.

It's open Monday to Saturday (Tuesday to Saturday from October to March) from 10 am to 1 pm and 3 to 6.30 pm (475 ptas).

PEDRALBES

This is a wealthy residential area north of Camp Nou.

Palau Reial

Close to Palau Reial metro station, across Avinguda Diagonal from the main campus of the Universitat de Barcelona, is the entrance to the **Parc del Palau Reial**, a verdant park open daily. In the park is the Palau Reial de Pedralbes, an early 20th century building that belonged to the family of

Eusebi Güell (Gaudí's patron) until they handed it over to the city in 1926 to serve as a royal residence – among its guests have been king Alfonso XIII, the president of Catalunya and General Franco.

Today it houses the **Museu de Ceràmica**, with a good collection of Spanish ceramics from the 13th to 19th centuries including work by Picasso and Miró. Spain inherited from the Muslims, and then further refined, a strong tradition in ceramics – here you can compare some exquisite work (tiles, porcelain tableware and the like) from some of the greatest centres of pottery production across Spain, including Talavera de la Reina in Castilla, Manises and Paterna in Valencia, and Teruel in Aragón. Upstairs is a display of fanciful modern ceramics from this century – here they have ceased to be a tool with aesthetic value and are purely decorative.

Across the corridor, the **Museu de les Arts Decoratives** brings together an eclectic assortment of furnishings, ornaments, and knick-knacks dating as far back as the Romanesque period (early Middle Ages). The plush and somewhat stuffy elegance of Empire and Isabelline style divans can be neatly compared with some of the more tasteless ideas to emerge on the subject of seating in the 1970s.

Both museums are open Tuesday to Sunday from 10 am to 3 pm (400 ptas each, 700 ptas for both).

Over by Avinguda de Pedralbes are the Gaudí-designed stables and porter's lodge for the **Finca Güell**, as the Güell estate here was called. They were done in the mid-1880s, when Gaudí was strongly impressed by Islamic architecture. They can only be visited as part of a tour (see the Getting Around chapter), although there is nothing to stop you admiring Gaudí's wrought iron dragon gate from the outside.

Museu-Monestir de Pedralbes

This peaceful old convent, now a museum of monastic life also housing part of the Thyssen-Bornemisza art collection, stands at the top of Avinguda de Pedralbes, 700m from Finca Güell. The easiest way here, if you are not walking up from Finca Güell, is to get the suburban FGC train to Reina Elisenda (the end of the line) from Catalunya station and then either walk (about 10 minutes) or pick up one of the buses running along Passeig de la Reina Elisenda de Montcada (such as No 22, 64 & 75).

The convent, founded in 1326, still houses a community of nuns who inhabit separate closed quarters. The museum entrance is on Plaça del Monestir, a divinely quiet corner of Barcelona; opening hours are Tuesday to Sunday from 10 am to 2 pm (700 ptas, 400 only for either the monastery *or* the Thyssen-Bornemisza collection).

The architectural highlight is the large, elegant, three-storey cloister, a jewel of Catalan Gothic architecture built in the early 14th century. You will be gently persuaded to head around it to your right, and the first chapel you come across is the Capella de Sant Miquel, whose murals were done in 1346 by Ferrer Bassá, one of Catalunya's earliest documented painters.

As you head around the cloister, you can peer into a restored refectory, a kitchen, stables, stores and a reconstruction of the old infirmary – all giving a good idea of convent life. Perhaps the hardest thing to imagine is spending your days in the cells on the ground and first floors. Here the devout nuns would spend much of their days in prayer and devotional reading.

The Col.lecció Thyssen-Bornemisza (entry from the ground floor), quartered in the (painstakingly restored) one-time dormitories of the nuns and the Saló Principal, is part of a wide-ranging art collection acquired by Spain in 1993. Most of it went to the Museo Thyssen-Bornemisza in Madrid; what's here is mainly religious work by European masters including Canaletto, Titian, Tintoretto, Rubens, Zurbarán and Velázquez. In total, 72 paintings and eight sculptures are on display. Together with the Madrid collection, they represent an extraordinarily eclectic approach to art procurement (if you get a chance to go to Madrid, the collection there, virtually across the road from El Prado, is a must). The sculptures and 17 paintings were produced by mostly anonymous medieval Italian artists. Next come some 20 pieces belonging to the early Renaissance period in Germany (including Cranach the Elder), accompanied by another 16 from northern Italy stretching into the 16th century. The collection is capped by a dozen late baroque works from the Venetian school.

THE OUTSKIRTS
Colònia Güell

Apart from La Sagrada Família, the last grand project Gaudí would turn his hand to was the creation of a kind of Utopian workers' complex outside Barcelona at Santa Coloma de Cervellò. His main role was to erect the colony's church – workers' housing and the local co-op were in the hands of other architects. He first thought about it in 1898, but work on the church's crypt started in 1908. It proceeded for eight years, at which point interest in the whole idea fizzled. The crypt today still serves as a working church.

This structure is an important part of Gaudí's oeuvre, little visited by tourists and yet a key to understanding what the master had in mind for his magnum opus La Sagrada Família. The mostly brick-clad columns that support the ribbed vaults are inclined in much the way you might expect trees in a forest to lean at all angles (reminiscent also of Parc Güell, which Gaudí was working on at much the same time), but Gaudí had worked out the angles in such a way that their load would be transmitted from the brick-ribbed vaulting in the ceiling to the earth without the help of extra buttressing. Similar thinking lay behind his plans for La Sagrada Família, whose final Gothic inspired structure would tower above anything ever done in the Middle Ages but not require so much as one buttress to hold it all up. Down to the wavy design of the pews, Gaudí's hand is visible (you can see an example of the seating in the Museu Nacional d'Art Modern de Catalunya in the Parc de la Ciutadella too).

And the primary colours in the curvaceous plant-shaped stained-glass windows are another reminder of the era in which the crypt was built.

The easiest way to get there is to take an FGC train (No S3; 140 ptas) from Plaça d'Espanya and get off at Molí Nou station, the last stop (train No S33 leaves about hourly, usually at a quarter past the hour, for Santa Coloma station, one further on). When you reach the station, exit by the underpass and turn right (north) up the BV-2002 road towards Santa Coloma de Cervelló. It's a 15-minute walk (the first five minutes on this traffic-choked road will be equivalent to your year's air pollution intake). You will walk along the walls of a light industrial complex called Recinto Colonia Güell, at the corner of which you turn left – follow this road as it veers to the right and you enter the small settlement – some of the houses and shops are unmistakable leftovers of the modernistas' planned workers' village. Keep heading straight uphill to reach the crypt.

Alternatively, you could get off the train one stop earlier at Sant Boi de Llobregat and catch the L76 bus right to Santa Coloma, but this will end up taking longer.

The Colònia Güell is open daily from 10 am to 1.15 pm and 4 to 6 pm, mornings only on Thursdays and holidays (100 ptas, free during Mass). If in doubt call ahead on ☎ 93 640 29 36.

Sant Cugat del Vallès

When the marauding Muslims tramped through the one-time Roman encampment turned Visigothic monastery of Sant Cugat del Vallès in the 8th century, they razed the lot to the ground. These things happen, so after the Christians got back in the saddle, work on a new monastic complex was stoically begun. What you see today is a combination of Romanesque and Gothic, in other words Transitional buildings. The lower floor of the cloister is a fine demonstration of Romanesque architecture and decoration and the principal reason for making the effort to come here (Sant Cugat may have been a favourite summer getaway for Barcelonins at the turn of the 19th century, but those days are long gone). The Gothic church and upper storey of the cloister also repay some quiet contemplation. The monastery is open daily from 9 am to noon and 4 to 8 pm.

To get here, take the FGC train from Plaça de Catalunya (lines S1, S2, S5 or S55) to Sant Cugat del Vallès (265 ptas; 30 minutes). From there you could wait for a local circle line bus, but the walk is hardly taxing. Head left out of the station along Avinguda d'Alfonso Sala Conde de Egara and turn right down Carrer de Ruis i Taulet, followed by a left into Carrer de Santiago Rusiñol, which leads to the monastery.

ACTIVITIES

For information on where you can practise sports in Barcelona, try the Servei d'Informació Esportiva (☎ 93 402 30 00), Avinguda de l'Estadi 30-40 (in the same complex as the Piscines Bernat Picornell on Montjuïc). They are open weekdays from 8.30 am to 3 pm.

Swimming & Gym

The Olympic pool on Montjuïc, the Piscines Bernat Picornell (☎ 93 423 40 41), is open to the public daily from 7 am until midnight Monday to Friday, until 9 pm Saturday, and 7.30 am to 2.30 pm Sunday (1200 ptas which includes use of the good gym inside). Access to the outdoor pool alone costs 650 ptas in summer *only*. It opens Monday to Saturday from 10 am to 6 pm (9 am to 9 pm in summer) and on Sundays 10 am to 2 pm (9 am to 8 pm). If you are about for any length of time and want regular access to the pool, gym and other facilities, think about taking out membership. You need to have a local bank account, as the monthly charge is made by direct debit (*domiciliació bancària*). You pay 3800 ptas to join and the same each month.

The nearby open-air Piscina Municipal de Montjuïc, used for diving and water polo in the 1992 games, has been closed to the public since 1996, although local youngsters regularly break in to beat the heat.

They are contemptuous of the lone guard who can do little more than watch helplessly and threaten to call the police.

Another pool option for lap swimmers are the Banys Sant Sebastià (☎ 93 221 00 10), down by La Barceloneta beach. The main (indoor) pool is open daily from 7 am to 11 pm, Sunday from 8 am to 5 pm (1000 ptas, which includes use of the gym). You can also become a member under conditions similar to those already outlined.

Other Sports

Bowling Bowling Barcelona (☎ 93 330 50 48), Carrer de Sabino Arana 6 (map 1; metro: Maria Cristina), is the place to come if you like launching round objects at pins.

Squash You can sweat it out on the court at a couple of places in Barcelona. Try the Poliesportiu Perill (☎ 93 459 44 30) at Carrer de Perill 16-22 (map 2; metro: Diagonal).

Table Tennis Ping Pong habitués can find out where the handiest place to play is by calling the Federació Catalana de Tennis de Taula (☎ 93 280 03 00). The Poliesportiu Municipal l'Espanya Industrial next to the so-called park of the same name in Sants (map 3; metro: Sants-Estació) has tables.

Tennis For more conventional tennis, there are several options in Barcelona. About the most pleasant and relatively convenient is the Tennis Municipal Pompeia (☎ 93 423 97 47), Avinguda del Marques de Comillas 29-41, on Montjuïc (map 6).

COURSES

The CIAJ youth information service – Centre d'Informació i Assessorament per a Joves (☎ 93 402 78 00) – at Carrer de Ferran 32 (map 5) in the Barri Gòtic (open Monday to Friday from 10 am to 2 pm and 4 to 8 pm) has information on various courses available throughout the city.

Language Courses

Some of the best-value Spanish language courses are offered by the Universitat de

Barcelona, which runs intensive courses (40 hours tuition over periods ranging from two weeks to a month; 45,000 ptas) all year. Longer Spanish courses, and courses in Catalan, are also available. For more information you can ask at the university's Informació office at Gran Via de les Corts Catalanes 585 (metro: Universitat), open Monday to Friday from 9 am to 1 pm and 4 to 8 pm, or (for Spanish) its Instituto de Estudios Hispánicos (☎ 93 403 55 19; fax 93 403 54 33), or (for Catalan) its Servei de Llengua Catalana (☎ 93 403 54 77; fax 93 403 54 78) – both in the same building as Informació.

The university run Escola Oficial d'Idiomes de Barcelona (☎ 93 329 24 58; fax 93 441 48 33) at Avinguda de les Drassanes s/n (metro: Drassanes) is another place offering economical 80-hour summer Spanish courses, as well as longer part-time courses in Spanish and Catalan.

International House (☎ 93 268 45 11; fax 93 268 02 39; spanish@bcn.ihes.com) is at Carrer de Trafalgar 14. Intensive courses start at 48,000 ptas a week. They have another branch at Avinguda Diagonal 612 (☎ 93 202 26 00) and can organise ccommodation with families or in pensiones.

Ads for courses and private tuition are posted on the noticeboard at the abovementioned university building, Come In bookshop at Carrer de Provença 203, and the British Council.

Other Courses

The best place to start looking for information on courses of any type in Barcelona is at the CIAJ (see under Courses, earlier). It has piles of files listing courses on everything from Deutsch to Dance. A couple of examples follow, but CIAJ is really where you need to enquire. Bear in mind that most available courses are aimed at residents rather than people passing through. Your Spanish, and preferably Catalan, would need to be in working order.

La Cafetera de l'Esbart Català de Dansaires
(☎ 93 303 10 01, Passatge del Crèdit 8). This group organises courses in Catalan dance for anyone from beginners to advanced, and is of special interest to professionals. Usually the sessions are held on Monday.

Institut del Teatre
(☎ 93 268 20 78, Carrer de Sant Pere més baix 7). The institute offers serious courses in various aspects of theatre – for long termers with a view to breaking into theatre.

Centre Cívic Drassanes
(☎ 93 441 22 80, Carrer Nou de la Rambla 43). This civic centre puts on all sorts of courses and workshops ranging from Didgeridoo to Windows 98.

Barcelona Centre d'Imatge
(☎ 93 311 92 73, Carrer de Pons i Gallarza 25). Various levels offered in photography

Àrea Espai de Dança i Creació
(☎ 93 210 78 50, Carrer d'Alegre de Dalt 55). One of the best spots in town to learn contemporary dance – some English is spoken

Places to Stay

Barcelona attracts a growing number of tourists with every passing year, so at times it can get a little squeezy. The peak (high season) periods are Setmana Santa (Easter week) summer (especially July-August), Christmas and New Year, and finding a room then can be a pain. Local tourism authorities happily claim an average year-round room-occupation rate of around 80%. The effect is that, with a little searching, you'll usually soon find something in your budget range – but you will probably need a little patience. To make the task easier, it is of course better to arrive in the morning – checkout time in most places is around midday.

You will find virtually every type of accommodation: party-time 'youth hostels' (and a handful of the more decorous HI version too); hidden-away pensiones; good mid-range hostales and hotels with character (faded or spruced up); as well as the usual five-star crowd – some of these with a good deal of charm, although others of the this-could-be-anywhere-in-the-world variety.

Seasons & Reservations

Prices at any type of accommodation may vary with the season. Some places have separate price structures for the high season (temporada alta), mid-season (temporada media) or the low season (temporada baja), all usually displayed on a notice in reception or close by. (Hoteliers are not actually bound by these displayed prices. They are free to charge less, which they quite often do, or more, which happens fairly rarely.)

The prices for accommodation in this book are a guide only. Always check room charges before putting your bags down.

Taxes

Virtually all accommodation prices are subject to IVA, the Spanish version of value-added tax, which is 7%. This is often included in the quoted price at cheaper places, but less often at more expensive ones.

To check, ask: '¿Está incluido el IVA?' ('Is IVA included?'). In some cases you will only be charged the IVA if you ask for a receipt.

PLACES TO STAY – BUDGET
Camping

The nearest camp site is the big **Cala Gogó** (☎/fax 93 379 46 00), 9km south-west of the centre at Carretera de la Platja s/n, El Prat de Llobregat, near the airport. It's open from February to November and charges 1900 ptas per site plus 580 ptas per person. You can get there by bus No 65 from Plaça d'Espanya, or by suburban train from Plaça de Catalunya to El Prat, then a 'Prat Playa' bus.

There are some better – but still vast – sites a few kilometres fartherout, to the south-west on the coastal C-246 road, the Autovía de Castelldefels (not the A-16 autopista heading for Sitges, and not the C-245 through central Viladecans and Gavà). All are reachable by bus No L95 from the corner of Ronda de la Universitat and Rambla de Catalunya. They include (with prices for a car, a tent and two adults):

El Toro Bravo (☎ 93 637 34 62, Carretera C-246, Km 11, Viladecans); open all year; a tad shabby; 2800 ptas

Filipinas (☎ 93 658 28 95, Carretera C-246, Km 12, Viladecans); open all year; one of the best for value for money; 2800 ptas

La Ballena Alegre (☎/fax 93 658 05 04, Carretera C-246, Km 12.4, Viladecans); open Easter to end of September; also good; 3800 ptas

La Tortuga Ligera (☎ 93 633 06 42, Avenida Europa 69, Gavà); open all year except December; 2750 ptas

Albatros (☎ 93 633 06 95, Carretera C-246, Km 15, Gavà); open May to September; 3100 ptas

Eleven kilometres north-east of the city, **Camping Masnou** (☎ 93 555 15 03, Carretera N-II, Km 639.8, El Masnou) is open all year. It's 200m from El Masnou train station (reached by suburban rodalies/cercanías trains from Catalunya station on

Plaça de Catalunya) and charges 2560 ptas for a car, tent and two adults.

Youth & Backpacker Hostels

Barcelona has four HI hostels and several non-HI hostels. All require you to rent sheets (150 to 350 ptas) If you don't have your own sheets or a sleeping bag, and some lock their gates in the early hours so aren't suitable if you plan to partyon late. Except at the Kabul, which doesn't take bookings, it's advisable to call ahead in summer.

The non-HI *Youth Hostel Kabul (map 6, ☎ 93 318 51 90, fax 93 301 40 34, Plaça Reial 17)* is in the Barri Gòtic. It's a rough and ready place but does have, as its leaflets say, a 'great party atmosphere' and no curfew. If sleep is your priority, you're better off somewhere else. The price is 1700 ptas, plus 1000 ptas key deposit. Security is not great but safes are available for valuables. There's room for about 150 people in bare and basic bunk rooms holding up to 10 each (keep an eye on your belongings). There's a small restaurant, and washing machines. In July and August you should be there by 10 am to get a place.

The biggest and most comfortable hostel is the 183-place *Alberg Mare de Déu de Montserrat (map 1, ☎ 93 210 51 51, fax 93 210 07 98, Passeig Mare de Déu del Coll 41-51)*. It's 4km north of the centre, a 10-minute walk from Vallcarca metro or a 20-minute ride from Plaça de Catalunya on bus No 28, which stops almost outside the gate (the last bus leaves Plaça de Catalunya at 1.30 am). The main building is a former private mansion with a wonderful mudéjar-style lobby. Most rooms sleep six. The main problem here is that they prefer you to stay no more than three days so others can enjoy the place too. A hostel card is needed: if you're under 25 or have an ISIC card, B&B is 1700 ptas; otherwise it's 2275 ptas. The hostel is in HI's IBN. You can also book through the central booking service of Catalunya's official youth hostels organisation, the Xarxa d'Albergs de Joventut (☎ 93 483 83 63, fax 93 483 83 50). (Note: the other Barcelona hostels, even the HI ones, are not in the Xarxa.)

Alberg Juvenil Palau (map 6, ☎ 93 412 50 80, Carrer del Palau 6) in the Barri Gòtic (metro: Liceu) has a friendly atmosphere and just 40 places in separate-sex bunk rooms. Cost is 1300 ptas, including breakfast. There's a kitchen and a good common room-cum-eating room.

Hostal de Joves (map 1, ☎ 93 300 31 04, Passeig de Pujades 29) faces the north end of Parc de la Ciutadella, a few minutes walk from the Estació de França and Arc de Triomf metro station. It has 68 bunk places in small dorms, and a kitchen with a sociable dining area. The price – 1500 ptas including breakfast – is the same for all. The hostel closes at 2 am on Friday and Saturday nights, 1 am other nights.

Abba Youth Hostel (map 6, ☎ 93 319 45 45, Passeig de Colom 9) offers beds in separate-sex dorms for 1300 ptas, including breakfast. It's handy to the Barri Gòtic and waterfront, but not to the metro.

Another handy but fairly spartan place off Carrer de la Boqueria is the *Albergue Arco (map 6, ☎ 93 301 31 93, Carrer de l'Arc de Santa Eulàlia 1)*. It is open 24 hours a day and a bed in a separate-sex dorm costs 1400 ptas. You have use of a washing machine (300 ptas a load) and a microwave. It is particularly popular with Japanese guests.

Alberg Pere Tarrès (map 1, ☎ 93 410 23 09, fax 93 419 62 68, Carrer de Numància 149), 1km north of Estació Sants and 600m from Les Corts and Maria Cristina metro stations, has 90 places in bare dorms of four to eight bunks. B&B costs from 1500 to 2000 ptas, depending on age and whether you have a hostel card. The building has been renovated and is in good nick, with courtyard, cooking and washing facilities. The gates are shut from 10 am to 4 pm and from 11.30 pm to 8.30 am (they're opened briefly to let guests in at 2 am).

The small and distant *Alberg Studio (map 1, ☎ 93 205 09 61, fax 93 205 09 00, Carrer de la Duquessa d'Orleans 58)*, off Passeig de la Reina Elisenda de Montcada, 4km north-west of Plaça de Catalunya, is open only from 1 July to 30 September, and has about 40 places. It stays open 24 hours and charges 1500 ptas. FGC trains run to nearby Reina Elisenda station from Catalunya station.

Hostales, Pensiones & Hotels

In the busier periods (see earlier) it's worth ringing ahead to book at the smaller places. Many of these adjust prices according to demand and, if you intend to stay several days, some may make a small reduction (it's worth asking). Some charge 100 to 350 ptas extra for a shower if you don't take a room with its own. Many places have three or four-bed rooms that are little dearer than a double. Bathrooms in these places are generally in the corridor and shared.

The prices below are for high season. The more expensive places can drop prices considerably in off season, while the smaller pensiones hardly vary in price at all.

La Rambla Little *Pensión Noya (map 6, ☎ 93 301 48 31, Rambla de Canaletes 133)*, at the top of La Rambla, above Restaurante Nuria, has 15 smallish but clean rooms at 2200/4500 ptas for singles/doubles in high season. Front rooms overlooking La Rambla can be noisy (metro: Catalunya).

Down near the bottom of La Rambla at No 4, the friendly *Hostal Marítima (map 6, ☎ 93 302 31 52)* is a time-honoured back-packers' lodging with a dozen worn but adequate rooms. You pay a flat 2000 ptas per person. The entrance is on Passatge de la Banca leading to the Museu de Cera (metro: Drassanes).

Barri Gòtic This central, atmospheric area has many of the better budget places. A few of those listed below are not, strictly speaking, in the Barri Gòtic but within a couple of minutes walk of it.

Pensión Estal (map 6, ☎ 93 302 26 18, Carrer de Santa Anna 27) is a friendly place on a quiet street with a mixed bag of rooms going for 2500/4000 ptas with shared bathroom. Some of the doubles have balconies and own bath (5500 ptas) but singles tend to be dingy (metro: Catalunya).

Hostal Lausanne (map 6, ☎ 93 302 11 39, Avinguda del Portal de l'Àngel 24) is a friendly, helpful place with good security. Popularity has made prices sneak up, but on balance this remains a good place. Clean rooms without bath cost 3500/4900 ptas. The doubles with bath are overpriced now at 8900 ptas (metro: Catalunya).

Hostal Fontanella (map 6, ☎/fax 93 317 59 43, Via Laietana 71) is a friendly, immaculate place, with 10 rooms costing 2900/5000 ptas or 4200/6600 ptas with bathroom (metro: Urquinaona).

Pensión-Hostal Fina (map 6, ☎ 93 317 97 87, Carrer de la Portaferrissa 11), in another quiet street, has 28 plain, clean rooms for 2750/3750 ptas, or 4750 ptas for a double with bath (metro: Catalunya or Liceu). *Hostal-Residencia Rembrandt (map 5, ☎/fax 93 318 10 11)*, at No 23, has good rooms at 2700/4000 ptas, or 3000/5000 ptas with shower. Doubles with bathroom cost 5500 ptas (metro: Catalunya or Liceu).

Hostal Paris (map 6, ☎/fax 93 301 37 85, Carrer del Cardenal Casañas 4) has 42 mostly large rooms for 3000/4000 ptas, or 4000/5800 ptas with bathroom. Prices can go down a couple of hundred ptas at quiet times. There's also a TV room (metro: Liceu).

Hostal Galerias Maldà (map 6, ☎ 93 317 30 02, Carrer del Pi 5), upstairs in the arcade, is a rambling family house with 21 rooms, some of them really big. It's one of the cheapest places in town, at 1500/3000 ptas, and has one great single set in a kind of tower for 1000 ptas (metro: Liceu).

Pensión Dalí (map 6, ☎/fax 93 318 55 80, Carrer de la Boqueria 12), has doubles for up to 4800/3700 ptas with/without loo and shower. There are large sitting and TV rooms (metro: Liceu). *Pensión Europa (map 6, ☎ 93 318 76 20)*, at No 18, has some rather small and bare singles for 2000 ptas and better doubles with bath for 4800 ptas. There's a big sitting room with TV (metro: Liceu).

Pensión Bienestar (map 6, ☎ 93 318 72 83, Carrer d'En Quintana 3), has clean, ordinary rooms, at 1300/2400 or 1500/2600 ptas depending on size (metro: Liceu).

Pensió Colom 3 (map 6, ☎ 93 318 06 31,

Carrer de Colom 3), almost on Plaça Reial, has converted into an unofficial basic youth hostel with dorm beds for 1400 ptas. They have a few pool tables (metro: Liceu). A couple of doors up, *Pension Villanueva (map 5, ☎ 91 301 50 84, Plaça Reial 2)*, is cheap and quiet, but involves a climb up three flights of stairs. At their most expensive, doubles with bathroom are 4500 ptas.

Hostal Levante (map 6, ☎ 93 317 95 65, Baixada de Sant Miquel 2), off Plaça de Sant Miquel, is a large, clean hostel, popular among travellers, charging up to 2500/4000 ptas, or 5000 ptas for doubles with bath (metro: Liceu).

Casa Huéspedes Mari-Luz (map 6, ☎ 93 317 34 63, Carrer del Palau 4) has friendly management, a sociable atmosphere, and room for 52 people in doubles and dorms. The dorms are a little oppressive, but the doubles are fine at 3800 ptas (double bed) and 4800 ptas (two beds) (metro: Liceu or Jaume I).

Pensión Alamar (map 6, ☎ 93 302 50 12, Carrer de la Comtessa de Sobradiel 1), has 13 rooms, some with balcony, for 1700/3500 ptas. It's cheap and basic, but you can use the kitchen and washing machine too (metro: Liceu).

Pensión Fernando (map 6, ☎ 93 301 79 93, Carrer de l'Arc del Remedio 4), is on Carrer de Ferran, in spite of the address. It is one of several places half-heartedly masquerading as a youth hostel. The singles without bath are pokey but cheap at 2000 ptas, while the doubles – a little more spacious and with bath – cost 5000 ptas.

Hostal Layetana (map 6, ☎ 93 319 20 12, Plaça de Ramon Berenguer El Gran 2) is friendly and well kept, with 20 good sized rooms at 2200/3500 ptas, or 4900 ptas for doubles with bathroom (metro: Jaume I).

A good little deal, smack in the heart of the Call, (the old Jewish quarter), is *Hotel Call (map 6, ☎ 93 301 34 86, Carrer de l'Arc de Sant Ramon del Call 4)*. The rooms are comfortable and all have bath and phone. They cost 3425/4815 ptas. This place tends to fill quickly, so show up before midday to have a hope of getting in (metro: Liceu).

Hotel Rey Don Jaime I (map 6, ☎ 93 310 62 08, Carrer de Jaume I 11) is not a bad deal in the upper budget range if you can get a quiet room – the street noise can be a bit much in the front room. Singles/doubles with shower and loo cost 4100/6200 ptas (metro: Jaume I).

El Raval *Hotel Peninsular (map 6, ☎ 93 302 31 38, Carrer de Sant Pau 34)* is a bit of an oasis on the fringe of the Barri Xinès. Once part of a convent, it has a plant-draped atrium extending the full height and most of the length of the hotel. The 80 rooms are clean and spacious. They cost 5000/6300 ptas in high season, with continental breakfast included (metro: Liceu).

Hostal Residencia Opera (map 6, ☎ 93 318 82 01, Carrer de Sant Pau 20), is a bit tatty but it's worth trying if other places are full. Rooms are 2500/4000 ptas, or 3000/5000 ptas with bath (metro: Liceu).

Hostal La Terrassa (map 6, ☎ 93 302 51 74, Carrer de la Junta de Comerç 11), is another big hostel, with basic but well kept rooms costing 2100/3600 without shower and 3200/4200 ptas with (metro: Liceu).

Upping the class a little is *Hosteria Grau (map 6, ☎ 93 301 81 35, Carrer dels Ramelleres 27)*. Cheapish singles without bath cost 3300 ptas, and doubles range from 4750 ptas (bath and loo in passageway) to 6250 ptas (with bath and loo). The latter rooms, in particular, are quite good. All rooms are heated, which is an issue in winter (metro: Catalunya).

La Ribera *Pensión Lourdes (map 6, ☎ 93 319 33 72, Carrer de la Princesa 14)*, has about 20 clean rooms for 1900/3000 ptas (metro: Jaume I).

Hostal Nuevo Colón (map 6, ☎ 93 319 50 77, Avinguda del Marquès de l'Argentera 19), opposite Estació de França, has cheerfully done-up rooms for 2800/4000 ptas, or 4000/5500 ptas with bath (metro: Barceloneta).

L'Eixample A few cheapies are spread strategically across this upmarket part of the city north of Plaça de Catalunya.

One of the cheapest in town, if you can get a room, is *Pensión Cerdeña (map 2, ☎ 93 318 56 03, Carrer de Girona 35)*, where a no-frills double will set you back all of 3000 ptas. Singles are harder to come by (metro: Girona). If you have no luck there (or in the couple of other hostales in the same building), head down the road to tiny *Pensión Girona (map 2, ☎ 93 265 02 59, Carrer de Girona 24)*, where singles/doubles cost 2500/5500 ptas. The latter have bathrooms (metro: Girona or Arc de Triomf).

Hostal Goya (map 5, ☎ 93 302 25 65, Carrer de Pau Claris 74), has 12 nice, good sized rooms at 2600/3800 ptas (loners can get a double for 2800 ptas) or 3700/4400 ptas with shower and loo (metro: Urquinaona).

Hostal Palacios (map 2, ☎ 93 301 30 79, Gran Via de les Corts Catalanes 629 bis) has 25 decent rooms. Singles without bath cost 2900 ptas. A few singles with shower are 4000 ptas and doubles with the whole shebang are 5620 ptas exactly (metro: Catalunya or Urquinaona).

Hostal San Remo (map 5, ☎ 93 302 19 89, Carrer d'Ausiàs Marc 19) is a good little place. Rooms range in price from 4000 to 5000 ptas and all have their own bathroom, as well as air-con and heating. There's a bar downstairs.

Hostal Oliva (map 2, ☎ 93 488 01 62, Passeig de Gràcia 32) is a friendly little place on the 4th floor, clean and well kept. Some of the varied rooms are refurbished and modern, others are older but still fine. Singles/doubles are 3100/5700 ptas, doubles with bath are 6700 ptas (metro: Passeig de Gràcia).

A leafier location is *Hostal Neutral (map 4, ☎ 93 487 63 90, Rambla de Catalunya 42)*. Singles cost 3000 ptas but only have a wash-basin. The doubles cost 5350 ptas and have a shower and loo (metro: Universitat).

Another pensión of reasonable quality, fartherwest on a quiet corner, is the pleasant *Hostal Cisneros (map 4, ☎ 93 454 18 00, Carrer d'Aribau 54)*. Simple, clean rooms without bath start at 3745/4500 ptas, while those with conveniences reach

4815/6420 ptas. It's handy to the centre too, just three blocks into l'Eixample from Plaça de la Universitat.

Nearby *Pensión Aribau (map 4, ☎ 93 453 11 06, Carrer d'Aribau 37)*, offers reasonable singles/doubles for 2500/5000 ptas. The singles only have a basin but do come with a TV if you're interested, while the doubles have shower, loo, TV and even a fridge (metro: Universitat).

Near Estació Sants *Hostal Sofia (map 4, ☎ 93 419 50 40, at Avinguda de Roma 1-3)* is just across the square in front of the station. The 12 sparkling clean rooms cost 3000/5500 ptas, or 6500 ptas for doubles with bathroom (metro: Sants-Estació).

Hostal Sans (map 1, ☎ 93 331 37 00, Carrer de Antoni de Capmany 82), a five-minute walk south-west of the station, is a modern place with rooms for 2200/3200 ptas, or 4200/4900 ptas with bathroom (metro: Plaça de Sants).

Gràcia If you want to stay out of the tourist core of Barcelona and mix with more of a local crowd, you might want to try staying up in Gràcia. You have a handful of choices here. *Hostal San Medín (map 2, ☎ 93 217 30 68, Carrer Gran de Gràcia 125, metro: Fontana)* is a simple place with spartan but clean singles/doubles going for 3500/5800 ptas. Another good one farther down the road is *Pensión Norma (map 2, ☎ 93 237 44 78, Carrer Gran de Gràcia 87)*. You can get singles/doubles without bathroom for 3000/4000 ptas or doubles with *en suite* for 5000 ptas.

PLACES TO STAY – MID-RANGE

All rooms in this range have bathrooms.

La Rambla

The *Hotel Continental (map 6, ☎ 93 301 25 70, fax 93 302 73 60, Rambla de Canaletes 138)* has 35 pleasant, well-decorated rooms, all with cable TV, microwave, fridge, safe and fan. Room rates with good breakfast start at 6900/9000 ptas in summer and rise for doubles which have Rambla views. (metro:

PLACES TO STAY

Catalunya). Seems OK to us, but some readers have reported being disappointed.

Hotel Lloret (map 6, ☎ 93 317 33 66, fax 93 301 92 83, Rambla de Canaletes 125) has 50 varied rooms; some are worn and not very big. All have air-con and TV. They cost 5200/7800 ptas – a little less in off season – (metro: Catalunya).

Hotel Internacional (map 6, ☎ 93 302 25 66; fax 93 317 61 90, La Rambla 78-80) on Plaça Boqueria has 60 simple, clean rooms with TV at 6530/12,840 ptas (the doubles are frankly over-priced). They have a breakfast room and bar with a balcony over La Rambla (metro: Liceu).

Hotel Oriente (map 6, ☎ 93 302 25 58; fax 93 412 38 19, La Rambla 47), is famous for its modernista design and has a fine skylit restaurant and other public rooms, but staff can be offhand. The bedrooms are slightly past their prime but still comfortable, with tiled floors and bathrooms, safes and TV. Singles/doubles are 7000/12,000 ptas plus IVA (metro: Liceu).

Hotel Cuatro Naciones (map 6, ☎ 93 317 36 24, fax 93 302 69 85, La Rambla 40) has adequate rooms for 6420/8025 ptas. It was built in 1849 and was once – a long time ago – Barcelona's top hotel. Buffalo Bill preferred it to a wagon when he was in town back in 1889 (metro: Liceu).

Barri Gòtic

Hotel Roma Reial (map 6, ☎ 93 302 03 66, Plaça Reial 11) has decent rooms, all with bath, at 4800/6800 ptas in high season.

Borderline price-wise is *Hotel Jardi (map 6, ☎ 93 301 59 00, Plaça de Sant Josep Oriol 1)*. Doubles with a balcony over this lovely square are 6600 ptas, but prices can rise to more than 8000 ptas in high season. The main problem here is the noise from buskers and the like on summer nights – so this might not be for you if you require early nights (metro: Liceu).

Hotel Nouvel (map 6, ☎ 93 301 82 74, fax 93 301 83 70, Carrer de Santa Anna 18-20) has some elegant modernista touches and good air-con rooms with satellite TV for 10,300/15,750 ptas plus IVA. Prices include breakfast (metro: Catalunya).

Hotel Suizo (map 6, ☎ 93 315 04 61, fax 93 310 40 81, Plaça de l'Àngel 12) is old on the outside but quite modern within and has a restaurant and snack bar. Rooms – comfortable, if unspectacular – are 11,000/14,000 ptas plus IVA (metro: Jaume I).

Hotel Rialto (map 6, ☎ 93 318 52 12; fax 93 318 53 12, Carrer de Ferran 40-42) is a classic 19th century mansion typical of what was built here when this boulevard was rammed across the Barri Gòtic in 1823. Barcelona's most illustrious artistic son, Joan Miró, was born in this very house, and if you were staying any closer to the historic epicentre of the city you'd be lodging in the Palau de la Generalitat itself! Singles/doubles are well appointed and cost 10,800/14,000 ptas (including breakfast) plus IVA (metro: Liceu or Jaume I). Newer and with less personality, but charging the same prices and perfectly reasonable, is *Hotel Gótico (map 6, ☎ 93 315 22 11, fax 93 310 40 81, Carrer de Jaume I, 14)*, on the other side of Plaça de Sant Jaume (metro: Jaume I) .

Just off the waterfront, *Hotel Metropol (map 6, ☎ 93 310 51 00, fax 93 319 12 76, Carrer Ample 31)* is not a bad bet at this level. Rooms are smallish but comfortable and they also have a car park. Singles/doubles are 9700/12,900 ptas plus IVA (but a lot more in the Easter week).

El Raval

Hotel Mesón de Castilla (map 4, ☎ 93 318 21 82, fax 93 412 40 20, Carrer de Valldonzella 5), has some lovely modernista touches – stained glass and murals in its public rooms, Gaudíesque window mouldings – and 56 good, quaintly-decorated rooms with breakfast for 9800/12,600 ptas plus IVA. There's easy parking too (metro: Universitat).

Right at the top end of this barri and a brief stroll away from La Rambla and Plaça de Catalunya, *Hotel Lleó (map 4, ☎ 93 318 13 12, fax 93 412 26 57)* is a fine mid to high-cost establishment with comfortable rooms, wheelchair access and bar. Singles/doubles cost 11,600/14,500 ptas plus IVA.

Hotel San Agustín (map 6, ☎ 93 318 16 58, fax 93 317 29 28, Plaça de Sant Agustí

3) is a modern place on a quiet square, with rooms for 8500/12,500 ptas plus IVA, including breakfast. All rooms have air-con and satellite TV (metro: Liceu).

Hotel España (map 6, ☎ 93 318 17 58, fax 93 317 11 34, Carrer de Sant Pau 9-11) is famous for its two marvellous dining rooms designed by the modernista architect Lluís Domènech i Montaner. One has big sea-life murals by Ramon Casas, the other has floral tiling and a wood-beamed roof. The 60 plus comfortable rooms cost 5400/10,300 ptas including breakfast (metro: Liceu).

Near Parc de la Ciutadella

Hotel Triunfo (map 6, ☎ 93 315 08 60, Passeig de Picasso 22) is not a bad bet and good for price, especially if you can get a room with views across to the park. Rooms cost 5500/8500 ptas.

L'Eixample

A fine choice for a bit of old-fashioned style is *Hotel Gran Via (map 5, ☎ 93 318 19 00, fax 93 318 99 97, Gran Via de les Corts Catalanes 642)* with 53 good-sized rooms at 9000/12,000 ptas plus IVA and a big, elegant lounge opening on to a roof terrace. Breakfast is available for 700 ptas (metro: Catalunya).

Near Estació Sants

Hotel Roma (map 4, ☎ 93 410 66 33, Avinguda de Roma 31) is a comfortable, upper mid-range option, handy for the train station. Rooms will cost you 10,200/15,300 ptas in high season.

PLACES TO STAY – TOP END

You can get top-end quality at mid-range prices in Barcelona by taking advantage of some swingeing price cuts for double rooms – 50% or even more – at these hotels' off-peak times when business travellers are absent.

La Rambla

The top hotel on La Rambla is the elegant *Le Meridien (map 6, ☎ 93 318 62 00, fax 93 301 77 76)* at No 111. Its top floor presidential suite is where the likes of Michael Jackson, Madonna and Julio Iglesias stay. Normal singles/doubles are 26,000/32,000 ptas plus IVA (metro: Catalunya or Liceu).

El Raval

Hotel Gravina (map 4, ☎ 93 301 68 68, fax 317 28 28, Carrer de Gravina 12) is on a generally quiet side street within easy reach of La Rambla. Rooms are a little small but perfectly comfortable with spotless *en suites*, air-con, TV and a safe in the wardrobe. You're looking at 11,500/17,500 ptas plus IVA. The price normally does *not* include their buffet breakfast – but with a little gentle nudging they can be persuaded to throw it in for the price.

Barri Gòtic

Hotel Colón (map 6, ☎ 93 301 14 04, fax 93 317 29 15, Avinguda de la Catedral 7) is a good choice for its location which is facing the cathedral. The 146 comfortable and elegant rooms cost 15,500/23,000 ptas plus IVA. There's a restaurant and piano bar (metro: Jaume I).

L'Eixample

Hotel Balmes (map 2, ☎ 93 451 19 14; fax 93 451 00 49, Carrer de Mallorca 216) is a good, modern hotel with white bricks much in evidence in the interior. Average-sized rooms with air-con, nice tiled bathrooms and satellite TV, are comparatively good value at 12,600/16,500 ptas plus IVA. There's garage parking, a coffee shop, a garden with bar and swimming pool and a restaurant (metro: Passeig de Gràcia).

The renovated *Hotel Regente (map 2, ☎ 93 487 59 89; fax 93 487 32 27, Rambla de Catalunya 76)* is also an attractive deal. Rooms with air-con and satellite TV cost 14,900/17,500 ptas plus IVA. The rooms feature wood panelling and have a nice feel (metro: Passeig de Gràcia).

The *St Moritz Hotel (map 2, ☎ 93 412 15 00, fax 93 412 12 36, Carrer de la Diputació 262 bis)*, is another upmarket hotel with 92 rooms at 16,900/19,900 ptas plus IVA. It has a restaurant and a pleasant terrace bar (metro: Catalunya or Passeig de Gràcia).

The *Hotel Majèstic (map 2, ☎ 93 488 17 17, fax 93 488 18 80, Passeig de Gràcia 70)*, is a sprawling, comfortable place with a nice line in modern art on the walls and a rooftop swimming pool. The 300 plus rooms, all air-con with satellite TV, range from 13,500/15,000 ptas to 19,000/22,000 ptas (including breakfast) plus IVA (metro: Passeig de Gràcia).

The *Comtes* (or *Condes*) *de Barcelona Hotel (map 2, ☎ 93 488 22 00, fax 93 488 06 14, Passeig de Gràcia 73-75)* is one of Barcelona's best hotels. It has two separate buildings facing each other across Carrer de Mallorca. The older one occupies the Casa Enric Batlló, built in the 1890s but now stylishly modernised. The air-con, soundproofed rooms have marble bathrooms. A double can be had for 20,500 ptas plus IVA. The same room for use as a single costs 1000 ptas less (metro: Passeig de Gràcia).

The *Hotel Ritz (aka Husa Palace; map 2, ☎ 93 318 52 00, fax 93 318 01 48, Gran Via de les Corts Catalanes 668)*, is the top choice for old-fashioned elegance, luxury, individuality and first-class service. It has been going since 1919. Singles/doubles are 28,500/32,000 ptas. Other rooms with tiled step-down 'Roman baths' cost almost double, and suites can go for in excess of 200,000 ptas. Add IVA to all prices (metro: Urquinaona).

A less expensive choice for old-fashioned elegance is *Hotel Avenida Palace (map 5, ☎ 93 301 96 00; fax 93 318 12 34, Gran Via de les Corts Catalanes 605)*. Doubles are fine at 24,000 ptas plus IVA, but single occupation costs a measly 2000 ptas less (metro: Catalunya).

Alternatively, if you can cough up 20,900 ptas for a double, consider the recently refurbished *Hotel Ducs de Bergara (map 5, ☎ 93 317 34 42, Carrer de Bergara 11)*. The building is a fine modernista piece with an 18th century artesonado ceiling and some nice art déco touches (metro: Catalunya).

One of the classiest addresses in town is the *Hotel Claris (map 2, ☎ 93 487 62 62, fax 93 215 79 70, Carrer de Pau Claris 150)*. Of course you pay for the pleasure, to the tune of 27,500/34,100 ptas plus IVA. Breakfast is another 2500 ptas (metro: Passeig de Gràcia).

The big attraction at *Hotel Astoria (map 2, ☎ 93 209 83 11, fax 93 202 30 08, Carrer de Paris 203)* is the buffet breakfast. The rooms, all nicely decked out and with full *en suites*, cost 14,200/16,500 ptas plus IVA. The buffet breakfast, at 1250 ptas, is truly good value by anyone's standards.

Port Olímpic

Barcelona's most fashionable, if rather impersonal, lodgings is the *Hotel Arts Barcelona (map 1, ☎ 93 221 10 00, fax 93 221 10 70, Carrer de la Marina 19-21)*, in one of the two sky-high towers that dominate the Port Olímpic. It has over 450 rooms and charges up to 40,000 ptas plus IVA for a double (metro: Ciutadella).

LONG-TERM RENTALS

The Universitat de Barcelona *(Gran Via de les Corts Catalanes 585; metro: Univer sitat)*, the Centre d'Informació i Assessorament per a Joves (☎ 93 402 78 00, Carrer de Ferran 32; map 6) and the British Council *(Carrer d'Amigó 83, near Muntaner FGC train station)* all have notice boards advertising flat shares and rooms to let. The free English-language monthly *Barcelona Metropolitan* (see Newspapers & Magazines in the Facts for the Visitor chapter) carries rental classifieds.

Otherwise, check out *Primeramà*, the weekly classifieds paper. The last few pages of the *Suplement Immobiliària* (real estate supplement) carry ads for share accommodation under the rubrique *Lloguer/ Hostes i vivendes a compartir*. Ads tend to be in Castilian rather than Catalan. Rooms can come as cheap as 25,000 ptas a month, but for something halfway decent, not too far from the centre, you're looking at a minimum of 35,000 ptas. You need to add bills (gas, electricity, water, phone and comunidad – building maintenance charges).

Places to Eat

FOOD

Eating, especially if you are not hamstrung by a rigidly tight budget, is a highlight of any stay in Barcelona. After a day spent trying to fathom the genius of Gaudí or the peculiarities of Picasso, what better counterpoint than hunkering down for a protracted stay at the tables of Barcelona's delightfully varied restaurants?

Food terminology in this chapter is given in Catalan/Castilian or Catalan alone, except in the few cases where the Castilian term is used in both languages. The idea is to reflect what you are most likely to see/hear in the streets of Barcelona, not to descend into the murky depths of linguistic polemics.

When to Eat

You may not arrive in Barcelona with jetlag, but your tummy will think it has abandoned all known time zones.

Breakfast (*esmorzar/desayuno*) is generally a no-nonsense affair however, taken at a bar on the way to work. Lunchtime (*menjar/comida*) is basically from 2 to 4 pm and is the main meal of the day. No local would contemplate chomping into dinner (*sopar/cena*) before 9.30 pm. Most (but not all) kitchens close by midnight.

Don't panic! If your gastric juices can't hold out, you can easily track down bar snacks or fast food (local and international) outside these times. And, anxious to ring up every tourist dollar possible, plenty of restaurants cater for northern European stomach habits – although you often pay for this with mediocre food and the almost exclusive company of other tourists.

Where to Eat

Many bars and some cafés offer some form of solid sustenance. This can range from *entrepans/bocadillos* (filled rolls) and *tapes/tapas* (bar snacks) through to more substantive *raciones* (basically bigger versions of a tapa), and full meals in *menjadors/comedores* (sitdown restaurants) out the back. *Cerveseries/cervezerías* (beer bars), *tavernes/tabernas* (taverns), *tascas* (snack bars) and *cellers/bodegas* (cellars) are just some of the kinds of establishment in this category.

For a full meal you will most frequently end up in a *restaurant/restaurante*, but other names will pop out at you. A *marisquería* specialises in seafood, while a *mesón* (a 'big table') might indicate (but not necessarily!) a more modest eatery.

What to Eat

Breakfast A coffee with some sort of pastry (*pasta/bollo*) is the typical breakfast. You may get a croissant or some cream-filled number. Some people prefer a savoury start – you could go for a *bikini/sandwich mixto* – a toasted ham and cheese. A Spanish *tostada* is simply buttered toast (you might order something to go with it). The Catalan version, a *torrada*, is usually more of an open toasted sandwich with something on it besides butter (depending on what you ask for). Some people go for an all-Spanish favourite, *xurros amb xocolata/churros con chocolate*, a lightly deep-fried stick of plain pastry immersed in thick, gooey hot chocolate. They are sold at stands around town.

Lunch & Dinner Many straightforward Spanish dishes are available here as elsewhere in the country. The travellers' friend is the *menú del día*, a set price meal comprising three or more courses, with a drink usually thrown in. This is often only available for lunch and can range in price from around 800 ptas to 5000 ptas at posh establishments. A *plat combinat/plato combinado* is a simpler version still – a one-course meal consisting of basic nutrients – the 'meat-and-three-veg' style of cooking. You'll see pictures of this stuff everywhere. It's filling and cheap but has little to recommend it in culinary terms.

You'll pay more for your meals if you order à la carte but the food will be better. The menu (*la carta*) begins with starters such as *amanides/ensaladas* (salads), *sopes/sopas* (soups) and *entremeses* (hors d'oeuvres). The latter can range from a mound of potato salad with olives, asparagus, anchovies and a selection of cold meats – almost a meal in itself – to simpler cold meats, slices of cheese and olives.

Later courses on the menu are often listed under headings like: *pollastre/pollo* (chicken); *carn/carne* (meat); *mariscs/mariscos* (seafood); *peix/pescado* (fish); *arròs/arroza* (rice); *ous/huevos* (eggs); and *verdures/verduras* (vegetables). Meat may be subdivided into *porc/cerdo* (pork), *vedella/ternera* (beef), and *anyell/cordero* (lamb).

Desserts have a lower profile; *gelats/helados* (ice cream), fruit and flans are often the only choices in cheaper places. Sugar addicts should look out for a couple of local specialities (see next section) where possible.

Catalan Cuisine Basques may well disagree, but Catalunya has a reputation for producing some of Spain's finest cuisine. Catalunya is geographically diverse and therefore provides a variety of fresh, high-quality seafood (though due to high demand, most seafood is now crated in from other parts of Spain and even Europe), meat, poultry, game, fruit and vegetables. These can come in unusual and delicious combinations: meat and seafood (a genre known as *mar i muntanya* – 'sea and mountain'), poultry and fruit, fish and nuts. Quality Catalan food tends to require a greater fiscal effort.

The essence of Catalan food lies in its sauces for meat and fish. These sauces may not be mentioned on menus as they're so ubiquitous. There are five main types: *sofregit* (fried onion, tomato and garlic); *samfaina* (sofregit plus red pepper and aubergine or courgette); *picada* (based on ground almonds, usually with garlic, parsley, pine or hazel nuts, and sometimes breadcrumbs); *allioli* (pounded garlic with olive oil, often with egg yolk added to make more of a mayonnaise); and *romesco* (an almond, tomato, olive oil, garlic and vinegar sauce, also used as a salad dressing).

Catalans find it hard to understand why other people put butter on bread when *pa amb tomàquet* – bread sliced, then rubbed, with tomato, olive oil, garlic and salt – is so easy.

Here are some typical dishes:

Starters
amanida Catalana
    Catalan salad; almost any mix of lettuce, olives, tomatoes, hard-boiled eggs, onion, chicory, celery, green pepper and garlic, with fish, ham or sausage, and mayonnaise or an oil-and-vinegar dressing
calçots amb romesco
    calçots are a type of long onion, delicious as a starter with romesco sauce. Catalans sometimes get together for a *calçotada*, the local version of a BBQ!
escalivada
    red peppers and aubergines (sometimes onions and tomatoes too), grilled, cooled, peeled, sliced and served with an olive oil, salt and garlic dressing
esqueixada
    salad of shredded salted cod (*bacallà*) with tomato, red pepper, onion, white beans, olives, olive oil and vinegar

Main Dishes
arròs a la cassola or *arròs a la Catalana*
    Catalan paella, cooked in an earthenware pot, without saffron
botifarra amb mongetes
    pork sausage with fried white beans
cargols
    snails, almost a religion in parts of Catalunya; often stewed with *conill* (rabbit) and chilli
escudella
    a meat, sausage and vegetable stew, the liquid of which mixed with noodles or rice, is served as a soup, followed by the rest served as a main course known as *carn d'olla*
fricandó
    a pork and vegetable stew
mandonguilles amb sipia
    meatballs with cuttlefish, a subtly flavoured land-sea combination
pollastre amb escamerlans
    chicken with shrimps, another amphibious event
sarsuela (zarzuela)
    mixed seafood cooked in sofregit with seasonings – a Barcelona invention

Desserts

crema Catalana	a cream custard with a crisp, burnt-sugar coating
mel i mató	honey and fresh cream cheese – simple but delicious
music	a serving of dried fruits and nuts with a glass of sweet muscatel wine

Other good things to look out for include *ànec/pato* (duck), *oca* (goose) and *canalons* (Catalan cannelloni). *Fideuas* (noodles) are usually served with tomato and meat/sausage or fish, as rice is with paella. Wild mushrooms are a Catalan passion – people disappear into the forests in autumn to pick them. There are many, many types; the large succulent *rovellons* are a favourite. Here are more words (with, where they differ, their Castilian equivalents) to help you with Catalan-only menus:

ametller (almendra)	almond
anyell (cordero)	lamb (see *xai*)
bou (buey)	beef
caldereta	a seafood stew
carxofe (alcachofa)	artichoke
castanya (castaña)	chestnut
ceba (cebolla)	onion
costella (chuleta)	cutlet
cranc (cangrejo/centello)	crab
entrepà	bocadillo
farcit (relleno)	stuffed
formatge (queso)	cheese
fregit (frito)	fried
fuet	salami-type sausage
gelat (helado)	ice cream
llagosta (langosta)	lobster
llenties (lentejas)	lentils
llet (leche)	milk
llonganissa (longaniza)	pork sausage
oli (aceite)	oil
ostra	oyster
ous (huevos)	eggs
pastís (pastel)	cake/pie
pebre (pimienta)	pepper
peix (pescado)	fish
pernil de la comarca	country-cured ham
pop (pulpo)	octopus
rap (rape)	monkfish
suquet	stew (like a French bouillabaisse)
torrada (tostada)	open toasted sandwich
truita (trucha)	omelette/tortilla, or trout (trucha)
xai	lamb

Foreign Cuisines

Barcelona can't compete with New York, Sydney, London or Paris, but it does offer a fair smattering of foreign restaurants. In case you want a break from the local stuff, a few of the better addresses have been sprinkled in among the recommendations below.

DRINKS
Nonalcoholic

Clear, cold water from a public fountain or tap is a Spanish favourite – but check that it's *potable* (fit to drink). For tap water in restaurants, ask for *aigua d'aixeta/agua de grifo*. *Aigua/agua mineral* (bottled water) comes in innumerable brands, either *amb/con gas* (fizzy) or *sense/sin gas* (still). A 1.5L bottle of agua mineral *sense/sin gas* costs around 75 ptas in a supermarket, but out and about you may be charged as much as 175 ptas for the same.

Coffee Coffee in Spain is strong and slightly bitter. A *cafè amb llet/café con leche* (generally drunk at breakfast only) is about 50% coffee, 50% hot milk. Ask for *grande* or *doble* if you want a large cup, *en got/en vaso* if you want a smaller shot in a glass, or *sombra* if you want lots of milk. A *café solo* is a short black; *cafè tallat/café cortado* is a short black with a little milk. For iced coffee, ask for *cafè amb gel/café con hielo*; you'll get a glass of ice and a hot cup of coffee, to be poured over the ice – which, surprisingly, doesn't all melt straight away!

Tea As in the rest of Spain, Barcelonins prefer coffee, but increasingly it is possible to get hold of many different styles of tea and *infusiones* (herbal concoctions). Locals tend to drink tea black. If you want milk, ask for it to come separately (*a parte*) to avoid ending up with a cup of tea-flavoured watery milk.

PLACES TO EAT

Soft Drinks *Suc de taronja/zumo de naranja* (orange juice) is the main, freshly squeezed juice available. It's often served with sugar. To make sure you are getting the real thing, ask for the juice to be *natural*, otherwise you run the risk of getting a puny little bottle of runny concentrate.

Refrescs/refrescos (cool drinks) include the usual international brands of soft drinks, local brands such as Kas, and *granissat/granizado* (iced fruit crush).

A *batido* is a flavoured milk drink or milk shake. *Orxata/horchata* is a Valencian drink of Islamic origin. Made from the juice of *chufa* (tiger nuts), sugar and water, it is sweet and tastes like soya milk with a hint of cinnamon. You'll come across it both fresh and bottled: Chufi is a delicious brand. A naughtier version is called a *cubanito* and involves sticking in a blob of chocolate ice-cream.

Alcoholic

Wine Spain is a wine-drinking country and *vi/vino* (wine) accompanies almost every meal. Spanish wine is strong because of the sunny climate. It comes *blanc/blanco* (white), *negro/tinto* (red), or *rosat/rosado* (rosé). In general it is cheap, although there is no shortage of expensive wines. A 500 ptas bottle of wine, bought from a supermarket or wine merchant, will be better than average. The same money in a restaurant will get you a mediocre drop. Cheap *vi de taula/vino de mesa* (table wine) sells for less than 200 ptas a litre, but wines at that price can be pretty rank.

Catalunya's whites are better than its reds, but the area is best known for *cava*, the fine local version of Champagne (see the Excursions chapter for more on Catalunya's main wine and cava area and how to identify quality wines).

You can order wine by the glass *(copa)* in bars and restaurants. At lunch or dinner it is common to order a *vi/vino de la casa* (house wine) – usually by the litre or half litre.

Beer The most common way to order *cervesa/cerveza* (beer) is to ask for a *caña*, which is a small draught beer (*cervesa/*

cerveza de barril). A larger beer (about 300ml) is sometimes called a *tubo* (which comes in a straight glass). A pint is a *jarra*. If you just ask for a cerveza you may get bottled beer, which is more expensive. A small bottle of beer is called a *flascó/botellín*. The local brew is Estrella Damm (of which there are several variants), while San Miguel, made in western Catalunya's Lleida, is also widely drunk. The Damm company produces 15% of all Spain's beer, as does San Miguel.

A *clara* is a shandy – a beer with a hefty dash of lemonade.

Other Drinks *Sangría* is a wine and fruit punch, sometimes laced with brandy. It's refreshing going down but can leave you with a sore head. You'll see jugs of it on tables in restaurants but it also comes ready-mixed in bottles at around 300 ptas for 1.5L. *Tinto de verano* is a mix of wine and Casera, a brand of lemonade or sweet, bubbly water. You don't see it so much in Barcelona, although it is common in other parts of Spain.

There is no shortage of imported and Spanish-produced top-shelf stuff – *coñac* (brandy) is popular.

PLACES TO EAT – BUDGET

One traveller's budget restaurant may be another's splurge, so these categories are a little arbitrary. Those hoping to satisfy their hunger for around 1000 ptas could try the following places (in a few cases you can opt to spend a little more – say up to around 2000 ptas – and broaden your range of choices).

Remember that, although most places recommended for tapas are placed in the budget category, if you eat a lot of tapas – which on average can cost 150 to 300 ptas – by the time you're on your fourth or fifth (and the accompanying drinks) you'll have well and truly crashed the 1000-ptas barrier!

La Rambla

Viena (map 6, Rambla dels Estudis 115), is a popular café with stools around a central counter and good *barretas* (baguettes) for 300 to 500 ptas.

Cafè de l'Òpera (map 6, La Rambla 74), opposite the Liceu opera house, is La Rambla's most interesting café, with elegant 1920s décor. It gets busy at night (see Bars), but is quieter for morning coffee and croissants. There are also bocadillos, from 350 ptas, and tapas.

Restaurant Nuria (map 6, Rambla de Canaletes 133) just down from Plaça de Catalunya, is a big, busy place doing pasta from 500 ptas, fish and meat courses from 700 ptas. It offers a three-course *menú* for 1100 ptas.

Barri Gòtic

This area is peppered with good eateries, some of them excellent value. Unless otherwise stated, all the following spots can be found on map 6.

Pastry Shops & Coffee Bars Tempting pastry and/or chocolate shops, often combined with coffee bars, abound all over the Barri Gòtic. There's a special concentration along Carrer and Baixada de la Llibreteria, north-east off Plaça de Sant Jaume. Among the least resistible pastry/chocolate places are: *Santa Clara (Carrer de la Llibreteria 21)* and *La Colmena (corner of Baixada de la Llibreteria and Plaça de l'Àngel)*. Two places with particularly good coffee in this area are *Bon Mercat (corner of Baixada de la Llibreteria and Carrer de la Freneria)*, and *Il Caffè di Roma (map 6, Plaça de l'Àngel)*.

Xocolateria La Xicra, (Plaça de Sant Josep Oriol 2), has great cakes, various coffees, teas and *xocolata* (hot chocolate, 230 ptas) so thick it's listed on the menu under *postres* (desserts). Nearby, two other good places to sit down for a coffee and croissant are *Granja La Pallaresa (Carrer de Petritxol 11)* and *Croissanterie del Pi (Carrer del Pi 14)*.

A great little place to sip a wide variety of teas and herbal infusions is *Salterio (Carrer de Sant Domènec del Call 4)*, just in off Carrer de Ferran.

Take-away Felafel & Kebabs *Disco-Bar Real (corner of Plaça Reial and Carrer de Colom)* has a takeaway counter doing good felafel for 250 ptas. *Buen Bocado (Carrer dels Escudellers 31)* has felafel for 300 ptas and shawarma for 400 ptas. It's open evenings only, until 2 am. The nameless *felafel & kebab takeaway (Carrer dels Escudellers, just east of Carrer dels Obradors)*, charges 50 ptas less for each.

Restaurants *Santa Ana (Carrer de Santa Anna 8)* is a bright, friendly place with quick service. Pizzas and sizeable plats combinats are 700 to 900 ptas, baguettes 300 to 400 ptas, all plus IVA.

Self-Naturista, at No 13, is a popular self-service vegetarian restaurant with a four-course lunch *menú* for 810 ptas.

The Bagel Shop (Carrer de la Canuda 25), just in off La Rambla, is the only place in town where your lox and cream cheese bagel will be the genuine article.

El Gallo Kiriko (Carrer dels Cecs de la Boqueria 19) is an inexpensive Pakistani restaurant. A good tandoori chicken with chips or salad, or couscous with chicken, beef or vegetables, is just 450 ptas. Curries with rice are 600 ptas.

Little *Bar-Restaurant Cervantes (Carrer de Cervantes 7)* does a good three-course lunch *menú* with plenty of choice, plus a drink, for 900 ptas. The basic *Cal Kiko (corner of Carrer de Cervantes and Carrer del Palau)* does a four-course *menú* for 725 ptas.

Facing each other across Carrer del Vidre off the south end of Plaça Reial are two cheap, busy little places: *Restaurante Senshe Tawakal*, which serves lentils and vegetables, or chicken and chips for 450 ptas and couscous for 550 ptas; and *Restaurante Rincón de Ríos Baixas*, with economical daily dishes such as paella for 500 ptas. Both stay open until 2 or 3 am.

Bar Comercio, across Carrer dels Escudellers from La Fonda, is a much plainer affair but will do you a decent feed – salads 300 to 400 ptas, mussels 475 ptas, chicken or rabbit 500 to 550 ptas.

Carrer de la Mercè, running roughly west from the main Correus i Telègrafs (post

PLACES TO EAT

office) is a good place to hunt around for great little northern Spanish *tascas* and *sidrerías*. Most of these are run by immigrants from Galicia and Asturias. **Tasca El Corral**, at No 19, and **Sidrería La Socarrena**, at No 21, are both worth checking out, but there are many others. **Bar Celta**, No 16, is cheap – you can fill up on tapas for under 1000 ptas.

El Raval

All of the following are on map 6.

Xaica Pizzeria (*Carrer de Jovellanos 7*) does good-sized pizzas for one for 550 to 825 ptas and a three-course *menú* for 995 ptas.

Restaurant Tallers (*Carrer dels Tallers 6*) is a clean, modest place with an adequate four-course lunch *menú* for 850 ptas.

Bar Restaurante Romesco (*Carrer de l'Arc de Sant Agustí*), just off Carrer de Sant Pau, is a no-frills, almost hole-in-the-wall joint serving up good portions of home-style cooking at great prices: such as chicken and chips for 400 ptas, or squid, cuttlefish or baby octopus dishes for 500 to 700 ptas.

Restaurante Els Tres Bots (*Carrer de Sant Pau 42*) is grungy but cheap, with a *menú* for 875 ptas. Along the same street at No 31, *Restaurante Pollo Rico* has a downstairs bar where you can get a quarter chicken, an omelette or a veal steak with chips, bread and wine, from 500 ptas; and a more salubrious but only slightly more expensive upstairs restaurant. *Kashmir Restaurant Tandoori*, at No 39, does tasty curries and biryanis from around 800 ptas.

Bar Kasparo (*Plaça de Vicenç Martorell 4*), is a quiet little Australian-run place where you can get great mixed salads and other healthy light food – perfect in summer on this quiet pedestrianised square.

Sant Antoni

Horchatería Sirvent, (*map 5, Carrer del Parlament 56*), is *the* haven of *horchata* in Barcelona and the best you'll try without catching the Euromed down to this drink's spiritual home: Valencia. You can get it by the glass or take it away by the bottle. They also sell ice cream, granizados and *turrón* (nougat).

La Ribera

All of the following are on map 6.

Comme-Bio (aka *La Botiga*) ☎ *93 319 89 68, Via Laietana 28*) is a modern, chemical-additive-free vegetarian restaurant and wholefood shop. Its good, four-course 1125 ptas daily *menú* includes a help-yourself salad bar; many à la carte dishes, including pizzas and spinach-and-Roquefort crêpes, cost around 900 ptas, or there are tofu and *seitán* (a vegetable protein) dishes for 1210 to 1475 ptas.

Lluna Plena (*Carrer de Montcada 2*) is a brick-walled, cellar-style place with good Catalan and Spanish food, open Tuesday to Saturday. It's packed for its four-course 1050 ptas lunch *menú* and often in the evenings too. For à la carte eating you could go for escalivada or esqueixada (around 450 ptas), followed by a quarter chicken (300 ptas), or rabbit (500 ptas) a la brasa.

Granja Xador (*Carrer de l'Argenteria 61-3*), around the corner from Santa Maria del Mar, is a bright, modern place with a big choice of plats combinats costing from 575 to about 775 ptas.

Restaurante Mar de la Ribera (*Carrer dels Sombrerers*), right by Santa Maria del Mar, does a decent three-course *menú* for 1000 ptas, including half a bottle of wine. It's a pleasant place with ceramics and paintings on the walls.

Several more eateries are sprinkled in among the bars on and around Passeig del Born and Plaça de les Olles east of Santa Maria del Mar. Among them is the cheap and speedy *Can Busto* (*map 6, Carrer de Rera Palau 3*), with a three-course *menú* for 900 ptas and many individual items from 400 ptas up. A little farther off the beaten track, *Restaurante Económico* (*Plaça de Sant Agustí Vell 13*) is a popular local hangout where a full set lunch can come in at under 1000 ptas.

L'Eixample

This is another area with loads of good places to eat. A good place to start a visit to L'Eixample is at the 9th floor cafeteria at *El Corte Inglés* department store on Plaça de

Catalunya (map 5). It's reasonably priced and has tremendous views.

Tapas, Snacks & Coffee You'll find a number of glossy but informal tapas places near the bottom end of Passeig de Gràcia (map 5). At No 24 is *Quasi Queviures (Qu Qu)*, with a big choice including sausages and hams, pâtés and smoked fish. Many tapas cost over 400 ptas, but portions are decent. At No 28 is *Ba-Ba-Reeba*, similar but less Catalan, and serving baguettes too. *Cerveseria Tapa Tapa* at No 44 (map 2), on the corner of Carrer del Consell de Cent, is another big, bright place with a great range of tapas from 250 ptas. Some of these places can feel a little barn-like and are owned by the same people.

Lizarran (map 2, Carrer de Mallora 257) is a lively spot with reasonable tapas. It is part of a chain but, as chains go, the quality isn't bad. This branch gets particularly busy at night.

For an excellent coffee on Passeig de Gràcia pop into *Cafè Torino* at No 59 (map 2), on the corner of Carrer de València – a neat, friendly place, popular with a mildly chic, young clientele.

Restaurants *Bar Estudiantil (map 4, Plaça de la Universitat)* does economical plats combinats, eg chicken, chips and *berenjena* (aubergine), or *botifarra*, beans and red pepper, each for around 600 ptas. This place is open until late into the night and is a genuine student hangout.

El Café de Internet (map 2, ☎ 93 302 11 54, Gran Via de les Corts Catalanes 656) has a double bill of food and the Internet. Before, during or after your meal or snack, you can use an Internet terminal upstairs for 600 ptas a half-hour. Downstairs, there's a lunch *menú* for 950 or 1050 ptas, or you can just go there for a bocadillo and coffee.

L'Hostal de Rita (map 2, ☎ 93 487 33 60, Carrer d'Aragó 279) a block east of Passeig de Gràcia, is an excellent mid-range restaurant. The 950-ptas four-course lunch *menú* is a good deal. À la carte mains are 700 to 1000 ptas. The owners of this restaurant

also now own the *Restaurant Madrid Barcelona* virtually over the road at No.282, and they have turned it into another reasonably priced deal. Mains come in under 1000 ptas, although if you have wine and dessert you are likely to end up with a bill of 2000 ptas. It is so popular that they set up odd little cardboard stools outside for customers who are waiting for a table.

FrescCo (map 2, Carrer de València 263), half a block east of Passeig de Gràcia, packs 'em in with its all-you-can-eat buffet of salads, soups, pizza, pasta, fruit, ice cream and drinks for 975 ptas.

Bar Ariño 2 (map 4, Carrer d'Aribau 82) is one of the more economical eateries in l'Eixample. The three-course *menú*, eg macaroni or soup, a meat dish and dessert, is 800 ptas.

La Flauta (map 4, ☎ 93 323 70 38, Carrer d'Aribau 23) is known for its fine tapas and tasty baguettes with all manner of fillings.

La Gran Tasca (map 2, ☎ 93 451 54 00, Carrer de Balmes 129 bis) is a big, bright restaurant-cum-tapas bar, busy in the evening with people heading for a night out. Tapas are 275 ptas-plus, a main dish of a quarter chicken, or rabbit, or a meat brochette, costs from 500 to 600 ptas.

Around La Sagrada Família

This area (map 2) is not a great culinary cubby hole, but if starvation strikes during your visit, *La Baguetina Catalana, (corner of Carrer de Provença and Carrer de Sardenya)*, does good baguettes for 300 to 400 ptas, while *La Casa del Jamón, (corner of Carrer de Mallorca and Carrer de la Marina)*, has an appetising range of tapas and raciones.

Gràcia

These places are all on map 2.

La Miel (Carrer de Bonavista 2), is popular for its good pancakes (*crepas*) from 450 to 700 ptas.

Bar Candanchu (Plaça de Rius i Taulet 9) has a restaurant with many plats combinats and paella for 1100 ptas. *Mario Pizza,* on the same square, does pizzas for 700 to 900 ptas.

Equinox Sol (Plaça del Sol 14) does a good trade in felafel for 300 ptas and shawarma for 375 ptas – also baba-ghanug, humus and shish kebabs at similar prices. Don't be put off by the bright, plasticky décor. You can stock up on wholefoods in *La Botiga del Sol (Carrer de Maspons)* at the corner of Plaça del Sol, then take a few steps west on Maspons to sip tea and herbal infusions in a youthful, Granada-like ambience at *Tetería Jazmín*.

El Tastavins (Carrer de Ramon y Cajal 12), does good home-style cooking in a bright, neat environment. Starters such as spinach with Roquefort are mainly 600 to 1000 ptas, and there is a *menú del día* for 850 ptas.

Two inexpensive small restaurants just off Plaça de la Virreina are *Cal Majó (Carrer de l'Or 21)* and *Casa de Pizzas*, at No 19. Cal Majó's dishes of the day will probably include such Catalan specialities as escalivada, fricandó and mandonguilles amb sipia for 800 to 1000 ptas.

Aroma (corner Travessera de Gràcia and Carrer de Xiquets) specialises in coffees and teas from around the world. You can drink in (with snacks) or take away.

Sarrià

Bar Tomàs (map 1, Carrer Major de Sarrià 49, FGC: Sarrià), is the best place in Barcelona for *patatas bravas* (potato bits dripping with a slightly spicy sauce mixed with mayonnaise). The place itself is an unassuming bar – they do other tapas as well.

Restaurant Chains

There are a few good local restaurant chains where you can get a quick, decent snack or meal with minimum effort. A few of the branches are listed below.

Bocatta – sells hot and cold baguettes with a big range of fillings, mostly 300 to 400 ptas. Branches are at La Rambla 89 (map 6); Carrer de Santa Anna 11 (map 6); Plaça de Sant Jaume (map 6); the corner of Carrer de Comtal and Carrer d'En Amargòs

(map 6) and Rambla de Catalunya between Carrer de Mallorca and Carrer de València (map 2); most branches open daily from 8 am to midnight.

Pans & Company – provides similar fare and prices to Bocatta. Branches are at La Rambla 123 (map 6), Carrer de Ferran 14 (map 6), and on Carrer dels Arcs off Plaça Nova (map 6), Ronda de la Universitat 7 (map 4), Rambla de Catalunya 13 (map 4), Passeig de Gràcia 39 (map 2) and Carrer de Provença 278 (map 2).

Pastafiore – pizza and pasta: a half *(media)* pizza is 395-575 ptas but you'll need a whole *(entera)* one for 550-865 ptas if you're hungry; pasta is around 475-675 ptas but tends to be less appetising. Branches are at Rambla de Canaletes 125 (map 6), Carrer de Provença 278 (map 2) and Travessera de Gràcia 60 (map 2).

Self Catering

There's great fresh food of all types at the *Mercat de la Boqueria* on La Rambla (map 6), open Monday to Saturday from 8 am to 8 pm. In La Ribera (map 6), *Mercat de Santa Caterina* is open Monday to Saturday from 7 am to 2 pm. In Gràcia there's a big *covered food market* at the corner of Travessera de Gràcia and Carrer de la Mare de Déu dels Desemparats.

Simago near the north end of La Rambla (map 6) is a convenient central supermarket.

PLACES TO EAT – MID-RANGE

Opening your purse wide will improve your options greatly. At the places listed below you can expect to pay anything from 2000 to 3500 ptas for a full meal with all the trimmings.

Barri Gòtic

All the places listed here can be found on map 6.

A Basque favourite is *Irati (Carrer del Cardenal Cassanyes 17)*. Their set menu is 1500 ptas, or you can enjoy the great tapas and a zurrito of beer, or six. A couple of doors down is the psychedelic *Juicy Jones*, where a vegetarian set menu costs 975 ptas, or you can just sip their juices.

Mesón Jesús (Carrer dels Cecs de la Boqueria 4), between Plaça de Sant Josep Oriol and Carrer de la Boqueria, is a cosy little place with a down-home ambience. It does a good 1250 ptas three-course set *menú*, including a drink.

Can Culleretes (☎ 93 317 30 22, Carrer d'En Quintana 5) is Barcelona's oldest restaurant, founded in 1786. It's still going strong, with old-fashioned décor and good Catalan food. A three-course *menú*, including half a bottle of wine, will cost around 2000 ptas.

Les Quinze Nits (☎ 93 317 30 75, Plaça Reial 6) is a stylish, bistro-like restaurant, on the borderline between smart and casual, with a long menu of good Catalan and Spanish dishes at reasonable prices. Three courses with wine and coffee typically come to about 2500 ptas. This place has such a reputation that long queues can often be seen outside.

La Fonda Escudellers (☎ 93 301 75 15, corner of Carrer dels Escudellers and Passatge dels Escudellers) is run by the same people as Les Quinze Nits on Plaça Reial, and has similar menu, prices, hours, ambience and standards.

The best Italian food in town can be had at *Ristorante Il Mercante di Venezia (☎ 93 317 18 28, Carrer de Josep Anselm Clavé 11)*, where a set menu costs 1180 ptas. *Restaurant Porto Mar (☎ 93 301 82 27, No 19)*, is a cheerful Brazilian spot where you tuck into *churrasco* (read: 'slab-o-meat'). Mains cost up to 1650 ptas, but you can have a mediocre *menú* for as little as 995 ptas. *Margarita Blue (☎ 93, 317 71 76, Carrer de Josep Anselm Clavé 6)* does imaginative versions of Mexican food and doubles as a bar.

El Paraguayo (☎ 93 302 14 41, Carrer del Parc 1), just off Carrer Ample, is a great place for succulent slabs of meat bigger than your head. Try the *entraña*; the word means 'entrails' but the meal is in fact a juicy slice of prime beef folded over onto itself and accompanied by a herb sauce. The *dulce de leche* (a South American version of caramel) desserts are to die for. Expect to pay around 2000 ptas a head.

Restaurant Clàssic Gòtic (Carrer de la Plata 3) is located in a low, vaulted, 16th century building where Picasso used to work. The lunch *menú* is 1200 ptas. Or you can splash out on a meal and floor show in the evening.

Restaurant Pitarra (Carrer d'Avinyó 56) serves up quality Catalan food. The old house was where the late 19th century playwright Serafí Pitarra did most of his work, hence the restaurant's name. It's a little expensive, with mains ranging up to 1975 ptas.

El Salón (☎ 93 315 21 59, Carrer de l'Hostal d'En Sol 6) is with little doubt one of the city's most popular eateries – even on a Monday night you are advised to book ahead or get in early for either the 9 pm or 11 pm shift! The problem with the first shift is that they oblige you to finish up by 11 pm – a tad rude.

Poble Sec
Restaurant Elche (map 7, ☎ 93 441 30 89, Carrer de Vila i Vilà 71), does some of Barcelona's best paella. Several varieties are on offer, mostly around 1400 to 1700 ptas per person (minimum of two people).

La Ribera
All these places can be found on map 6.

Restaurante Bunja Raya (☎ 93 319 31 69, Carrer dels Assaonadors 7) makes a nice change with its Malaysian and Indonesian cooking. It has a set menu for 1795 ptas. *Pla de la Garsa (☎ 93 315 24 13, Carrer dels Assaonadors 13)*, is an old-style Catalan restaurant with attractive tiles, lamps and paintings. The 1350 ptas lunch *menú* gives you three courses plus good wine and cheese.

For a bit of a splurge on superb, mainly Catalan and French cooking, you can't do much better than *Senyor Parellada (☎ 93 310 50 94, Carrer de l'Argenteria 37)*, an informally chic restaurant. You should book for dinner. Mains start at 1800 ptas. You might start with mushroom and fish crêpes or monkfish soup, followed by duck breast with cherry vinegar, and round it off with a crema Catalana or mel i mató.

PLACES TO EAT

Centre Cultural Euskal Etxea (Placeta de Montcada 1) is a fine San Sebastián-style bar where you can wash down the scrummy tapas with glasses of the Basque wine, *txacoli*. If you plan to make this your main meal, be prepared to part with 2000 to 3000 ptas.

L'Eixample

The *Centro Asturiano (map 2, Passeig de Gràcia 78)* is a great little club tucked away up on the first floor. It occasionally opens its doors to the lunchtime rabble for the solid 1150 ptas *menú del día*. The open air interior patio is a wonderful spot to eat, but you can eat inside too.

There's one in every city, and for portions of American-style food as big as your head, the *Hard Rock Cafe (map 6, ☎ 93 270 23 05, Plaça de Catalunya 21)* may well be the place for you. You can buy the T-shirt next door.

For some of the better quality Chinese food in Barcelona (the city has plenty of the cheap and cheerful variety), try *Swan (map 2, ☎ 93 488 09 77, Carrer de la Diputació 269)*.

Gràcia

These are all on map 2.

Taverna El Glop (☎ 93 213 70 58, Carrer de Sant Lluís 24) is a rustic spot (locals say it's a bit passé but the food is good) specialising in torrades, grilled meats and salads. A meal with drinks costs 2500 to 3000 ptas.

La Singular (☎ 93 237 50 98, Carrer de Franciso Giner 50) does fantastic salads (with salmon, tuna or pâté) as mains. If you throw in a few tapas and have wine and coffee you'll be looking at 2500 ptas a head.

Bar Bodega Manolo (Carrer del Torrent de les Flors 101) has to be one of the most unprepossessing looking joints in Gràcia. Hold your horses, because they do great home-made meals Thursday to Saturday nights – you'll pay around 2000 ptas. During the day they do a straightforward *menú del día* for around 1000 ptas.

Port Vell & La Barceloneta

In the Maremàgnum complex on the Moll d'Espanya (map 5), a couple of popular waterside eateries are *Tapasbar* and *El Chipirón (☎ 93 225 80 40)*. Both specialise in (average) seafood. Several fast-food places lurk here, too.

Fronting the Palau de Mar (map 5) is a line of al fresco dining options mostly specialising in (fine) seafood. One of the best is *La Gavina (☎ 93 221 05 95)*, where you can expect to pay around 3000 ptas a head for a full meal with wine. Their fideuas are particularly scrummy.

Restaurant Set (7) Portes (map 5, ☎ 93 319 30 33, Passeig d'Isabel II 14) is a classic Barcelona restaurant, founded in 1836. The atmosphere is old-fashioned with wood panelling, tiles, mirrors and plaques naming some of the famous – such as Orson Welles – who have eaten here. Paella (1400 to 2300 ptas) is the speciality but there's other fish, seafood and meat at similar prices. It's near-essential to book.

La Barceloneta has some good seafood restaurants. Many, such as *El Rey de la Gamba (map 6, ☎ 93 221 64 17)*, are on Passeig de Joan de Borbó facing Port Vell. Most main dishes here (it's at No 46) are 1000 to 2000 ptas plus IVA.

Port Olímpic

The harbour here is lined on two sides by dozens of restaurants and tapas bars, extremely popular in spring and summer. They are not cheap but some are good. One of the more economical places is *La Taverna del Cel Ros (map 1)*, which has a three-course *menú* for 975 ptas plus IVA. The irritating thing with most of the restaurants here is the touting done by bored waiters in slack periods.

Just south of the Port Olímpic, beneath the giant copper *Peix* (Fish) sculpture, is *Planet Hollywood (map 1, ☎ 93 221 11 11)*, one of a chain part-owned by Arnold Schwarzenegger and Silvester Stallone. Here you can eat pasta and pizza as well as burgers and Tex-Mex (900 to 1500 ptas for most things) and admire décor of Hollywood costumes, props and stills. The Cyborg used in *Terminator 2: Judgement Day* revolves revoltingly in a glass cylinder at the restaurant's upper entrance.

Tibidabo

Plaça del Doctor Andreu (map 1) at the foot of the Tibidabo funicular is a good place to halt on your way to or from Tibidabo. The best views are from the *Mirablau Terrazza*, an open-air café by the tramvia blau stop, and the *Mirablau* bar next door. A couple of more expensive restaurants across the street are the only alternative.

PLACES TO EAT – TOP END

Although Barcelona is not to be compared with cities like London, it is possible here to part company with reasonable sums of money for food if you so wish. Eating at the restaurants listed below will see your wallet lightened by anything from 3000 ptas. In some cases, if you choose carefully, you might be able to bring the bill down below that mark, but not by much.

Barri Gòtic

All of the following are on map 6.

Els Quatre Gats (☎ 93 302 41 40, *Carrer de Montsió 3 bis)* was a famous turn-of-the-century artists' hangout (see the boxed text) now reincarnated as a fairly expensive restaurant. It was restored a few years ago to its original appearance and displays reproductions of some of its former customers' portraits, painted by other former customers. Starters/snacks such as esqueixada, or escalivada amb torrada, are close to 1000 ptas, and main fish and meat dishes cost 1100 to 2700 ptas. But you can stick to a drink if you just want to sample the atmosphere.

Les Quatre Barres (☎ 93 302 50 60, *Carrer d'En Quintana 6)* also serves up excellent Catalan food – 3000 or 4000 ptas for a meal with drinks.

El Gran Café (☎ 93 318 79 86, *Carrer d'Avinyó 9)* has classy modernista décor and good Catalan/French food. À la carte main dishes are 1200 to 3000 ptas, but there's an entire lunch *menú* for the same price.

Los Caracoles (☎ 93 302 31 85, *Carrer dels Escudellers 14)* started life as a tavern in the 19th century and is one of Barcelona's best known restaurants – although it's now frequented by tourists rather than by the celebrities whose photos adorn its walls. It's still good and lively and offers a big choice of seafood, fish, rice and meat; a typical full meal is 3000 or 4000 ptas, although you could get away with less. Try the snails.

La Ribera

Cal Pep (map 6, ☎ 93 310 79 61, *Plaça de les Olles 8)* has great tapas and a small dining room with good seafood where a three-course Catalan meal with drinks will be around 3500 ptas.

For the best *fondues* in town, go straight to *La Carassa* (map 6, ☎ 93 310 33 06, *Carrer de Brosoli 1)*. It's a cosy, intimate little place but so popular that there are often two shifts, one at 9 pm and another at 11 pm. If you get in for the first, they'll boot you out at 11 to make way for the next round.

L'Eixample

The restaurant of the classy *Hotel Ritz* (map 2, ☎ 93 318 52 00, *Gran Via de les Corts Catalanes 668)* has particularly good seafood – the daily *menú* is 3350 ptas.

You could easily miss *Tragaluz* (map 2, ☎ 93 487 01 96, *Passatge de la Concepció 5)*, but don't. It serves inventive Mediterranean cuisine (with an Italian leaning) and mouth-watering desserts – what about the *tarta de manzana con helado de dulce de leche* (apple pie with caramel ice cream)?! A meal costs about 5000 ptas a head with wine. Downstairs is a fine Japanese snack bar.

Gargantúa i Pantagruel (map 4, ☎ 93 453 20 20, *Carrer d'Aragó 214)* is warm and inviting and serves quality Catalan country cooking. Expect to spend about 3500 ptas.

Barcelona's first Japanese restaurant is still one of its best. *Yamadori* (map 4, ☎ 93 453 92 64, *Carrer d'Aribau 68)* will set you back about 5000 ptas.

PLACES TO EAT

The Coolest Cats in Town

Modernisme has survived in the imagination as a wholly architectural and design phenomenon. In its time, however, it was a much broader, albeit in some respects effete, artistic 'movement'. On canvas, Ramon Casas and Santiago Rusiñol were the leading lights, although neither could really pretend to greatness. Casas was something of a dandy, and a well-lined one at that. He and Rusiñol had both spent time in Parisian artistic circles, as had many other hopefuls and hangers-on. Among their pals were Miguel Utrillo, another painter, and Pere Romeu. The latter was an intriguing character who had given up painting and developed an interest in shadow puppetry. His hobbies ranged from swimming to cycling, from cabaret to sports cars.

From 1892 until 1899, Rusiñol, who thought he had developed new, symbolic ways of expression through his art, organised *festes modernistes* down in what was destined to become the eternal playground of Sitges. Somehow, these eccentric little get-togethers of artists, musicians, writers and party-goers seemed a little insubstantial and so, in 1897, it was decided to establish a permanent base.

Casas had the dosh, so he bought an early modernista house (Josep Puig i Cadafalch's first creation) on Carrer de Montsió and entrusted its management to Romeu. It became a restaurant, bar and meeting place for the luminaries of Barcelona Modernisme, and came to be known as Els Quatre Gats, (the Four Cats). In Catalan the expression means 'a handful of people'. That handful consisted of Casas, Rusiñol, Romeu and Utrillo who proceeded to organise all sorts of cultural get-togethers, from art exhibitions to concerts by such emerging composers as Isaac Albéniz and Enric Granados. The young Picasso, in whom the Cats saw great potential, had his first exhibition here in 1900. Of course Romeu put on puppet shows,

as often as not for children. A couple of anti-establishment magazines also emerged and one of them, *Pèl & Ploma* (Paper & Pen), published an article on Picasso in 1901.

It was fun while it lasted, but it didn't last terribly long. By 1903 Els Quatre Gats had closed. The building was later taken over by a rather conservative art circle and underwent several metamorphoses before ending up as what it is today, a somewhat pricey restaurant feasting on its brief but, nowadays, much glamourised past.

PLACES TO EAT

Gràcia

Botafumeiro (map 2, ☎ 93 218 42 30, Carrer Gran de Gràcia 81) is reputedly a place where the shellfish is about as good as it gets in all Barcelona. It would want to be, as you will abandon the best part of 10,000 ptas a head for the pleasure.

Considerably more modest but a local classic of Catalan cuisine – try the *botifarra amb mongetes – Cal Juanito (map 1, ☎ 93 213 30 43, Carrer de Ramon i Cajal 3)* is a delightful place with classic tile décor, wooden rafters and walls covered in plates signed by all the great and good who have munched here over the decades. About 4500 ptas a head.

La Barceloneta

For a real treat (and splurge) make for *Can Solé (map 5, ☎ 93 221 50 12, Carrer de Sant Carles 4)*. The food is superb, the desserts are to die for and the service is little short of amazing – when you're half way through your fish, they come and remove it and discreetly strip away all the bones for you. You can fill up on a salad and first course of paella alone (1450 ptas). Expect to pay about 5000 ptas for four courses, wine and coffee.

Poble Nou

Restaurant Els Pescadors (map 1, ☎ 93 225 20 18; Plaça de Prim 1) is a fine seafood place on a small square still surrounded by local fishermen's houses in Poble Nou. The mainly seafood menu is excellent and diners are attracted from far and wide to this otherwise fairly grubby, post-industrial part of town. You'll pay about 4500 ptas for a full meal.

Entertainment

BARS

You could write a whole book on Barcelona's bars (but it might not be good for your health), which run the gamut from wood-panelled wine cellars to bright waterfront places and trendy haunts sporting gimmicky modern design (designer bars). Each is a different scene. Some bars are very local, some are full of foreigners, some are favoured by students, others by the well-dressed middle classes. Some play great music, others are places for a quiet talk. Most bars are at their liveliest from about 11 pm to 2 or 3 am, especially Thursday to Saturday. The following will keep you busy for a while and you'll soon start discovering your own favourite nooks.

You can pay anything up to 300 ptas for a bottle of beer – a lot depends on when and at what time you buy it. Mixed drinks tend to start at 400 ptas.

La Rambla

Cafè de l'Òpera (map 6, La Rambla 74), opposite the Liceu opera house, is the busiest and classiest place on an otherwise largely tacky strip. It has been in action since at least 1929 and was formerly preceded by a restaurant, founded in 1876.

Barri Gòtic

Bar del Pi (map 6, Plaça de Sant Josep Oriol) is a characterful little bar with a mixed local clientele. You can drink outside on one of the Barri Gòtic's nicest plazas.

For a low-key drink earlier in the evening, *La Pineda (map 6, Carrer del Pi 16)* is a happy haunt with great hams which seem to drip off the ceiling.

Bar Pilarica (map 6, Carrer de la Dagueria 26) must be the smallest bar in Barcelona but it's groovy for a passing drink. For something more spacious, try *Cafè de l'Acadèmia (map 6, Plaça de Sant Just)*, facing the church.

Glaciar (map 6), in a corner of Plaça Reial, gets busy with a young crowd of foreigners and locals in the evening and stays open till 2 or 3 am. The more basic *Bar Reixas* in the opposite corner of the square is also popular. You can get cheap drinks at *Restaurante Senshe Tawakal* (see Places to Eat).

Tiny *Bar Malpaso (map 6, Carrer d'En Rauric)*, just off Plaça Reial, is packed at night with a young, casual crowd and plays great Latin and African music. Another hip low-lit place with a more varied clientele is *Schilling (map 6, Carrer de Ferran 23)*. Mixed drinks are about 700 ptas at both.

Bar L'Ascensor (map 6, Carrer de Bellafila 3), off Carrer de la Ciutat east of the Ajuntament, is a cosy little place with good taped music and a young clientele. The entrance – as the name might suggest – is a demounted lift.

On entering *El Limón Negro (map 6, Carrer dels Escudellers Blancs 3)* you may notice the rather disconcerting mannequin hanging on the wall, dishevelled, pubenda revealed. Don't worry, just sit down for a drink or get a bite upstairs.

A few yards closer to the waterfront you can raise the red lantern at *Shanghai (map 6, Carrer de N'Aglá 9)*, a humming but cosy place for a beer ... or sake. In warmer months, the terrazas on Plaça de George Orwell (at the east end of Carrer dels Escudellers) are pleasant places to drink away the evening – if you score a table!

Dot (map 6, Carrer Nou de Sant Francesc 7) is one of the hippest hangouts of the moment, often with DJ Angel Dust. It generally is open to about 3 am, a little later on Fridays and Saturdays, and each night the musical theme changes, from 'easy listening' on Sundays to 'space funk' on Fridays.

Parnasse (map 6, corner of Carrer d'En Gignas and Carrer d'En Groc) is tucked away in the backstreets near the main post office. You can drink anything from malt whiskey to orgasms. They also have a few terminals for connecting to the net (600 ptas for half an hour).

(continued on page 167)

DAMIEN SIMONIS

DAMIEN SIMONIS

DAMIEN SIMONIS

DAMIEN SIMONIS

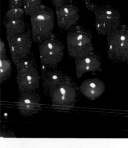

DAMIEN SIMONIS

DAMIEN SIMONIS

...ands and hooded members of religious fraternities are typical of the Easter processions such as
...nese that leave the Esglesia de Sant Agustí in Barcelona's El Raval district on Good Friday.

Death in the afternoon? The spectacle of skill, bravery and killing usually starts at 6 pm.

SPECTATOR SPORTS

BULLFIGHTS

Death in the Afternoon is not a favourite Catalan theme, but there are some fights on summer Sunday afternoons at the Plaça Monumental, on the corner of Gran Via de les Corts Catalanes and Carrer de la Marina (metro: Monumental). The 'fun' usually starts at 6 pm. Tickets are available at the arena from Wednesday to Saturday from 10.30 am to 2 pm and 6 to 7 pm; Sundays from 10 am, or by phoning ☎ 902-33 22 11. Prices range from 2500 ptas to 12,000 ptas – the latter is for the front row in the shade – any closer and you'd be fighting the bulls yourself.

Toro, Toro, Toro

For many, bullfighting is a sickening affair; others view it as a noble battle. Whichever way you look at it, there is little doubt about the cruelty of it, nor about the risks that bullfighters (*toreros*) run.

The *corrida* (bullfight) is a spectacle with a long history. It is not, as some suggest, simply a ghoulish alternative to the slaughterhouse. Aficionados maintain that the bull is better off dying at the hands of a *matador* (killer) than in the *matadero* (abattoir).

Bred for conflict, the toro bravo, *or fighting bull, is nevertheless treated like a king until the final, fatal day.*

The corrida is about many things – death, bravery, performance. It is certainly bloody and cruel and there is nothing worse than to see a matador and his sidekicks mess up the kill. Although it has its roots in ancient Roman 'games', *la lidia*, as the art of bullfighting is also known, took off in an organised fashion in Spain in the mid-18th century. In the 1830s, Pedro Romero, the greatest *torero* (bullfighter) of the time was, at the age of 77, appointed director of the Escuela de Tauromaquia de Sevilla, the country's first bullfighters' college. It was around this time, too, that breeders succeeded in creating the first reliable breeds of *toro bravo* or fighting bull.

The Fight The bullfight generally begins at 6 pm, hence the title of Hemingway's manual on the subject, *Death in the Afternoon*. As a rule, six toros and three matadors are on the day's card. If any are considered not up to scratch they are booed off (the president will display a green hand-kerchief) and replacements brought on. Each fight takes about 15 to 20 minutes.

Traditionally, young men have aspired to the ring in the hope of fame and fortune, much as boxers have done. Most attain neither. Only champion matadors make good money, and some make a loss, for the matador must rent or buy his outfit and equipment, pay for the right to fight a bull and pay his *cuadrilla* (team).

If you see a major fight you will notice the team is made up of quite a few people. Firstly, there are several *peones*, junior bullfighters under the orders of the main torero, who is the matador. The peones come out to distract the bull with great capes, manoeuvre him into the desired position and so on.

Then come the *picadores*, mounted on horseback. Charged by the bull, which tries to eviscerate the (nowadays) heavily padded and blind-folded horse, the picador shoves his lance into the withers of the bull. The peones then return to the scene to measure their courage against the (hopefully) charging bull.

The picador is shortly followed by the *banderilleros*. Two banderilleros will each successively race towards the charging bull and attempt to plunge a pair of colourfully decorated *banderillas* (short prods with harpoon-style ends) into the bull – again aiming for the withers. This spurs the animal into action and the matador will seek to profit from it, executing more fancy manoeuvres.

The picador goads the bull and tests its courage by shoving a lance into its withers to weaken it.

The dress of the matador could be that of a flamenco dancer. At its most extravagant, the *traje de luces* (suit of lights) can be an extraordinary display of bright, spangly colour. All the toreros, with the occasional exception of the matadors, wear the black *montera* (the Mickey Mouse ears hat). The torero's standard weapons are the *estoque* or *espada* (sword) and the heavy silk and percale *capa* (cape). You will notice, however, that the matador, and the matador alone, uses a different cape with the sword – a smaller piece of cloth held with a bar of wood called the *muleta* and used for a number of different passes, or *faenas*.

How well he is doing can be judged by the cries from the crowd. The various moves must be carried out in certain parts of the stadium, which is divided into three parts: the *medios* (centre); *tercios* (an intermediate, chalked-off ring); and *tablas*, the outer ring.

When the bull seems tired and unlikely to give a lot more, the matador chooses his moment for the kill. Placing himself head-on he aims to sink the sword cleanly into the animal's neck *(estocada)* for an instant kill. It's easier said than done.

A good performance followed by a clean kill will have the crowd on its feet waving handkerchiefs in the air in clear appeal to the president to award the matador an *oreja* (ear) of the animal. The president usually waits to see how great is the crowd's enthusiasm before flopping a white handkerchief onto his balcony. If the fight was exceptional, the matador might *cortar dos orejas* – cut two ears off. On rare occasions the matador may be awarded the tail as well.

The sad carcass is dragged out by a team of dray-horses and the sand raked in preparation for the next toro. The meat ends up in the butcher's.

Names to look for include: Jesulín de Ubrique, a true macho whose attitudes to women don't go down well with everyone; Enrique Ponce, a serious class act; Joselito and Manuel Diaz (El Cordobés).

FOOTBALL

 Barcelona Football Club has not only one of Europe's best teams, Barça, but also one of its best stadiums, the 120,000 capacity Camp Nou in the west of the city (metro: Collblanc). Games are quite an occasion as long as the opposition is good enough to fire up the home team and the crowd. Check the daily press for upcoming games. Tickets, available at the stadium and through some banks, cost from around 3000 to 8000 ptas – the cheapest are in the one small standing section, a long, long way above the pitch. For more information call ☎ 93 496 36 00. The city's other club, Espanyol, based at the Estadi Olímpic on Montjuïc (map 7), traditionally plays a quiet second fiddle (in the top division) to Barça, although lately the players have been improving their game. A local derby, or better still a match against arch-rivals, Real Madrid, is a guarantee that sparks will fly – although getting tickets can be difficult.

The Boots of Barça

In 1895, a group of English residents kicked off a local football tournament in Barcelona. This odd activity, imported from Perfidious Albion, caught on. The first local club to be formed was Palamós (still in 2nd division) in 1898. On 29 November of the following year, FC Barcelona came into being.

Competition didn't really get going until the following year when three more groups formed. These were: L'Hispània, l'Irish and the Societat Espanyola de Futbol (which kept changing its name but always retained the 'Espanyol' bit). Interestingly, the latter team was the only one to permit only Spanish players. The bulk of FC Barcelona's players were English, German and Swiss, with only a few token Catalans. Some would mutter that things haven't changed much today! L'Hispània was mostly Scottish and there are no prizes for guessing who filled the ranks of l'Irish.

In November 1900, the dozen or so teams that had mushroomed formed a league, with four of them (including FC Barcelona) in the first division. The Copa Macaya, Catalunya's first championship, which was fought out the following month, saw the Scots of l'Hispània take the honours. Thus began Catalan football.

In the meantime, football was spreading across the rest of Spain. In

In the meantime, football was spreading across the rest of Spain. In the first national championships, Barcelona went under to Biscaia 2-1 in 1902.

By 1910, FC Barcelona was the premier club in a rapidly growing local league. The red and blue colours were already well known and the first signs of professionalism in the game emerged – paid transfers of players are recorded and Espan - yol's management charged spec- tators. Barça had 560 members (about 110,000 today), who were all mighty chuffed at the team's victory at that year's nation- al championship.

Antagonism between Catalan FC Barcelona and Castilian Spanish Espanyol (not to mention from Madrid's premier team, Real Madrid) was often cause for violent contests before the civil war (FC Barcelona fans will tell you it was a con- stant struggle against dodgy decisions in the national league). After Franco's victory in 1939, things didn't get any easier, but massive migration in the 1950s and 1960s brought new players and supporters – it was one way for new- comers to integrate into local society.

Barça remains one of Spain's great teams – one of only three (along with Real Madrid and Atlético de Bilbao) never to have been relegated to 2nd division. Since the league got fully under way in 1928, Barça has taken 15 cups (including the 1998 champi- onship), second only to arch-rivals Real Madrid, with 27 cups. Between them the two have virtually monopolised the game – only six other teams have managed to come out on top (three of them only once or twice) in 60 years of competition.

In keeping with the internationalisation of football, Barça remains in Dutch hands under Louis van Gaal after the retirement of master player and trainer Johan Cruyff. In the early games of the 1998-99 season the team was looking a little sluggish, but it's early days yet.

CASTLES IN THE AIR

It's a little difficult to know how to classify making human castles, but to many a Catalan, the *castellers* are as serious in their sport as any footballer.

The 'building' of *castells* is particularly popular in central and south- ern Catalunya and the number this activity's fans is growing. Teams (*colles*) from various parts of Catalunya compete in the summer and you are most likely to see castellers in town festivals (*festes majors*).

Erecting human towers is not a new pastime. The golden age of this activity was in the 1880s when the most daring castellers raised nine human storeys. Now, 57 colles have been registered by the Coordinadora de Colles Castelleres. Of these, two teams, la Vella and the Jove dels Xiquets de Valls, can trace their roots back a century. The latest team is the Castellers de Badalona (a town just north of Barcelona), which began in 1997. 'Castle-fever' is spreading – teams have sprung up, as it were, in Mallorca and France, and as far away as Mexico and Argentina.

It's very much an amateur sport. The club will pay team members' travel costs and supply a team jersey, but that's as far as the remuneration goes. It was once an exclusively male preserve but women now form up to a quarter of some colles.

The 'Castles'

The idea is to 'build' human layers of a 'castle' and then to successfully undo it without everyone tumbling in a heap. This is much easier said than done. The first level of the *tronco* (trunk) is a wide and solid scrum of people, together known as the *pinya*. The most popular teams 'playing' at home can get a thousand people chiming in to be part of the pinya!

A monument to Castellers in Vilafranca del Peredis, Catalunya

Above this you build your castle. About the best any team has recorded is a *quatre de nou* or *tres de nou*: a four-by-nine or three-by-nine castle. That means nine storeys of people, three or four in the core levels tapering to two then one person at the top. Often the base *pinya* does not provide enough buttressing, so you get more of the same on the second level. That is called the *folre*. Hence, very often the result is, say, a *quatre de nou amb folre* (a four-by-nine with folre). Teams who, on those rare occasions, can do without the folre, get extra merit. Sometimes a team will add some support to the third level (*manilles*). When one is built without any extra support at the lower levels it is termed *net* (clean).

If all goes well, the whole structure is topped off by a kid (*anxaneta*) who serves as a pinnacle, or *agulla*. When the anxaneta waves his arm the castell is complete. If it can be dismantled without collapsing in a heap, the castell is *descarregat*.

There are more permutations of this activity than crenellations on your average stone castle. Teams sometimes concentrate on a level, say seven, ranging from a *nou de set* (nine people by seven storeys) through to the really tricky two and one-person levels. Those involving two castellers per storey are *torres* (towers) and those with one per level are *pilars* (pillars). It is rare to get either above six or seven storeys. To keep team members humming, someone usually belts out some strident tunes on a *gralla*, something like a kazoo.

It is tempting to think the sky's the limit on what castellers can achieve, but perhaps it is more prosaically a question of human strength and persistence. The virtually unthinkable, a *tres de deu*, has not been achieved since the 19th century. Another challenge is *quatre de nou sense folre* (a four-by-nine without folre), also unheard of for more than 100 years.

When & Where

You don't often see castellers in action in Barcelona, although teams converge on Plaça de Catalunya in June for non-competition displays (for the exact dates check with the tourist office) and occasionally for festes in the city's barris. One of the best teams to look for is Els Castellers de Vilafranca del Penedès (see also the Excursions chapter), which appears at festas all over Catalunya. In Vilafranca, the main festa takes place around the end of August.

The standard afternoon program involves three competing colles, each with four castles to make – around three hours of sweaty work. The action takes place in town squares – just turn up and join the crowd. The season lasts roughly from February to December. Every two years there is a championship day at Tarragona's bullring, usually around October. The next meet is due in the year 2000.

DAMIEN SIMONIS

(continued from page 160)

People in need of an early morning heart-starter (or pre-sleep hair of the dog) can call in at **Bar Los de Extremadura** *(map 6, Carrer Ample 51)*, which has little to recommend it except that it is open for a tipple from about 6 am.

El Raval

This area has a number of old harbour-style bars – dark, wood-panelled and bare except for the odd mirror and vast arrays of bottles behind the bar. These now tend to be bohemian hang-outs rather than dens of low-life, but are atmospheric places to drink. One not to miss is **Bar Marsella** *(map 6, Carrer de Sant Pau 65)*, which opened its doors in 1820 and still specialises in *absenta* (absinthe), a beverage hard to find because of its supposed narcotic qualities. Your glass of absinthe (400 ptas) comes with a lump of sugar, a fork and a little bottle of mineral water (100 ptas). Hold the sugar on the fork, over your glass, and drip the water onto the sugar so that it dissolves into the absinthe, which turns yellow. The result should be a warm glow in you and a mellow atmosphere in the bar. The Marsella is open from 6 pm to about 2 am nightly.

Nearby is **The Quiet Man** *(map 6, Carrer del Marquès de Barberà 11)*, a relaxed Irish pub attracting both locals and foreigners (500 ptas for a pint of Guinness). There's live music some nights. Another Irish joint is the **Shamrock** *(map 4, Carrer dels Tallers 72)*.

Another good place is **Casa Almirall** *(map 4, Carrer de Joaquín Costa 33)*, which has been going since the 1860s; it's dark and intriguing, with *modernista* décor and a mixed clientele. **Bar Pastís** *(map 6, Carrer de Santa Mònica 4)* is a tiny old bar with a French cabaret theme (lots of Piaf in the background). It's been going on and off since the end of WWII.

L'Ovella Negra *(map 6, The Black Sheep, Carrer de les Sitges 5)*, is a noisy, fun, barn-like tavern with a young crowd and pool and *futbolín* (table soccer).

Café Que Pone Muebles Navarro, (which translates as 'Café where the Sign says Navarran Furniture'), *(map 6, Carrer* de la Riera Alta 4-6)* is an art gallery-cum-lounge-cum-bar where you can get great cheesecake! It's an odd place but worth a look. It is open until midnight (closed Mondays).

If by 2.30 am, when all these places have shut their doors, you still need a drink and you don't want a disco, your best bet (except on Sundays) is the **London Bar** *(map 6, Carrer Nou de la Rambla 36)*, which sometimes has live music and is open until about 5 am (bottled beer 450 ptas). This is a classic of the barri and has been open since 1909. It started as a hangout for circus hands (!) and in later years was frequented by the likes of Picasso, Miró and Hemingway in search of some local colour. At **Kentucky** *(map 5, Carrer de l'Arc del Teatre)*, all sorts of local types collect at this long American-style bar and mix with stray foreigners. Beer costs 300 ptas, it's tacky and always packed – perfect!

La Ribera

El Nuestro Raco, *(map 6, Carrer de la Bòria 22)*, is a curious little place for a quiet drink. It specialises in *cremat de ron* (a rum concoction) at 450 ptas a go.

El Xampanyet *(map 6, Carrer de Montcada 22)*, is the city's best known cava bar – a small, cosy place with nice tiled walls and good tapas as well as cava, which costs around 500 ptas for a typical bottle but is also available by the glass.

Next door, at No 20, the baroque magnificence of the **Palau de Dalmases** is matched only by the luxurious plushness inside. You almost feel you should don a powdered wig to sip on your cockails here, and on some nights you'll have classical music playing in the background. The snag is price – a glass of no-name wine will cost 1000 ptas! Come for the music and masked opera performance on Thursday night and 2500 ptas will get you the show and a drink.

El Nus *(map 6, Carrer dels Mirallers 5)* is a small, dim, chic bar in the narrow old streets near the Església de Santa Maria del Mar, done out with pictures of its Maharishi-lookalike owner – good for a quiet drink after dinner.

Along and near Passeig del Born (map 6), which links the Església de Santa Maria del Mar and the former fresh produce market El Born, you'll find stacks of bars. Most of them are fairly new but done with a dash of style. *Bar Rosal*, No 29, is a good example. It includes bread and hummus on the snack menu. You can get full meals in a couple of these bars too. Also worth a try on the same road are *El Copetín*, No 19, for cocktails and *Miramelindo*, No 15 – a spacious tavern where you can actually hear yourself talk as well as drink.

La Tinaja (map 6, Carrer de l'Esparteria 9), set inside an old vaulted warehouse, looks as if it's been going for decades but it started doing business in summer 1998. Nearby *Mudanzas* (map 6, Carrer de la Vidrieria 15), has been around for a lot longer. It's a popular little bar and quite often you can hear live music here. Around the corner, shady Plaça de les Olles is a charming little hideaway square in summer when the *terrasses* are in operation.

A more modern hideaway is *Local* (map 6), on the square off Carrer de Santa Maria, a curvy bar with a mellow atmosphere. You can be pretty sure of getting a drink here any night of the week until around 3 am.

In a class of its own is the nearby wine bar *La Vinya del Senyor* (map 6, Plaça de Santa Maria del Mar). Come here to taste a selection of wines and cavas, accompanied by simple snacks. There are so many places around here that you can keep busy trying out new ones all night.

If you should head north off Passeig del Born, you probably would never think to trudge up Carrer del Rec (map 6). Do it. At No 49 is *Borneo*, a laid-back bar with wide windows onto the street. Across the road and a few doors up at No 24 is *Gimlet*, where they do some mean cocktails.

If you feel like some UK ales and a spot of Sky sport in a cavernous new place, try *The Blackhorse Pub* (map 6, Carrer de l'Allada Vermell 16). It's not a bad spot.

Port Olímpic

Just wander round the harbour here and take your pick of the many bright and busy spots, all with tables out front in the open air; some have good music inside too. Problem is, the area is a little artificial and touristy.

L'Eixample

La Bodegueta (map 2, Rambla de Catalunya 100) is a classic wine cellar. Bottles and barrels line the walls and stools surround marble tables.

La Fira (map 4, Carrer de Provença 171) is a designer bar with a difference. You enter through a hall of distorting mirrors and inside you'll find that everything is fairground paraphernalia. It sounds corny but the atmosphere is fun.

Gràcia

Café del Sol and *Eldorado* are the lively bars on Plaça del Sol (map 2). The former has a vaguely bohemian crowd, tapas and tables outside. The outside part shuts by 2 am, inside you have another hour's drinking. Just off the square at Carrer del Planeta 39, *La Ñola* is a lively neighbourhood bar that has been around for ages.

The main bar on Plaça de Rius i Taulet is *Bar Chirito de Oro*. Not far off is *Alfa* (map 2, Carrer Gran de Gràcia 36) a happening place where you can drink and dance until 3 am.

Café Salambó (map 2, Carrer de Torrijos 51) is a gentle designer bar imitating a village bar, with benches at low tables, and has an upper level with pool tables. It's a favourite of writers, being owned by Carme Balcells, literary agent of Gabriel García Márquez, Milan Kundera and others who have spent time in Barcelona. There's food too – 1150 ptas for a three-course menú.

Farther up the hill are bars and cafés with potential, around the corner of Carrer de Torrijos and Carrer de la Perla. A block north, *Café La Virreina* on the leafy Plaça de la Virreina is a relaxed place with a mixed-ages crowd, 1970s rock music, cheap hot bocadillos, and tables outside.

Montjuïc

The Poble Espanyol has several bars that get lively. The most original is *Torres de Ávila* (map 7), inside the tall entrance towers themselves. Created by the top Barcelona designer Javier Mariscal (he was responsible for the Olympics mascot Kobi in 1992), it has several levels and all sorts of surreal touches, including an egg-shaped room and glass lifts that you fear will shoot you through the roof. It's open from 10 pm to 4 am.

Western Gràcia/Avinguda Diagonal

The area around Carrer de Marià Cubí gets busy with locals on weekends. It's a little on the *pijo* (well-off kids) side, but can be fun all the same. And it's not likely to be filled with tourists! Don't bother earlier in the week, as the area tends to be dead.

Mas i Mas, *(map 3, Carrer de Marià Cubí 199)* is one of the area's best known drinkeries. Another must is *Universal*, across the road at No 182. It opens Monday to Saturday until 4.30 am. Sometimes it has live music. The street is lined with bars of various types and should keep you well occupied for a night. Nearby are some discos for carrying on later into the night (see later).

Poble Nou

Here's another part of town that the flood of foreigners doesn't really reach. Carrer de Zamora (metro: Marina or Bogatell) is the place to head. If you like your bars barnlike, the *Megataverna Ovella Negra*, No 78, is the place to be from Thursday to Saturday until 3 am. There's a handful of other bars around here and Zeleste disco is nearby (see later).

LIVE MUSIC

There's a good choice most nights of the week. Most places with live music also have bars – a beer is usually between 300 and 600 ptas; many also have dance space, with the bands playing before or between disco sessions, for which you won't have to pay any extra. Starting times are rarely before 10 pm, more often midnight or 1 am. Normal entry charges range from nothing to 1500 ptas or so – the higher prices usually include a drink or two. You may pay more for visiting name bands. Big touring bands often play in the 17,000 capacity Palau Sant Jordi on Montjuïc. The Teatre Mercat de les Flors (at the foot of Montjuïc) is another much-used venue.

To find out what's on, look in *Guía del Ocio*'s 'Música' section, and check posters and leaflets in places like Glaciar bar on Plaça Reial. Here are some of the most reliable places, both for music and general liveliness:

Barri Gòtic

Barcelona Pipa Club (map 6, Plaça Reial 3): jazz Thursday to Saturday around midnight (usually 1000 ptas plus drinks); open from 10 pm (ring the bell to get in) to 2 or 3 am; like someone's flat inside

Harlem Jazz Club (map 6, Carrer de la Comtessa de Sobradiel 8): music from around 11 pm to 2 am nightly except Monday – often jazz, but also some rock and Latin (entry free, a drink compulsory)

Jamboree (map 6, Plaça Reial 17): varied jazz and funk nightly, usually at 9 pm and midnight (1000 to 1800 ptas, usually including first drink); disco later

Sala Tarantos, next door to the Jamboree: class flamenco some nights – most often Friday and Saturday at midnight (around 1500 ptas)

Poble Sec

Club Apolo (map 7, Carrer Nou de la Rambla 113): world music – chiefly African, Latin and Spanish – several nights a week around 10.30 pm (2000 ptas for big name bands), followed by live salsa or (on Friday and Saturday) a disco.

Western Gràcia/Avinguda Diagonal

These are all within a few blocks of Avinguda Diagonal; the nearest stations are Diagonal (metro), Hospital Clínic (metro) and Gràcia (suburban train).

La Antilla Cosmopolita (map 2, Carrer de Muntaner 244): full of Latin Americans and Caribbeans dancing salsa; live bands at

12.30 am or later several nights a week (normally 1500 ptas)

La Boîte (map 3, Avinguda Diagonal 477): jazz or blues – sometimes jams – several nights a week at midnight (1200 to 2500 ptas); disco later

Luz de Gas (map 2, Carrer de Muntaner 246): live soul, country, salsa, rock, jazz or pop most nights at midnight or 1 am (usually 1500 ptas)

El Clot

Savannah (map 1, Carrer de la Muntanya 16; metro: Clot): rock or punk bands a few nights a week, often around 10.30 pm (usually 1000 to 1300 ptas); disco later

Poble Nou

Zeleste (map 1, Carrer dels Almogàvers 122; metro: Marina); huge club converted from a warehouse, regularly hosting visiting rock and pop bands, as does its smaller neighbour Zeleste 2 round the corner at Carrer de Pamplona 88; name bands are usually on around 10 pm, for 1500 to 2500 ptas

DISCOS

Barcelona's discos come alive from about 2 or 3 am until 5 or 6 am, and are best on Friday and Saturday nights. Some have live bands, often starting about midnight, to fill the place before the real action begins. (Places where the bands are an attraction in their own right are listed in the Live Music section). Disco cover charges range from nothing to as much as 3000 ptas. It depends partly on how busy the place is and whether the bouncers like the look of you. If you go early, you'll often pay less. Drinks are expensive, of course: anything up to 800 ptas for a beer. Some discos ask for smart dress and won't let you in in sneakers or runners.

Guía del Ocio lists many discos in its 'Tarde & Noche' section. Where's hot changes as fast as it does everywhere but among the following places are some *de toda la vida* (ie, they've been around for ages).

Barri Gòtic & Ramblas

Jamboree (see under Live Music): from around 1.30 am, after the nightly jazz, a lively disco with two spaces – one for Latin rhythms, one for rock – till 5 am or so; entry from nothing to 1500 ptas.

Karma (map 6, Plaça Reial 10): young, student-type basement place with good music; open from around 11 pm to 4 am; usually 1000 ptas including a drink. It can get so packed you can barely move – thank God for the air-conditioning!

Moog (map 6, Carrer de l'Arc del Teatre 3): another good disco – upstairs Latin and dance hits from as far back as the 70s; downstairs strobe lights and techno. It's open until about 7 am on weekends and entry is 1000 ptas (as are the mixed drinks!).

La Ribera

Luz de Luna (see under Live Music): a fun salsa place where early in the week you can sip on piña coladas and other South American mixes and dance on the luridly decorated dance floor. Mid-week, it fills up from around 2 am but closes by about 4 am. Fridays and Saturdays you can shake and wiggle until 6 am. Cocktails cost around 600 ptas.

Fellini (Map 5, Estació de França): have to catch an early train? Well you could go to this rather loud young persons' disco until 8 am on weekends and then walk straight onto the train! This disco is in the same building as the station and house is the general theme. Entry is 1000 ptas until 4 am and 1500 ptas thereafter.

Poble Sec

Club Apolo (see under Live Music): ethnic, funk, house, soul, R&B disco Friday and Saturday from 1.30 am, live salsa Wednesday and Thursday at 12.30 am, following a main live band; 1000 ptas including a drink (free if you stay on after the main band).

Port Vell

A bevy of bars and discos open in the Maremàgnum complex (map 5) until the wee hours. In July and August, most of the action is here and spreads along the waterfront. One of the places to watch for is *Boîte Nayandei*, open nightly until 5 am. If you want to listen to hits of past decades and get views of the port, try *Hits Box*. This place has seven bars

– each in the shape of an instrument. The performers who sometimes attempt to 'recreate' groups of the past – with the aim of getting punters in the mood – can be a little embarrassing. Other possibilities range from Irish pubs to salsa spots (such as *Mojito Bar*). With such a concentration of places you can chop and change if you want, although cover charges on some are a disincentive. All in all, the crowd in the noisier discos is young to very young, but 'older' folks will find company in some of the less over-the-top establishments. Mixed drinks in these places begin around the 800 ptas mark, beer 500 ptas (you may be offered flyers for a free *second* drink in some places).

La Barceloneta

Havana Beach Club (map 1), on the Platja de San Sebastiá in La Barceloneta, is great for coctails, tapas and the sea breeze while you dance.

L'Eixample

CR (map 4, Carrer de València 234): relaxed bar-cum-disco with standard disco music and a mixed-ages, fairly clean-living crowd; entry free.

Nick Havanna (map 2, Carrer del Rosselló 208): big 1980s 'designer bar' with a video bank at one end of the dance space and glass-backed urinals flushed by veritable cascades of water; open nightly from 11 pm to 4 or 5 am, often with bands or salsa/merengue classes at midnight; free entry.

Satanassa (map 4, Carrer d'Aribau 27): 'antidesign' haunt of androgynous people (with a notable gay leaning), with gaudy erotic murals; open from about 11 pm to 4 or 5 am; free entry.

Velvet (map 2, Carrer de Balmes 161): smallish designer bar and disco inspired by the film *Blue Velvet*, with 1960s music; busy with a fairly straight crowd; free entry.

Around Avinguda Diagonal

Otto Zutz (map 2, Carrer de Lincoln 15), west of Via Augusta: for beautiful people (bouncers will decide how beautiful you are) and those who favour wearing black; often bands at midnight with no cover –

you can stay after the band finishes without paying; beer 800 ptas.

La Antilla Cosmopolita (see under Live Music): salsa scene, popular with Latin Americans and Caribbeans, with live bands often on late; usually 1500 ptas including a drink.

La Boîte (see under Live Music): disco after the nightly jazz or blues.

The Music Box (map 3, Avinguda Diagonal 618): farther west (and a favourite with the Carrer de Marià Cubí bar crowd), this thumping disco hits its straps from about 2 to 5 am (early in the week is not so hot).

Fibra Óptica (map 3, Carrer de Beethoven): virtually next door to The Music Box, it opens nightly from midnight and has two dance areas.

Salsa Salsa (map 3, Carrer de Bori i Fontestà): around the block for those who prefer Latin dance rhythms to the disco scene.

Gràcia

KGB (map 1, Carrer de Ca l'Alegre de Dalt 55): hard rock warehouse-type scene; open from 10 pm to 8 am for tireless all-nighters

Tibidabo

Mirablau (map 1, Plaça del Doctor Andreu), at the foot of the Tibidabo funicular: bar with great views and a small disco floor; open daily from 11 am until 4.30 or 5 am; entry free

El Clot

Savannah (see under Live Music): good dance music nightly from 8 pm, Sunday until midnight, Tuesday to Thursday to 3 am, Friday and Saturday to 5 am (closed Monday).

Poble Nou

Zeleste (see under Live Music): vast ex-warehouse on several levels including a huge dance space and a long, quiet bar with waiter service; best from around 2.30 to 5 am, Friday and Saturday nights

GAY & LESBIAN VENUES

Three good gay bars, virtually one on top of the other, are *Punto BCN (map 4, Carrer de*

ENTERTAINMENT

Muntaner 63-65) in l'Eixample and *Dietrich* and *Este Bar (map 4, Carrer del Consell de Cent 255 and 257 respectively)* around the corner. Punto BCN is a relaxed place to meet people, as indeed is Este Bar. Dietrich is more of a theatre café, often with entertainment, and it's quite camp. It is open until about 3 am.

Café de la Calle (map 2, Carrer de Vic 11) is a cosy meeting place for lesbians and gay men. *Antinous (map 6, Carrer Josep Anselm Clavé 6)* is a gay bookshop-cum-café.

If *Bar La Concha (map 6, Carrer de la Guàrdia 14)*, in El Raval, were a theme bar, the theme would be the actress from Castilla-La Mancha, Sara Montiel. The place is covered in more than 250 photos of her, which seem to be the big attraction for a largely gay and transvestite crowd. The music ranges from pasodobles to modern Spanish hits, and the place is open until 3 am.

A good lesbian bar is *Bahía (map 2, Carrer de Seneca 12)*, open until about 2.30 am.

Discos

The two top gay discos are *Metro (map 4, Carrer de Sepúlveda 185)* near Plaça de la Universitat, and *Martin's (map 2, Passeig de Gràcia 130)*. Metro attracts some lesbians and heteros as well as gay men; it's packed for its regular Monday-night cabarets. Martin's is gay men only. Both are open from midnight to 5 am and have 'dark rooms'. Popular with a young gay crowd is *Arena (map 4, Carrer de Balmes 32)*. It opens at midnight and closes around 5 am. *Satanassa* (see under Discos) has a heavy gay leaning. *La Sardina Borracha*, which means the 'drunk sardine' *(map 4, Carrer de Salou 23)* is a gay men's disco, open from 6 pm until late.

CLASSICAL MUSIC & OPERA

Guía del Ocio has ample listings, but the monthly *Informatiu Musical* leaflet has the best coverage of classical music (as well as other genres). You can pick it up at tourist offices and the Palau de la Virreina arts information office at La Rambla de Sant Josep 99 (map 6), which also sells tickets for many events. You will see from the leaflet that recitals take place all over the city and beyond – in theatres, museums, monasteries and so on.

Although Barcelona's great opera house, the Gran Teatre del Liceu, La Rambla (map 6), is still out of action (following a fire on 31 January 1994), there are occasional small-scale operas at places such as Palau de la Música Catalana, Teatre Victòria and Teatre Malic (detailed later).

The good news is that the Liceu is due to re-open in October 1999. The reconstruction will have cost around 17 billion ptas, but directors say that it will be one of the most technologically advanced theatres in the world. Let's hope the fire extinguishing systems are just as fabulous.

The chief venue for classical and choral music is the *Palau de la Música Catalana (map 6, Carrer de Sant Pere mes alt 11)* in La Ribera, which has a busy and wide-ranging program. Attending a concert here is also a fine way to see the gorgeous interior of this modernista building.

The *Palau Sant Jordi* on Montjuïc is used for bigger concerts and the *Mercat de les Flors (Carrer de Lleida 59)*, at the foot of Montjuïc, is an important venue for music, dance and drama (both map 7).

The easiest way to get hold of tickets for most of the above venues and other theatres throughout the city is through the Caixa Catalunya's Tel-Entrada service on ☎ 902-10 12 12. You can also book on the Internet at www.telentrada.com. Many theatres and performance spaces offer discounts of 20-25% to holders of Euro<26 cards and to senior citizens (you'll need some ID and age requirements may differ from place to place – always ask).

CINEMAS

Foreign films, shown with subtitles and original soundtrack rather than dubbed, are marked 'v.o.' *(versión original)* in movie listings. Cinemas to check for these include the *Alexis (Rambla de Catalunya 90, map 2)*; *Arkadín (Travessera de Gràcia 103, map 2)*; *Capsa (Carrer de Pau Claris 134, map 2)*; *Casablanca (Passeig de Gràcia 115, map 2)*; *Icària-Yelmo (Carrer de Salvador Espriu 61, map 1)*; *Maldà (Carrer* del Pi 5, map 6); **Renoir-Les Corts** (*Carrer de Eugeni d'Ors 12, map 3*); and **Verdi** (*Carrer de Verdi 32, map 2*).

The **Filmoteca** (*Avinguda de Sarrià 3, map 4*), specialises more in film seasons that concentrate on particular directors, styles and eras of film. If you want to see classics in the original language, then **Méliès Cinemes** (*Carrer de Villarroel 102, map 4*) is for you.

A ticket is usually 600 to 750 ptas but most cinemas have a weekly *día del espectador* (viewer's day; often Monday or Wednesday) when they charge 400 to 600 ptas.

THEATRE

Theatre is nearly all in Catalan or Spanish (*Guía del Ocio* specifies which). More meaningful than straight drama to the average visitor might be Barcelona's music hall/cabaret scene, a tradition dating from the turn of the century and still alive and well at theatres on and near Avinguda del Paral.lel like the **Teatre Arnau** (*map 7, ☎ 93 441 48 81, Avinguda del Paral.lel 60*); the **Llantiol** (*map 5, ☎ 93 329 90 09, Carrer de la Riereta 7*); and **Teatre El Molino** (*map 7, Carrer de Vila i Vilà 99*).

The **Teatre Lliure** (*map 2, ☎ 93 218 92 51, Carrer del Torrent de l'Olla*) in Gràcia is dedicated to theatre in Catalan – if you get into the language you can see anything from the classics to the latest in avant garde productions. Actors play on a stage in the middle of the theatre, surrounded by the audience.

Artenbrut (*map 2, ☎ 93 457 97 05, Carrer del Perill 9-11*) concentrates more on new and rising directors. Performances are usually in Catalan and occasionally in Castilian. **Teatre Malic** (*map 6, ☎ 93 310 70 35, Carrer de la Fusina 3*) is a relatively small spot that offers a packed program including music, alternative theatre and a mix of better known local talent and emerging genius.

Originally destined to become *the* home of Catalan theatre, Ricard Bofill's ultra neoclassical **Teatre Nacional de Catalunya** (*map 1, ☎ 93 306 57 06, Plaça de les Arts 1, metro: Glòries*) opened its doors in 1997. So far it has put on a mixed bag of not always exciting theatre. Disappointingly mainstream to some, it absorbed 14% of the city's theatre-going public in 1998.

The **Teatre Victòria** (*map 7, ☎ 93 443 29 29, Avinguda del Paral.lel 67-69*) often stages ballet and contemporary dance but otherwise is used by well known companies such as Tricicle.

The **Teatre Principal** (*map 6, ☎ 93 301 47 50, La Rambla 27*), opened again in 1998 after a long absence and tends to stage a hodgepodge of theatre and musicals.

The next big shake-up in theatre is due in 2000. Then, the Teatre Lliure will open a big new theatre space in Montjuïc, as will the Institut del Teatre. Together with the Mercat de les Flors they will form the Ciutat del Teatre (Theatre City) which, it is hoped, will attract big and better companies, as well as bigger and better audiences.

DANCE
Sardana

The *sardana*, Catalunya's national dance, is danced every week – except sometimes in August – on Plaça de la Seu in front of the cathedral at 6.30 pm on Saturday and noon on Sunday, and in Plaça de Sant Jaume at 6 pm on Sunday. These are not shows for tourists but feature ordinary Catalans doing something they enjoy and which expresses their Catalanity. The dancers join hands to form ever-widening circles, placing their bags or coats in the centre. The dance is intricate but, in true Catalan style, not flamboyant. The steps and the accompanying brass and reed music are rather sedate, at times jolly, at times melancholy, rising to occasional crescendos, then quietening down again.

Flamenco

Barcelona is not a major centre for this sultry Andalucían dance, but a few tacky *tablaos* are scattered about. If this is the only way you can see it, perhaps it's better than nothing. **El Tablao de Carmen** (*☎ 93 325 68 95, Carrer dels Arcs*) is in the Poble Espanyol (map 7) while the **Cordobés** (*map 5, ☎ 93 317 66 53*) is at La Rambla 35. Book ahead.

Shopping

Although perhaps not in the same league as London, Paris or Milan, Barcelona is certainly up there among Europe's stylish cities. The city is a natural magnet for the fashion-conscious and there is no shortage of design outlets for even the most tireless consumer.

Everything from books to jewels, *haute couture* (both local and international) designer furniture, cava and condoms is on offer. Several markets animate *plaçes* around the centre of town.

Most of the mainstream stores can be found on a shopping 'axis' which looks something like the hands of a clock set at ten to six. From the waterfront it leads up La Rambla through Plaça de Catalunya and on up Passeig de Gràcia (see map 1). At Avinguda Diagonal you turn left. From here as far as Plaça de la Reina Maria Cristina (especially the final stretch from Plaça de Francesc Macià) the Diagonal is jammed with places where you can empty your bank account. The T1 Tombbus service has been laid on for the ardent shopper (see the Getting Around chapter) and eventually a tram may run the length of Avinguda Diagonal too.

The best shopping areas in central Barcelona are Passeig de Gràcia and the streets to its south-west (including the Bulevard Rosa arcade, map 2, just north of Carrer d'Aragó), and Barri Gòtic streets such as Carrer de la Portaferrissa, Carrer de la Boqueria, Carrer del Call, Carrer de la Llibreteria and Carrer de Ferran, and around Plaça de Sant Josep Oriol (all map 5). You'll also find some interesting shops specialising in Latin American, African and other crafts.

Department store bargain-hunters note that the winter sales officially start on or around 10 January and their summer equivalents on or around 5 July.

ANTIQUES

If you can't break away from the old town, Carrer de Banys Nous in the Barri Gòtic (map 5) is lined with antique shops and is a good area to start. The side streets in the immediate area, including Carrer de la Palla, also hide a bevy of antique shops. While you're wandering along Carrer de la Palla, glance up at No 21 – it was once the Hospital de Sant Saver – founded back in 1462.

But there are alternatives. Bulevard dels Antiquaris, Passeig de Gracìa 55 (part of the Bulevard Rosa arcade complex) is jammed with antique shops, most of a general nature (furnishings, paintings, decorative items) with a few specialists: Brahuer (jewellery), Govary's (porcelain dolls), Dalmau (wooden frames) and Victory (crystal).

ART GALLERIES

You could start hunting for art in several places. Along Carrer de Montcada (map 6) are several galleries, the biggest being Galeria Maeght at No 25. Others include the Galeria Surrealista, next door to the Museu Picasso, the Sala Montcada of the Fundació La Caixa at No 16, Galeria Beaskoa next door and Galeria Montcada (jammed in next to the Palau Dalmases).

Another one to look for in this part of town, near the former Mercat del Born, is Galeria Tristan Barbará, Carrer de La Fusina 11 (map 6). Flassaders, at No 44 on the street of the same name, is an interesting gallery of contemporary art (map 6).

Predictably enough, the presence of the Museu d'Arte Contemporanea de Barcelona in El Raval is turning the surrounding area into an artsy zone. You'll find a half dozen small galleries and designer stores on Carrer del Doctor Dou, Carrer d'Elisabets and Carrer dels Àngels (map 6).

The classiest concentration of galleries – about a dozen of them – is on the short stretch of Carrer del Consell de Cent between Rambla de Catalunya and Carrer de Balmes (map 4).

The *Guía del Ocio* guide (for more on this useful publication, see the Entertainment chapter) carries a limited list of art galleries.

ART PRINTS & POSTERS

For many, a big Miró print or a Picasso poster would make the perfect souvenir or gift. The Fundació Joan Miró, Museu Picasso and MACBA are all well stocked. The souvenir shops in the main tourist office and Palau de la Virreina (see Souvenirs later) also carry limited offerings.

For high-quality postcards of Barcelona, prints and the like, Estamperia d'Art on Plaça del Pi (map 6) is a good place to investigate.

BARÇA

For some, football is the very meaning of life. If you fall into that category your idea of shopping heaven may well be La Botiga del Barça, Carrer de Arístides Maillol s/n (map 1, near the team's Museu del Futbol at the Camp Nou stadium,) and their branch in the Maremàgnum complex (map 6). There you can get shirts, keyrings, footballs, the works – anything you could think of featuring the famous red and blue colours.

BOOKS

There is no shortage of decent bookshops in Barcelona but the local product is a little pricey, so people used to UK and US prices for English-language titles should hesitate before plunging in. The cost of printing in Spain is high, so books in Spanish will be expensive here and still more so abroad. Those keen on Catalan have come to the right place. A wealth of specialist bookshops cater to particular requirements and quite a few outlets sell general literature in other European languages too.

La Rambla

Llibreria & Informació Cultural de la Generalitat de Catalunya, Rambla dels Estudis 118 (map 5) – a good first stop for books and pamphlets on all things Catalan, although a lot of it is highly specialised and technical stuff

Llibreria de la Virreina, in the Palau de la Virreina, La Rambla de Sant Josep 99 (map 5) – an assortment of art/architecture and art history books, many with at least some relevance to Barcelona

Barri Gòtic & El Raval

Cómplices, Carrer de Cervantes 2 (map 6) – gay and lesbian books

Documenta, Carrer del Cardenal Casañas 4 (map 6) – novels in English and French, maps

Próleg, Carrer de la Dagueria 13 (map 5) – women's bookshop

Quera, Carrer de Petritxol 2 (map 6) – specialist in maps and guides, including for hiking and trekking

Salas Llibreteria, Carrer de la Unió 3 (map 6) – new and used books in several languages

MACBA, Plaça dels Àngels (map 5) – this place is an excellent source of books on a whole range of visual arts and architectural subjects

L'Eixample

Herder, Carrer de Balmes 26 (map 5) – one of the city's best general bookstores, with a wealth of material and foreign language books too

Happy Books, Carrer de Provença 286 in l'Eixample (map 2), – another place with a bit of everything. The big advantage with this place is the prices. Not only are the books cheap but occasionally they have some on special offers for even sillier prices. The patio and café inside the bookshop make this place worth a look even if you don't want to stock up on literature. Other branches are around the corner at Passeig de Gràcia 77 and Carrer de Pelai 20 (map 5).

Altaïr, Carrer de Balmes 71 (map 5) – great travel bookshop with maps, guides and travel literature

BCN, Carrer d'Aragó 277 (map 3) – literature and travel guides in English; some French literature; good for dictionaries

Come In, Carrer de Provença 203 (map 2) – specialist in English-teaching books; also plenty of novels and books on Spain, in English and French

Laie, Carrer de Pau Claris 85 (map 6) – novels and books on architecture, art and film in English, French, Spanish and Catalan

Librería Francesa, Passeig de Gràcia 91 (map 2) – lots of novels and guidebooks in French, English, Spanish and Catalan

The English Bookshop, Carrer d'Entença 63 (map 5) – a good range of literature, teaching material and children's books

Gràcia

Bookstore, Carrer de la Granja 13 (Greater Barcelona map) – second-hand English-language books

CAMPING & OUTDOOR

For every kind of tent you can imagine, head for Alquiler Tiendas Camping, Carrer del Planeta 5 in Gràcia (map 2). They sell, rent and repair the things.

To get equipped for mountain climbing and the like, try Campamà, Carrer del Comte d'Urgell 95 (map 4).

CANDLES

Even if you are not interested in all the mounds of wax, you may want to pop in to Cereria Subirà, Baixada de la Llibreteria 7 (map 6) just to say you have been in the oldest shop in Barcelona. It started in 1761.

CLOTHING & FABRICS

If you are after international fashion, Avinguda Diagonal (map 3) is the place to look. Calvin Klein is at No 484 (map 2), Giorgio Armani at Nos 490 (map2) and 620, Gianni Versace at No 606 (map 3) and Gucci at No 415 (map 2). Jean Pierre Bua, at No 469, hosts designers ranging from Jean Paul Gaultier through to Helmut Lang.

Max Mara fans will want to head for Passeig de Gràcia 23 (map 2).

Loewe, at Avinguda Diagonal 570 (map 3), is one of Spain's leading and oldest fashion stores, founded in 1846. There's another branch, opened in 1943, in the modernista Casa Lleo Morera on Passeig de Gràcia (map 2). You could also try Ortiga, (map 3) Carrer de Borí i Fontestà 10, for prêt-a-porter evening dresses. Adolfo Domínguez, Passeig de Gràcia 32, is a star name in Spanish fashion and Gonzalo Comelier, on the corner of Passeig de Gràcia and Carrer de Caps, is known for men's clothing.

Zaire is another well-known local name for women's fashion. It is a chain and you'll find several across town including branches in l'Illa del Diagonal shopping complex (see Department Stores below), Avinguda Diagonal 584 and at Avinguda del Portal de l'Àngel 24 (map 6). Antonio Miró, Carrer del Consell de Cent 349 (map 2), concentrates on light, natural fibres to produce smart, unpretentious men's and women's fashion – jackets are a strong point.

Jeanne Weis at Carrer d'En Rauric 8 (map 6) north of Carrer de Ferran (Barri Gòtic) is a tiny shop with some nice lines in African printed fabrics, cushions and shirts. Jacquard du Monde at Avinguda del Portal de l'Àngel 5 (map 6, Barri Gòtic) has colourfully patterned sweaters from around 8000 ptas.

CERAMICS

A couple of interesting ceramics and pottery shops are hidden north of the Catedral. Ceràmiques i Terrisses Cadí, Carrer de les Magdalenes 23 (map 6) has a diverse range of plates, jugs and so on. If they have nothing of interest, the shop across the road, marked simply Cerámica, might.

CONDOMS

Barcelona even has several exotic condom shops, one of them on one of the prettiest squares of the Barri Gòtic – La Condoneria at Plaça de Sant Josep Oriol 3 (map 6). Here you can purchase condoms of every colour and shape you could dream of (and some that might never have occurred to you).

A slightly less colourful array of prophylactics is also available at Condon Center, Carrer del Carme 66 in El Raval (map 6).

CRAFTS

If you want to take a look at high quality Catalan crafts (artesania) to get some inspiration for future shopping expeditions, pop into the Centre Català d'Artesania (☎ 93 215 71 78) at Passeig de Gràcia 55 (map 2). It is dedicated to promoting and maintaining Catalan craft traditions. The centre usually hosts exhibitions of current work.

Nature Selection at Carrer del Consell de Cent 304 between Passeig de Gràcia and Rambla de Catalunya (map 2, l'Eixample) has a big stock of ethnic bags (leather and cloth), jewellery, pots, drums, carvings, glass, baskets, tablecloths, rugs and more. Casa Miranda, Carrer de Banys Nous 15 (map 6) has woven baskets of all shapes and sizes.

orre de Calatrava, Anella Olímpica, Montjüíc

DAMIEN SIMONIS

Dona i Ocell by Joan Miró, Parc Joan Miró

DAMIEN SIMONIS

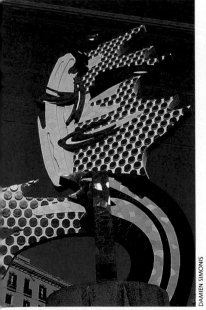

arcelona's Head by Roy Lichtenstein, Port Vell

DAMIEN SIMONIS

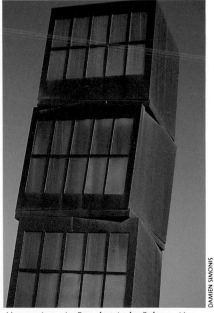

Homenatge a La Barceloneta by Rebecca Horn

DAMIEN SIMONIS

Festa de la Mercè, featuring *gegants* **(top left & middle right)**, Capgros or Big Head **(bottom left)** and **(bottom right)** the Parade of Bestie de Foc & Dimonis (Beast of Fire and Demons).

For African crafts, try Galeria Àfrica Negra, Carrer dels Banys Vells 5 in La Ribera (map 6).

DEPARTMENT STORES
The single best place to look for anything you need is the El Corte Inglés department store on Plaça de Catalunya (maps 5 & 1) – nine floors of everything, open Monday to Saturday from 10 am to 9.30 pm. It has have another important branch in the northwest of town on Plaça de la Reina Maria Cristina and a third on Avinguda Diagonal.

Marks & Spencer (map 1) is at Avinguda Diagonal 545. A couple of doors down at No 549 is FNAC, the French-owned store specialising in CDs, tapes, videos and books. Actually, the two shops form part of a huge new shopping mall – l'Illa del Diagonal – considered to be one of the city's more interesting post-Olympic architectural developments.

If you like shopping emporia, the Centre de les Glòries, (map 1) by the massive roundabout and metro stop of the same name, is probably for you. It counts 250,000 sq m of space in the grounds of the former Hispano Olivetti factory and is also home to a range of bars and eateries to take your mind off shopping for a while.

DESIGN
Vinçon, next door to La Pedrera at Passeig de Gràcia 96 (map 2), has the slickest designs in furniture and household goods, both local and imported. Not surprising really, since the building belonged to the turn-of-the-century artist Ramon Casas – painter and leading member of the *quatre gats*. People who like this kind of stuff tend to hang around inside quite a while.

Bd Ediciones de Diseño, Carrer de Mallorca 291 is worth a look, even if you have left your credit cards at home. Here you will find a collection of pieces for the home by some of Barcelona's leading designers. Opened in 1972, this prize-winning store is located in a modernista house built by Domènech i Montaner and restored in 1979.

When hanging around La Ribera, design-buffs should also mark off a little time for Aspectos, Carrer de Rec 28 (map 6), which has a broad range of stuff from furniture to art déco knicknacks for the home. The Art*quitect* showroom at Carrer del Comerç 31 (map 6) is interesting for those interested in building design.

Lulaky, Carrer del Consell de Cent 329 (map 4), has adopted the concept of the café-bookshop but in this case you'll find kitchenware, cutlery, crockery and the like. It all has a designer feel and in this case the café, which is downstairs, actually serves meals too.

FOOD & DRINK
Serious champagne sippers should pop by Xampany, Carrer de València 200 (map 4). It stocks more than 100 types and brands of cava and all the associated drinking utensils you can imagine.

If coffee is more your tipple, head for El Magnífico, Carrer de l'Argenteria 64 (map 6). These guys have been toasting all sorts of coffee for most of this century. Across the road at No 59 they have a tea shop, Sans & Sans Colonials.

Nuts to you at Casa Gispert, Carrer dels Sombrerers 23 (map 6) where they've been roasting almonds and selling all manner of dried fruit since 1851.

For longtermers in Barcelona who are interested in whipping up their own culinary storms at home but are having trouble finding all the ingredients, Marks & Spencer, Avinguda Diagonal 545, has an interesting food section and El Corte Inglés is also OK in this regard.

Superstore Asia Foods, Carrer dels Tallers 77 (map 4) in El Raval, is chock full of ingredients, otherwise hard to come by, for cooking up Asian meals. If Italian is your thing, try out Da Giorgio, Plaça del Doctor Ignasi Barraquer, south off Avinguda Diagonal (map 3).

JEWELLERY
Joyería Bagués, Passeig de Gràcia 41 (map 2, in the Casa Amatller), is a reliable name in high quality rocks. If you want to check out a more international name, try Cartier at

Carrer del Consell de Cent 351 (map 2), next door to Casa Lleo Morera. For gold jewellery, Vasari, Passeig de Gràcia 73 (map 2), is reliable.

If you wander down along the museum trail on Carrer de Montcada, you'll find several silver specialists on the same street.

LATE-NIGHT STORES

The concept of the 24-hour general store is yet to reach Barcelona, but an approximation is VIPS, an import from Madrid. It's at Rambla de Catalunya 5 (map 4) and opens Monday to Thursday from 8am to 2 am; Fridays from 8 am to 3 am; weekends from 9 am to 3 am. Locals says it is not a big success here. Down in Madrid it thrives – do Madrileños hang out later with a greater need for munchies? You may be more familiar with 7-Eleven. The one at Carrer de Roger de Llúria 2 (map 5) is open seven days from 7 am to 3 am.

LLADRÓ & MAJORICA

These are possibly the two best known Spanish brand names in the world. Lladró porcelain is coveted as much as the Majorica pearls that compete with it for display space in several stores around Barcelona. García, La Rambla 4 (map 6), is a handy spot to take a look at these products. For a broader and higher quality selection of Majorica jewellery, head for the Majorica store on the intersection of Avinguda Diagonal and Carrer de Còrsega (map 1).

MARKETS

The large Els Encants Vells (the old charms) flea market (also known as the Fira de Bellcaire) is held every Monday, Wednesday, Friday and Saturday from 8 am to 6 pm (8 pm in summer) next to Plaça de les Glòries Catalanes (metro: Glòries). The markets were shifted here in August 1928 from Avinguda Mistral, near Plaça d'Espanya, because the sight of such a jumble sale did not fit in with the town fathers' visions for the 1929 World Exhibition – such eyesores had to be removed. There are plans to shift them again – to the inner ring

of the confusing Plaça de les Glòries Catalanes roundabout. You can find everything from wardrobes to sex guides here – all at *preus de ganga* (bargain basement prices).

In the Barri Gòtic, there's a crafts market in Plaça de Sant Josep Oriol on Thursday and Friday, an antiques market in Plaça Nova on Thursday, and a coin and stamp collectors' market in Plaça Reial on Sunday morning (all on map 6). On the western edge of El Raval, the Mercat de Sant Antoni (map 4) dedicates Sunday morning to old maps, stamps, books and cards.

MUSIC

Since Virgin Megastore shut down in August 1998, the only big department store in the centre of town with any sort of CD collection is El Corte Inglés. Otherwise, you could try the FNAC (see Department Stores) which is rather far away from the centre of town. One of the biggest record stores is Planet Music, with more than 50,000 CDs, at Carrer de Mallorca 214 (map 2).

Several small shops specialising in indie and other niche music can be found on or around Carrer de les Sitges and especially on Carrer dels Tallers (El Raval), which boasts a dozen music stores. Castelló, at Nos 3 and 79, is a large family business that has been going since 1935. The family has seven stores all told and it is said to account for a fifth of the retail record business in all Catalunya. Rock & Blues, at No 10 (map 6), is a haven for good old vinyl. Hysteria, No 19, concentrates on what locals term black metal, doom and hardcore – eloquent genre names for all that is heavy metal and harder still! Sound Track, No 45 (map 5), is the home of second-hand vinyl, CDs and cassettes. CD-Drome, nearby at Carrer de Valldonzella 3 (map 4), specialises in house, hip-hop, trip-hop and other hops.

MUSICAL INSTRUMENTS

New-Phono, Carrer Ample 37, in the Barri Gòtic (map 6), has been selling instruments under one name or another since 1834. The shop is housed in what was once the stables of a noble family.

PERFUME

Regia, Passeig de Gràcia 55 (map 2), is reputed to be one of the best perfume stores in the city. There are a couple of other branches farther out of the centre.

PHOTOGRAPHY

Arpi, La Rambla 38 (map 6), has five floors given over to all things photographic (still, video and cinema). It is a standard port of call for professional snappers. For a good, second-hand collection, try Casanova, Carrer de Pelai 18 (map 4).

SHOES

There's a gaggle of relatively economical shoe shops on Avinguda del Portal de l'Àngel, off Plaça de Catalunya (map 6), Camper, at Carrer de València 249 (map 2), just off Passeig de Gràcia, has a good range of Doc Marten-type boots, mostly around 10,000 ptas a pair.

SOUVENIRS

We all succumb at one stage or another to a little kitsch. If you are in that sort of mood, the easiest thing to do is head for La Rambla. The place is lined with shops that will sell you all sorts of junk. Among the more popular items are bullfight posters with your name painted on them. Football fans can collect a Barça shirt (although you may want to check out the Barça-dedicated store first – see above).

Before you flash your cash at La Rambla's merchants, have a look inside Barcelona Original, the souvenir boutique in the building of the Centre d'Informació Turisme de Barcelona at Plaça de Catalunya. It has an interesting range of quality stuff, including ceramics, watches, art prints, coffee table books and the like. Also, most of the major museums and art galleries have shops attached where you can, as it were (sometimes literally), 'buy the T-shirt'. Some of the stuff on sale is good quality.

Excursions

Catalunya, the autonomous region of which Barcelona is the capital, has a little of everything: tacky package coastal resorts and remote cliff-side beaches, skiing and trekking, a plethora of towns and villages boasting jewels of Romanesque and Gothic art and architecture, ancient ruins to the north and south of Barcelona, and one of Europe's top gay party towns. What appears below is merely a taste of what is accessible on day trips out of Barcelona. Lonely Planet's *Spain* contains many more hints on heading farther afield.

ACCOMMODATION

Room and camping ground prices, should you want to stay more than a day, are for the high season, when it's often advisable to ring ahead to ensure a room. On the coast, prices can drop significantly in low season.

Catalunya has a wide network of *cases de pagès* (or *casas rurales* in Castilian). These are farmhouses and other rural lodgings that often provide economical and good accommodation in country areas. You can pick up a complete guide to them at the regional tourist office (Palau Robert) in Barcelona.

The 24 member hostels of Catalunya's official youth hostel network, the Xarxa d'Albergs de Joventut, all share a central booking service (☎ 93 483 83 63, fax 93 483 83 50) at USIT Unlimited, Carrer de Rocafort 116-122, Barcelona (metro: Rocafort).

At Xarxa hostels you need an HI card. With a few minor exceptions, all have the same price structure: if you're under 25 or have an ISIC, B&B is 1475 ptas in the low season and 1700 ptas in the high season; otherwise it's 1950 ptas low season, 2275 ptas high season.

GETTING AROUND

General information on transport around Catalunya is given in the Getting There & Away chapter. Specifics appear under each destination.

NORTH OF BARCELONA
Girona

Northern Catalunya's largest city, Girona (Gerona in Castilian, population 75,000), sits in a valley 36km inland from Palafrugell. Its impressive hillside medieval centre above the Riu Onyar makes it well worth a visit.

The Roman town of Gerunda lay on the Via Augusta, the highway from Rome to Cádiz (Carrer de la Força in Girona's old town follows part of the line of the Via Augusta). Taken from the Muslims by the Franks in 797, Girona became capital of one of Catalunya's most important counties, falling under the sway of Barcelona in the late 9th century.

Information The tourist office (☎ 972 22 65 75) is towards the south end of the old town, at Rambla de la Llibertat 1. It's open Monday to Friday from 8 am to 8 pm, Saturday from 8 am to 2 pm and 4 to 8 pm, Sunday from 9 am to 2 pm.

Catedral The fine baroque façade of the cathedral stands at the head of a majestic flight of steps rising from Plaça de la Catedral. Most of the building, however, is much older. Repeatedly rebuilt and altered down the centuries, it has Europe's widest Gothic nave (23m). The cathedral's museum, through the door marked 'Claustre Tresor', contains masterly Romanesque *Tapís de la Creació* (Tapestry of the Creation). The 400 ptas fee for the museum also admits you to the beautiful 12th century Romanesque cloister.

Museu d'Art Next door to the cathedral, in the 12th to 16th century Palau Episcopal, the art museum's collection ranges from Romanesque woodcarving through to early 20th century painting. It's open Tuesday to Saturday from 10 am to 6 pm (to 7 pm in summer), Sunday and holidays from 10 am to 2 pm (200 ptas).

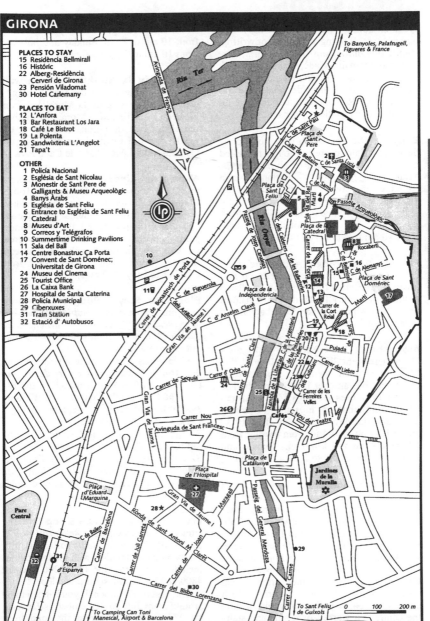

GIRONA

PLACES TO STAY
15 Residència Bellmirall
16 Històric
22 Alberg-Residència
   Cerverí de Girona
23 Pensión Viladomat
30 Hotel Carlemany

PLACES TO EAT
12 L'Anfora
13 Bar Restaurant Los Jara
18 Café Le Bistrot
19 La Polenta
20 Sandwixteria L'Angelot
21 Tapa't

OTHER
1 Policía Nacional
2 Església de Sant Nicolau
3 Monestir de Sant Pere de
   Galligants & Museu Arqueològic
4 Banys Àrabs
5 Església de Sant Feliu
6 Entrance to Església de Sant Feliu
7 Catedral
8 Museu d'Art
9 Correos y Telégrafos
10 Summertime Drinking Pavilions
13 Sala del Ball
14 Centre Bonastruc Ça Porta
17 Convent de Sant Doménec;
   Universitat de Girona
24 Museu del Cinema
25 Tourist Office
26 La Caixa Bank
27 Hospital de Santa Caterina
28 Policía Municipal
29 Ciberxuxes
31 Train Station
32 Estació d' Autobusos

EXCURSIONS

Església de Sant Feliu Girona's second great church, in part unflatteringly disguised by scaffolding at the time of writing, stands downhill from the cathedral. The 17th century main façade, with its landmark single tower, is on Plaça de Sant Feliu, but the entrance is at the side. The nave has 13th century Romanesque arches but 14th to 16th century Gothic upper levels.

Banys Àrabs The 'Arab baths' on Carrer de Ferran Catòlic are, although modelled on earlier Muslim and Roman bathhouses, actually a 12th century Christian affair in Romanesque style. Opening hours are Tuesday to Saturday from 10 am to 7 pm (summer only), Sunday and holidays from 10 am to 2 pm; the rest of the year daily from 10 am to 2 pm (200 ptas).

Passeig Arqueològic Across the street from the Banys Àrabs, steps lead up into lovely gardens that follow the city walls up to the 18th century Portal de Sant Cristòfol gate, from which you can walk back down to the cathedral.

Monestir de Sant Pere de Galligants Down across the little Riu Galligants, this 11th and 12th century Romanesque monastery has another lovely cloister. The monastery houses Girona's Museu Arqueològic (archaeology museum). Opening hours are Tuesday to Saturday from 10.30 am to 1.30 pm and 4 to 7 pm (winter from 10 am to 2 pm and 4 to 6 pm), Sunday and holidays from 10 am to 2 pm (200 ptas).

Call (Jewish Quarter) Until 1492, Girona was home to Catalunya's second most important medieval Jewish community (after Barcelona) and the Jewish quarter, the Call, was centred on Carrer de la Força. For an idea of medieval Jewish life and culture, visit the Centre Bonastruc Ça Porta, entered from a narrow alley off the upper side of Carrer de la Força. Named after Jewish Girona's most illustrious figure, a 13th century Cabbalist philosopher and mystic, the centre – a warren of rooms and stairways around a courtyard – has exhibitions and a café. It's open Monday to Saturday from 10 am to 8 pm, Sunday and holidays from 10 am to 2 pm (200 ptas).

Passeig de la Muralla You can walk along a good length of the top of the city walls – the Passeig de la Muralla – from Plaça de Josep Ferrater i Mora, just south of the Universitat de Girona building at the top of the old town, down to Plaça del General Marvà near Plaça de Catalunya.

Museu del Cinema Spain's first cinema museum houses the Col.lecció Tomàs Mallol, which includes not only displays tracing the history of cinema, but a parade of hands on items for indulging in shadow games, optical illusions and the like – great for kids. The museum opens daily, except Monday, from 10 am to 8 pm; 6 pm from October to May (400 ptas).

Places to Stay – Budget The nearest camping ground is *Camping Can Toni Manescal* (☎ *972 47 61 17, Fornells de la Selva*), 7km south. It only holds 140 people but is open all year.

Girona has a good modern youth hostel, the *Alberg-Residència Cerverí de Girona* (☎ *972 21 80 30*), well placed in the old town at Carrer dels Ciutadans 9. It's only available from July to September. High season rates are charged all year.

One of the nicest, cheaper places in the old town is *Pensión Viladomat* (☎ *972 20 31 76, Carrer dels Ciutadans 5*). Comfortable singles/doubles without bath are 2000/4000 ptas, and there are a few doubles with bath for 6000 ptas.

Places to Stay – Middle & Top End The attractive little *Residència Bellmirall* (☎ *972 20 40 09, Carrer de Bellmirall 3*), is in a lovely medieval building with singles/doubles including breakfast for 4540/7200 ptas, or 4800/7800 ptas with shower and loo.

The best deal in town, if you happen to be around from July to September, is *Històric* (☎ *972 20 91 59*), across the road from

Residència Bellmirall. It rents out four-bed apartments with lounge, fridge and stove for 3500 ptas a person.

Top of the tree is *Hotel Carlemany* (☎ 972 21 12 12, Plaça de Miquel Santaló), with doubles for 15,470 ptas plus IVA.

Places to Eat The cafés under the arcades on Rambla de la Llibertat and nearby Plaça del Vi are good places to soak up a bit of atmosphere. Several of those on Rambla de la Llibertat offer decent paellas for 850 ptas or more.

The bright *Sandwitxeria L'Angelot* (Carrer de la Cort Reial 3) is popular for its pancakes and salads from 475 ptas. Across the street, *Tapa't* has a great range of tapas from 225 ptas. You can tuck into some vegetarian goodies at *La Polenta (Carrer de la Cort Reial 6)* – mains range from 600 to 1000 ptas.

Café Le Bistrot (Pujada de Sant Domènec), on one of the most picturesque stairways in the old town, is a treat. Vaguely bohemian, it serves salads, *pizzes de pagès* (good little bread-base pizzas) and crêpes, all for between 500 and 700 ptas.

Bar Restaurant Los Jara (Carrer de la Força 4) and *L'Anfora,* just up the hill at No 15, both have four-course menús for around 1500 ptas.

Getting There & Away Barcelona Bus (☎ 972 20 24 32) runs to/from Barcelona's Estació del Nord (1¼ hours) and Figueres (50 minutes) three to seven times daily. SARFA (☎ 972 20 17 96) runs buses to most parts of the Costa Brava.

Girona (train station ☎ 972 20 70 93) is on the train line between Barcelona, Figueres and Portbou on the French border. There are around 20 trains a day to Figueres (30 to 40 minutes; 320 to 370 ptas in 2nd class) and Barcelona (1½ hours; 765 to 880 ptas).

Figueres

Another 26km north along the A-7 autopista, or by train, is Figueres (Figueras in Castilian), a bit of a dive with a one-man show – Salvador Dalí. In the 1960s and 70s he created here, the town of his birth, the extraordinary Teatre-Museu Dalí.

Information The tourist office (☎ 972 50 31 55), Plaça del Sol is open Monday to Saturday from 9 am to 8 pm.

Teatre-Museu Dalí Salvador Dalí was born in Figueres in 1904 and went to school there. Although his career took him for spells to Madrid, Barcelona, Paris and the USA, he remained true to his roots and lived well over half his adult life at Port Lligat, near Cadaqués on the coast east of Figueres. Between 1961 and 1974 Dalí converted Figueres' former municipal theatre, ruined by a fire at the end of the civil war in 1939, into the Teatre-Museu Dalí.

Even on the outside, the building aims to surprise, from the collection of bizarre sculptures at the entrance on Plaça de Gala i Salvador Dalí to the pink wall along Pujada del Castell, topped by a row of Dalí's trademark egg shapes and what appear to be female gymnast sculptures. From July to September the museum is open from 9 am to 7.15 pm daily and for most of this period there are night sessions from 10 pm to 12.30 am. Queues are long on summer mornings. From October to June the museum is open from 10.30 am to 5.15 pm daily (closed Mondays until the end of May, and on 1 January and 25 December). Entry is 1000 ptas (800 ptas October to May), and 1200 ptas for the summer night sessions.

Inside, the ground floor (Level 1) includes a semicircular garden area on the site of the original theatre stalls. In its centre is a classic piece of weirdness called *Taxi Plujós* (Rainy Taxi), composed of an early Cadillac – said to have belonged to Al Capone – and a pile of tractor tyres, both surmounted by statues, with a fishing boat balanced precariously above the tyres. Put a coin in the slot and water washes all over the inside of the car. The Sala de Peixateries (Fish Shop Room) off here holds a collection of Dalí oils, including the famous *Autoretrat tou amb tall de bacon fregit* (Self-Portrait with Fried Bacon) and *Retrat de Picasso* (Portrait of Picasso). Beneath the former stage of the theatre is the crypt, with Dalí's plain tomb.

The stage area (Level 2), topped by a glass geodesic dome, was conceived of as Dalí's Sistine Chapel. The large backdrop – egg, head, breasts, rocks, trees – was part of a ballet set, one of Dalí's many ventures into the performing arts. If proof were needed of Dalí's acute sense of the absurd, the painting *Gala mirando el Mar Mediterráneo* (Gala looking at the Mediterranean Sea) appears, from the other end of the room, with the help of coin-operated viewfinders, to be a portrait of Abraham Lincoln.

One floor up (Level 3) you come across the Sala de Mae West, a living-room whose components, viewed from the right spot, make up a portrait of Ms West – a sofa for her lips, two fireplaces for nostrils, two impressionist paintings of Paris for eyes.

Other Attractions The Museu de l'Empordà at Rambla 2 combines archaeological finds from Greek, Roman and medieval times with a sizeable collection of art – mainly by Catalan artists but there are also some works lent by the Prado in Madrid.

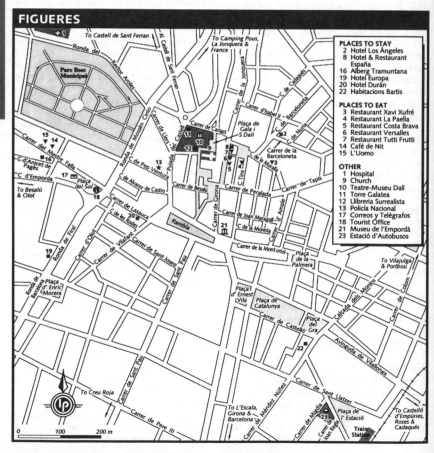

FIGUERES

PLACES TO STAY
2 Hotel Los Ángeles
8 Hotel & Restaurant España
16 Alberg Tramuntana
19 Hotel Europa
20 Hotel Durán
22 Habitacions Bartis

PLACES TO EAT
3 Restaurant Xavi Xufré
4 Restaurant La Paella
5 Restaurant Costa Brava
6 Restaurant Versalles
7 Restaurant Tutti Frutti
14 Café de Nit
15 L'Uomo

OTHER
1 Hospital
9 Church
10 Teatre-Museu Dalí
11 Torre Galatea
12 Llibreria Surrealista
13 Policía Nacional
17 Correos y Telégrafos
18 Tourist Office
21 Museu de l'Empordà
23 Estació d'Autobusos

The museum is open from Tuesday to Saturday from 11 am to 1 pm and 3 to 7 pm; Sundays from 11 am to 1.30 pm (300 ptas). You can also visit the large 18th century **Castell de Sant Ferran**, on a low hill 1km north-west of the centre.

Places to Stay – Budget *Camping Pous* (☎ 972 67 54 96), north of the centre on the N-II towards La Jonquera, is small and charges 2000 ptas for site, car and two adults. It closes in December.

The *Alberg Tramuntana* youth hostel (☎ 972 50 12 13, *Carrer d'Anicet de Pagès 2*) is two blocks west of the tourist office. It holds only 56 people (in dorms of four to 24) but is open nearly all year; high season rates are charged from July to September. It is one of the few hostels you can book through the IBN system.

Habitacions Bartis (☎ 972 50 14 73, *Carrer de Méndez Núñez 2*), on the way into the centre from the bus and train stations, has adequate singles/doubles for 1500/2500 ptas plus IVA.

Better is the almost elegant *Hotel España* (☎ 972 50 08 69, *Carrer de la Jonquera 26*), which has decent rooms for up to 4000/6600 ptas with shower, and a few cheaper ones without.

Places to Stay – Middle *Hotel Los Ángeles* (☎ 972 51 06 61, *Carrer de Barceloneta 10*) is good value with roomy singles/doubles for 3980/6770 ptas plus IVA. *Hotel Europa* (☎ 972 50 07 44, *Ronda Firal 37*), is another respectable mid-range hotel. Rooms with bath are 3250/5600 ptas plus IVA. *Hotel Durán* (☎ 972 50 12 50; fax 972 50 26 09, *Carrer de Lasauca 5*), just off the top end of the Rambla, has a bit more style. Comfortable, homely singles/doubles are 6200/8900 ptas plus IVA.

Places to Eat Carrer de La Jonquera, just down the steps east of the Teatre-Museu Dalí, is lined with restaurants – among them are *Restaurant España*, *Restaurant Tutti Frutti*, *Restaurant Versalles* and *Restaurant Costa Brava* offering reasonable

three-course menús for 700 to 900 ptas. *Restaurant La Paella*, two short blocks east on Carrer de Tins, does a menú for 950 ptas.

A qualitative leap upwards is *Restaurant Xavi Xufré (Carrer de la Muralla 7)*, where you can get a standard menú for 1000 ptas, or try the gastronomic version for 2300 ptas. The excellent restaurant of the *Hotel Durán* (see Places to Stay) is better still, but you won't get much change from 3500 ptas for a full meal.

Entertainment Two of the grooviest café-bars in town are right next to one another on Carrer del Mestre Falla – *Café de Nit* and *L'Uomo*.

Getting There & Away Barcelona Bus (☎ 972 50 50 29) runs to Girona (50 minutes) seven times a day, and on to Barcelona six times a day (2¼ hours).

Figueres is on the Barcelona-Girona-Portbou railway.

Costa Brava

The rugged Costa Brava stretches from Blanes (about 60km north-east of Barcelona) to the French border. Although parts of it are truly awful holiday resorts jam-packed with the cheap charter crowd in search of sand, sun and drinks (Lloret de Mar is a prime example of what to avoid), there are some equally spectacular locations.

If you're driving, it is quite possible to choose a spot anywhere along the coast for a day trip. Those relying on public transport may find it a bit of a stretch and should plan on staying over at least one night. Remember that in the peak months of July and August, finding accommodation can be difficult – if places listed below give no joy, get a hold of the full list of accommodation from tourist offices in Barcelona.

Tossa de Mar Marc Chagall called it Blue Paradise. A small white village backing on to a curved bay that ends in a headland protected by medieval walls and towers, Tossa is the first truly pleasant stop on the road north along the Costa Brava. In summer, boats with

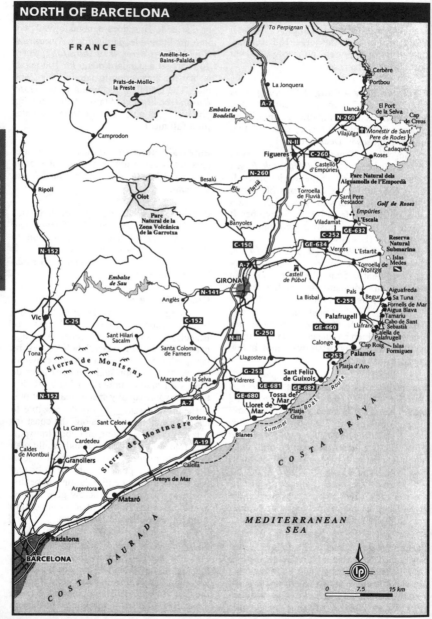

NORTH OF BARCELONA

glass bottoms will take you to some enchanting little coves and beaches to the south and north of the main beach, Platja Gran.

The bus station is just off Plaça de les Nacions sense Estat (Stateless Nations Plaza). Almost next door, at Avinguda del Pelegrí 25, is the tourist office (☎ 972 34 01 08).

There are five camping grounds around Tossa, each holding between 800 and 1700 people, but you're unlikely to find any of them open between mid-October and Setmana Santa. Nearest to town, and one of the cheapest, is *Camping Can Martí* (☎ *972 34 08 51, Rambla Pau Casals*), 1km back from the beach. Most of the 80 or so hostales and hotels are open only from Easter to October. One of the cheapest places here is *Pensión Moré* (☎ *972 34 03 39, Carrer de Sant Elm 9*) which has good-sized singles/doubles for 1300/2600 ptas; bathrooms are shared. *Fonda Lluna* (☎ *972 34 03 65, Carrer de la Roqueta 20*) is good value at 1900/3800 ptas for small rooms with bath (breakfast included). *Hotel Diana* (☎ *972 34 18 86; fax 972 34 11 03, Plaça d'Espanya 6*) is a relaxed, small-scale, older hotel fronting Platja Gran. It has a Gaudí fireplace in the lounge and offers doubles costing 11,200 ptas with sea views or 10,100 ptas looking onto the square.

On the beachfront, Passeig de Mar, the *Capri* serves up some better value food and offers a bit of almost everything – salads from 600 ptas, pizzas, pasta, meat or seafood from around 950 ptas. *Restaurant Bahía (Passeig de Mar 19)*, does some of Tossa's best food. It has a set menú for 1885 ptas.

SARFA runs to/from Barcelona's Estació del Nord up to 10 times daily. The trip takes 1¼ hours and costs 985 ptas. In summer you could get a *rodalies/cercanías* train to Blanes and pick up a boat for Tossa. Crucetours (☎ 972 37 26 96 or ☎ 909-76 60 91) and Viajes Marítimos (☎ 908-93 64 76) both run boats.

Palafrugell & Around The coast around Palafrugell is one of the most spectacular on the Costa Brava and there are several low-key beach resorts that truly warrant some effort. A little way inland, Palafrugell is the local transport hub. From there you can fan out to **Calella de Palafrugell, Llafranc, Tamariu, Aigua Blava** and **Fornells de Mar.**

There is a sprinkling of places to stay at most beaches, as well as in Palafrugell itself.

SARFA (☎ 972 30 06 23) runs buses from Barcelona's Estació del Nord (two hours; 1500 to 1705 ptas) to Palafrugell seven to 12 times daily. Or you can go to Girona first and switch buses there.

In summer, half-hourly buses link Palafrugell to Calella and Llafranc. Only three or four buses a day run to Tamariu.

For the remaining beaches, you need to get to Begur first. Three of the Barcelona-Palafrugell services continue on to Begur. From there, a Bus Platges (beach bus) service runs to Aigua Blava and Fornells, from late June to mid-September.

L'Escala & Empúries L'Escala is a pleasant medium-sized resort on the south shore of the Golf de Roses. It's close to the ancient town of Empúries (Ampurias in Castilian).

Empúries, founded around 600 BC, was probably the first, and certainly one of most important, Greek colonies in Iberia. The colony came to be called Emporion (literally, market). In 218 BC, Roman legions set foot on the peninsula here to cut off Hannibal's supply lines in the Second Punic War. By the early first century AD, the Roman and Greek settlements had merged. Emporiae, as the place was then known, was abandoned in the late 3rd century AD, after raids by Germanic tribes. Later, an early Christian basilica and cemetery stood on the site of the Greek town. Then, after over a millennium of use, the whole place disappeared altogether, to be rediscovered by archaeologists at the turn of the 20th century.

Many of the ancient stones now laid bare don't rise more than knee high. You need a little imagination – and perhaps the aid of a taped commentary (600 ptas from the ticket office) – to make the most of this site.

In spring and summer the site is open from 10 am to 8 pm, with a pedestrian entrance from the seafront promenade in front of the ruins – just follow the coast from L'Escala to reach it. At other times, opening hours are 10 am to 6 pm and the only way in is the vehicle approach from the Figueres road, about 1km from central L'Escala (400 ptas).

The nearest camping ground to the centre of L'Escala is the small *Camping La Escala* (☎ *972 77 00 84, Camí d'Ample 21*), about 700m south of La Platja. It charges 2950 ptas plus IVA for two adults with a car and tent and is open from April to September. The *Alberg d'Empúries* youth hostel (☎ *972 77 12 00, Les Coves 41*) is just south of the Empúries ruins. It has room for 68 people in dorms of six or more. High-season rates are charged from April to September. A good bet, although often booked out in high season, is *Hostal Mediterrà/Mediterráneo* (☎ *972 77 00 28, Carrer de Riera 22-24*), a block west of Carrer del Pintor Joan Massanet. Singles/doubles with shower cost 1800/ 3550 ptas in summer.

L'Escala is famous for its *anchoas* (anchovies) and good fresh local fish. The seafront restaurants are mostly expensive but, if your wallet is fat enough, try *Els Pescadors* on Port d'En Perris, the next bay west from La Platja (five minutes walk), which does superb baked and grilled fish and seafood, *suquet* and rice dishes. You will pay from 3000 to 4000 ptas a head unless you opt for the menú del día at 1680 ptas.

SARFA has one bus from Barcelona (via Palafrugell) on weekdays (1½ hours), rising to three on Sundays. Five a day run to Figueres (50 minutes), where you can pick up a train for Barcelona.

from	to	time
Figueres	Girona	50 mins
Figueres	Barcelona	2¼ hrs
Tossa	Barcelona	1¼ hrs
Palafrugell	Barcelona	2 hrs
L'Escala	Barcelona (via Palafrugell)	2½hrs
Cadaques	Barcelona	2¼ hrs

Cadaqués The northern end of the Costa Brava is more barren and, for some tastes, more startling than the coast farther south.

The sprawling white village of Cadaqués is one of the highlights of the entire coast. Salvador Dalí spent a lot of time here and in nearby Port Lligat, attracting a stream of celebs to the place.

The pretty town centre is well worth a stroll, and you'll also find a couple of art museums cashing in on the Dalí theme. If you take a 20 minute walk from Cadaqués you can visit the **Casa Museu Dalí** in Port Lligat. Visits must be booked (☎ 972 25 80 63) and you are allowed a grand total of about 30 minutes inside as you are guided through. The house is open from mid-March to 1 November daily, except Monday, from 10.30 am to 6 pm. From mid-June to mid-September the hours are extended to 9 pm, and the house remains open seven days a week.

Camping Cadaqués (☎ *972 25 81 26*), about 1km from central Cadaqués on the road to Port Lligat, has room for about 500 people and can get pretty crowded. Two adults with a tent and a car pay 2880 ptas plus IVA. It opens from Setmana Santa to September. In Cadaqués, *Hostal Marina* (☎ *972 25 81 99, Carrer de Frederic Rahola 2*), is a good bet, with singles/doubles at 3000 ptas per person, all with bath. In Port Lligat, near the small beach, *Residencia/ Aparthotel Calina* (☎ *972 25 88 51*) has a range of pleasant modern rooms and one-room apartments costing from 8100 to 10,350 ptas a double.

SARFA (☎ 972 25 87 13) has buses to/from Barcelona (2¼ hours) two to five times daily.

WEST OF BARCELONA
Montserrat

Montserrat (Serrated Mountain), 50km north-west of Barcelona, is a 1236m mountain of truly weird rock pillars, shaped by wind, rain and frost from a conglomeration of limestone, pebbles and sand that once lay under the sea. With the historic Benedictine Monestir de Montserrat, one of Catalunya's most important shrines, perched at 725m on its side, it makes a great outing from Barcelona.

The most dramatic approach is by the

cable car that swings high across the Llobregat valley from Aeri de Montserrat station, served by regular trains from Barcelona. From the mountain, on a clear day, you can see as far as the Pyrenees, Barcelona's Tibidabo and even, if you're lucky, Mallorca. It can be a lot colder up on Montserrat than in Barcelona.

Orientation & Information The cable car from Aeri de Montserrat arrives on the mountain just below the monastery. Just above the cable car station is a road and the information office (☎ 93 835 02 51), open daily from 9 am to 6 pm, with a good free leaflet-map on the mountain and monastery. Past here, a minor road doubles back up to the left to the lower station of the Funicular de Sant Joan. The main road curves round and up to the right, passing the blocks of *Cel.les* (see Places to Stay & Eat), to enter

Plaça de Santa Maria at the centre of the monastery complex.

Monestir de Montserrat The monastery was founded in 1025 to commemorate an apparition of the Virgin on the mountain. Wrecked by Napoleon's troops in 1811, then abandoned as a result of anticlerical legislation in the 1830s, it was rebuilt from 1858. Today, a community of about 80 monks lives here. Pilgrims come from far and wide to venerate the monastery's Black Virgin (La Moreneta), a 12th century Romanesque wooden sculpture of Mary with the infant Jesus. La Moreneta has been Catalunya's official patron since 1881.

The two-part **Museu de Montserrat**, on Plaça de Santa Maria, has an excellent collection ranging from an Egyptian mummy and Gothic retablos to art by El Greco, Monet, Degas and Picasso. It's open weekdays from 10 am to 6 pm; weekends and

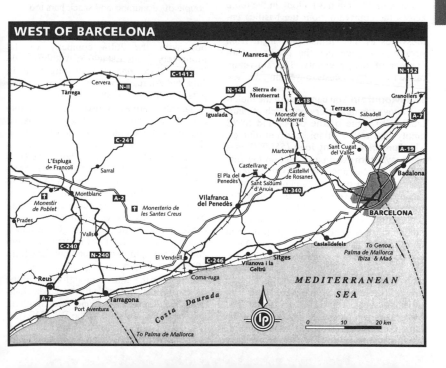

WEST OF BARCELONA

holidays from 9.30 am to 6.30 pm (500 ptas, 300 for students).

From Plaça de Santa Maria you enter the courtyard of the 16th century **basilica**, the monastery's church. The basilica's façade, with its carvings of Christ and the 12 Apostles, dates from 1900-01, despite its 16th century plateresque style. Daily from 8 to 10.30 am and noon to 6.30 pm (and weekends from 7.30 to 8.30 pm), you can file past the image of the Black Virgin, high above the basilica's main altar. Follow the signs to the Cambril de la Mare de Déu, to the right of the main basilica entrance.

The **Montserrat Boys' Choir**, or Escolania, reckoned to be Europe's oldest music school, sings in the basilica every day at 1 and 7 pm, except in July. The church fills up quickly, so try to arrive early. It is a rare treat, as the choir does not perform often outside Montserrat – five concerts a year and a world tour every two.

On your way out have a look in the room across the courtyard from the basilica entrance, filled with gifts and thank-you messages to the Montserrat Virgin from people who give her the credit for all manner of happy events. The souvenirs range from plaster casts to wedding dresses.

The Mountain You can explore the mountain above the monastery on a web of paths leading to some of the peaks and to 13 empty and rather dilapidated hermitages. The **Funicular de Sant Joan** (550/875 ptas one way/return) will carry you up the first 250m from the monastery. If you prefer to walk, the road past the funicular's bottom station will lead you up and round to its top station in about one hour (3km).

From the Sant Joan top station, it's a 20 minute stroll (signposted) to the **Sant Joan hermitage**, with fine westward views. More exciting is the one hour walk north-west, along a path marked with occasional blobs of yellow paint, to Montserrat's highest peak, **Sant Jeroni**, from where there's an awesome sheer drop on the north side. The walk takes you across the upper part of the mountain, with a close-up experience of some of the weird rock pillars. Many have

been given names: on your way to Sant Jeroni, look over to the right for La Prenyada (the pregnant woman), La Mòmia (the mummy), L'Elefant (the elephant), the phallic Cavall Bernat, and El Cap de Mort (the death's head).

Places to Stay & Eat If you want to stay over, there are several options (all ☎ 93 835 02 01) at the monastery. A small camping ground 300m along the road past the lower Sant Joan funicular station is open from Setmana Santa to October. The cheapest rooms are in the *Cel.les de Montserrat*, three blocks of simple apartments for two to 10 people. A two-person apartment costs from 3900 to 5350 ptas in high season. Overlooking Plaça de Santa Maria are the *Hotel El Monestir*, with singles/doubles in high season from 3290/6015 ptas; and the comfortable *Hotel Abat Cisneros*, with rooms from 6520/10,755 ptas in high season. You'll find a couple of restaurants and snack bars too.

Getting There & Away There's a daily bus with the Julià company to the monastery from Estació d'Autobusos de Sants in Barcelona at 9 am (plus 8 am in July and August) for a return fare of 1300 ptas. It returns at 5 pm.

The alternative is a trip by train and cable car. Trains run from Plaça d'Espanya station in Barcelona to Aeri de Montserrat, five to 10 times a day (peak frequency on summer weekdays) – a 1½ hour ride (you can get the direct R5 train or the R6 to Martorell Enllaç and connect there with the R50 for Aeri de Montserrat). Return tickets for 1770 ptas include the cable car between Aeri de Montserrat and the monastery. The cable car goes about every 15 minutes, Monday to Saturday from 10 am to 1.45 pm and 3 to 6.35 pm; Sunday and holidays from 10 am to 6.15 pm.

Probably the most straightforward route by car from Barcelona is by Avinguda Diagonal, Via Augusta, the Túnel de Vallvidrera and the A-18. Turn on to the BP-1213, just past Terrassa, and follow it 18km north-west to the C-1411. Then head a couple of kilometres south on this road to Monistrol de Montserrat, from where a road snakes about 7km up the mountain to the monastery.

There is talk of building a new *cremallera* train line up the hill from Monistrol. One of these steep incline lines ran from 1892 to 1957 and planners hope the new one will cut down car and bus traffic to what is, with 2.5 million visitors a year, Catalunya's second most visited spot.

Wine Country

Some of Spain's best wines come from the area centred on the towns of Sant Sadurní d'Anoia and Vilafranca del Penedès. Sant Sadurní d'Anoia, a half-hour train ride west of Barcelona, is the capital of *cava*, Spanish 'champagne'. Vilafranca del Penedès, 12km on down the track, is the heart of the Penedès DO, which produces noteworthy light still whites. A number of wineries open their doors to visitors and there'll often be a

free glass included in the tour, and plenty more for sale. It's a little ad hoc and often you need to call ahead to arrange a visit.

Simply touring around the area in the hope of bumping into wineries is unlikely to yield results. See the Vilafranca del Penedès section later for tips on where to gather information before embarking on a wine excursion.

Getting There & Away Up to three rodalies trains an hour run from Barcelona Sants to Sant Sadurní and Vilafranca (about 45 minutes). By car, take the A-2, then the A-7 and follow the exit signs.

Sant Sadurní d'Anoia A hundred or so wineries around Sant Sadurní produce 140 million bottles of cava a year – something like 85% of the national output. Cava is made by the same method as French Champagne and is gaining ground in international

EXCURSIONS

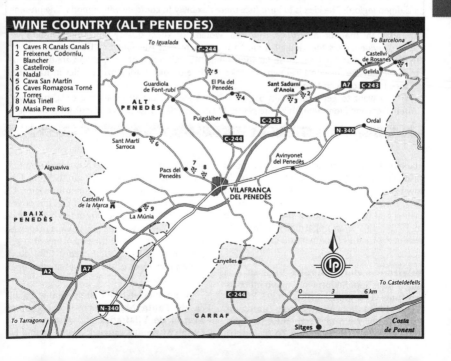

WINE COUNTRY (ALT PENEDÈS)

1 Caves R Canals Canals
2 Freixenet, Codorníu, Blancher
3 Castellroig
4 Nadal
5 Cava San Martín
6 Caves Romagosa Torné
7 Torres
8 Mas Tinell
9 Masia Pere Rius

EXCURSIONS

What's in a Label?

If your bottle is labelled DO (*denominación de origen*), you can be sure of reasonable quality. In Catalunya there are nine DO wine areas. DO refers to those areas that have maintained consistent high quality over a long period. Only some wines from Spain's premier wine-growing region, La Rioja, go one better – DOC, or *denominación de origen calificada*. These labels are indicative only. Some fine wines have no such tags.

Other categories of wine, in descending order, are: *denominación de origen provisional* (DOp), *vino de la tierra*, *vino comarcal*, and *vino de mesa* (ordinary table wine).

Vino joven is wine made for immediate drinking while *vino de crianza* has to have been stored for certain minimum periods. *Reserva* requires storage of at least three years for reds and two years for whites and rosés. *Gran reserva* is a title permitted for particularly good vintages. These wines must have spent at least two calendar years in storage and three in the bottle. They're mostly reds.

In Catalunya, the nine DO wines come from points all over the region, but the bulk of them come from the Penedès area, which pumps out almost two million hectolitres a year. The other eight DO wine-growing areas, spread as far apart as the Empordà area around Figueres in the north and the Terra Alta zone around Gandesa in the south-west, together have an output of about half that produced in Penedès.

The Catalan regional government is contemplating introducing a new, more generic label, VCPRD (*vinos de calidad producidos en una región determinada* – quality wines produced in a defined region). The idea is to introduce more flexibility to compete with imports. The present DO rules make the mixing of grape varieties from various zones near impossible. Winemakers are adamant that the new rules, if passed, would not affect quality but rather, would give Spanish winemakers the kind of room to manoeuvre that Australian and Californian winemakers have. For it is from those far shores that the chill winds of competition are beginning to blow and are making local wineries take stock, although traditional enemies in Italy and France have not been forgotten.

If you want to get information on the Internet about Catalan wines and cava, try www.interceller.com. From here, there are plenty of links to related subjects and individual wineries.

markets. Catalan vintners claim cava exports rose 30% in 1997! If you happen to be in town in October, you may catch the Mostra de Caves i Gastronomia, a cava and food-tasting fest that was held for the second time in 1998 – this is an opportunity to taste the products of a lot of competition caves.

Vilafranca del Penedès Vilafranca is larger than Sant Sadurní and much more interesting. The tourist office (☎ 93 892 03 58) on Plaça de la Vila is open Tuesday to Friday from 9 am to 1 pm and 4 to 7 pm, and Saturday from 10 am to 1 pm. In summer it also opens on Saturday from 5 to 8 pm and Sunday from 10 am to 1 pm. This is a good place to look for information on wineries. Tourist office staff can direct you to several places aside from the big boys so you can see how wine and cava is made and get a glass or two at the end. They also sell a booklet called *L'Alt Penedès* (800 ptas), which lists most of the area's wineries open to the public.

A block north, the mainly Gothic **Basilica de Santa Maria** faces the combined **Museu de Vilafranca** and **Museu del Vi** (Wine Museum) across Plaça de Jaume I.

Porta Reial, Monestir de Poblet, SW Catalunya

Catedral, Montcada, Conca de Barberá, Catalunya

DAMIEN SIMONIS

DAMIEN SIMONIS

The Monestir de Montserrat, one of Catalunya's most important shrines

BETHUNE CARMICAHEL

Monument to Castellers, Vilafranca del Peredis

Statue of El Greco, waterfront, Sitges,

Mural, Carrer dels Sedassos, Tarragona,

Gegants at the *Festa de Moros i Cristians*, Lleid

For information on wineries and wines in the area, you could approach Penedès Denominació d'Origen (☎ 93 890 48 11, fax 93 890 47 54), Carrer d'Amalia Soler 27. This is an association of all DO wineries in the region. Its website is www.totweb.com/do.penedes/ or you can email them at dopenedes@ troc.es.

A good place to get a handle on the area's wines is the Celler Cooperatiu Vilafranca del Penedès (☎ 93 817 10 35), Carrer del Bisbe Morgades 18-24. It's about a five minute walk from the tourist office.

Visiting Wineries To do a tour of the area you will need your own transport. As already hinted, you should not expect to wander into any old winery you pass. Many open their doors to the public, if at all, only at limited times during the weekend. The more enthusiastic ones will show you around the place, give you an idea of how wines and/or cava are made and finish off with a glass or two. Since cava is the area's single biggest product, it stands to reason that many of the wineries that open to the public specialise in this bubbly rather than in still wines.

The following list is by no means exhaustive but should get you started:

Freixenet
(☎ 93 891 70 00, www.freixenet.es) This is the best known cava company (although not everyone agrees its bubbly is the best), based next to the train station in Sant Sadurní d'Anoia at Carrer de Joan Sala 2. It is one of about 20 wineries in Sant Sadurní itself that open, at times, to visitors, although many require you to book ahead. Free tours are given Monday to Thursday (also Friday mornings, Saturday and Sunday in December) at 9, 10 and 11.30 am and 3.30 and 5 pm.

Codorníu
(☎ 93 818 32 32, www.codorniu.es) Bottled for the first time in 1872, and it remains one of the best caves around. The Codorníu headquarters, a modernist building at the entry to Sant Sadurní town by road from Barcelona, is open for free visits Monday to Friday from 9 am to 5 pm, Saturday and Sunday from 9 am to 1 pm.

Torres
(☎ 93 817 74 87) Three kilometres north-west

An Old Oak Tree

When, back in 1498, Javier Codorníu bought the land that he would turn into the first vineyards of Sant Sadurní d'Anoia, the single greatest feature of his purchase was a hundred-year-old oak tree.

In the following centuries a good number of the surrounding country's business deals were solemnly sworn in the shade of the grand old tree. They say that in those days a witnessed handshake was as cast iron a guarantee as anyone could expect.

By the time the first cava was bottled in 1872, the tree had become the symbol of the Raventós i Blanc family that now ran the winery, and also of the Can Codorníu farm. For Manuel Raventós, the grandson of the original producer of the farm's cava, protecting the ancient oak has taken priority even over the business of winemaking. After around 600 years, the grand old oak tree of Can Codorníu is not only in good health, it's even growing!

of the town centre of Vilafranca on the BP-2121 road near Pacs del Penedès, this is the area's premier winery. The Torres family tradition reaches back to the 17th century, but the family company, in its present form, was founded in 1870. It revolutionised Spanish winemaking back in the 1960s by introducing new temperature-controlled stainless-steel technology and French grape varieties that helped produce much lighter wines than the traditional heavy Spanish plonk. One of the biggest names in world wine production, the Torres enterprise is no longer content to restrict itself to home territory. It has wineries in California and Chile and is even planning a foray into China – that famous wine-drinking nation! It produces an enormous array of red and white wines of all qualities, using many grape varieties, including: chardonnay, sauvignon blanc, Merlot, cabernet sauvignon, Pinot Noir and more locally specific ones such as parellada, garnacha and tempranillo. Torres is open for visits Monday to Friday from 9 am to noon and 3 to 5 pm; Saturday and Sunday from 9 am to 1 pm.

EXCURSIONS

Blancher
(☎ 93 818 32 86, www.troc.es/blancher) Plaça del Pont Romà 5, Sant Sadurní d'Anoia. Just off the town's main road, La Rambla de la Generalitat, this rather huge place has been going since 1955. Visits will lead you around the plant and there is also a small museum. On weekends there are hourly tours from 10.30 am to 1.30 pm. During the week you need to call ahead.

Nadal
(☎ 93 898 80 11, www.nadal.com) Nadal is just outside the hamlet of El Pla del Penedès. It has been producing cava since 1943. The centrepiece of the place is a fine *masia*, where you can join organised visits to be acquainted with vine growing, harvest and the whole process of producing the sparkling wine. A tasting will round off the visit. On weekdays you can join in at 10 and 11 am, noon and 4, 5 and 6 pm; on Saturday from 10.30 am to 12.30 pm.

Mas Tinell
(☎ 93 817 05 86) Here is a good drop that ended up on the table for the Infanta Cristina's wedding. Mas Tinell also does some still wines and is technically open to visitors Monday to Saturday from 9 am to noon and 3 to 6 pm, although it's preferred that you call ahead.

Caves Romagosa Torné
(☎ 93 899 12 53) Farther up the road from Mas Tinell, at Finca La Serra on the road to Sant Martí Sarroca. Again, although it produces other wines, cava is the star. Open weekdays from 9 am to 1 pm and 4 to 8 pm; holidays from 10 am to 2 pm.

Cava San Martín
(☎ 93 898 82 74) Just off the C-244, about 10km north of Vilafranca, this small, friendly outfit produces several varieties of wine, including whites, reds and rosés. Again though, it is most proud of its bubbly. It's best to call ahead.

Masia Pere Rius
(☎ 93 891 82 74) This cute little *masia* (or Catalan country farmhouse) lies just outside La Múnia on the B-212 about 5km south-west of Vilafranca. It shows how cava is made and will invite you to taste some of the wines as well as the bubbly. Open Monday to Saturday from 10 am to 8 pm; Sunday and holidays from 10 am to 3 pm.

Caves R Canals Canals
(☎ 93 775 54 46) In Castellví de Rosanes, just off exit 25 from the A-7 heading south from Barcelona, this cave opens for visits on Saturday and Sunday morning. You have to call ahead.

Castellroig
(☎ 93 899 51 28) About 1km west of Sant Sadurní d'Anoia along the C-243, the winery offers tastings of its cava, but clearly with a view to selling it.

Conca de Barberà

This hilly, green back-country district comes as a refreshing surprise in the otherwise drab flatlands of south-west Catalunya. Vineyards and woods succeed one another across green rolling hills, studded with occasional medieval villages and monasteries.

Monestir de Poblet The jewel in the crown in the Conca de Barberà is this imposing fortified monastery. It was founded by Cistercian monks from southern France in 1151.

The walls of this abbey devoted to Santa Maria, as well as being a defensive measure, also symbolised the monks' isolation from the vanities of the outside world. Within the triple line of walls stand out several magnificent buildings. The Gothic **Capilla de Sant Jordi** is also known as 'la dorada' because bronze panels on the chapel were overlaid with gold to suitably impress the visiting emperor Felipe II in 1564. In the **Palau del Rei Martí**, the most captivating element is the exquisitely crafted Gothic windows. The oldest part of this sprawling abbey is the **cloister**, a transitional work showing clearly enough its Romanesque origins.

The monastery is open daily from 10 am to 12.30 pm and 3 to 6 pm; 5.30 pm in winter (500 ptas, 300 for students). One-hour guided tours (in Catalan and/or Spanish) start every 15 to 30 minutes.

If you have time you should explore the surrounding area, particularly the walled town of **Montblanc**, 8km away.

Over Easter and the summer months you can stay across the road from the monastery at the cheerful *Hostal Fonoll* (☎ 977 87 03 33). Singles/doubles start at 1995/2750 ptas without bathroom, 3900/5000 ptas with.

Regular trains from Barcelona to Tarragona via Reus (line Ca4) stop at Montblanc and L'Espluga de Francolí – the latter a 40 minute walk to the monastery.

SOUTH OF BARCELONA
Sitges

Sitges attracts everyone from jet-setters to young travellers, honeymooners to week-ending families, Barcelona night owls to an international gay crowd – anyone after a good time. The beach is long and sandy, the nightlife thumps until breakfast and there are lots of groovy boutiques if you need to spruce up your wardrobe. In winter Sitges can be dead but it wakes up with a vengeance for *carnaval*, when the gay crowd puts on an outrageous show.

Sitges has been fashionable in one way or another since the 1890s, when it became an avant-garde art-world hang-out. It has been Spain's most anticonventional, anything-goes resort since the 1960s.

Orientation The main landmark is the Es-glésia de Sant Bartomeu i Santa Tecla parish church, atop a small rocky elevation that separates the 2km-long main beach to the south-west from the smaller, quieter Platja de Sant Sebastià to the north-east. The old part of town climbs gently inland

SITGES

PLACES TO STAY
1 Camping El Rocà
5 Romàntic Hotel
9 Hostal Mariàngel
13 Hostal Parelladas
17 Hostal Bonaire
18 Hostal Rivamar

PLACES TO EAT
6 La Granja de Sitges
7 Restaurant La Viña
11 Los Vikingos
14 Eguzki
16 Restaurant Miami
19 Hotel La Santa Maria

OTHER
2 Hospital Sant Joan
3 Train Station
4 Tourist Office
8 Museu Romàntic
10 Correos y Telégrafos
12 Parrots Pub
15 Trailer Disco
20 Policía Local
21 Museu Cau Ferrat
22 Museu Maricel del Mar
23 Església de Sant
    Bartomeu i Santa Tecla

EXCURSIONS

from the church area, with the train station some 500m back, at the top of Avinguda d'Artur Carbonell.

Information The tourist office (☎ 93 811 76 30), Carrer de Sínia Morera 1, opens daily in July and August from 9 am to 9 pm; other months, Monday to Friday from 9 am to 2 pm and 4 to 6.30 pm (Saturday from 10 am to 1 pm). You can pick up a free map of gay-oriented bars, hotels, restaurants and shops, the *Plano Gay de Sitges*, at several spots around town including Parrots Pub on Plaça de la Industria.

Museums The **Museu Cau Ferrat** on Carrer de Fonollar was built in the 1890s as a house-cum-studio by Santiago Rusiñol, a co-founder of Els Quatre Gats in Barcelona, and the man who attracted the art world to Sitges.

Next door is the **Museu Maricel del Mar**, with art and artistry from the middle ages to the 20th century. The museum is part of the Palau Maricel, a stylistic fantasy built around 1910 by Miquel Utrillo. The **Museu Romàntic** at Carrer de Sant Gaudenci 1 recreates the lifestyle of a 19th century Catalan landowning family and contains a collection of several hundred antique dolls.

From late June to early September all three museums are open Tuesday to Sunday from 10 am to 9 pm; at other times, Tuesday to Sunday from 9.30 am to 2 pm, plus Tuesday from 4 to 6 pm and Sunday from 4 to 8 pm (200 ptas at each).

Beaches The main beach is divided by a series of breakwaters into sections with different names. A pedestrian promenade runs its whole length. Sitges also has two nude beaches – one exclusively gay – about 20 minutes walk beyond the Hotel Terramar at the far end of the main beach.

Places to Stay Sitges has over 50 hotels and hostales, but many close from around October to April, then are full in July and August.

Camping El Rocà (☎ 93 894 00 43, *Avinguda de Ronda s/n*), is in the upper part of town north of the railway, 1km from the beach. It has room for 600 people, at 630

ptas per adult, per car and per tent. It's open from April to September.

Two friendly places popular with travellers, both on the central Carrer de les Parellades, are *Hostal Mariàngel* (☎ 93 894 13 57), No 78 and *Hostal Parelladas* (☎ 93 894 08 01) at No 11. The Mariàngel has rooms from 2000/3750 ptas to 3000/5000 ptas (with shower). The Parelladas has singles without shower for 2400 ptas and doubles with bathroom for 5000 ptas.

One place open all year is *Hostal Bonaire* (☎ 93 894 53 26, *Carrer de Bonaire 31*), where doubles are 4000 ptas with washbasin or 5500 ptas with bathroom.

Hostal Rivamar (☎ 93 894 34 08, *Passeig de la Ribera 46*) is right on the seafront. Doubles with bathroom, if you're lucky enough to get one, are 7000 ptas plus IVA.

The *Romàntic Hotel* (☎ 93 894 83 75, *Carrer de Sant Isidre 33*), comprises three adjoining 19th century villas, sensuously restored in period style, with a leafy dining courtyard. It's popular with gay visitors, although not exclusively so. There are about 60 rooms with shower starting from 7300/10,100 ptas.

Places to Eat You'll be lucky to find a menú del día for less than 1200 ptas. The self-service *Los Vikingos (Carrer del Marques de Montroig 7-9)*, does tolerable pasta, pizzas and seafood from 725 ptas. *Hotel La Santa Maria (Passeig de la Ribera 52)* has a vast Catalan and Spanish restaurant, partly open-air, with starters like *xató* (a local fish salad in piquant dressing), *escalivada* and *esqueix-ada*, and a full range of meat and fish mains, all from around 1000 ptas.

Carrer de Sant Pau has a string of good restaurants including the Basque *Eguzki* at No 3, which offers good tapas and a mixed menu of seafood and meat mains ranging from 800 to 1600 ptas. *Restaurant Miami*, No 11, has a decent four course menú for 1300 ptas.

La Granja de Sitges, Plaça del Cap de Vila, is a lively tapas spot. *Restaurant La Viña*, Carrer de Sant Francesc 11, also has a range of generous tapas starting at around 400 ptas.

Entertainment Much of Sitges' nightlife happens on one short pedestrian strip that is packed with humanity right through the night in summer: Carrer del 1er de Maig, Plaça de la Industria and Carrer del Marques de Montroig, all in a short line off the seafront Passeig de la Ribera. Carrer del 1er de Maig – or Calle del Pecado (Sin Street) – vibrates to the volume of 10 or so disco-bars, all trying to outdo each other in decibels.

Carrer de Sant Bonaventura has a string of gay bars, mostly behind closed doors. *Trailer*, Carrer del Àngel Vidal 36, is a popular gay disco.

Getting There & Away Four rodalies trains an hour, from about 6 am to 10 pm, run from Barcelona Sants to Sitges, taking 30 minutes and costing 305 ptas (350 ptas on weekends). The best road from Barcelona is the A-16 tollway.

Tarragona

Tarragona was first occupied by the Romans, who called it Tarraco, in 218 BC. In 27 BC Emperor Augustus made it the capital of his new Tarraconensis province – most of what's now Spain – and lived here till 25 BC while directing campaigns in Cantabria and Asturias. It would not have been long afterwards that Tarragona's most famous son, Pontius Pilate, was born here. Tarragona was abandoned when the Muslims arrived in 714 AD, but reborn as the seat of a Christian archbishopric in 1089. Today, with 111,000 people, it's a mainly modern city, but its rich Roman remains and fine medieval cathedral make it an absorbing place.

Orientation The main street is Rambla Nova, which runs roughly north-west from a cliff top overlooking the Mediterranean. A couple of blocks to the east, and parallel, is Rambla Vella, which marks the beginning of the old town and which, incidentally, follows the line of the Via Augusta, the Roman road from Rome to Cádiz.

The train station is half a kilometre south-west of Rambla Nova, near the seafront, and the bus station is about 2km inland, on Plaça Imperial de Tàrraco.

Information The main tourist office (☎ 977 24 50 64), Carrer Major 39, is open Monday to Friday from 10 am to 2 pm and 4.30 to 7 pm, Saturday, Sunday and holidays from 10 am to 2 pm (and extra hours from July to September).

Catedral Tarragona's cathedral is a treasure house. Built between 1171 and 1331 on the site of the Roman city's temple, it combines Romanesque and Gothic features, as typified by the main façade on Pla de la Seu. The entrance is by the cloister on the north-west side of the building. At our last check the cathedral was open for tourist visits from Monday to Friday for hours that vary with the season but always include 10 am to 1 pm and (except from mid-November to mid-March) 3 to 6 pm. The 300 ptas charge includes a detailed booklet.

The cloister has Gothic vaulting and Romanesque carved capitals. Rooms off the cloister house the Museu Diocesà, with an extensive collection extending from Roman hairpins to some lovely 12th to 14th century polychrome woodcarvings of a breastfeeding Virgin.

The interior of the cathedral, over 100m long, is Romanesque at the north-east end and Gothic at the south-west.

Museu d'Història de Tarragona This comprises four separate Roman sites around the city. A good one to start with is the **Museu de la Romanitat** on Plaça del Rei, which includes part of the vaults of the Roman circus, where chariot races were held. The circus 300m long, stretched from here to beyond Plaça de la Font. Close to the beach is the well preserved **Amfiteatre**, where gladiators battled each other, or wild animals, to the death. In its arena are the remains of 6th and 12th century churches, built to commemorate the martyrdom of the Christian bishop Fructuosus and two deacons who were burnt alive here in 259. By Carrer de Lleida are remains of a **forum**.

The **Passeig Arqueològic** is a peaceful walk round part of the perimeter of the old town between two lines of city walls; the inner ones are mainly Roman while the outer ones were put up by the British in the War of the Spanish Succession.

From June to September, all these places are open Tuesday to Saturday from 9 or 10 am to 8 pm (the Passeig Arqueològic to midnight); Sundays from 10 am to 2 pm. In other months they tend to open from 10 am to 1.30 pm and at least two afternoon hours (Sunday and holidays 10 am to 2 pm).

A single 475 ptas ticket (free for students) is good for all four, along with the modest **Museu d'Art Modern**, Carrer de Santa Anna 8, and the 14th century noble mansion now serving as the **Museu Casa Castelarnau**, Carrer dels Cavallers 14.

Museu Nacional Arqueològic de Tarragona This carefully presented museum on Plaça del Rei gives further insight into Roman Tarraco. Exhibits include the large, almost complete *Mosaic de Peixos de la Pineda* showing fish and sea creatures. The museum is open Tuesday to Saturday from 10 am to 1 pm and 4.30 to 7 pm, Sunday and holidays 10 am to 2 pm (100 ptas, free on Tuesday).

Beaches The town beach, Platja del Miracle, is reasonably clean but can get terribly crowded. Platja Arrabassada, 1km north-east across the headland, is longer and Platja Llarga, beginning 2km farther out, stretches for about 3km. Bus Nos 1 and 9 from the Balcó stop on Via Augusta go to both.

Places to Stay There are eight camping grounds on or close to the beach within 11km north-east of the city along the N-340. Nearest is *Camping Tàrraco* (☎ 977 23 99 89) behind Platja Arrabassada, but others, such as *Camping Las Palmeras* (☎ 977 20 80 81) at the far end of Platja Llarga, are better.

The *Alberg Sant Jordi* youth hostel (☎ 977 24 01 95, Avinguda del President Lluís Companys 5), about 300m north-west of the bus station, has 192 beds but during the academ-

ic year most are taken up by students. The high season is from April to August.

Plaça de la Font in the old town has three good pensions. Cheapest is *Pensión Marsal* (☎ 977 22 40 69), at No 26. Basic singles/doubles with shower are 1650/3300 ptas. *Pensión Forum* (☎ 977 23 17 18), No 37, charges 2500/4500 ptas for much the same. *Hostal Noria* (☎ 977 23 87 17), No 53, is a bit better value at 2600/4300 ptas but is often full.

The three star *Hotel Lauria* (☎ 977 23 67 12, Rambla Nova 20) is a worthwhile splurge at 5500/10,000 ptas plus IVA, with a good location and a pool.

Places to Eat The *Pensión Marsal* has a respectable four-course lunch or dinner menú for just 700 ptas. For Catalan food, head for the stylish *Restaurant Bufet El Tiberi (Carrer de Martí d'Ardenya 5)*, which offers an all-you-can-eat buffet for about 1400 ptas per person. Nearby *Mesón Andaluz (Carrer de Pons d'Icart 3)* is a backstreet local favourite, with a good three-course menú for 1100 ptas. *Café Cantonada (Carrer de Fortuny 23)* has a lunch menú for 900 ptas; next door, *Restaurant Cantonada* has pizzas and pasta from around 600 ptas.

A popular little place is *Pizzeria Lina (Carrer de Fortuny 8)*, which has a set menu for 775 ptas. It does pizza, couscous and a ragbag of other dishes.

Several good spots line Rambla Nova. *Viena*, No 50, has good croissants and a vast range of *entrepans* from 250 ptas. *Tapas Art*, No 26, has good tapas from 200 ptas. *La Rambla*, No 10, has a set menu for 1500 ptas or you can eat à la carte for around 3000 ptas. Across the road, *Restaurant Mirador* has a swankier set menu for 2500 ptas.

Entertainment *El Cau* is a cool hangout in a Roman circus vault on Carrer de Trinquet Vell.

Getting There & Away About 20 regional and long-distance trains a day run to/from Barcelona Passeig de Gràcia (one to 1½ hours; the cheapest fare is 630 ptas in 2nd

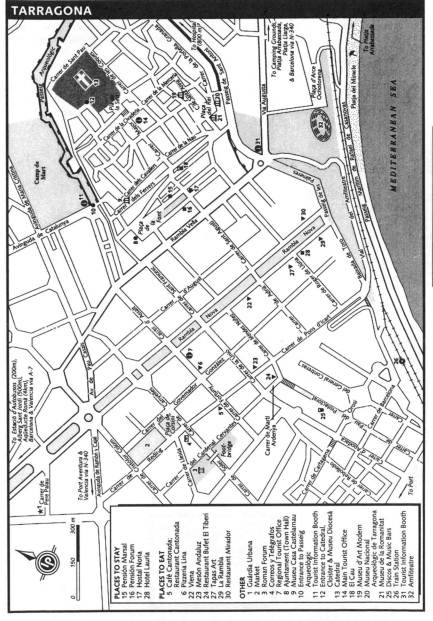

TARRAGONA

EXCURSIONS

MEDITERRANEAN SEA

PLACES TO STAY
15 Pensión Marsal
16 Pensión Forum
17 Hostal Noria
28 Hotel Lauria

PLACES TO EAT
5 Café Cantonada;
   Restaurant Cantonada
6 Pizzeria Lina
22 Viena
23 Mesón Andaluz
24 Restaurant Bufet El Tiberi
27 Tapas Art
29 La Rambla
30 Restaurant Mirador

OTHER
1 Guàrdia Urbana
2 Market
3 Roman Forum
4 Correos y Telégrafos
7 Regional Tourist Office
8 Ajuntament (Town Hall)
9 Museu Casa Castellarnau
10 Entrance to Passeig
   Arqueològic
11 Tourist Information Booth
12 Entrance to Catedral,
   Cloister & Museu Diocesà
13 Catedral
14 Main Tourist Office
18 El Cau
19 Museu d'Art Modern
20 Museu Nacional
   Arqueològic de Tarragona
21 Museu de la Romanitat
25 Discos & Music Bars
26 Train Station
31 Tourist Information Booth
32 Amfiteatre

0   150   300 m

class). About eight stop at Sitges (one hour from Tarragona). There are buses too but the train is easier.

Port Aventura

Port Aventura (☎ 902-20 22 20), 7km west of Tarragona, is Spain's biggest and best funfair-adventure park. If you have 4100 ptas to spare (3100 ptas for children aged from five to 12), it makes an amusing day out, especially if you have ankle-biters in tow. The funfair is only open from Setmana Santa to October, daily from 10 am to 8 pm; to midnight from around mid-June to mid-September. Night tickets, valid from 7 pm, are 2500 ptas.

Trains run to Port Aventura's own station, about 1km walk from the site, several times a day from Tarragona and Barcelona (1200 ptas return). By road, take exit 35 from the A-7, or the N-340 from Tarragona. Parking is 500 ptas.

Language

Barcelona is a bilingual city, with both the local Catalan and Spanish (more accurately Castilian – *castellano*) spoken by just about everyone. Indeed, for every Catalan intent on speaking the local tongue there seems to be another who'll favour Castilian. It *is* true that the signs and menus you read will more often than not be in Catalan.

Foreigners will encounter no ill-feeling for muddling through in Castilian – that in itself is appreciated. If you go the whole hog and try your hand at Catalan, you should earn extra brownie points. It's worth the effort to try at least one, as English is not as widely spoken as many travellers seem to expect.

Castilian Spanish

Pronunciation

Vowels

Unlike English, each of the vowels has a uniform pronunciation which doesn't vary. For example, the letter 'a' has one pronunciation rather than the numerous ones we find in English, such as in 'cake', 'care', 'cat', 'cart' and 'call'. Many words have a written accent. This acute accent (as in *días*) indicates a stressed syllable; it does not change the sound of the vowel. Vowels are pronounced clearly even if they are in unstressed positions or at the end of a word.

a	somewhere between the 'a' in 'cat' and the 'a' in 'cart'
e	as in 'met'
i	somewhere between the 'i' in 'marine' and the 'i' in 'flip'
o	similar to the 'o' in 'hot'
u	as in 'put'

Consonants

Some consonants are the same as their English counterparts. The pronunciation of other consonants varies according to which vowel follows. The Spanish alphabet also contains the letter ñ, which is not found in the English alphabet. Until recently, the clusters **ch** and **ll** were also officially separate consonants, and you're likely to encounter many situations – eg in lists and dictionaries – in which they are still treated that way.

b	soft, as the 'v' in 'van'; also (less commonly) as in 'book' when word-initial or when preceded by a nasal such as 'm' or 'n'
c	as the 'th' in 'thin'
ch	as in 'choose'
d	sometimes not pronounced at all
g	as in 'go' when initial or before 'a', 'o' or 'u'; elsewhere much softer. Before 'e' or 'i' it's a harsh, breathy sound, a bit like 'ch' in Scottish *loch*.
h	always silent
j	a harsh, guttural sound similar to the 'ch' in Scottish *loch*
ll	similar to the 'y' in 'yellow'
ñ	a nasal sound like the 'ni' in 'onion' or the 'ny' in 'canyon'
q	always followed by a silent 'u' and either 'e' (as in *que*) and 'i' (as in *aquí*); the combined sound of 'qu' is like the 'k' in 'kick'
r	a rolled 'r' sound; longer and stronger when initial or doubled
s	often not pronounced, especially at the end of a word; thus *pescados* (fish) is pronounced 'peh-cow' in Andalucia
v	same as 'b'
x	as the 'x' in 'taxi' when between two vowels; as the 's' in 'say' before a consonant
z	as the 'th' in 'thin'

Greetings & Civilities

Hello.	*¡Hola!*
Goodbye.	*¡Adiós!*
Yes.	*Sí.*
No.	*No.*
Please.	*Por favor.*

Thank you.	*Gracias.*
You're welcome.	*De nada.*
Excuse me.	*Perdón/Perdone.*
Sorry/Excuse me.	*Lo siento/* *Discúlpeme.*

Useful Phrases

Do you speak English?	*¿Habla inglés?*
Does anyone speak English?	*¿Hay alguien que hable inglés?*
I (don't) understand.	*(No) Entiendo.*
Just a minute.	*Un momento.*
Could you write it down, please?	*¿Puede escribirlo, por favor?*
How much is it?	*¿Cuánto cuesta/vale?*

Getting Around

What time does the ... leave/arrive?	*¿A qué hora sale/ llega el ...?*
boat	*barco*
bus (city)	*autobús/bus*
bus (intercity)	*autocar*
train	*tren*
metro/ underground	*metro*

next	*próximo*
first	*primer*
last	*último*
1st class	*primera clase*
2nd class	*segunda clase*

I'd like a ... ticket.	*Quisiera un billete ...*
one-way	*sencillo*
return	*de ida y vuelta*

Where is the bus stop?	*¿Dónde está la parada de autobús?*
I want to go to ...	*Quiero ir a ...*
Can you show me (on the map)?	*¿Me puede indicar (en el mapa)?*
Go straight ahead.	*Siga/Vaya todo derecho.*
Turn left.	*Gire a la izquierda.*
Turn right.	*Gire a la derecha.*
near	*cerca*
far	*lejos*

Around Town

I'm looking for ...	*Estoy buscando ...*
a bank	*un banco*
the city centre	*el centro de la ciudad*
the embassy	*la embajada*
my hotel	*mi hotel*
the market	*el mercado*
the police	*la policía*
the post office	*los correos*
public toilets	*los aseos públicos*
a telephone	*un teléfono*
the tourist office	*la oficina de turismo*

the beach	*la playa*
the bridge	*el puente*
the castle	*el castillo*
the cathedral	*la catedral*
the church	*la iglesia*
the hospital	*el hospital*
the lake	*el lago*
the main square	*la plaza mayor*
the mosque	*la mezquita*
the old city	*la ciudad antigua*
the palace	*el palacio*
the ruins	*las ruinas*
the sea	*el mar*
the square	*la plaza*
the tower	*el torre*

Accommodation

Where is a cheap hotel?	*¿Dónde hay un hotel barato?*
What's the address?	*¿Cuál es la dirección?*
Could you write it down, please?	*¿Puede escribirla, por favor?*
Do you have any rooms available?	*¿Tiene habitaciones libres?*

I'd like ...	*Quisiera ...*
a bed	*una cama*
a single room	*una habitación individual*
a double room	*una habitación doble*
a room with a bathroom	*una habitación con baño*
to share a dorm	*compartir un dormitorio*

How much is it ...?	¿Cuánto cuesta ...?
per night	por noche
per person	por persona
Can I see it?	¿Puedo verla?
Where is the	¿Dónde está el baño?
bathroom?	

Food

breakfast	desayuno
lunch	almuerzo/comida
dinner	cena
I'd like the set	Quisiera el menú
lunch.	del día
Is service included?	¿El servicio está
	incluido?
I'm a vegetarian.	Soy vegetariano/
	vegetariana. (m/f)

Time & Dates

What time is it?	¿Qué hora es?
today	hoy
tomorrow	mañana
yesterday	ayer
in the morning	de la mañana
in the afternoon	de la tarde
in the evening	de la noche
Monday	lunes
Tuesday	martes
Wednesday	miércoles
Thursday	jueves
Friday	viernes
Saturday	sábado
Sunday	domingo
January	enero
February	febrero
March	marzo
April	abril
May	mayo
June	junio
July	julio
August	agosto
September	setiembre/
	septiembre
October	octubre
November	noviembre
December	diciembre

Health

I'm ...	Soy...
diabetic	diabético/a
epileptic	epiléptico/a
asthmatic	asmático/a
I'm allergic to ...	Soy alérgico/a a ...
antibiotics	los antibióticos
penicillin	la penicilina
antiseptic	antiséptico
aspirin	aspirina
condoms	preservativos/
	condones
contraceptive	anticonceptivo
diarrhoea	diarrea
medicine	medicamento
nausea	náusea
sunblock cream	crema protectora
	contra el sol
tampons	tampones

Numbers

0	cero
1	uno, una
2	dos
3	tres
4	cuatro
5	cinco
6	seis
7	siete
8	ocho
9	nueve
10	diez
11	once
12	doce
13	trece
14	catorce
15	quince
16	dieciséis
17	diecisiete
18	dieciocho
19	diecinueve
20	veinte
21	veintiuno
22	veintidós
23	veintitrés
30	treinta
31	treinta y uno
40	cuarenta

50	*cincuenta*
60	*sesenta*
70	*setenta*
80	*ochenta*
90	*noventa*
100	*cien/ciento*
1000	*mil*

one million	*un millón*

Catalan

Pronunciation

Catalan sounds are not hard for an English-speaker to pronounce. You should, however, note that vowels will vary according to whether they occur in stressed or unstressed syllables.

Vowels

a	when stressed, as the 'a' in 'father'; when unstressed, as in 'about'
e	when stressed, as in 'pet'; when unstressed, as the 'e' in 'open'
i	as the 'i' in 'machine'
o	when stressed, as in 'pot'; when unstressed, as the 'oo' in 'zoo'
u	as the 'u' in 'humid'

Consonants

b	pronounced 'p' at the end of a word
c	hard before 'a', 'o', and 'u'; soft before 'e' and 'i'
ç	like 'ss'
d	pronounced 't' at the end of a word
g	hard before 'a', 'o' and 'u'; before 'e' and 'i', as the 's' in measure
h	silent
j	as the 's' in 'pleasure'
r	as in English in the middle of a word; silent at the end
rr	the roll of the tongue 'r', at the beginning of a word, or 'rr' in the middle of a word
s	as in 'so' at the beginning of a word; as 'z' in the middle of a word
v	as a 'b' in Barcelona; pronounced 'v' in some other areas
x	mostly as in English; sometimes 'sh'

Other letters are approximately as in English. There are a few odd combinations:

ll	repeat the 'l'
tx	like 'ch'
qu	like 'k'

Greetings & Civilities

Hello!	*Hola!*
Goodbye.	*Adéu!*
Yes.	*Sí.*
No.	*No.*
Please.	*Sisplau/Si us plau.*
Thank you (very much).	*(Moltes) gràcies.*
You're welcome.	*De res.*
Excuse me.	*Perdoni.*
May I?/Do you mind?	*Puc?/Em permet?*
Sorry. (forgive me)	*Ho sento/Perdoni.*
What's your name?	*Com et dius?* (inf) *Com es diu?* (pol)
My name's ...	*Em dic ...*
Where are you from?	*D'on ets?*

Language Difficulties

Do you speak English?	*Parla anglès?*
Could you speak in Castilian please?	*Pot parlar castellà sisplau?*
I (don't) understand.	*(No) ho entenc.*
Could you repeat that?	*Pot repetir-ho?*
Could you please write that down?	*Pot escriure-ho, sisplau?*
How do you say ... in Catalan?	*Com es diu ... en català?*

Getting Around

What time does the ... leave?	A quina hora surt ...?
flight	vol
train	tren
bus	autobús

I'd like a ... ticket.	Voldria un bitllet ...
one-way	d'anada
return	d'anar i tornar

Where is (the) ...?	On és ...?
bus station	l'estació d'autobusos
city centre	el centre de la ciutat
train station	l'estació de tren
tourist office	l'oficina de turisme
subway station	la parada de metro

How do I get to ...?	Com puc arribar a ...?
I want to go to ...	Vull anar a ...
Please tell me when we get to ...?	Pot avisar-me quan arribem a ...?

baggage claim	recollida d'equipatges
departures	sortides
exchange	canvi
platform	andana

Around Town

I'm looking for ...	Estic buscant ...
a bank	un banc
the city centre	el centre de la ciutat
the police	la policia
the post office	correus
a public toilet	els lavabos públics
a restaurant	un restaurant
the telephone centre	la central telefònica
the tourist office	l'oficina de turisme

What time does it open/close?	A quina hora obren/tanquen?

I want to change ...	Voldria canviar ...
some money	diners
travellers cheques	txecs de viatge

Accommodation

Is there a campsite/ hotel near here?	Hi ha algun càmping/ hotel a prop d'aquí?
Do you have any rooms available?	Hi ha habitacions lliures?

I'd like ...	Voldria ...
a single room	una habitació individual
a double room	una habitació doble
to share a dorm	compartir un dormitori

I want a room with a ...	Vull una habitació amb ...
bathroom	cambra de bany
double bed	llit de matrimoni
shower	dutxa

How much is it per night/person?	Quant val per nit/persona?
Does it include breakfast?	Inclou l'esmorzar?
Are there any cheaper rooms?	Hi ha habitacions més barates?
I'm going to stay for (one week).	Em quedaré (una setmana).
I'mleaving now.	Me'n vaig ara.

Food

breakfast	esmorzar
lunch	dinar
dinner	sopar

Can I see the menu please?	Puc veure el menú, sisplau?
I'd like the set lunch, please.	Voldria el menú del dia, sisplau.
The bill, please.	El compte, sisplau.

dessert	postres
a drink	una beguda
Bon appétit/Cheers!	Salut/Bon profit!

Some Popular Catalan Dishes

allioli
  garlic sauce
calçots
  shallots, usually served braised with an almond dipping sauce; a seasonal delicacy

War of Words

By the 12th century, Catalan was a clearly established language with its own nascent literature. It belongs to the group of western European languages that grew out of Latin, including
Italian, French, Castilian and Portuguese.

The survival or predominance of a language is frequently linked to centuries of political and
social events, and Catalan's history has been a little rocky.

It was most closely related to the *langue d'oc*, the southern French derivative of Latin that
long reigned supreme as the principal tongue in Gallic lands. The langue d'oc's most con-
spicuous survival is Provençal, a language often thought of as merely a dialect in modern
France and now spoken by only a few diehards.

Until the disaster of the Battle of Muret in 1213 (see History in Facts about Barcelona).
Catalan territory extended well across southern France, taking in Roussillon and reaching into
Provence. Catalan was spoken, or at least understood, throughout these territories, as well
as in modern Catalunya and Andorra.

In the following couple of hundred years, as the French losses were for a while compen-
sated for by Mediterranean empire building, the Catalans spread their language south into
Valencia, west into Aragón and east to the Balearic Islands (Islas Baleares). Traces of the language also remained in Sicily and Naples and the Sardinian town of Alghero is still a Catalan
-speaking outpost.

Optimists count about 10 million speakers of Catalan today – in Catalunya, Valencia,
Andorra, the Islas Baleares, the eastern strip of Aragón, a few northern enclaves of Murcia,
Roussillon (France) and Alghero.

Like most languages, Catalan has its dialects. The main distinction is between western and
eastern Catalan – the former used in Andorra, western and far southern Catalunya and the
Catalan-speaking parts of Aragón and Valencia, the latter in the rest of the Catalan world.
Those with expert ears subdivide these into 12 sub-dialects! Valencians prefer to call their
dialect *valencià* rather than *català*, while in the Balearic Islands you may hear of languages
called *mallorqui*, *menorqui* and *eivissenc* – actually the Catalan sub-dialects used in Mallorca, Menorca and Ibiza respectively. Whether you consider them separate languages or dialects
is, in a sense, irrelevant – if you come to understand the Catalan spoken in Barcelona, the differences between it and Catalan spoken elsewhere soon become apparent.

It gets even more complicated. In Sardinia and France, Italian and French are respectively the majority languages and the local tongues are rapidly becoming minority
languages. Many Valencianos actually prefer Castilian to Catalan – the whole pan-
Catalan phenomenon emanating from nationalist quarters in Barcelona is profoundly
irritating to the bulk of Valencianos. Indeed, beyond Catalunya, inland northern Valencia and Andorra, passers-by are as likely to hear Castilian spoken as Catalan. In and
around Barcelona itself, much of the population's origins lie in other parts of Spain and,
although the second generation has grown up learning Catalan, Castilian still tends to
be their first tongue.

Since the death of Franco in 1975 Catalunya has led a campaign to reinvigorate use
of the language. The Generalitat reckons 93% of the population in Catalunya understands it and 68% speaks it. In Valencia, about half the population speaks it, as does
67% in the Balearic Islands. The big problem is that not nearly so many can write it –
the true test of linguistic capacity. Even in Catalunya it is estimated that only 39% write
Catalan satisfactorily. If you find yourself watching chat programmes on local TV you

will occasionally strike comperes speaking Catalan and their interlocutors answering in Castilian.

The Catalans' campaign to revive their language has been at the centre of polemics since Jordi Pujol's nationalist Convergència i Unió (CiU) coalition took control of the Generalitat in 1980. To understand the conflict better, it has to be borne in mind that since 1714 Catalan has repeatedly been banned and the use of Castilian imposed, although frequently locals seemed little enough perturbed by this.

Renewed interest in the language came in intellectual circles with the Renaixença at the end of the 19th century and, in rural areas at least, use of the language never really slackened off. Franco again banned it, although by the 1960s he had loosened the reins a little. Still, until his demise, all education in Catalan schools was exclusively in Castilian.

It is hardly surprising that, since the birth of the regional autonomies (see History and Government & Politics in the Facts about Barcelona chapter), there has been a backlash. It is now virtually impossible to get a public service job without fluency in Catalan. Increasingly it is becoming necessary in the private sector. And just as Franco had all signs in Catalan replaced, Castilian road signs, publicity and the like are now harder and harder to find, although both languages have equal legal status.

Pujol stirred the pot still more in 1998. In January his *Llei de Política Lingüística* (Linguistic Policy Law) was passed by the Generalitat and although he reiterated that speakers of both languages would be guaranteed equal treatment, Pujol declared that he assumed the growing use of Catalan would imply the decline of Castilian.

Socialists and conservatives in and outside Catalunya cried out that Pujol was attempting to impose Catalan monolingualism. Just to add a little sauce to the debate, Pujol announced in June 1998 a system whereby at least 25% of mainstream international cinema would have to be dubbed into Catalan rather than Castilian (a law passed in September and in effect from March 1999).

Increasingly, all teaching in Catalan schools is done in Catalan. Castilian is a compulsory subject but is taught more like a second language in many cases. Pujol and company insist publicly that Catalunya will remain a bilingual territory, but the right-wing Partido Popular's culture minister in Madrid quipped that it would be a good idea to set up a Spanish institute in Barcelona to disseminate Castilian language and culture, along the lines of the British Council and Institut Francais!

A lot depends on your perspective. It does not seem unreasonable that public servants, teachers and the like must speak Catalan in Catalunya, bearing in mind that they must also be willing and able to deal with citizens in Castilian. On the other hand, such a ruling makes it virtually impossible for university lecturers, teachers and other professionals from other parts of Spain to apply for jobs in Catalunya – a clear case of discrimination in some Castilians' eyes.

Some aspects of the law reflect an almost Quixotic crusading nature in the CiU's programmes. The Second 'Additional Disposition' refers to the Generalitat's duty to 'insure the promotion, use and protection of the Catalan language and generalise and extend knowledge and use of it' in all Catalan territories (ie, all those listed above). There's a chicken-and-egg element to all of this, but one might well wonder what historical justification there could be for bolstering the use of Catalan in Alghero, when it was virtually enforced on locals there in the first place in an act of imperialism no less flagrant than any of those of which the Castilian Spaniards might be accused!

coca
a dense cake, especially popular during St Joan (John) celebrations, when it's decorated with candied peel or pine nuts

crema catalana
a light crème caramel with a burnt toffee sauce

ensaïmada mallorquina
a sweet Mallorcan pastry

escalivada
roasted red peppers and eggplant in olive oil

escudella i carn d'olla
a Christmas dish of soup and meatballs

fuet
a thin pork sausuage, native to Catalunya

mel i mató
a dessert of curd cheese with honey

mongetes seques i butifarra
haricot beans with thick pork sausage

pa amb tomàquet (i pernil)
crusty bread rubbed with ripe tomatoes, garlic and olive oil, often topped with cured ham

paella
remember, paella is Valencian in origin – if you only have it once, try to have it in Valencia

sobrassada
a spreadable red sausage; a speciality in Majorca

Drinks

almond drink	*orxata*
fruit juice	*suc*
mineral water (plain, no gas)	*aigua mineral (sense gas)*
tap water	*aigua de l'aixeta*
soft drinks	*refrescs*

coffee ...	*cafè ...*
with liquer	*carajillo (cigaló in north Catalunya)*
with a little milk	*tallat*
with milk	*amb llet*

black coffee	*cafè sol*
long black	*doble*
iced coffee	*cafè gelat*
decaffeinated coffee	*cafè descafeinat*
tea	*te*

Catalunya is famous for its *cava*, the region's 'champagne'.

a beer	*una cervesa*
a champagne	*un cava*
a rum	*un rom*
a whisky	*un whisky*
muscatel	*moscatell*
ratafia (liquer)	*ratafia*

a glass of ... wine	*un vi ...*
red	*negre*
rosé	*rosat*
sparkling	*d'agulla*
white	*blanc*

Shopping

Where can I buy ...? *On puc comprar ...?*

Where is the nearest ...?	*On és la/el ... més propera/proper?*
bookshop	*llibreria*
camera shop	*botiga de fotos*
department store	*grans magatzems*
greengrocer	*botiga de verdures (or fruiteria)*
launderette	*bugaderia*
market	*mercat*
newsagency	*quiosc*
pharmacy	*farmàcia*
supermarket	*supermercat*
travel agency	*agència de viatges*

condoms	*preservatius/condons*
deodorant	*desodorant*
razor blades	*fulles d'afaitar*
sanitary napkins	*compreses*
shampoo	*xampú*
shaving cream	*crema d'afaitar*
soap	*sabó*
sunblock cream	*crema solar*
tampons	*tampons*
tissues	*mocadors de paper*
toilet paper	*paper higiènic*
toothbrush	*raspall de dents*
toothpaste	*pasta de dents*

magazines	*revistes*
newspapers	*diaris*
postcards	*postals*

envelope	*sobre*
map	*mapa*
pen (ballpoint)	*bolígraf*
stamp	*segell*

Time, Dates & Numbers

One thing to remember when asking about times in Catalan: minutes past the hour (eg quarter past, twenty-five past) are referred to as being before the next hour. Thus 'half past two' becomes *dos quarts de tres* (two quarters to three) and 'twenty past nine' becomes *un quart i cinc de deu* (one quarter and five minutes to ten). This is repeated in minutes to the hour, where 'ten to five' becomes *tres quarts i cinc de cinc* (three quarters and five minutes to five).

What time is it?	*Quina hora és?*
It's one o'clock.	*És la una.*
It's two o'clock.	*Són les dues.*
It's quarter past six.	*És un quart de set.*
It's half past eight.	*Són dos quarts de nou.*

Monday	*dilluns*
Tuesday	*dimarts*
Wednesday	*dimecres*
Thursday	*dijous*
Friday	*divendres*
Saturday	*dissabte*
Sunday	*diumenge*

January	*gener*
February	*febrer*
March	*març*
April	*abril*
May	*maig*
June	*juny*
July	*juliol*
August	*agost*
September	*setembre*
October	*octubre*
November	*novembre*
December	*desembre*

0	*zero*
1	*un, una*
2	*dos, dues*
3	*tres*
4	*quatre*
5	*cinc*
6	*sis*
7	*set*
8	*vuit*
9	*nou*
10	*deu*
11	*onze*
12	*dotze*
13	*tretze*
14	*catorze*
15	*quinze*
16	*setze*
17	*disset*
18	*divuit*
19	*dinou*
20	*vint*
30	*trenta*
40	*quaranta*
50	*cinquanta*
60	*seixanta*
70	*setanta*
80	*vuitanta*
90	*noranta*
100	*cent*
1000	*mil*

Glossary

Items listed below are in Castilian (Spanish)/Catalan. In some cases only the Spanish (S) or Catalan (C) term appears, either because the word is the same in both languages or because the term given is the most commonly used. In some cases, only the Spanish is given as the only distinction from the Catalan is the addition of accents.

abierto/obert – open
ayuntamiento/ajuntament – city or town hall
albergue juvenil/alberg de joventut – youth hostel; not to be confused with *hostal*
alcalde – (S & C) mayor
altar mayor/major – high altar
apartado de correos/apartat de correus – post office box
artesonado – (S) *mudéjar* wooden ceiling with interlaced beams leaving a pattern of spaces for decoration
autonomía – (S) autonomous community or region: Spain's 50 *provincias* are grouped into 17 of these, of which one is Catalunya
autopista – (S & C) tollway
autovía – (S) toll-free dual-carriage highway

bakalao – (S) ear-splitting Spanish techno music (not to be confused with *bacalao*, salted cod)
Barcelonin – (C) inhabitant/native of Barcelona
barrio/barri – district, quarter of Barcelona
biblioteca – (S & C) library
bodega/celler – literally, a cellar (especially a wine cellar); also means a winery, or a traditional wine bar likely to serve wine from the barrel

capgròs – (C) huge-headed figure seen in traditional Catalan festivals
cajero automático/caixer automàtic – automatic teller machine (ATM)
call – (C) Jewish quarter in medieval Barcelona (and other Catalan towns)
calle/carrer – street
cambio/canvi – in general, change; also currency exchange
caña/canya – a small beer in a glass
capilla/capella – chapel
capilla mayor/capella major – chapel containing the high altar of a church
Carnaval/Carnestoltes – carnival; a period of fancy-dress parades and merrymaking ending on the Tuesday 47 days before Easter Sunday

carretera – (S & C) highway
carta – (S & C) menu
casa rural/casa de pagès – a village or country house or farmstead with rooms to let
castellers – (C) human-castle builders
catedral – (S & C) cathedral
cercanías/rodalies – local trains serving Barcelona's airport, suburbs and some outlying towns
cerrado/tancat – closed
cervecería/cerveseria – beer bar
claustro/claustre – cloister
comarca – (S & C) district, a grouping of municipios
comedor/menjador – dining room
comisaría/comissaria – National Police station
consigna – (S & C) left-luggage office or lockers
copas/copes – drinks (literally, glasses); *ir de copas/anar de copes* is to go out for a few drinks
coro/cor – choir (part of a church, usually in the middle)
correfoc – (C) fire-running, a part of many Catalan festes where people run about the streets chased by fire-breathing dragons and the like
Correos y Telégrafos/Correus i Telègrafs – post office
costa – (S & C) coast
cuenta/compte – bill (check)

duro – (S & C) hard; also a common name for a 5 ptas coin

entrada – (S & C) entrance
estación de autobuses/estació d'autobusos – bus station

feria/fira – (trade) fair
ferrocarril – (S & C) railway
FGC – (C) Ferrocarrils de la Generalitat de Catalunya, local trains operating alongside metro in Barcelona
fiesta/festa – festival, public holiday or party
fin de semana/cap de setmana – weekend ·
flamenco/flamenc – means flamingo and Flemish as well as flamenco music and dance

gallego/gallec – Galician; a native of Galicia
garum – (Latin) a spicy, vitamin-rich sauce made from fish entrails found throughout the former Roman Empire, including Barcelona
gegant – (C) a huge figure, usually representing

210

kings, queens and other historical figures, often seen parading around at festes
gitano – (S & C) the Roma people, formerly called Gypsies

hostal – (S & C) commercial establishment providing accommodation in the one to three star category; not to be confused with *albergue juvenil*

iglesia/església – church
IVA – *impuesto sobre el valor añadido/impost sobre el valor afegit*, or value-added tax (VAT)

librería/llibreria or **llibreteria** – bookshop
lista de correos/llista de correus – poste restante
litera/llitera – couchette or sleeping carriage
llegada/arribada – arrival

madrileño – (S) a person from Madrid
marcha/marxa – action, life, 'the scene'
marisquería – (S) seafood eatery
menú del día – (S) fixed-price meal available at lunchtime, sometimes in the evening too
mercado/mercat – market
modernisme – (C) modernism; the architectural and artistic style, influenced by Art Nouveau and sometimes known as Catalan modernism, whose leading practitioner was Antoni Gaudí
modernista – (S & C) an exponent of *modernisme*
Morisco/Morisc – a Muslim converted (often only superficially) to Christianity in medieval Spain
moro – (S & C) 'Moor' or Muslim (usually in a medieval context)
mudéjar – (S) a Muslim living under Christian rule in medieval Spain; also refers to their decorative style of architecture
muelle/moll – wharf or pier
museo/museu – museum

oficina de turismo/turisme – tourist office

Pantocrator – (Greek) Christ the All-Ruler or Christ in Majesty, a central emblem of Romanesque art
peña/penya – a club, usually of flamenco or football fans
pica pica – (C) - snacks/snacking
pinchos/pinxos – Basque for *tapas/tapes*
piscina – (S & C) swimming pool
plato combinado/plat combinat – literally 'combined plate', a largeish serve of meat/seafood/omelette with trimmings
playa/platja – beach
plaza de toros/plaça de braus – bullring
provincia – (S & C) province; Spain is divided into 50 of them
pueblo/poble – village
puente/pont – bridge; also means the extra day or two off that many people take when a holiday falls close to a weekend
puerta/porta – gate or door
puerto/port – port

REAJ – (S) Red Española de Albergues Juveniles, the Spanish HI youth hostel network
Reconquista – the Christian reconquest of the Iberian Peninsula from the Muslims (8th to 15th centuries)
refugi – (C) shelter or refuge, especially a mountain refuge with basic accommodation for hikers
RENFE – (S) Red Nacional de los Ferrocarriles Españoles, the national rail network
retablo – altarpiece
río/riu – river

sacristía – sacristy, the part of a church in which vestments, sacred objects and other valuables are kept
salida/sortida – exit or departure
sardana – (C) traditional Catalan folk dance
Semana Santa/Setmana Santa – Holy Week, the week leading up to Easter Sunday
sida – (S & C) AIDS
sierra/serra – mountain range

tapas/tapes – bar snacks traditionally served on a saucer or lid *(tapa)*
taquilla – (S & C) ticket window
tarjeta de crédito/targeta de crèdit – credit card
tarjeta telefónica – (S) phonecard
terraza/terrassa – terrace; often means a café's or bar's outdoor tables
tienda/botiga – shop
turismo/turisme – means both tourism and saloon car; *el turismo* can also mean the tourist office

urbanización/urbanització – suburban housing development

valle/vall – valley
v.o. – *versión original*, a foreign-language film subtitled in Spanish

LONELY PLANET

Phrasebooks

Lonely Planet phrasebooks are packed with essential words and phrases to help travellers communicate with the locals. With colour tabs for quick reference, an extensive vocabulary and use of script, these handy pocket-sized language guides cover day-to-day travel situations.

- handy pocket-sized books
- easy to understand Pronunciation chapter
- clear & comprehensive Grammar chapter
- romanisation alongside script to allow ease of pronunciation
- script throughout so users can point to phrases for every situation
- full of cultural information and tips for the traveller

'...vital for a real DIY spirit and attitude in language learning'
– *Backpacker*

'the phrasebooks have good cultural backgrounders and offer solid advice for challenging situations in remote locations'
– *San Francisco Examiner*

Arabic (Egyptian) • Arabic (Moroccan) • Australian *(Australian English, Aboriginal and Torres Strait languages)* • Baltic States *(Estonian, Latvian, Lithuanian)* • Bengali • Brazilian • Burmese • Cantonese • Central Asia • Central Europe *(Czech, French, German, Hungarian, Italian, Slovak)* • Eastern Europe *(Bulgarian, Czech, Hungarian, Polish, Romanian, Slovak)* • Ethiopian (Amharic) • Fijian • French • German • Greek • Hill Tribes • Hindi/Urdu • Indonesian • Italian • Japanese • Korean • Lao • Latin American Spanish • Malay • Mandarin • Mediterranean Europe *(Albanian, Croatian, Greek, Italian, Macedonian, Maltese, Serbian, Slovene)* • Mongolian • Nepali • Papua New Guinea • Pilipino (Tagalog) • Quechua • Russian • Scandinavian Europe *(Danish, Finnish, Icelandic, Norwegian, Swedish)* • South-East Asia *(Burmese, Indonesian, Khmer, Lao, Malay, Tagalog Pilipino, Thai, Vietnamese)* • Spanish (Castilian) *(also includes Catalan, Galician and Basque)* • Sri Lanka • Swahili • Thai • Tibetan • Turkish • Ukrainian • USA *(US English, Vernacular, Native American languages, Hawaiian)* • Vietnamese • Western Europe *(Basque, Catalan, Dutch, French, German, Greek, Irish)*

Lonely Planet Journeys

JOURNEYS is a unique collection of travel writing – published by the company that understands travel better than anyone else. It is a series for anyone who has ever experienced – or dreamed of – the magical moment when they encountered a strange culture or saw a place for the first time. They are tales to read while you're planning a trip, while you're on the road or while you're in an armchair in front of a fire.

These outstanding titles explore our planet through the eyes of a diverse group of international writers. JOURNEYS books catch the spirit of a place, illuminate a culture, recount a crazy adventure or introduce a fascinating way of life. They always entertain, and always enrich the experience of travel.

MALI BLUES
Traveling to an African Beat
Lieve Joris (translated by Sam Garrett)
Drought, rebel uprisings, ethnic conflict: these are the predominant images of West Africa. But as Lieve Joris travels in Senegal, Mauritania and Mali, she meets survivors, fascinating individuals charting new ways of living between tradition and modernity. With her remarkable gift for drawing out people's stories, Joris brilliantly captures the rhythms of a world that refuses to give in.

THE GATES OF DAMASCUS
Lieve Joris (translated by Sam Garrett)
This best-selling book is a beautifully drawn portrait of day-to-day life in modern Syria. Through her intimate contact with local people, Lieve Joris draws us into the fascinating world that lies behind the gates of Damascus. Hala's husband is a political prisoner, jailed for his opposition to the Assad regime; through the author's friendship with Hala we see how Syrian politics impacts on the lives of ordinary people.

THE OLIVE GROVE
Travels in Greece
Katherine Kizilos
Katherine Kizilos travels to fabled islands, troubled border zones and her family's village deep in the mountains. She vividly evokes breathtaking landscapes, generous people and passionate politics, capturing the complexities of a country she loves.

'beautifully captures the real tensions of Greece' – *Sunday Times*

KINGDOM OF THE FILM STARS
Journey into Jordan
Annie Caulfield
Kingdom of the Film Stars is a travel book and a love story. With honesty and humour, Annie Caulfield writes of travelling in Jordan and falling in love with a Bedouin with film-star looks.

She offers fascinating insights into the country – from the tent life of traditional women to the hustle of downtown Amman – and unpicks tight-woven western myths about the Arab world.

Lonely Planet Travel Atlases

L onely Planet has long been famous for the number and quality of its guidebook maps. Now we've gone one step further and produced a handy companion series: Lonely Planet travel atlases – maps of a country produced in book form.

Unlike other maps, which look good but lead travellers astray, our travel atlases have been researched on the road by Lonely Planet's experienced team of writers. All details are carefully checked to ensure the atlas corresponds with the equivalent Lonely Planet guidebook.

- full-colour throughout
- maps researched and checked by Lonely Planet authors
- place names correspond with Lonely Planet guidebooks
- no confusing spelling differences
- legend and travelling information in English, French, German, Japanese and Spanish
- size: 230 x 160 mm

Available now: Chile & Easter Island • Egypt • India & Bangladesh • Israel & the Palestinian Territories • Jordan, Syria & Lebanon • Kenya • Laos • Portugal • South Africa, Lesotho & Swaziland • Thailand • Turkey • Vietnam • Zimbabwe, Botswana & Namibia

---

Lonely Planet TV Series & Videos

L onely Planet travel guides have been brought to life on television screens around the world. Like our guides, the programs are based on the joy of independent travel, and look honestly at some of the most exciting, picturesque and frustrating places in the world. Each show is presented by one of three travellers from Australia, England or the USA and combines an innovative mixture of video, Super-8 film, atmospheric soundscapes and original music.

Videos of each episode – containing additional footage not shown on television – are available from good book and video shops, but the availability of individual videos varies with regional screening schedules.

Video destinations include: Alaska • American Rockies • Australia – The South-East • Baja California & the Copper Canyon • Brazil • Central Asia • Chile & Easter Island • Corsica, Sicily & Sardinia – The Mediterranean Islands • East Africa (Tanzania & Zanzibar) • Ecuador & the Galapagos Islands • Greenland & Iceland • Indonesia • Israel & the Sinai Desert • Jamaica • Japan • La Ruta Maya • Morocco • New York • North India • Pacific Islands (Fiji, Solomon Islands & Vanuatu) • South India • South West China • Turkey • Vietnam • West Africa • Zimbabwe, Botswana & Namibia

The Lonely Planet TV series is produced by: Pilot Productions
The Old Studio
18 Middle Row
London W10 5AT, UK

Lonely Planet On-line
www.lonelyplanet.com *or* AOL keyword: lp

Whether you've just begun planning your next trip, or you're chasing down specific info on currency regulations or visa requirements, check out Lonely Planet On-line for up-to-the minute travel information.

As well as mini guides to more than 250 destinations, you'll find maps, photos, travel news, health and visa updates, travel advisories, and discussion of the ecological and political issues you need to be aware of as you travel. You'll also find timely upgrades to popular guidebooks which you can print out and stick in the back of your book.

There's also an on-line travellers' forum where you can share your experience of life on the road, meet travel companions and ask other travellers for their recommendations and advice.

And of course we have a complete and up-to-date list of all Lonely Planet travel products including travel guides, diving and snorkeling guides, phrasebooks, atlases, travel literature and videos, and a simple on-line ordering facility if you can't find the book you want elsewhere.

Lonely Planet Diving & Snorkeling Guides

Known for indispensible guidebooks to destinations all over the world, Lonely Planet's Pisces Books are the most popular series of diving and snorkeling titles available.

There are three series: **Diving & Snorkeling Guides**, **Shipwreck Diving** series and **Dive Into History**. Full colour throughout, the **Diving & Snorkeling Guides** combine quality photographs with detailed descriptions of the best dive sites for each location, giving divers a glimpse of what they can expect both on land and in water. The **Dive Into History** series is perfect for the adventure diver or armchair traveller. The **Shipwreck Diving** series provides all the details for exploring the most interesting wrecks in the Atlantic and Pacific oceans. The list also includes underwater nature and technical guides.

LONELY PLANET

Guides by Region

Lonely Planet is known worldwide for publishing practical, reliable and no-nonsense travel information in our guides and on our Web site. The Lonely Planet list covers just about every accessible part of the world. Currently there are nine series: travel guides, shoestring guides, walking guides, city guides, phrasebooks, audio packs, travel atlases, diving and snorkeling guides and travel literature.

AFRICA Africa – the South • Africa on a shoestring • Arabic (Egyptian) phrasebook • Arabic (Moroccan) phrasebook • Cairo • Cape Town • Central Africa • East Africa • Egypt • Egypt travel atlas • Ethiopian (Amharic) phrasebook • The Gambia & Senegal • Kenya • Kenya travel atlas • Malawi, Mozambique & Zambia • Morocco • North Africa • South Africa, Lesotho & Swaziland • South Africa, Lesotho & Swaziland travel atlas • Swahili phrasebook • Trekking in East Africa • Tunisia • West Africa • Zimbabwe, Botswana & Namibia • Zimbabwe, Botswana & Namibia travel atlas
Travel Literature: The Rainbird: A Central African Journey • Songs to an African Sunset: A Zimbabwean Story • Mali Blues: Traveling to an African Beat

AUSTRALIA & THE PACIFIC Australia • Australian phrasebook • Bushwalking in Australia • Bushwalking in Papua New Guinea • Fiji • Fijian phrasebook • Islands of Australia's Great Barrier Reef • Melbourne • Micronesia • New Caledonia • New South Wales & the ACT • New Zealand • Northern Territory • Outback Australia • Papua New Guinea • Papua New Guinea (Pidgin) phrasebook • Queensland • Rarotonga & the Cook Islands • Samoa • Solomon Islands • South Australia • Sydney • Tahiti & French Polynesia • Tasmania • Tonga • Tramping in New Zealand • Vanuatu • Victoria • Western Australia
Travel Literature: Islands in the Clouds • Sean & David's Long Drive

CENTRAL AMERICA & THE CARIBBEAN Bahamas and Turks & Caicos • Bermuda • Central America on a shoestring • Costa Rica • Cuba • Eastern Caribbean • Guatemala, Belize & Yucatán: La Ruta Maya • Jamaica • Mexico • Mexico City • Panama
Travel Literature: Green Dreams: Travels in Central America

EUROPE Amsterdam • Andalucía • Austria • Baltic States phrasebook • Berlin • Britain • Central Europe • Central Europe phrasebook • Czech & Slovak Republics • Denmark • Dublin • Eastern Europe • Eastern Europe phrasebook • Edinburgh • Estonia, Latvia & Lithuania • Europe • Finland • France • French phrasebook • Germany • German phrasebook • Greece • Greek phrasebook • Hungary • Iceland, Greenland & the Faroe Islands • Ireland • Italian phrasebook • Italy • Lisbon • London • Mediterranean Europe • Mediterranean Europe phrasebook • Paris • Poland • Portugal • Portugal travel atlas • Prague • Romania & Moldova • Russia, Ukraine & Belarus • Russian phrasebook • Scandinavian & Baltic Europe • Scandinavian Europe phrasebook • Scotland • Slovenia • Spain • Spanish phrasebook • St Petersburg • Switzerland • Trekking in Spain • Ukrainian phrasebook • Vienna • Walking in Britain • Walking in Italy • Walking in Switzerland • Western Europe • Western Europe phrasebook
Travel Literature: The Olive Grove: Travels in Greece

INDIAN SUBCONTINENT Bangladesh • Bengali phrasebook • Bhutan • Delhi • Goa • Hindi/Urdu phrasebook • India • India & Bangladesh travel atlas • Indian Himalaya • Karakoram Highway • Nepal • Nepali phrasebook • Pakistan • Rajasthan • South India • Sri Lanka • Sri Lanka phrasebook • Trekking in the Indian Himalaya • Trekking in the Karakoram & Hindukush • Trekking in the Nepal Himalaya
Travel Literature: In Rajasthan • Shopping for Buddhas

LONELY PLANET

Mail Order

Lonely Planet products are distributed worldwide. They are also available by mail order from Lonely Planet, so if you have difficulty finding a title please write to us. North and South American residents should write to 150 Linden St, Oakland, CA 94607, USA; European and African residents should write to 10a Spring Place, London NW5 3BH, UK; and residents of other countries to PO Box 617, Hawthorn, Victoria 3122, Australia.

ISLANDS OF THE INDIAN OCEAN Madagascar & Comoros • Maldives • Mauritius, Réunion & Seychelles

MIDDLE EAST & CENTRAL ASIA Arab Gulf States • Central Asia • Central Asia phrasebook • Iran • Israel & the Palestinian Territories • Israel & the Palestinian Territories travel atlas • Istanbul • Jerusalem • Jordan & Syria • Jordan, Syria & Lebanon travel atlas • Lebanon • Middle East on a shoestring • Turkey • Turkish phrasebook • Turkey travel atlas • Yemen
Travel Literature: The Gates of Damascus • Kingdom of the Film Stars: Journey into Jordan

NORTH AMERICA Alaska • Backpacking in Alaska • Baja California • California & Nevada • Canada • Florida • Hawaii • Honolulu • Los Angeles • Miami • New England USA • New Orleans • New York City • New York, New Jersey & Pennsylvania • Pacific Northwest USA • Rocky Mountain States • San Francisco • Seattle • Southwest USA • USA phrasebook • Washington, DC & the Capital Region
Travel Literature: Drive Thru America

NORTH-EAST ASIA Beijing • Cantonese phrasebook • China • Hong Kong • Hong Kong, Macau & Guangzhou • Japan • Japanese phrasebook • Japanese audio pack • Korea • Korean phrasebook • Kyoto • Mandarin phrasebook • Mongolia • Mongolian phrasebook • North-East Asia on a shoestring • Seoul • South-West China • Taiwan • Tibet • Tibetan phrasebook • Tokyo
Travel Literature: Lost Japan

SOUTH AMERICA Argentina, Uruguay & Paraguay • Bolivia • Brazil • Brazilian phrasebook • Buenos Aires • Chile & Easter Island • Chile & Easter Island travel atlas • Colombia • Ecuador & the Galapagos Islands • Latin American Spanish phrasebook • Peru • Quechua phrasebook • Rio de Janeiro • South America on a shoestring • Trekking in the Patagonian Andes • Venezuela
Travel Literature: Full Circle: A South American Journey

SOUTH-EAST ASIA Bali & Lombok • Bangkok • Burmese phrasebook • Cambodia • Hill Tribes phrasebook • Ho Chi Minh City • Indonesia • Indonesian phrasebook • Indonesian audio pack • Jakarta • Java • Laos • Lao phrasebook • Laos travel atlas • Malay phrasebook • Malaysia, Singapore & Brunei • Myanmar (Burma) • Philippines • Pilipino (Tagalog) phrasebook • Singapore • South-East Asia on a shoestring • South-East Asia phrasebook • Thailand • Thailand's Islands & Beaches • Thailand travel atlas • Thai phrasebook • Thai audio pack • Vietnam • Vietnamese phrasebook • Vietnam travel atlas

ALSO AVAILABLE: Antarctica • Brief Encounters: Stories of Love, Sex & Travel • Chasing Rickshaws • Not the Only Planet: Travel Stories from Science Fiction • Travel with Children • Traveller's Tales

FREE Lonely Planet Newsletters

We love hearing from you and think you'd like to hear from us.

Planet Talk

Our FREE quarterly printed newsletter is full of tips from travellers and anecdotes from Lonely Planet guidebook authors. Every issue is packed with up-to-date travel news and advice, and includes:

- a postcard from Lonely Planet co-founder Tony Wheeler
- a swag of mail from travellers
- a look at life on the road through the eyes of a Lonely Planet author
- topical health advice
- prizes for the best travel yarn
- news about forthcoming Lonely Planet events
- a complete list of Lonely Planet books and other titles

To join our mailing list, residents of the UK, Europe and Africa can email us at go@lonelyplanet.co.uk; residents of North and South America can email us at info@lonelyplanet.com; the rest of the world can email us at talk2us@lonelyplanet.com.au, or contact any Lonely Planet office.

Comet

Our FREE monthly email newsletter brings you all the latest travel news, features, interviews, competitions, destination ideas, travellers' tips & tales, Q&As, raging debates and related links. Find out what's new on the Lonely Planet Web site and which books are about to hit the shelves.

Subscribe from your desktop: www.lonelyplanet.com/comet

Index

Text

Bold indicates maps.
Italics indicates boxed text.

Boxed Text

Dancing *sardanas*, the catalan traditional dance, Avenida de la Catedral

DAMIEN SIMONIS

Street corner in L'Eixample – ¡salnd!

BETHUNE CARMICHAEL

MAP 1

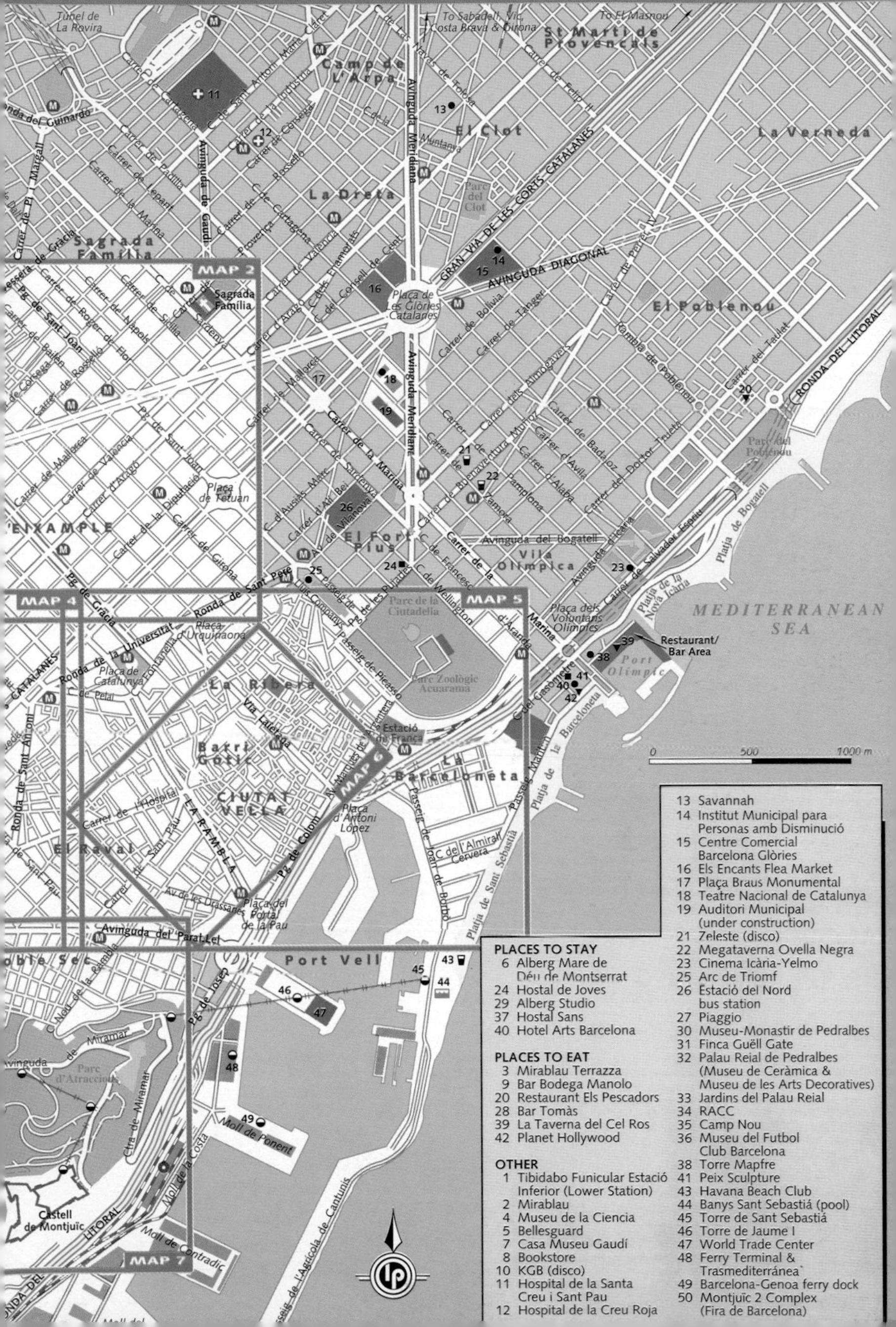

MAP 1

Tunel de
La Rovira

To Sabadell, Vic,
Costa Brava & Girona

To El Masnou

St Martí de
Provençals

Camp de
L'Arpa

13

El Clot

La Verneda

La Dreta

Parc
del
Clot

Sagrada
Família

MAP 2

Sagrada
Família

16

Plaça de
Les Glòries
Catalanes

14

15

AVINGUDA DIAGONAL

GRAN VIA DE LES CORTS CATALANES

El Poblenou

17

EIXAMPLE

18

19

Parc del
Poblenou

RONDA DEL LITORAL

20

21

22

El Fort
Pius

26

25

24

Vila
Olímpica

Avinguda del Bogatell

23

Platja de
la Nova Icària

MEDITERRANEAN
SEA

MAP 4

Plaça de
la Universitat

Plaça de
Catalunya

MAP 5

Plaça del
Voluntaris
Olímpics

La Ribera

Parc de la
Ciutadella

Barri
Gòtic

Parc Zoològic
Acuarama

Estació
de França

Plaça del
Port
Olímpic

39

Restaurant/
Bar Area

38

40 41
42

CIUTAT
VELLA

Plaça
d'Antoni
López

Barceloneta

El Raval

Avinguda del Paral·lel

Port Vell

43

45

44

46

47

Miramar

Parc
d'Atraccions

48

World Trade Center

49

Castell
de Montjuïc

MAP 7

0   500   1000 m

PLACES TO STAY
6 Alberg Mare de
   Déu de Montserrat
24 Hostal de Joves
29 Alberg Studio
37 Hostal Sans
40 Hotel Arts Barcelona

PLACES TO EAT
3 Mirablau Terrazza
9 Bar Bodega Manolo
20 Restaurant Els Pescadors
28 Bar Tomàs
39 La Taverna del Cel Ros
42 Planet Hollywood

OTHER
1 Tibidabo Funicular Estació
   Inferior (Lower Station)
2 Mirablau
4 Museu de la Ciencia
5 Bellesguard
7 Casa Museu Gaudí
8 Bookstore
10 KGB (disco)
11 Hospital de la Santa
   Creu i Sant Pau
12 Hospital de la Creu Roja

13 Savannah
14 Institut Municipal para
   Personas amb Disminució
15 Centre Comercial
   Barcelona Glòries
16 Els Encants Flea Market
17 Plaça Braus Monumental
18 Teatre Nacional de Catalunya
19 Auditori Municipal
   (under construction)
21 Zeleste (disco)
22 Megataverna Ovella Negra
23 Cinema Icària-Yelmo
25 Arc de Triomf
26 Estació del Nord
   bus station
27 Piaggio
30 Museu-Monastir de Pedralbes
31 Finca Güell Gate
32 Palau Reial de Pedralbes
   (Museu de Ceràmica &
   Museu de les Arts Decoratives)
33 Jardins del Palau Reial
34 RACC
35 Camp Nou
36 Museu del Futbol
   Club Barcelona
38 Torre Mapfre
41 Peix Sculpture
43 Havana Beach Club
44 Banys Sant Sebastiá (pool)
45 Torre de Sant Sebastiá
46 Torre de Jaume I
47 World Trade Center
48 Ferry Terminal &
   Trasmediterránea
49 Barcelona-Genoa ferry dock
50 Montjuïc 2 Complex
   (Fira de Barcelona)

MAP 2

MAP 4

MAP 2

LA SAGRADA
FAMÍLIA

Avinguda de Gaudí

Sagrada
Família

Plaça de
Gaudí

Carrer de Sant Antoni Maria Claret

Carrer de la Industria

Carrer de Còrsega

Carrer de Sardenya

Carrer de Lepant

Carrer de la Marina

M

35

34

La Sagrada
Família

36

Carrer de Nàpols

Passeig de Sant Joan

Carrer de Roger de Flor

Carrer de Provença

Plaça de
la Sagrada
Família

Carrer de la Sardenya

Carrer de València

Carrer d'Aragó

Passeig de Sant Joan

AVINGUDA DIAGONAL

Carrer de Bailèn

Carrer de Rosselló

Carrer de Mallorca

M

Verdaguer

Plaça Mossèn
Jacint
Verdaguer

Carrer d'Aragó

Verdaguer

M

33

Passeig de Sant Joan

37

L'EIXAMPLE

Carrer de València

Carrer de Bailèn

Carrer de Girona

Carrer del Bruc

Carrer del Consell de Cent

105

Plaça
de Tetuan

100

Girona

M

106

Carrer de Roger de Llúria

Carrer de la Diputació

99

98

107

Carrer de Pau Claris

Passeig de Mèndez Vigo

97

108

96

95

109

110

Passeig
de Gràcia

115

Carrer de Casp

M

94

Passeig de Gràcia

80

111

116

81

Rambla de Catalunya

90

112

114

Carrer de Roger de Marc

82

83

84

91

89

85

92

86

87

88

113

Carrer de Casp

MAP 5

GRAN VIA DE LES CORTS CATALANES

Rambla de Catalunya

MAP 5

MAP 2

MAP 2

PLACES TO STAY
25 Pensión Norma
26 Hostal San Medín
52 Hotel Astoria
58 Hotel Balmes
71 Comtes de Barcelona Hotel
   & Vasari
77 Hotel Regente
89 St Moritz Hotel
92 Hostal Oliva & Adolfo
   Domínguez
98 Hotel Majèstic
106 Hotel Claris
112 Hostal Palacios
114 Hotel Ritz (Husa Palace)
115 Pensión Cerdeña
116 Pensión Girona

PLACES TO EAT
4 Taverna El Glop
6 Cal Majó
7 Casa de Pizzas
10 El Tastavins
11 Cal Juanito
13 Equinox Sol
16 Tetería Jazmín
17 La Botiga del Sol
18 Aroma
19 Mario Pizza
21 Bar Candanchu
22 La Singular
24 Botafumeiro
34 La Baguetina Catalana
36 La Casa del Jamón
41 La Miel
49 Pastafiore
55 La Gran Tasca
66 Tragaluz
68 Pastafiore & Pans &
   Company
72 Lizarran
74 Bocatta
79 Cafè Torino
83 Pans & Company
91 Swan

93 Cerveseria Tapa Tapa
94 Restaurant Madrid
   Barcelona
97 L'Hostal de Rita
99 FrescCo
101 Centro Asturiano
113 El Café de Internet

OTHER
1 Casa Vicenç
2 Església de Sant Josep
3 Café la Virreina
5 Café Salambó
8 Cinema Verdi
9 Teatre Lliure
12 La Ñola
14 Café del Sol
15 Eldorado
20 Bar Chirito de Oro
23 Alquiler Tiendas
27 Otto Zutz
28 Cinema Arkadín
29 Café de la Calle
30 Alfa
31 Artenbrut
32 Poliesportiu Perill
33 Casa de les Punxes
   (Casa Terrades)
35 Museu Gaudí
37 Hertz Rentacar
38 Palau Quadras
   (Museu de la Música)
39 Casa Comalat
40 Majorica
42 Martin's
43 Cinema Casablanca
44 German Consulate
45 Bahía
46 Calvin Klein
47 Giorgio Armani
48 Institut Français de
   Barcelona
50 Luz de Gas
51 La Antilla Cosmopolita
53 Gucci

54 Velvet
56 Come In Bookshop
57 Planet Music
59 Avis rentacar
60 Museu Egipci
61 Nick Havanna
62 Alitalia
63 American Express
64 Palau Robert (Regional
   Tourist Office)
65 Librería Francesa
67 Happy Books &
   Happy Café
69 La Bodegueta
70 Happy Books & Canadian
   Consulate
73 Cinema Alexis
75 Casa Enric Batlló
76 Camper
78 Bulevard Rosa; Lufthansa;
   Regia; Centre Català
   d'Artesania
80 Fundació Antoni Tàpies
81 Casa Batlló
82 Casa Amatller & Joyería
   Bagués
84 Casa Lleo Morera, Cartier &
   Loewe
85 Antonio Miró
86 Natura Selection
87 Max Mara
88 Iberia
90 Café Interlight
95 Correos
96 BCN Bookshop
100 Italian Consulate
102 24-hour pharmacy
103 La Pedrera (Casa Mila)
104 Vinçon
105 Swedish Consulate
107 Cinema Capsa
108 Istituto di Cultura Italiano
109 Europcar Rentacar
110 Belgian Consulate
111 Pullmantur

MAP 3

PLACES TO STAY
23 Alberg Pere Tarrès

OTHER
1 Institute of North American
   Studies
2 British Council
3 Universal
4 Mas i Mas
5 Zara
6 Loewe
7 Jean Pierre Bua

8 El Corte Inglés
9 UK Consulate & La Boîte
10 Gianni Versace
11 International House Language
   School
12 The Music Box
13 Giorgio Armani
14 Fibra Óptica
15 Ortiga
16 Salsa Salsa
17 UPS Couriers
18 Da Giorgio

19 Marks & Spencer
20 FNAC
21 L'Illa del Diagonal
22 Bikini
24 Ronicar Rentacar
25 Netherlands Consulate
26 Japanese Consulate
27 El Corte Inglés
28 Bowling Barcelona
29 Australian Consulate
30 Swiss & Irish Consulates
31 Cinema Renoir-Les Corts

Palau Reial (ex-tinca Güell), Pedrables

MAP 3

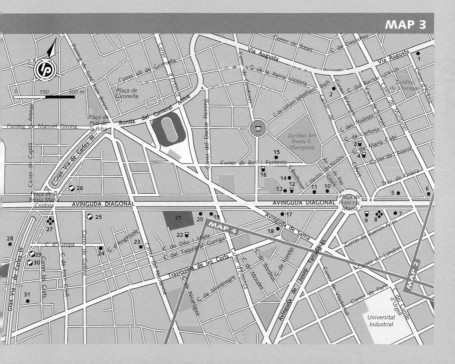

MAP 4

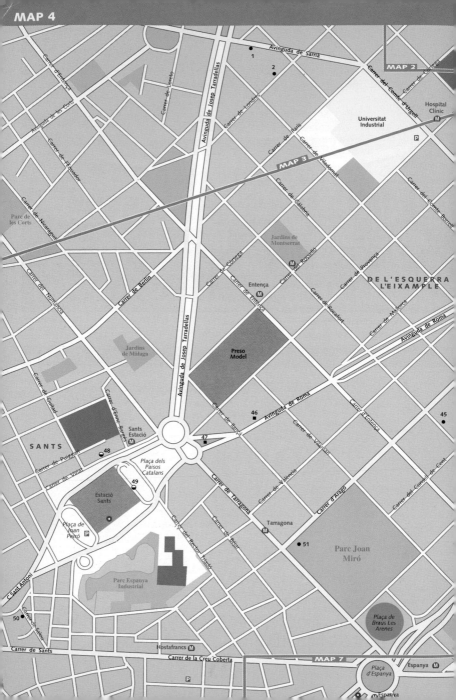

MAP 4

MAP 5

Plaça del
Doctor
Ferrer i
Cajigal

fospital Clínic
i Provincial

Plaça del
Doctor
Letamendi

Universitat
de Barcelona

To Plaça de
Catalunya

Carrer de Pelai

L'EIXAMPLE

Urgell Ⓜ

Rocafort Ⓜ

GRAN VIA DE LES CORTS CATALANES

SANT ANTONI

Carrer de la Ra Alta

Ronda de Sant Pau

Avinguda de Mistral

Avinguda del Paral·lel

0   100   200 m

MAP 7

MAP 4

NICK RAY

Port de Barcelona, near La Ramblas

MAP 5

Plaça Reial, surrounded by eateries, bars & nightspots

DAMIEN SIMONIS

MAP 5
MAP 2

▼ 1
▼ 2
7
6
▼ 9
10
11
3
5
8
12
4

Passeig de Gràcia
Carrer de Pau Claris
Carrer de Roger de Llúria
Carrer de Muntaner-Núñez

M Urquinaona
Carrer de

Ronda de Sant Pere
Plaça
d'Urquinaona

Rambla de Catalunya
Jardins de
La Reina
Victòria

Carrer de Casp
Carrer de Sant Pere
Carrer de l'Ortigosa

GRAN VIA DE LES CORTS CATALANES

14 13
15
16
17 ℹ
M Catalunya
Plaça de
Catalunya

Mercat
Sta Caterina

LA RIBERA

19
20
21
18

Carrer de la Universitat
Ronda de la Universitat

23
22 ▼

Carrer de Pelai

Carrer de les Tallers
Carrer de
Jonqueres

Carrer Comtal
Avinguda del Portal de l'Àngel
C de Cucurulla
C de Montsió
Carrer de Santa Maria

Via Laietana
Avinguda de F Cambó

BARRI GOTIC
Plaça de
la Seu
Avinguda de la Catedral
P   P

LA RAMBLA

Carrer de Montalegre
Carrer d'Elisabets
Carrer Xuclà
Fortuny

Carrer del Carme

Carrer del Pintor Fortuny

Plaça de la Vila
de Madrid

C de la Canuda

C de Portaferrissa

Jaume I M

Carrer de

Via Laietana

Antic
Hospital
Santa Creu

Mercat de
la Boqueria

Liceu M

EL RAVAL

Hospital

Plaça de
Sant Jaume

Plaça de
la Boqueria

CIUTAT VELLA

Plaça
Reial

MAP 4

Carrer del Carme
Carrer de Sant Jeroni
Carrer de la Riereta

Carrer de la Reina Amàlia

Ronda de Sant Pau

47

48
49

MAP 7

45
44
46

LA RAMBLA

Avinguda de les Drassanes

Drassanes M

Plaça
del Portal
de la Pau

Museum
Maritim

Passeig de Colom

Port

MAP 6

MAP 4

M Paral.Lel Funicular

Avinguda del Paral.Lel

Carrer de Vila i Vilà

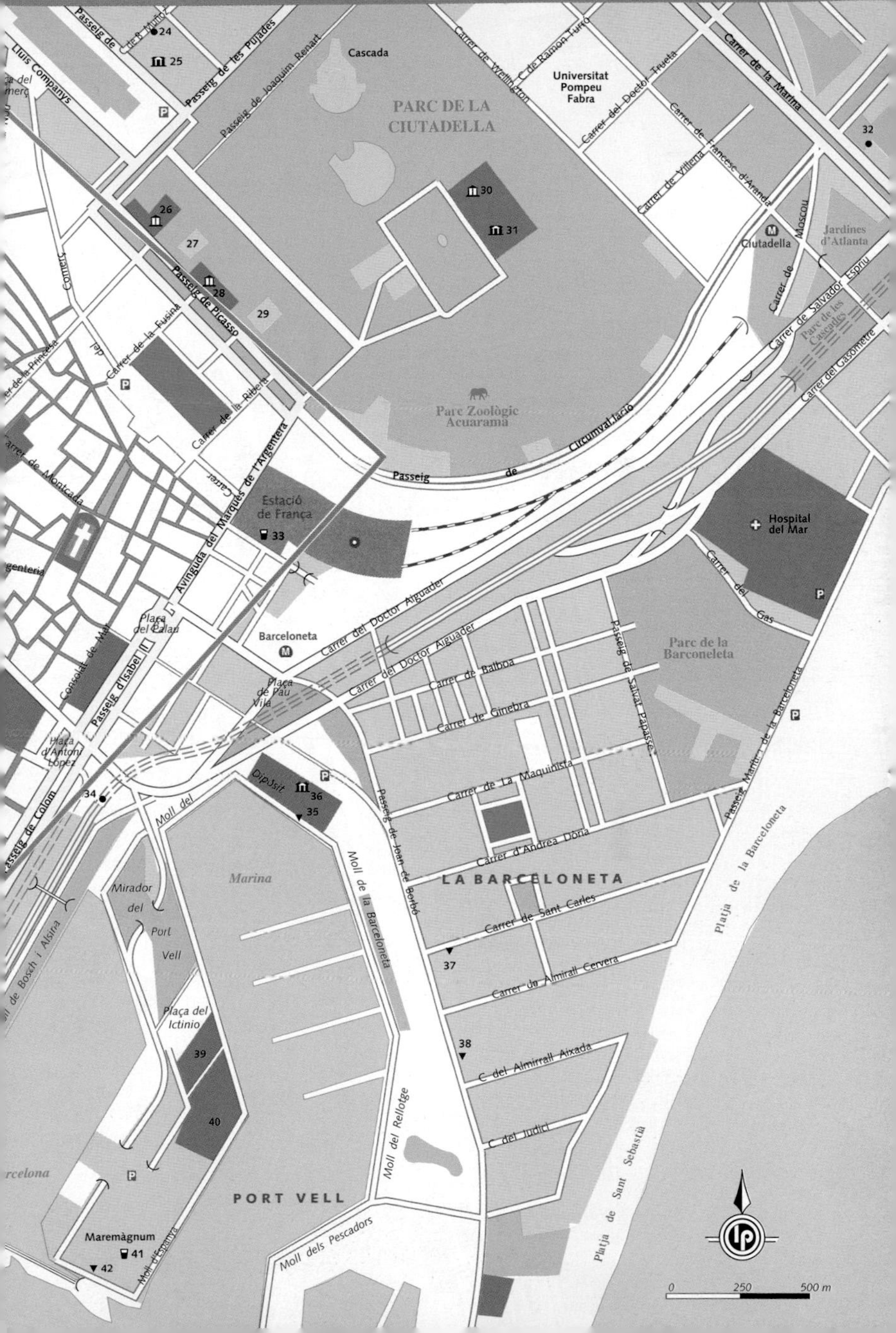

MAP 5

■ 24
🏛 25

Passeig de les Pujades

Cascada

Carrer de Wellington

C de Ramon Turró

Carrer de la Marina

Passeig de Joaquim Renart

PARC DE LA
CIUTADELLA

Universitat
Pompeu
Fabra

Carrer del Doctor Trueta

Carrer de la Marina

32 ●

Lluís Companys

P

Camins

🏛 26
27

🏛 30

🏛 31

Carrer de Villena Francesc d'Arand

M
Ciutadella

Jardines
d'Atlanta

Passeig de Picasso

28
29

Carrer de la Fusina

Carrer de la Ribera

Carrer de Salvador Espriu

Carrer de les Caselles

Carrer de Moscou

P

Carrer de la Princesa

Carrer de la Fusina

Avinguda del Marquès de l'Argentera

Parc Zoològic
Acuarama

Passeig de Circumval·lació

Carrer del Casanova

Carrer de Montcada

Estació
de França
🚩 33

Passeig   de

Carrer del Gas

Hospital
del Mar

gentera

Plaça
del Palau 🏛

Barceloneta
M

Carrer del Doctor Aiguader

Carrer del Doctor Aiguader

Carrer de Balboa

Parc de la
Barconeleta

P

Consolat de Mar

Passeig d'Isabel II

Plaça
de Pau
Vila

Carrer de Ginebra

Passeig de Joan de Borbó

Passeig de Sant Palaroni

P

Plaça
d'Antoni
López

34 ●

Moll del

Dipòsit
🏛 36
▼ 35

P

Carrer de la Maquinista

Passeig Martim de la Barceloneta

P

Passeig de Bosch i Alsina

Mirador
del
Port
Vell

Marina

Moll de la Barceloneta

Carrer d'Andrea Dòria

LA BARCELONETA

Platja de la Barceloneta

Carrer de Sant Carles

Plaça del
Ictinio

39

40

▼
37

Carrer de Almirall Cervera

rcelona

P

Moll del Rellotge

▼
38

C del Almirall Aixada

C del Judici

Platja de Sant Sebastià

PORT VELL

Moll dels Pescadors

Maremàgnum
🚩 41
▼ 42

Moll d'Espanya

0   250   500 m

MAP 6

Museu d'Art Contemporani

Plaça de Catalunya

▼ 42

Plaça de Wiver...

Plaça d' Ramon Amade

■ 41

RAMBLA DE CANALETES

3 ■
■ 1
2 ■
5 ■
7 ■
8 ■
9 ■
4 □
6 ●
10 ●
11 ▼

Plaça dels Àngels

Carrer d'Elisabets

Plaça de Vicenç Martorell

Carrer dels Tallers

Carrer dels Tallers

46 ■ 45
Carrer de Santa Anna
47 ■ 48

Carrer de la Canuda
49 ▼

Plaça de la Vila de Madrid
50 ■

Carrer del Peu de la Creu

Carrer de la Riera Alta

● 16

● 15
Carrer del Carme

Carrer del Doctor Dou

Carrer del Pintor Fortuny

Carrer del Àngels

14 ■

12 ▼
13 ▼

Església de Betlem

RAMBLA DELS ESTUDIS

✚

ℹ 60
● 59

Carrer de l'Hospital

Carrer del Carme

Jardins Doctor Fleming

Antic Hospital Santa Creu
✚

Plaça de la Gardunya

Palau de la Virreina
■

Mercat de la Boqueria

58 ■

57 ■

Carrer de la Portaferrissa

BARRI GOTIC

61 ▼

● 62

63 ■

Carrer del Pi

65 ■

64 ▼

Carrer de Sant Rafael

17 ■
● 18

Plaça de Sant Agustí

Carrer de l'Hospital

75 ▼
77 ■
76 ▼
78 ■ 80
79 ■
81 ■
82 ●

73 72
Plaça del Pi

Carrer

Església de Santa Maria del Pi

Plaça de Sant Josep Oriol

84 ●

83 ●

Carrer de Banys Nous

Carrer de la Boqueria

Plaça de Sant Felip Ne

Carrer de Santa Eulàlia

Església de Sant Agustí

19 ■

Plaça Boqueria
Ⓜ Liceu

112 ▼
111 ●

110 ▼
109 ▼
108 ▼

● 85

■ 103

● 10

24 23
22
21
20 ■

Gran Teatre del Liceu (under construction)

113 ▼

114 ▼

115 ▼

107 ●

106 ●
105 ■
104 ●

Carrer del

Carret

25 ■

26
27 ▼

Carrer de Sant Pau

Marqués de Barberà

28 ■

29 ●

116 ▼
120 ▼

121 ▼

124 ●

ℹ 125

■ 126

Carrer de Ferran

EL RAVAL

30 ●

31 ★

117 ■
118 ■
119 ■
144 ■ 145
146 ■
147 ■

122 ▼
123 ▼

140 ▼

136 ▼

137 ■

Plaça de Sant Miquel
ℹ 135

RAMBLA DELS CAPUTXINS

Plaça Reial

141 ●
142 ▼
143 ■

C de la Lleona

138 ▼
139 ▼
159 ▼

Carrer de Cervantes

32 ■

33 ■

Carrer Nou de la Rambla

Palau Güell
■

148 ●
149 ●

150 ▼
151 ▼

152 ▼

155 ▼
154 ▼
153 ▼

156 ■

157 ▼

158 ▼ 160 ▼
161 ▼
162 ●

163 ■

Plaça de George Orwell

Escudellers

34 ●

35 ●
36 ●

37 ●

38 ●

Carrer de l'Arc del Teatre

Plaça del Teatre

171 ▼

39 ●

Ⓜ Drassanes

RAMBLA DE SANTA MONICA

172 ■

173 ●

180 ✚

● 40

Museu de Cera
■

174 ■

175 ■
176 ■
177 178

Plaça del Duc de Medinaceli

179

Comandància de Marina

MUSEU MARITIM
■

Museu de Cera

MAP 6 - CIUTAT VELLA

EL RAVAL
PLACES TO STAY
3 Hosteria Grau
7 Pensión Noya & Restaurant Nuria
9 Hotel Lloret
14 Le Meridien
17 Hotel San Agustín
18 Hostal La Terrassa
19 Hostal Residencia Opera
21 Hotel España & Fonda Espanya
23 Hotel Peninsular
30 Hotel Oriente

PLACES TO EAT
2 Bar Kasparo
5 Restaurant Tallers
8 Pastafiore
11 Pans & Company
12 Viena
13 Simago Supermarket
22 Bar Restaurante Romesco
24 Restaurante Els Tres Bots
26 Kashmir Restaurant Tandoori
27 Restaurante Pollo Rico

OTHER
1 Hysteria
4 L'Ovella Negra
6 Rock & Blues
10 Castelló
15 Condon Center
16 Café Que Pone Muebles Navarro
20 Antiga Casa Figueras
25 Bar Marsella
28 The Quiet Man
29 Salas Llibreteria
31 Guàrdia Urbana
32 London Bar
33 Bar La Concha
34 Escola Oficial d'Idiomes de Barcelona
35 Kentucky
36 Moog
37 Teatre Principal
38 Tablao Cordobés
39 Bar Pastís

BARRI GÒTIC
PLACES TO STAY
41 Hotel Continental
43 Hostal Fontanella
44 Pensión Estal
48 Hotel Nouvel
51 Hostal Lausanne
57 Hostal-Residencia Rembrandt
58 Pensión-Hostal Fina
63 Hostal Galerias Maldà; Cinema Maldà
66 Hotel Colón
73 Hotel Jardi
82 Hostal Paris
87 Hostal Layetana
95 Hotel Suizo
97 Hotel Rey Don Jaime I
103 Hotel Call
104 Pensión Fernando
105 Albergue Arco
109 Pensión Bienestar
110 Pensión Europa
111 Pensión Dalí
112 Hotel Internacional
117 Pensión Villanueva
119 Pensió Colom 3 & Disco-Bar Real
126 Hotel Rialto
130 Hotel Gótico
137 Hostal Levante
142 Hotel Roma Reial
145 Hotel Cuatro Naciones
147 Youth Hostel Kabul
160 Casa Huéspedes Mari-Luz
161 Alberg Juvenil Palau
162 Pensión Alamar
170 Hotel Metropol
174 Hostal Marítima & García
185 Abba Youth Hostel

PLACES TO EAT
42 Hard Rock Cafe
45 Self-Naturista
46 Bocatta
47 Santa Ana
49 The Bagel Shop
52 Els Quatre Gats
53 Bocatta
56 Pans & Company
61 Granja La Pallaresa
64 Croissanterie del Pi
72 Xocolateria La Xicra
76 Irati
80 Juicy Jones
85 Mesón Jesús
94 La Colmena
96 Bon Mercat
99 Santa Clara
100 Bocatta
108 Can Culleretes
114 Cafè de l'Òpera
115 Les Quatre Barres
120 Les Quinze Nits
121 Pans & Company
131 Il Caffè di Roma
136 El Gran Café
138 El Gallo Kiriko
139 Bar-Restaurant Cervantes
150 Restaurante Rincón de Ríos Baixos
151 Bar Comercio
152 La Fonda Escudellers
153 Los Caracoles
154 Buen Bocado
155 Restaurante Senshe Tawakal
157 Felafel & Kebab Takeaway
159 Cal Kiko
166 El Salón
171 Restaurant Pitarra
175 Ristorante Il Mercante di Venezia
176 Restaurante Porto Mar
177 Margarita Blue
181 Bar Celta
182 Restaurant Classic Gòtic
183 Tasca El Corral
184 Sidrería La Socarrena

OTHER
50 Roman Tombs
54 Ceràmiques i Terrisses Cadí
55 Ceràmica
59 Institut Català de la Dona
60 Llibreria & Informaciò Cultural de la Generalitat de Catalunya; Casa de Comillas
62 Quera Bookshop
65 La Pineda
67 Casa de la Pia Almoina; Museu Diocesà
68 Casa de l'Ardiaca
69 Capella de Santa Llúcia
70 Església de Sant Sever
71 Museu del Calçat
74 Bar del Pi
75 Estamperia d'Art
77 24-hour Pharmacy
78 Museu de l'Eròtica
79 Centre Comercial New Park
81 Documenta Bookshop
83 La Condoneria
84 Casa Miranda
86 Museu Frederic Marès
88 Capella Reial de Santa Àgata
89 Saló del Tinell
90 Mirador del Rei Martí
91 Casa del Lloctinent
92 Casa Padellàs (Museu d'Història de la Ciutat)
93 Cereria Subirà
98 Temple Romà d'Agusrti
Continued on next page

MAP 6 - CIUTAT VELLA

Font Mágica, Montjuïc

GREG ELMS

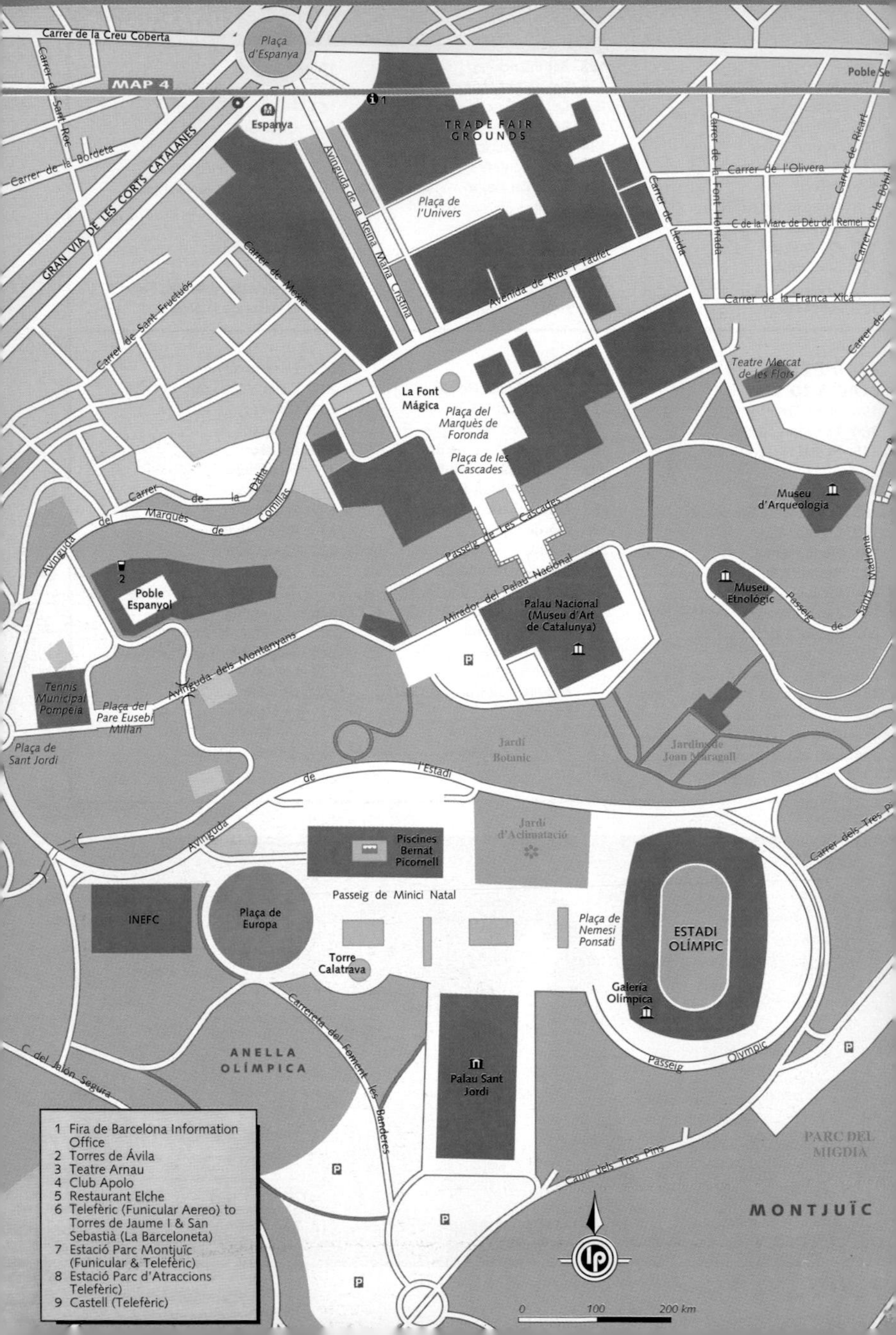

MAP 7

Carrer de la Creu Coberta

Plaça d'Espanya

MAP 4

Poble Se

GRAN VIA DE LES CORTS CATALANES

Espanya

Carrer de Sant Roc

Carrer de la Boleta

Carrer de Sant Fructuós

Carrer de Mina

Avinguda de Joan de Borbó

Avinguda de la Reina Maria Cristina

TRADE FAIR GROUNDS

Plaça de l'Univers

Carrer de l'Olivera

Carrer de Lleida

C de la Mare de Déu de Remei

Avinguda de Rius i Taulet

Carrer de la Franca Xica

Teatre Mercat de les Flors

La Font Màgica

Plaça del Marquès de Foronda

Plaça de les Cascades

Museu d'Arqueologia

Carrer de la Palla

Carret de Marquès de Coialla

Avinguda del Marquès

Passeig de les Cascades

Poble Espanyol

Mirador del Palau Nacional

Museu Etnològic

2

Palau Nacional (Museu d'Art de Catalunya)

Avinguda dels Montanyans

Tennis Municipal Pompeia

Plaça del Pare Eusebi Millan

Plaça de Sant Jordi

Jardí Botànic

Jardins de Joan Maragall

Avinguda de l'Estadi

Carrer dels Tres Pins

Piscines Bernat Picornell

Jardí d'Aclimatació

INEFC

Plaça de Europa

Passeig de Minici Natal

Plaça de Nemesi Ponsati

ESTADI OLÍMPIC

Torre Calatrava

Galería Olímpica

C del Julián Segura

ANELLA OLÍMPICA

Carretera del Foment

Avinguda de l'Estadi

Passeig Olímpic

PARC DEL MIGDIA

Palau Sant Jordi

Camí dels Tres Pins

MONTJUÏC

P

P

P

1 Fira de Barcelona Information Office
2 Torres de Ávila
3 Teatre Arnau
4 Club Apolo
5 Restaurant Elche
6 Telefèric (Funicular Aereo) to Torres de Jaume I & San Sebastià (La Barceloneta)
7 Estació Parc Montjuïc (Funicular & Telefèric)
8 Estació Parc d'Atraccions Telefèric
9 Castell (Telefèric)

0   100   200 km

MAP 7

POBLE SEC

MAP 4

MAP 5

Avinguda del Paral.lel

Paral.lel
(Funicular)

Teatre
Victòria

3

4

Teatre
El Morino

5

Carrer de Vila i Vilà

Carrer de Blai

Carrer de Tapioles

Carrer de Salvà

Carrer de Piquer

Carrer de Blesa

Carrer del Roser

Carrer de Margarit

Carrer Nou de la Rambla

Carrer d'Elkano

Carrer de Blai de Garay

Carrer de Magalhães

Passeig de Montjuïc

Plaça
del Sortidor

Carrer d'Annibal

Exposició

Ptge. de la Vinyeta

Passeig de la Font Trobada

Passeig de Miramar

Plaça de
Carlos
Ibañez

6

Plaça de
l'Armada

Avinguda de Miramar

Funicular

Jardins de
Miramar

P

ndació
n Miró

7

Avinguda de Miramar

Plaça de
Dante

Plaça de
Neptú

Terminus
No 61 Bus

PARC
D'ATRACCIONS

Jardins de
Mossèn Costa
i Llobera

Carretera de Miramar

Plaça del
Mirador

Teleféric de Montjuïc

Jardins de
Mossèn Cinto
Verdaguer

8

Jardins del
Mirador

Carretera de Miramar

P

RONDA DEL LITORAL

Estació
del Port

Carrer dels Tres Pins

Avinguda del Castell

9

Moll de la Costa

Carrer de la Cartoixa

Museu
Militar

21

CASTELL DE
MONTJUÏC

Carrer del Foc

RONDA DEL LITORAL

Moll de
Contradic

Passeig de l'Avinguda de Colom

MAP LEGEND

BOUNDARIES
.... International
.... State
.... Disputed

HYDROGRAPHY
.... Coastline
.... River
.... Creek
.... Lake
.... Intermittent Lake
.... Canal
.... Spring, Rapids
.... Waterfalls
.... Swamp

ROUTES & TRANSPORT
.... Freeway
.... Highway
.... Major Road
.... Minor Road
.... Unsealed Road
.... City Freeway
.... City Highway
.... City Road
.... City Street, Lane
.... Pedestrian Mall
.... Tunnel
.... Train Route & Station
.... Metro & Station
.... Tramway
.... Cable Car; Funicular
.... Walking Track
.... Walking Tour
.... Ferry Route

AREA FEATURES
.... Building
.... Park, Gardens
.... Cemetery
.... Market
.... Beach
.... Urban Area

MAP SYMBOLS
❂ **CAPITAL** .... National Capital
◉ **CAPITAL** .... State Capital
● **CITY** .... City
● **Town** .... Town
● Village .... Village
○ .... Point of Interest

■ .... Place to Stay
Λ .... Camping Ground
⌒⌒ .... Caravan Park
⌂ .... Hut or Chalet

▼ .... Place to Eat
🍺 .... Pub or Bar

✈ .... Airport
⊙ .... ATM, Bank
🏖 .... Beach
🚲 .... Bike Rental
🏰 .... Castle or Fort
✚ 🕌 .... Church
⌒⌒⌒ .... Cliff or Escarpment
♀ .... Embassy
✛ .... Hospital
🏛 .... Monument
☪ .... Mosque
▲ .... Mountain or Hill
🏛 .... Museum
🌴 .... National Park

← .... One Way Street
🅿 .... Parking
⛽ .... Petrol
★ .... Police Station
✉ .... Post Office
❖ .... Shopping Centre
🏛 .... Stately Home
🏊 .... Swimming Pool
✡ .... Synagogue
☎ .... Telephone
🚻 .... Toilet
❶ .... Tourist Information
◒ .... Transport
🐖 .... Zoo

Note: not all symbols displayed above appear in this book

LONELY PLANET OFFICES

Australia
PO Box 617, Hawthorn, Victoria 3122
☎ (03) 9819 1877 fax (03) 9819 6459
email: talk2us@lonelyplanet.com.au

USA
150 Linden St, Oakland, CA 94607
☎ (510) 893 8555 TOLL FREE: 800 275 8555
fax (510) 893 8572
email: info@lonelyplanet.com

UK
10a Spring Place, London, NW5 3BH
☎ (0171) 428 4800 fax (0171) 428 4828
email: go@lonelyplanet.co.uk

France
1 rue du Dahomey, 75011 Paris
☎ 01 55 25 33 00 fax 01 55 25 33 01
email: bip@lonelyplanet.fr
3615 lonelyplanet *(1,29 F TTC/min)*

World Wide Web: www.lonelyplanet.com *or* AOL keyword: lp
Lonely Planet Images: lpi@lonelyplanet.com.au